That Old Bilbao Moon
The Passion and Resurrection of a City

Joseba Zulaika

Center for Basque Studies
University of Nevada, Reno

This book was published with the generous financial assistance of the Basque Government

Occasional Papers Series, No. 24
Series Editors: Joseba Zulaika and Cameron J. Watson

Center for Basque Studies
University of Nevada, Reno
Reno, Nevada 89557
http://basque.unr.edu

Book design: Jose Luis Agote
Cover design: Daniel Montero
Front cover based on a photo by Goretti Etxaniz

Library of Congress Cataloging-in-Publication Data

Zulaika, Joseba.
That old Bilbao moon : the passion and resurrection of a city / Joseba Zulaika.
pages cm -- (Occasional papers series; no. 24)
Includes bibliographical references and index.
Summary: "Touching on anthropology, ethnology, history, philosophy, and personal history, this book is the author's meditation on his own postwar generation in the Basque Country's largest city"-- Provided by publisher.
1. Bilbao (Spain)--Social life and customs--20th century. 2. Bilbao (Spain)--Social conditions--20th century. 3. Bilbao (Spain)--Biography. 4. Zulaika, Joseba. I. Title.

DP402.B5Z85 2014
946'.6308--dc23

2014036262

To Goretti

That old Bilbao moon . . .
It was the most beautiful!
It was the most beautiful!
It was the most beautiful!
In the world!

—Bertolt Brecht

CONTENTS

Return to Bilbao: A Carnival Morning

It was the spring of 1999 and a Carnival Monday morning when I returned for a visit to San Felicísimo ("Saint Happiest")—the Bilbao monastery where in the 1960s, as a teenager and for almost a decade, I tried hard to become a saint, but was finally expelled, an atheist and suicidal.

Three decades later, I was back in Bilbao on one of my periodic return trips from the United States, where I worked at the University of Nevada and had become a citizen, when I decided to visit the religious friends whom I hadn't seen for so long. As I entered the convent's patio, full of the noise of the all-night Carnival revelers nearby, I found myself conversing with Iñaki, the monk who had made a deal with my mother to intern me in the seminary. This was in the Bilbao now ruled by Doctor Deseo's songs: "Heart of Tango," "Fugitives from Paradise," "Set Fire to Bilbao," "Closest to Hell," "Wild Moons," "To Die in Bilbao":

To die in Bilbao, nothing can be better

To burn one's life and be reborn in your arms again.

Under the spell of San Felicísimo's familiar palm trees I was suddenly overcome by a sense of déjà vu—as if everything that had happened there in the past, in that Bilbao defined by Gabriel Aresti as the "lowest hell," was conspiring to bring me and my former friends to this moment, I saw my generation once again at a turning point, as if on the threshold of a final decision in a moment of crisis. Inside those monastic walls we had experienced intense religious desire that later, after the Fall, seemed like a delirious comedy—a carnivalesque production at the edge of heaven and hell that still demanded, as if by *repeating* ourselves forward and by deferred action, some sort of resolution. We had to reproduce the structure of Dante's *Vita Nuova*—some written in the past, some written in the present. I strongly felt it all had happened for the only thing that mattered now: the writing of this moment—a book to turn the shipwreck into a new point of departure.

Between 1968 and 1970 I was one of twenty-five youths living in San Felicísimo in Bilbao's Deusto neighborhood. We understood well Dalí's

Church and convent of San Felicísimo in Bilbao.

perfidious saying that "those who have not smelled the odor of sanctity are traitors." Our pursuit of sanctity, which for many of us culminated in atheism, taught us that transcending religion was the truly most religious act in our lives. "Conversion" had been key to our allegorical journey through Dante's Hell, Purgatory, and Paradise. But it was after *de*-conversion that our true Dantesque journey began. "Why not climb up this blissful mountain here, / the beginning and the source of all man's joy?"—we heard Dante say all those years; but it was Aresti's *Maldan behera* (Downfall) that marked the beginning of our true metamorphosis.

After I was expelled from the convent, I spent a year in London, dejected and writing poetry on the myth of Paradise Lost. Other former seminarians ended up in ETA. Now I was back for a visit to San Felicísimo. While I was walking with Iñaki just a few feet from the cell where I had experienced my religious and erotic traumas, he began talking about Nietzsche—the enemy! The monks had taught us to submit to the burning intensity of a text—the magic to be found through identification with an author. Yet it was through reading Miguel de Unamuno and Freud and Dostoyevsky and especially Nietzsche, the Anti-Christ, that everything the monks had patiently instilled in us was undone. Nietzsche was the name for the subjective split—the time loop created by the event that renders the subject into a work yet to be completed. His *Zarathustra* commanded us to be suspicious of all truths, Christian truths in particular.

The rhetoric of love was for the weak; nothing good could come from life-denying resentment. But Nietzsche himself had been broken by Ariadne's love. His famous one-line declaration of love to Cosima Wagner—"Ariadne, Ich liebe dich. Dionysus"—written from the asylum after his breakdown, echoes his desolation while linking Ariadne with the labyrinth of love. For the apocalyptic author who freed us from our Christian subject, "Ariadne was the one great conundrum that Nietzsche could never solve—the enigma of woman and the riddle of love." Nietzsche introduced us to *A Season in Hell*, to the Rimbaud who wrote: "Love is to be reinvented, that is clear"—a reinvention that "was indissolubly an artistic, existential and political move."

Captive amoreux was how Jean Genet defined himself. Prisoners of love—that has been my Bilbao generation's fundamental impasse regarding motherland, God, family, culture. If you truly love me, the command was, you must surrender your life. There was no law for love. As Bertolt Brecht wrote in his ironic "Bilbao Song,"

> That old Bilbao moon
> Where love was worthwhile . . .

Friedrich Nietzsche (1844–1900).

Frank Gehry's "shipwreck" in Bilbao.

From a lover's standpoint, the object of love is suddenly transubstantiated into something entirely new, the commonplace transfigured into a revelation, out of nothing and without any empirical change—the Thing that is more than the Thing itself. That very "gap" in being is the opening to *the Real*—in love, art, or politics—and to the formation of a new subject.

A memoir, an ethnography, an essay, a manifesto that aims to track and challenge my generation's consciousness, this Dantean narration presents "characters," including its author, who are real people but whose lives do not conform to ideal cultural models. They are rather figures under the threat of disintegration who require for their survival the confrontation with their subjectivities. Except for names and peripheral details changed to protect individual privacy, every conversation and event here narrated is ethnographically "factual." And yet, this non-fictional text deals essentially with the subject's "fundamental fantasies." The hallucinatory quality of some of the generational narratives described here proves that fantasy is not equal to some imaginary not-real, but that "it constitutes a dimension of the real."

What were the defining traits of "my generation"? We came of age in the 1960s; our basic education was framed by religion; our politics was overshadowed by ETA; we experienced the art world under the influence of sculptors Jorge Oteiza and Eduardo Chillida; our primary identity was Basque; Unamuno and Gabriel Aresti were indispensable literary references; the impasse between moralistic celibacy and the desire for sexual liberation dominated our erotic life; the ideological struggle was between the models presented by the national liberation movements and those of the international socialism and the emancipation of the working classes. Far from having a unified voice, there is much internal struggle in each of the vital historical subjects who have shaped this generation—nationalist, socialist, ETA, Christian, atheist, humanist, or feminist. In time, the inevitable problems of violence, nationalisms (Basque, Spanish), the class struggle, the role of women would create deep splits within this generation, but the sense that we all belonged to the same society would remain, the conviction that we all would swim or sink in the same boat. In its utopian desires and violent destruction, this generation would find its most emblematic image in Gehry's Bilbao "shipwreck," as he himself defined his masterpiece, a project many of us opposed initially but which emerged as the promise of a new city: a building of cuts and torsions, an architecture of the labyrinth.

The generation of the sixties was an *event* in the history of the Basques and their city, Bilbao. It became early the collective subject of a truth process that included a radical reinvention of politics, culture, knowledge, and love. It was from the beginning a militant generation possessed by a conviction for freedom, the consequences of which we couldn't know. We fought Franco's dictatorship. We were defeated in our youthful revolutionary goals of national independence and socialist utopia. My Bilbao generation, addicted to sacrifice, in time became a blind, raging Minotaur trapped in a maze of cultural circumstance and political desire.

Despite the wreckage, the command persisted: you must change your life, you must transform your city. Literary exemplars of such transfiguration are Dante's *Divine Comedy* and William Blake's visionary city *Jerusalem*, where "Beatrice is Blake's City, yet a Woman." Dante's passage through Hell, Purgatory, and Paradise is a story that with its twists of perspective is a *comedy* in the end and not a tragedy, and which I employ here as a formal device, in the manner that Seamus Heaney and other writers did, to convey the complex transformations of my generation—a Dantesque voyage, which began:

Midway along the journey of our life

I woke to find myself in a dark wood,

for I had wandered off from the straight path.

Dante and Virgil at the Gates of Hell. Illustration of the *Divine Comedy* by William Blake.

Revolution or Death

"Why does history take this course?" Marx asked himself, before replying, "So that humanity may happily separate itself from its past." Or, as Kafka would have it, so that the Messiah's coming would no longer be necessary. The Messiah for my 1960s generation was ETA.

It was in the early 1950s that a small group of young, politically minded students began meeting in Bilbao. Franco's regime had been solidified, thanks to its 1953 agreement with the United States. The students named their semi-clandestine organization Ekin (Action), and decided that learning Euskara, their native language, was the first business of the day. Speaking Euskara was their inaugural act of transgression in a Bilbao where anything Basque was fiercely repressed. They began studying Basque history and institutions, in particular the Old Law of Bizkaia (the traditional and customary laws of Bilbao's province), as well as the vanguard European intellectual movements of the time. The students distanced themselves from the activism, folklorism, and sentimentalism of the Basque Nationalist Party's youth. While the Basque Nationalist Party was conservative and ideologically pro–middle class, Ekin was socialist and proletarian and not religiously affiliated. Ekin members were soon going from town to town giving lectures and organizing study courses. They were reading Unamuno's *The Tragic Sense of Life*, Maritain's *Man and the State*, and Berdiaev's *The Sense of History*. They believed Saint Paul to be the most genuine of prophets. By the summer of 1959, the Bilbao students wrote to the Basque government-in-exile in Paris that they had created a new political organization by the name of ETA (*Euskadi Ta Askatasuna*—"Euskadi and Freedom").

These young activists of the newly born ETA carried in their pockets a small volume known as *The White Book* for the color of its cover, which summarized their cause. Its insistence on the primacy of "conscience" and "responsibility" sets it closer to the *Spiritual Exercises* of the Basque founder of the Jesuits, Saint Ignatius of Loyola, than to anything of their own day. Responsibility, according to ETA, was a philosophical "category," the domain of freedom and decision. *The White Book* integrated the demands of Christian commitment and modern existentialist freedom—Loyola-*cum*-Sartre. Its paramount goal was to create a new subject capable of fighting Franco's regime— a subject to be exercised both in intellect and will, a subject made of events that happen to and transform the individual. Essentially, ETA

ETA's logo, "Euskadi ta Askatasuna."

BNP - religious
conservative
middle class
ETA - socialist

members agreed with Loyola—what mattered did not consist "in knowing much" but in "understanding the realities profoundly." The ideological pillars of the new patriotism were an Ignatian irrevocable decision to surrender one's will for the cause; Sartrian absolute freedom; and the Sabinian oath to offer one's life for the fatherland. If each of these components was in itself explosive, the sworn commitment that ETA members made to all three was dynamite.

One of the founders of ETA and its main ideologue until the middle 1960s was José Luis Álvarez Enparantza, an engineering student in Bilbao in the early 1950s whose pen name was Txillardegi. During the formative years of ETA he published a novel, *Leturia-ren egunkari ezkutua* (Leturia's Secret Diary, 1957), which was a breakthrough in Basque literature because of its existentialist themes staged in urban settings. It narrates the failed love between the protagonists Leturia and Miren, which ends in her sickness and death and his suicide. Under the influence of writers such as Soren Kierkegaard, Unamuno, Jean-Paul Sartre, and Albert Camus, Txillardegi explores the themes of freedom and the necessity to choose, which lead to failure. After marrying Miren, then abandoning her to go to Paris and experiment with a life of his own, Leturia comes to the realization that "my heart needed something Absolute," and falling in love with a woman was only a symptom of that need. It is the fascination with the love object that creates something "more beautiful than the object that caused love," and gets dressed as the Absolute. It is "when you reach the goal that the fascination ends" and makes the road more desirable than the goal itself—"Now I understand the fascination for the impossible love: let us choose the impossible, and thus the flower of seduction will never wither." In a text that Txillardegi characterized as a "witness" to the subjective and intellectual issues of the period, his protagonist debates the conflicting demands that derive from intelligence (which turns the subject into the center of his world) and sentiment (which demands the surrender of one's life for others).

This is a key debate whose final resolution Txillardegi borrows from his mentor Unamuno's *The Tragic Sense of Life:* "he denies to thought the capacity to find truth," observes Txillardegi, "and he takes the road of sentiment alone." Since Leturia is unable to choose, he thinks it better that he surrender, while adopting the analogy of the dog in relation to his master: "I have to ask not 'Who is my servant?' but 'Whose servant am I?' This is the salvation." In the end, Leturia's love for Miren is a thinly veiled metaphor for his love of the motherland: "Miren needs me; my motherland needs me; my people need

Cover of Txillardegi's first novel.

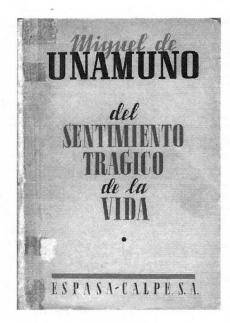

Cover of Unamuno's influential book.

me. I belong to them, and without them I am nothing." He recognizes, "I am guilty, yes," for having abandoned his Miren/Motherland, and he promises that, if she survives, "I will redeem my sins with love. With love . . . with love . . . Who used to speak always about love? I am afraid to admit it: Christ!"

Leturia is barely a Christian, and Txillardegi's protagonist in his next novel, *Peru Leartzako* (1960), is no longer one. The previous generation of Basque nationalists who fought the war was guided by the slogan "God and Ancient Laws." For the ETA generation, God was no longer the big Other. What propelled them, more than ethnic memory, were the philosophical problems discussed by Paris intellectuals. Even though he was inspired by atheists such as Unamuno and Sartre, Leturia repeats Christ's formula: "And what is love? To lay down your life."

The White Book spoke to more than a theory of a new revolutionary subject. The book announced to its readers that it was time for *le passage à l'acte*—the trial by fire. The second chapter examined in detail various methods of action, including those developed by the Communists and Catholic Action. This wasn't action for action's sake, but a coming-about after a decade of reflection. ETA could learn from the Communists, Catholics, and nationalists, but it was something radically different from any of them. Several ETA members were practicing Catholics. How the ethical problem of political violence should be handled was integral to *The White Book,* which quotes profusely from Catholic moralists such as Maritain. ETA held meetings to consider the arguments of Gandhi's nonviolent methods but the text was clear: "We have to offer resistance by all means, even by violence, if needed, and by other means that could be considered immoral, but which in our situation are not." By the end of 1959, the first bomb attacks against Francoist monuments and newspaper offices and against Spanish government headquarters in Bilbao, Vitoria-Gasteiz, and Santander had begun.

Forcing a radical change of perspective in the nationalist subject was equivalent to the Kierkegaardian opposition between "ethnic memory" and "repetition": "We cannot avoid recognizing what we have been, but the most important thing is what we are, what we want to be." A retrospective nationalism, anchored in folklore, surviving through nostalgia, was anathema to ETA. It was time to realize "that we are in 1961, and not in 1936." The racism of Sabino Arana, founder of the Basque Nationalist Party, was scandalous, as was the older generation's disinterest in Basque language and culture. The change that was needed was not merely ideological but, crucially, subjective—and nothing less than revolutionary.

The new subjectivity of the ETA nationalists emphasized the primacy of the person over nation and state. This initial ETA was free of the fetishes that would later characterize it—activism, violence, independentism. The book affirmed expressly that the future of a "resurrected" Euskadi did not depend on the achievement of a sovereign nation-state, because "conceptually, the modern State is currently in acute decline, leaning toward its disappearance." For that initial ETA, the state should always be "underneath" the people. In short, God, Prehistory, the Land of the Ancestors, the Old Laws, the State—these big Others were unessential. The only worthy past for this new Basque subject was the one to be realized existentially now in the present.

The fathers' war was no longer ETA's war, and yet ETA's commitment could not be understood without acknowledging the wound of the fathers' defeat and trauma. The site of the vanquished fathers' apocalypse was Gernika (Guernica in Spanish)—a town of seven thousand inhabitants twenty miles from Bilbao, site of the provincial Parliament and the centuries-old Tree, symbolic of Basque popular democracy. The town was obliterated in 1937 by Franco with the help of Hitler's Condor Legion. The fathers' impotence could only be avenged with a new type of action and subjectivity. For the fathers, war had been the constitutive moment of the national consciousness, but now a new kind of war was needed with a new kind of revolutionary strategy. This war had to bring about the liberation of the motherland once and for all—it had to be the *last* war. The paradigm of war became the dominant political and subjective perspective—everything was measured in terms of *borroka* (struggle). *Borroka* would overshadow the thinking of every party, every activity, every project.

"I return from Death. What we tried to bury grows here," wrote the sculptor Jorge Oteiza, working in Bilbao during the early 1950s. The words predicted a post-Gernika generation forced to return from Death while destined to its own crucible—Revolution or Death. The Bilbaino Unamuno was the thinker behind Oteiza and the first generation of ETA leaders, his tragic sense of life their dominant ethos. Suddenly, an entire generation had been overtaken by the willful promise of a Revolution; softly hidden underneath the joyous enthusiasm was the almost imperceptible call to surrender our lives. The newly started historical process could only be written as tragedy, Gernika being its axiom.

Gernika: A Birthday Present for Hitler

Gernika was the event that condensed Basque history and politics for my generation. On April 26, 1937, Nazi planes coming to the aid of Franco bombed and burned the town to the ground. One of the reporters who saw Gernika in flames was George Steer. His "Telegram from Guernica" appeared on April 28, 1937, in the *Times* of London and the *New York Times*. Steer's report provoked an outcry around the world. Both houses of Congress condemned it in Washington.

Almost a year earlier, on July 25, 1936, a week after Franco's uprising began, Hitler was attending the annual Wagnerian Bayreuth Festival when he received Franco's request for military aircraft. At 10 p.m., after Hitler had seen *The Ring of the Nibelungen* opera cycle—in which Brünnhilde was put to sleep by her father, Wotan, on a mountaintop, surrounded by a ring of magic fire that could only be crossed by the hero, Siegfried—he met with Franco's emissary, Francisco Arranz. The following day Hitler met with his top officers and decided to support Franco by sending military planes and personnel to Seville. This act of support was coded "Operation Magic Fire."

Guernica, the most ancient town of the Basques and the center of their cultural tradition, was completely destroyed yesterday afternoon by insurgent air raiders. . . .

In the form of its execution and the scale of the destruction it wrought . . . the raid on Guernica is unparalleled in military history. Guernica was not a military objective. . . . The object of the bombardment was seemingly the demoralization of the civil population and the destruction of the cradle of the Basque race.

Rankin, *Telegram from Guernica*, 2.

Gernika razed to the ground.

One of those officers was Hermann Göring, who had a personal stake in convincing Hitler that the Luftwaffe air force he commanded should be the Third Reich's military weapon par excellence in the upcoming war. In Göring's view, Franco's rebellion in Spain could serve as the perfect testing ground for his theory of air power. An attack on Gernika in particular would showcase the pivotal role of "carpet bombing," according to the theory of "total war." Hitler's birthday was April 20, and Göring planned Gernika's destruction for the day before as a birthday present for him (it had to be on a Monday, the day that farmers from the area gathered in Gernika for the weekly market). For unknown reasons, the attack was postponed until the following Monday, April 26, and accordingly the military parade in Berlin celebrating Hitler's birthday was also postponed to the same Monday. The fate of Gernika, the ancient symbol of Basque popular democracy, was to become a sacrificial birthday offering for Hitler. The Wagnerian magical fire would carry out the double mission of burning bodies in Gernika and inflaming spirits in Berlin.

After the conclusion of the Spanish Civil War, Hitler saluted the pilots who carried out the air raids with words of praise: "Your fight in Spain was a lesson to our opponents." Churchill, who actively opposed any aid for Bilbao, called Gernika "an experimental horror." Göring admitted at the Nuremberg war crimes trials that Gernika had been a testing ground for German weaponry and strategy. Karl von Knauer, the officer in charge of the attack, used his experience in Gernika to prepare a tactical manual emphasizing lower-level attacks for German bomber pilots. The same man who conceived the bombing of Gernika, Wolfram von Richthofen, now possessed the know-how to destroy Rotterdam, Warsaw, Belgrade, Crete, and Stalingrad. The forces leading toward the Holocaust and Hiroshima were already in play in the small Bizkaian town. The massacre in Gernika signaled the fall of Bilbao and the defeat of the Basque army; it was a prelude to Franco's victory over the Republican forces.

One of the sobbing Basque soldiers collecting burned bodies in Gernika after the bombing was Joseba Elosegi. In his autobiography, Elosegi talks about a woman, covered in dust, screaming "My son, my son!" She ran away wailing with the dead child in her arms after Elosegi found the boy's blood-soaked corpse in the rubble. The eyes of that woman and the sight of Gernika burning haunted Elosegi for the rest of his life—until September 18, 1970. That day, while Franco was watching a pelota game in Donostia-San Sebastián, Elosegi set himself on fire and jumped from the seats above onto the playing court shouting "Gernika! Gernika!" and "Long live free Euskadi!" to remind the dictator of his atrocity. The embers of "Operation Magic Fire" had not yet died.

French historian Pierre Vilar pointed out the intimate bond between Gernika and Bilbao: "Why did the destruction of Gernika become, in turn, an *event-symbol* . . .? It has been said at times that the world 'has known worse things,' but Gernika was the *first* to be destroyed, and by *German planes*. This fact had such implications that those who were responsible for it *denied* it, their supporters *believed* their denial and the spineless people *behaved as if they also believed it*. The effect of this denial may have saved Bilbao from the total destruction that had been announced by Mola." If Bilbao was the Basques' worldly city of commerce, industry, and finance, Gernika with its Parliament and its Tree was the political city of the Basques' ancient law. The first Basque president, José Antonio de Aguirre, took his presidential oath twice on the same day, once in Bilbao and then in Gernika—historically and symbolically, both places were two aspects of the same polis.

Christopher Holme wrote a poem, "Gernika, April 26 1937," which begins, "The world ended tonight." George Orwell told Arthur Koestler that history stopped with the Spanish Civil War. Arthur Miller wrote, "In the half-century to come, the shadow upon all the wars of liberation would always be Spain." For the Basques, the slaughter in Gernika was the "end of history"—the apocalypse.

When the Spanish military revolted in July 1936, Basque nationalists, overcoming strong religious objections but mindful of their nationalist aspirations, sided with the Spanish Republicans. On October 7, the nationalist Aguirre was elected the first Basque president. Walking from the Parliament in the company of his multiparty government, he stood under the Tree of Gernika and swore the oath of loyalty. Aguirre was the man of Gernika. Indalecio Prieto was the other "man of Gernika." When President Aguirre swore the Basque Statute of Autonomy in Gernika, which implied the historic creation of Euskadi as an autonomous political entity, the Socialist Prieto supported it from Madrid's government. He understood and loved Gernika and its historic significance, but from his own political perspective.

After the destruction of Gernika in April 1937, five divisions of the Basque army defended Bilbao's twenty-mile front. Bilbao's defenses formed a sort of Bizkaian Maginot Line called the *cinturón de hierro* (iron ring), which was finally destroyed by heavy German air attacks and tens of thousands of artillery shells. "They summed up for us the fate of Bilbao," wrote Steer, and now they "had been beaten by the combined forces of Germany, Italy and Castile, while others, even declared allies, folded their hands to watch." Bilbao's iron ring was unable to stop Hitler's magic ring of fire, from Wagner's Nibelungen cycle, which had inspired his support for Franco. A convulsed, suicidal Prieto called Aguirre to order him to blow up the bridges, including the one in the Deusto district and the one by the city hall just built by Bastida, to keep the enemy from Bilbao. He wanted the city—his city—to resist to the very end, even if he had to destroy its water supply and the blast furnaces that had created its wealth. Aguirre resisted Prieto's pleas. As the airplanes were dropping their bombs on Bilbao, the militiamen were cursing and swearing at them: "Excrement of God!" Bilbao fell on June 19, 1937.

One of the victims of Gernika was "Lauaxeta"—the pen name of Estepan Urkiaga, a well-known poet working in Bilbao for Aguirre's Basque government. The Gernika bombing was followed by a propaganda war in which Franco and the Germans claimed that the town had been bombed and burned by its Republican Basque defenders. It was Lauaxeta's role to show evidence to the contrary to the international media. As he led a French journalist to the charred town, both men were arrested. The journalist was freed and Lauaxeta was executed. Before facing the firing squad at dawn, Lauaxeta spent the night writing a farewell poem to his country—"Agur, Euzkadi" (Goodbye, Euskadi), which concluded:

> Let the spirit go to luminous heaven
> Let the body be thrown to the dark earth.

In another poem, "Azken oyua" (The Last Howl), Lauaxeta wrote:

> Oh Lord, please grant me this death;
> Let the smell of the roses be for cowards.
> Send me blessed freedom.

Lauxeta's axiom and testament was his line "Everything must be given to the freedom we love." Freedom was a political sacrament.

Lauaxeta was an admirer of Federico García Lorca, with whom he corresponded and whose work he translated into Basque. Prominent in Lorca's poetry is the moon as an icon of eroticism and death. For Lorca, "the moon is the material embodiment of death and apocalypse that abolishes the dichotomy of life/death," its ominous

Agur, Euskadi

Beautiful were the Basque landscapes
beautiful the wide open sea;
but right now more beautiful to me
is the glory of this death!
Let not my will,
but yours be done.
Let the spirit go to luminous heaven
Let the body be thrown to the dark
earth.
—Author's translation

presence pervasive. In his poem "Colors," Lorca's moon is multicolored: it is violet over Paris, yellow over dead cities, "deep and bloody" over the desert, white when it is a "true moon," and

> there is a green moon
> that's moon of the legends.

With a nod to Lorca perhaps ("Green, I want you green. / Under the gypsy moon") Brecht's Bilbao moon was also green—"through the roof the moon was shining green"; "they've shut the green moon out because of rain."

One of Lorca's poems that Lauaxeta translated into Euskara was "The Rider's Song," a premonition of their coming deaths. Another bilbaino poet who identified the moon with death was Unamuno. In his long religious poem *The Christ of Velázquez* he has the dead Christ say, "I am the moon." He repeatedly describes the pallor of Christ's dead body: "the dead Man who doesn't die / white like the moon at night." And when dealing with his blood on the cross, he adds: "The moon turned into all blood."

One enraged reader of Steer's "Telegram from Guernica" was Pablo Picasso. In early January he was commissioned to do a painting for the Spanish pavilion at the 1937 World's Fair in Paris. He began with two plates of an etching, *The Dream and Lie of Franco*, mocking the general's pretensions to greatness. But his work on that project remained unfinished, impeded by his stormy personal life. On April 27, 1937, news of Gernika's destruction reached Paris, and there was a large demonstration and protest march through the city. Picasso read the news and saw photos of the destroyed town in *Ce Soir*. The following day he did six sketches that were the start of *Guernica*. While confronting the gravity of the fascist horror in Spain, Picasso could paint only one subject now—Gernika. He unleashed a creative energy that brought together the Crucifixion, martyrdom, the *corrida,* and the Minotaur. He completed several sketches with the main figures being a bull, a horse, a fallen warrior, and the central image of a woman with a lamp. The wounded horse, figure of the victim in the *corrida,* was made to carry most of the weight of suffering. In later sketches, a woman with a dead child is added; in some of them, the woman is climbing or descending a ladder from the cross. In another, later discarded, a fallen warrior becomes Christ crucified with His fist clenched and raised to the heavens.

In its final version, *Guernica* metamorphizes Picasso's Minoan imagery into an immortalized cry against the horrors of war. A dead warrior lies decapitated. A horse in its death throes lies above the dead soldier. An impassive bull hovers over the figure of a mother with a dead child in her arms. And at the center, a woman holds a lamp, like Ariadne in Picasso's earlier Minotauromachies. While he was working on the figures of the painting, Picasso described them "as though [they] were alive." In a sense they were, for not only did the painting combine Picasso's art and imagination, but his love life at the time as well. *Guernica* was Picasso's sacrament; he said that, if people got too close, "when they scratch it a drop of blood will form." This was Picasso's requiem for his generation—the icon of the Gernika century.

Guernica was preceded by a series of etchings, the best-known of which is *Minotauromachy* (1935). It displays a fierce minotaur with a sword in his mouth, a female *torera,* and a girl, Ariadne (Nietzsche's labyrinth), raising a candle—as if representing illumination's combat against the dark forces of violence and evil. The Minotaur had become an obsessive theme for Picasso during the 1930s. When, with his surrealist friends, writers Michel Leiris and Georges Bataille, Picasso launched the journal *Minotaure* in May 1933, the publication used Bataille's title and Picasso's front cover. Fascinated by bullfighting all his life, Picasso found that the archeological discoveries of Crete (with its mythical Minotaur) provided new creative imagery. He would later sketch several Minotaurs in his *Vollard Suite* series, and according to Lisa Florman, the Minotaur transcends the opposition of vision and carnality in some of his other plates, such as *Battle of Love*: "vision and touch are reconciled . . . a mode of vision that is thoroughly carnal and characterized by all the rapaciousness of a bull. The Minotaur thus represents a synthesis or transcendence." But in the later *blind* Minotaur, the sightless eyes descending on the face of a head thrown back become the failure of such a synthesis. This blind Minotaur was to become not only the expression of Picasso's own battle of love but also the emblem of my ETA generation.

Long before Picasso's *Guernica,* other artists through the millennia had painted horses on the dark walls of Gernika's caves. Just a few miles from Gernika's center, two archeologists, Telesforo de Aranzadi and José Miguel de Barandiarán, in the 1920s and 1930s discovered and explored the Cave of Santimamiñe, one of many containing prehistoric

Picasso, *Minotauromachy* (1935).

Cover of the first issue of *Minotaure* (1933).

remains. This cave, with its hidden horses, came to be known as the "sanctuary" of Basque prehistory—the fetishistic underground where a primordial identity could be projected. There is one foundational discipline underneath Basque nationalism and identitarian politics: anthropology. Gernika's historic relevance and its transformation into a worldwide "event-symbol" cannot be fully grasped without reference to its anthropological romance.

A prehistoric Basque Country served as a fundamental fantasy of origins for modern Basques torn by the ills of modern Bilbao's industry and modernization. This anthropological tradition, with the concept of race as its anchor, gave ground to a Basque ahistorical subject that concealed the present. In a time when the modern subject is defined as a tearing apart, an identity based on the premodern premise of plenitude becomes the ultimate cultural impasse. Basque anthropology could be seen as marking an opposition to Bilbao's capitalism, a *symptom* at the heart of capitalism as the universal term. During Franco's times, anthropology became the axiomatic discipline asserting Basque identity as opposed to the dictatorship's Spanish homogeneity.

But race was not only the canonical fetish of Gernika's Basque anthropological totality. It was also central to the worldview of the Nazis bombarding Gernika. The very notion of race was a child of the European Enlightenment. Promoted by Kant in 1775, scientific thought began to assert the permanence of race. No other people were as intrigued by the Basques as the Germans. Long before the German Condor Legion came to Gernika, there had been intense German scholarly interest in the Basques. The great linguist Wilhelm von Humboldt visited the Basque Country during the years 1799–1801 and extolled the "Basque nation," its language, and *volksgeist* in the most admiring tones. He was followed by a long tradition of German intellectuals fascinated with the Basques. German enthusiasm did not diminish with the Nazis, whose search for a new European order of "uncontaminated" races found a prime candidate in the Basques.

Gernika's anthropological romance was thus not only a Basque affair. Rousseau wrote that Gernika had "the happiest people in the world [with] troops of peasants regulating the affairs of state under an oak, and conducting themselves wisely." The second American president, John Adams, visited Bilbao in 1779 and presented Gernika as an historical examplar of "federal democracy" in his three-volume work that would be read by the authors of the U.S. Constitution. In 1810 the

British romantic poet William Wordsworth wrote a poem to "The Oak of Guernica," extolling it as the guardian of "Biscay's ancient liberty."

The night of the fall of Bilbao on June 19, George Steer, the British journalist who seven weeks earlier had witnessed Gernika on fire and written of its destruction for the world press, made one last visit to the Basque government's empty offices in the Hotel Carlton on the Gran Vía. He picked up photographs and souvenirs of Aguirre—including the president's pen and his last notepad. With them Steer began writing his classic *The Tree of Gernika.* Next to the hotel, on Ercilla Street, now stands a life-sized statue of President José Antonio Aguirre, installed in 2004.

Steer was the last witness to the fallen city. His wife, Margarita, and their unborn child had died earlier that year in a London clinic. Grief-stricken, for weeks he had visited his wife's dead body until finally, in early April, he took it to Biarritz in the French Basque Country to be buried. Then he joined the war as a reporter. Careless with his own life on the front line, Steer came under fire on several occasions.

As he exited the Hotel Carlton that June night when everything was lost, Steer found himself walking the predawn streets alone. The bridges had been dynamited at 2 a.m., and all the lights were out. That night, when two hundred thousand people were being evacuated westward, "the enemy came out in the soft moonlight and machine gunned the length of the road to Santander, flying very low." Steer described the moment of departure:

Statue of President Aguirre on Ercilla Street, next to the Carlton Hotel.

> Here at least there was moonlight, a clear view along the
> gleaming ribbon road, the companionship of the softly flowing
> river and of many other mortals also fleeing west. I wandered
> alone about the streets, trying to drink in this silence and
> darkness. Here I was, a small fidgety animal, in a great city
> which was only not a desert because every corner of it echoed
> to the sound of my feet. But in other ways it was a desert,
> unpeopled except by a moonlight mirage, which on the leaves
> and litter of its sidewalks pretended a variety without life-blood
> or marrow.

Haunted by the memory of his dead wife, Steer continued to walk in that hour of final defeat, comforted by the river and mesmerized by the mirage of Brecht's "that old Bilbao moon." The time had come to say goodbye to Bilbao; "it was cold, approaching dawn, when to look at the stream of the Nervión made one shiver." This was Rimbaud's "The Drunken Boat":

The Dawns are heartbreaking.

Every moon is atrocious and every sun bitter.

Steer convinced a chauffeur to take him down a nearly impassable road. They were fired upon. In front of him were thousands upon thousands of militiamen marching away from Bilbao "under the onset of a great emotion." This was Dante's Bilbao: "Come see your city. . . . in mourning now, / widowed, alone, lamenting night and day:/ 'My Caesar, why have you abandoned me?'" The Bilbao poet Ángela Figuera added:

But I couldn't do anything. Death showed up.

I clamored to God. I clamored. But it was in vain.

I gave birth to Cain and Abel. I gave birth to WAR.

Cruel Beauty was the title of her book of poems.

Goering and von Richthofen's birthday present to Hitler on that 26 of April of 1937 would cast a long historical shadow over my generation. Just days after the bombing of Gernika, when he was four, Julen Madariaga was evacuated to Algorta, fifteen kilometers from Bilbao. He was the son of one of Bilbao's upper-middle-class families. One night, on a fishing boat armed with cannons for self-protection, Julen was taken with his mother and four brothers to Bayonne, France; later he left with his family from the port of La Rochelle in southern France on board the SS *Oropesa*, headed for a decade of exile in Chile. Also during those days, on May 21, 1937, the SS *Habana* left for Southampton with 3,840 children on board, escorted by two British naval vessels. This was particularly risky because the Spanish armada had imposed a blockade on Bilbao. Relatives of the thousands of departing children were watching from Punta Galea, on the far side of Bilbao's Abra estuary, as the Spanish warship *Canarias* lingered nearby in the darkness. It would surely have blocked the escape of the boat with its cargo of children had the British battle cruiser HMS *Hood* not placed itself between the fishing boat and the warship. It entered Southampton silently on Sunday, May 23, so as to not wake the children, who would soon be taken to Stoneham Camp and from there distributed among ninety-four "colonies," which were in essence camps where the children were lodged and cared for. An estimated thirty thousand children were sent to France, Belgium, the Soviet Union, Mexico, and Switzerland, carrying letters, photos, souvenirs, and memories of their loved ones still in the Basque Country.

All during this time the British government pursued a policy of neutrality relative to the turmoil in Spain. The Conservatives then in power had no appetite for a leftist Spanish Republican government, and under British pressure, France's Socialist government under Leon Blum and twenty-four other European governments accepted a pact of "non-intervention." Franklin Roosevelt did nothing to assist the Republic, while U.S. corporations like Ford, General Motors, Firestone, Texaco Oil, and other businesses helped Franco's fascists. Roosevelt later admitted that he had made "a grave mistake" and that soon afterward he had paid a price for it because the Western democracies' spineless response ended up emboldening Hitler. The word *Gernika* became taboo. The only exception to the policy of non-intervention was the generosity and good will extended toward refugee children. It showed the contradictions of the humanitarian stance—let Franco and Hitler massacre them in Gernika/Bilbao, but we will feed the children if they manage to escape elsewhere. Orwell summed it up in a 1942 essay: "The outcome of the Spanish war was settled in London, Paris, Rome, Berlin—at any rate not in Spain. . . . The war was actually won for Franco by the Germans and Italians."

Even bringing food to Bilbao, let alone arms, was too dangerous for the allies. On the other hand, the German Condor Legion contingent was made up of eighteen thousand young men, all volunteers. Hitler loaned Franco seven hundred airplanes, and the Italians sent airplanes as well. The Basques had only five planes at the beginning of the defense of Bilbao. There were no scruples for support on the insurgents' side. Yvonne Cloud wrote that "loyalties are political loyalties to the Basque children." Their destiny was determined by politics—the neutrality and "humanitarianism" of the Western democracies amounted to denial of the bloodletting in Spain. These impotent children, an embarrassment to the European democracies, became the custodians of their parents' political truths.

On the morning of June 19, 1937, as the news that Bilbao had fallen arrived at Stoneham Camp, the guards were unsure how to proceed. Some were against informing the children; others thought they should have a night's respite and be told in the morning. The majority felt it was best to let them know before bedtime so they could weep in the night and wake up to a new day. At 7:45 p.m., the announcement was made. The children did not react. Then one of the Basque priests gave the same message in Spanish: "We very much regret that enemy troops are now in the town of Bilbao . . ." and a loud shriek interrupted him. The children began to wail and cry "Mother! Mother!" long into the night. Cloud writes of scenes of weeping and despair, moaning, and cries that rose to hysteria, a howling crowd of children abandoned to grief and swaying rhythmically. Some began throwing stones and sticks at the loudspeaker. About three hundred children ran wildly from the camp into the road and to the nearby woods to fall down and cry. The remaining children, more than three thousand of them, went to their tents where they lay sobbing until morning.

Are you for or against us? The children's wailing posed the question. Are you for fascism or liberty, for a humanitarian or a political solution? Names—Franco, Hitler, Bilbao—were like bombs thrown at the children. At one point, Cloud saw two hundred children return the cry of *Salud!* (Cheers!) from a passing car by raising their fists. Those fists were only the beginning of their rebellion. The exiled children of Gernika were the future ETA teenagers of Bilbao.

The children of war in Stoneham Camp raising their fists.

Aita Patxi/von Richthofen: The Cross and the Trash

Father Frank, a Passionist monk known as "Aita Patxi," was a chaplain called in 1936 to administer religious services to the Republican army. Born in a farm in the Bizkaian town of Arrireta, he was in Gernika on the day of the bombing. Wolfram von Richthofen, a lieutenant colonel sent to Spain by Hitler, was in charge of the Condor Division that flew the planes over Gernika and helped to plan the strategy of the attack. While von Richthofen was directing the bombs dropped from above, Aita Patxi, crucifix in hand, was assisting the soldiers and civilians being massacred below.

Aita Patxi and von Richthofen each kept a diary of their war experiences. The 1936–39 Spanish Civil War was, for von Richthofen, essentially a training camp for the impending World War II. Parts of his diary were published in Klaus Maier's *Guernica* and illustrate what Benjamin called the fascist "aestheticization of politics"—when humanity "is capable of experiencing its own destruction as an aesthetic enjoyment of the highest order." At Aguirre's insistence, whom he met in the trenches of the Bizkaian hills during the spring of 1937, Aita Patxi wrote an autobiographical account of his war memories two decades after Gernika. The juxtaposition of both texts speaks for itself.

These fragments from von Richthofen's April diary, the month Gernika was bombed, illustrate his attitude toward his assignment:

4.4.1937. I have gone to Otxandio. Marvelous effects of the bombardment, and of the fighter plane and of the A/88 . . . Dead and mutilated people everywhere; heavy trucks, carrying part of the munitions, blown up.

24.4.1937. Elorrio has been evacuated by the enemy, one of our battalions is further advanced 500 meters in red territory. It is very entertaining to see, at the beginning of the sunset, the fire that comes out of the rifle mouths. . . . First they were bombarded once by the Italians, but then they were spared because of their pretty palaces.

25.4.1937. Finally the bomber planes arrive; the Ju dropped heavy bombs over Ermua very beautifully. . . . Again the Italians miss the target and bomb Eibar by mistake. . . . Elgueta, which was taken care of completely by the Italians on the 23rd, has a horrendous aspect. Very good results of the bombardment, the hits fell very tightly.

Wolfram von Richthofen.

26.4.1937. Eibar, touching. . . . With the exception of a few houses, the center of the town was completely burned out. The beginning of the fire and the collapse of some houses was a very interesting phenomenon.

27.4.1937. [The day after the bombing of Gernika] After lunch, a nice trip to the coast of Deba, where the headquarters of the Italian General Staff are, and to Ondarroa, the frontline, where there is also a command post.

Magnificent coast, which recalls Amalfi. . . . Toward Zarautz, where I find Sander and lodge for the night. Beautiful grand hotel at the edge of a pretty sea, with a good room and good food. There, magnificent.

In the morning again we discuss everything point by point. The transmission of news from unit to unit is a matter of concern. . . . It is not worth having transmissions of our own for this *zarzuela* operetta.

In the afternoon, Sander, Jaenecke and myself play cards.

28.4.1937. Also in the afternoon, precise information that Gernika has been literally razed to the ground.

29.4.1937. In the afternoon, playing cards with Sander and Jaenecke; the latter always ransacks us.

Aita Patxi's memories relating to April 25 and April 26 follow. (He labels Franco's troops "Spaniards," but he knew of course that those who fought against the rebel army and for the Republic were also Spaniards.)

DEATH AND RESURRECTION. It was exactly like that for me. In that moment of tribulation, with the Spaniards shooting and shooting at me, it was for me as if I had *died and been resurrected*. . . .

TERRIBLE BOMBING. . . . As I was with three soldiers, with the Cross in my hands, the Spanish airplanes began to drop bombs and more bombs. What horror! One of the bombs fell right next to me and left me unconscious on the ground. I didn't know whether I was alive or dead. . . . I began to look for the Cross in the mud, and after I found it I got up to help the pitiful soldiers. They were all calling out again and again, sobbing. How could I be quiet? . . .. My blood was boiling. With the Cross in my hands, I went to everyone and I gave it to them to kiss, while telling them at the same time to put their lives in the hands of God and to ask help from the Virgin Mary and that she would protect them. Some had blood pouring out of their mouth; others had lost their legs and arms. After kissing the Cross, to those who could take it I gave them the Host of Our Lord, and to the others the final rites and the extreme unction. When the bombings were over, those of us who were alive took first the wounded and then the dead to the plain below. I don't know the names of all the dead and wounded. . . . These were the final words of Tomás Torrezuri: LONG LIVE A FREE EUZKADI.

TOWARD GERNIKA. At nightfall, they told us that we had to go toward Gernika, and so we began walking. On the road we were all praying the Rosary, I would initiate it and they would all answer me. . . . Then a few trucks arrived and they took us to Bilbao.

GERNIKA BURNING. (Monday). April 26. . . . So we left Bilbao. But when we arrived in Gernika, we were told we could not advance because the Spaniards were there nearby. Thus we had to stay in Gernika. It must have been 10 or 11 in the morning . . . it was bright, there was splendid sunshine. . . . At about 3 p.m. the Spaniards began the air raids to set Gernika on fire. They began to drop bombs, to set the houses on fire, and to machine-gun. What anguish! We didn't know where to go. . . . I had the Cross in my hands and I prayed the Rosary with everyone and I gave the last rites to everyone. What weeping and wailing!

Aita Patxi.

In tragic irony, von Richthofen and Aita Patxi were both fighting a titanic battle within a symbolic universe presided over by the cross: von Richthofen's Iron Cross, the symbol Hitler had rescued for his Luftwaffe war planes (the Knight's Cross of the Iron Cross was the award Hitler gave him), versus Aita Patxi's bloodied crucifix. The symbolic struggle was the raised crucifix of Aita Patxi at the front of the Basque soldiers defending Gernika versus the raised crucifix of the *Cruzada* (crusade) led by Franco (and including many Basque brothers affiliated with the insurgent army) razing Gernika to the ground. It was the essential gap inside the same symbol. It was the *coincidentia oppositorum*—the apocalypse.

It is hard to conceive of a greater subjective traumatic gap belonging to the same symbolic universe than the one effected by Aita Patxi/Aguirre and von Richthofen. The powerful advantage of technology and a new culture of modernity allowed the victorious von Richthofen to conduct warfare in the anonymous manner of a bureaucracy, almost as if it were a work of art with its focus on technical perfection and aesthetic pleasure. The vanquished Aita Patxi and Aguirre had, in contrast, only the power of their old-fashioned Christianity, their claim to universal justice, and the conviction that their cause could not be conquered by defeat or death—the radical belief and utter defiance through resurrection.

But in the crossroads of Spanish politics, where the antagonism between Christianity and Marxist socialism represented a major cultural faultline, Aita Patxi and Aguirre's faith would be sorely tested as the Catholic Church openly sided with the fascists. "This is a fight between Christ and Lenin," the Vatican secretary of state, Cardinal Pacelli, later Pope Pius XII, told the Basque delegation headed by President Aguirre. Had Aguirre sided with Franco and Hitler and not with the leftist Spanish Republic, Pacelli would have been far warmer. The Basque nationalists, who had just attended mass and taken Communion in the Saint Ignatius Room at the Jesuits' residence in Rome, were baffled that their religious commitment was being questioned and that Pacelli refused to meet with them. Aguirre, who had attended a Jesuit high school and university, was Christian to the core, yet, as he was told by the Vatican, his politics were "red." "Until Fascism is defeated, Basque Nationalism will remain at its post," Aguirre had promised the Republican deputies at the Cortes of Valencia weeks before, in October 1936. His religious paradox, like Aita Patxi's, was that he was forced to be truly "Leninist" because he

The Iron Cross, symbol of the German Army.

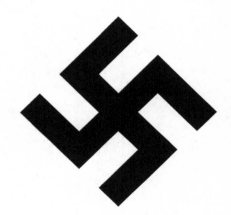

The swastika.

Iron Cross with Oak Leaves, Hitler's supreme medal to reward his generals.

was truly "Christian." Aita Patxi and Aguirre were *repeating Lenin* in their partisan universality.

Aita Patxi was, after the war and until his death in 1974, a well-known fixture in Bilbao's religious world. Residing in San Felicísimo, he was considered a saint by everyone for his visits to the sick and his constant prayers. He is currently in the process of beatification.

Aita Patxi was my confessor during the novitiate year previous to taking religious vows—poverty, chastity, and obedience, plus propagating Christ's Passion. If not for his saintly aura, he would have been a comic figure from the Middle Ages. An unworldly, dour man, his troglodyte religiosity was grotesque. As part of his observance, he would never look you straight in the eye and was incapable of small talk, limiting his speech to saying "in the presence of God" or praying the Rosary. If he encountered someone in the convent's corridor, his only acknowledgement was to tip his small black cap. His edifying presence frequently provoked open laughter among us novices, as if reminding us of Christianity's inherent character of divine comedy. Everything about his faith and heroism seemed remote and quaint. He could well have said with Dostoevsky's Prince Myshkin, "Blessed is he who takes no offence at me."

Aita Patxi conducted his first mass dressed in red, an expression of his desire for martyrdom—like Kierkegaard, being a Christian was for him neither more nor less than being a martyr. He thought the occasion had arrived when he was called to serve as a chaplain in the war. In December 1936, Aita Patxi changed his Passionist habit, with its heart-shaped escutcheon of the Passion on the breast, Rosary beads hanging from the belt, and long cloak and sandals, for the uniform of the soldier-chaplain—backpack, blanket, shoes, mess kit, and canteen. He gave his military superiors the impression of a pallid, sickly, and extremely shy man, someone of little worth. His intrusive piety, praying Rosaries and offering masses, provoked the scorn of anarchists and communists alike. But the true measure of the man would emerge when they were engulfed in the carnage of war.

To those who knew him, Aita Patxi's true gift was his religious radicalism—to the point of inhumanity. The "road to sanctity" required that the all-too-human senses of sight, hearing, speech, taste, touch, and smell be brutally denied. The human had to be reduced to ashes in order for the divine to take hold. The sense of the inhuman was reflected most memorably during his captivity when, as later reported by sev-

Christian crucifix.

The *lauburu*.

The Tree of Gernika.

José Antonio Aguirre.

Indalecio Prieto.

Estepan Urkiaga, "Lauaxeta."

Julen Madariaga.

eral witnesses, he offered to take the place of a prisoner who had been condemned to face a firing squad—a gesture that was to be repeated by Maximilian Kolbe in Auschwitz in the summer of 1941. The man, a communist from Asturias who had escaped the Spanish concentration camp at San Pedro de Cardeña near Burgos, was recaptured and condemned to death. He refused the last spiritual rites. Those in charge of the prisoner thought he might accept them from Aita Patxi, whom even the nonbelievers by now respected. Indeed, the Asturian soldier did not refuse Aita Patxi's company. But then, in his religious madness, Aita Patxi offered himself to the fascists in the communist's stead, saying that the condemned man had a wife and five children to care for. His offer was accepted and a simulacrum of a firing-squad shooting was carried out (Aita Patxi "was smiling and happy")—a simulacrum that is reminiscent of Dostoyevsky's mock execution. But in the end, the officers refused to carry out the execution and Aita Patxi "learned the next day that the Asturian had been shot at dawn."

But even "charity" was not enough to capture Aita Patxi's enigma, his utter abjection and remoteness from this world, the horror of his comic figure. Lacan expressed it best: "A saint's business, to put it clearly, is not *caritas.* Rather, he acts as trash (*déchet*); his business being *trashitas* (*il décharite*)"—*trashity* being a condensation of trash and charity. If anything, Aita Patxi's bizarre life was the embodiment of "trash." But Lacan introduced the figure of the saint as trash not to denigrate it but to best define his own priestlike occupational role: "The psychoanalyst truly wants to be shit." Both figures evoke the double-faced reality of the tabooed *homo sacer*—cursed and exalted, trash and divine at once.

In his religious absolutism, Aita Patxi had been traversed by a God who was so traumatic that he had become a monstrous figure. Aita Patxi's saintly madness, one could add, went even further than von Richthofen's murderous madness. As Charles Péguy wrote, saints are "bitten harder and deeper, filled infinitely more than the criminal, than the cruel is bitten and filled with cruelty. . . . The holy is marked infinitely more than the cruel. The saintly is devoured where the cruel is only bitten."

Aita Patxi—how can I forget?—was also the man who prayed for me when he was my confessor during my novitiate. He was deeply wounded by our desertion when most of us forsook the religious life and left the convent. Despite the sense of dread that the memory of his religiosity elicits in me, I cannot but admire his antifascist struggle and love the man I envision raising his bloodied crucifix against von Richthofen's Nazi planes. Although unable to be a true witness to his spirituality, I write here to bear testimony to the immensity of his "passion and resurrection" in Gernika.

Hiroshima, Mon Amour

The fixation with Basque origins was one more result of archeology's impact on Europe's intellectual culture after the epoch-making findings of Arthur Evans in Knossos, Crete, at the turn of the twentieth century. Evans's matriarchal and pacifist theories would have their counterparts in the work of Basque ethnography. But not only archeologists had become fixated upon ancient Greece during the later part of the nineteenth century. In 1872 Nietzsche wrote *The Birth of Tragedy*, in which he deployed the Dionysian and Apollonian components of classical Greek tragedy in order to transcend the nihilism of the modern era. The archeologists of Knossos, with Heinrich Schliemann at the forefront, and the writers, artists, and psychoanalysts enchanted with Cretan mythology found in Nietzsche a true prophet of modernism. Nietzsche's initial hero was Richard Wagner, for whose wife, Cosima, he wrote his final "Ariadne, I love you. Dionysus," and whose music inspired him to prophesize the return of pre-Socratic values to a post-Christian world—the same music that moved Hitler in Bayreuth to order his "Operation Magic Fire" in support of Franco's crusade. But the truest prophecy by Nietzsche was written in his autobiographical *Ecce Homo*: "One day there will be associated with my name the recollection of something frightful . . . I am not a man, I am dynamite . . . there will be wars such as there have never been on earth." Gernika was only the prelude to Nietzsche's full prophecy.

It wasn't enough that President Aguirre was betrayed by the Church and the European democracies. He would soon learn that von Richthofen's words after destroying Gernika—it was "a complete technical success," the bombs producing "marvelous effects"—would be replicated by his own savior, the United States, after "Little Boy" was dropped from the *Enola Gay* over Hiroshima—a bomb that most U.S. top military commanders opposed because they saw it as unnecessary to end the war. "This is the greatest thing in history," an excited President Truman had remarked in jubilation. The pilot who dropped the bomb, Paul Tibbets, said, "If Dante had been with us on the plane, he would have been terrified."

The success was such that it merited a repeat performance, and "Big Boy" was dropped three days later on Nagasaki—chosen instead of Kokura, the original target city, because of poor visibility there. The pilot reported, "Results clear and successful in all respects. Visible effects greater than any tests." When he was asked about any regrets, Truman replied, "not the slightest in the world," and when asked whether the decision had been difficult, he said, "Hell no, I made it like that," and he snapped his fingers. This was the same holocaust logic that Franco and Hitler had inaugurated in Gernika, now applied to a target many times larger: arbitrarily select a city, then sacrifice and obliterate it along with hundreds of thousands of people, and thus "send a message" to the enemy. Soon the scientists who made the bomb possible—Oppenheimer, Szilard, Einstein—were horrified by the monster they had created and begged the president not to use it, only to be met with scorn for having become cry-baby scientists. "We in America," wrote Lewis Mumford at the time, "are living among madmen. Madmen govern our affairs in the name of order and security." This madness would extend to the Cold War, one of whose consequences was the underpinning of Franco's regime by the United States, and would have a direct impact on my Bilbao generation.

Aguirre, the man of Gernika who must have felt that anything done to defeat Hitler was necessary and right, was now ideologically obliged to turn a blind eye to his own protector's atrocity. What was done to vanquish European fascism had to be right, even if it might entail answering hell with hell. It would take the eyes of Aguirre's contemporary, Bilbaino Jesuit Pedro Arrupe, then living in Hiroshima, to see the novelty of the Event in all its horror. The Jesuits were intrinsic to Bilbao's religious fabric, and Arrupe had joined the order at the age of eighteen. He was assigned to Japan as a missionary. When the atomic bomb exploded, Arrupe was the master of novices in a Jesuit center at Nagatsuka, four miles from Hiroshima. Using the skills he had learned as a former medical student at the University of Madrid, and with help from the novices, he transformed the center into a clinic where he attended to thousands of victims.

It wasn't only Arrupe who linked Hiroshima to Gernika. It was also connected in the experience of Robert Oppenheimer, the director of the Manhattan Project that would produce the atomic bomb at

Pedro Arrupe. Hiroshima

Los Alamos. One of the members of the Lincoln Brigade who died in the Spanish war was Joe Dallet, whose widow, Kitty, would later marry Oppenheimer. To the surprise of many, the left-wing pacifist Oppenheimer became the ardent soldier and champion of the Cold War by his dogged determination to develop the bombs to be dropped over Hiroshima and Nagasaki. "From Spain to Los Alamos was a short step," wrote Freeman Dyson, a physicist who worked under Oppenheimer for twenty years. "Oppenheimer was as proud of his bombs as Joe Dallet had been proud of his guns. Oppenheimer became the good soldier that Kitty loved and admired." Oppenheimer himself said that Gernika signaled the beginning of the atomic era. It was indeed a short step between Gernika and Hiroshima.

Arrupe became an active witness to the destruction of Hiroshima. What Aguirre saw in Gernika, Arrupe contemplated on August 6, 1945—the day of the Feast of the Transfiguration. He was thirty-seven. What he learned that day—the modern state's celebration of technologically sophisticated mass murder—changed him forever. In 1950, he traveled the world giving testimony of that day. His later revolutionary "re-foundation" of the Jesuit Order in the 1960s as its general head was the deferred action of the inner explosion that Arrupe experienced in Hiroshima.

"I was in my room with another priest at 8:15 when suddenly we saw a blinding light, like a flash of magnesium," Arrupe recounted. "We heard a formidable explosion similar to the blast of a hurricane." While his novices rushed to the outskirts of the city for food and supplies, Arrupe treated—without anesthetics—contusions, wounds from wood and glass imbedded in bodies, all kinds of burns, and infected blisters produced by the radiation. "The suffering was frightful, the pain excruciating, and it made the bodies writhe like snakes, yet there was not a word of complaint. They all suffered in silence." He had room for only 150 wounded in his Jesuit house-turned-clinic.

Hiroshima became Arrupe's gospel, the text that made him *see*. The bedrock of Jesuit spirituality emerges from the mystical experiences of "seeing" that Saint Ignatius had after his conversion in Manresa, in September 1522, by the Cardoner River. Arrupe wrote about "the transcendental importance" of that "sort of Pentecost" for Ignatius. His own illumination would be by Hiroshima's river on the night "Little Boy" was dropped—a sight not even Dante could have imagined:

> We were to witness more horrible scenes that night. As we
> approached the river, the spectacle was awful beyond words.
> Fleeing the flames and availing themselves of low tide, the
> people lay across both shores, but in the middle of the night the
> tide began to rise, and the wounded, exhausted now and half
> buried in mud, could not move. The cries of those drowning are
> something I shall never forget.

Arrupe continued his pilgrimage through the Dantesque city toward the Jesuit convent, where all of its priests were injured. He arrived at five in the morning, the time to celebrate Mass: "In turning around to say *Dominus Vobiscum*, I saw before my eyes many wounded, suffering terribly. . . . I do not think I have ever said mass with such devotion." It was with that "The Lord be with you" that Arrupe saw history as a combination of political horror and mystical passion and resurrection—a vision of the evil of modern life that was not so much about religious decadence or moral laxity as about the horror of modern militarism disguised as belief in civilization and the defense of moral values.

What he saw was the unnamable. As relief trains started arriving from Tokyo and Osaka, Arrupe began to ask what had happened and

It was five in the afternoon. An indescribable spectacle met our gaze: a macabre vision which staggered the imagination. Before us lay a city completely destroyed. We walked through its streets, stepping on ruins under which embers still felt warm. Any carelessness on our part could be fatal.

Much more terrible, however, was the tragic sight of those thousands of injured people begging for help. One such was a child who had a piece of glass imbedded in the pupil of his left eye, and another who had a large wooden splinter protruding like a dagger from between his ribs. Sobbing, he called out: 'Father, save me!'

Another victim was caught between two beams with his legs calcified up to the knees. . . . More heartbreaking, perhaps, were the cries of the children calling to their parents.

Arrupe, *Essential Writings*, 44.

they told him very mysteriously that it was "the atomic bomb?" And what was that? "They knew nothing but the name. It was a new word that was coming for the first time into the vocabulary.

As he entered Hiroshima, "we soon began to raise pyramids of bodies and pour fuel on them to set them afire." Arrupe was a thoroughly modern one from Bilbao's upper bourgeoisie, the top student of his class at the most prestigious medical school in Madrid before he joined the Jesuits. Arrupe's vision of evil went beyond Hitler; indeed, all of modern culture and technology were implicated in Hiroshima. Arrupe set himself the task of leading his religious order through a historic re-foundation that sided with the dispossessed and the poor—a "radical Christianity" that, in the words of Thomas Altizer, "refuses a redemption which is confined to individual selfhood, and seeks an apocalyptic transformation of the world." This man would personify the avant-garde of a turbulent post–Vatican II Conciliar Church.

Arrupe's inner revolution was born from his experience of messianic time beyond historic time. "It was 8:10," he wrote. "That clock, silent and immobile, has been for me a symbol. The explosion of the first atomic bomb can be considered an event beyond history. It is not a memory, it is a perpetual experience that does not stop with the tic tock of the clock. . . . Hiroshima has no relation to time: it belongs to eternity." Decades later, as the leader of the Jesuit Order, Arrupe would be at the forefront of a "liberation theology" that radically questioned the Church's historical involvement in the structures of power and domination. At the core of this new theology is an apocalyptic and *kenotic* (empty) vision of a humiliated God, in which the biblical "My God, why have you forsaken me?" turns into "My God, why have you forsaken *yourself!*"

I met one of these liberation theology priests, Javi, at Bilbao's soccer field, San Mamés, after one of Athletic's disastrous losses. I had purchased Javi's latest work in a Bilbao bookstore where I read about God's "impotence in the world" and about how "God's *kenosis* on the cross leads to an authentic revolution in the image we have of God," leading to a Jewish mystical theme: "the one of God's *self-limitation* to give space to the existence and autonomy of the world." Javi had earlier asked: "Why Gernika? Why Auschwitz? Why Hiroshima? . . . Why ETA's violence?" He added, "This unending series of questions appears to postulate a declaration of bankruptcy of faith in God

Pedro Arrupe

and a complete discredit of the Augustinian name for God: 'I am your salvation.'"

Hiroshima, like Gernika, was an apocalypse; through the influence of Arrupe and his followers, it would have a direct impact on Bilbao. The footbridge between the Jesuit University of Deusto and Abandoibarra, next to the Guggenheim, was named after Arrupe. If Gernika taught my generation the need to defend ourselves from fascism and foreign intervention, then Hiroshima and the Cold War made it obvious that, beyond a national-cultural perspective, "the unthinkable," the end of time, was now a distinct possibility.

Wigs and Bullets

Aguirre's fate was the political catechism in which my ETA generation was schooled. Nobody would question his democratic, Christian, and patriotic credentials, yet his defeat made a mockery of harboring any hopes of international support for overthrowing Franco's regime. The Spanish Civil War ended in the spring of 1939, and the Basque government-in-exile moved to Paris. Then World War II began, and Aguirre experienced a harrowing escape. He was visiting his family in Belgium when the Nazis invaded; he joined one of the caravans of refugees hurrying along the roads toward France while being bombed from the air. "This same air power had made the Basque roads during our war a mockery to civilization," Aguirre would later write. In fact, someone Aguirre knew was actively involved in the air war over France—von Richthofen, the master bomber who had honed his skills over Gernika and then destroyed Warsaw and other cities from the air. Gernika, Belgium, Europe—it was all the same for von Richthofen, and also for Aguirre.

While Aguirre eluded the Nazis, and French and Spanish forces searched for him, he dreamed of America, "the promised land," the "continent which . . . attained a marvelous personality," a "country of salvation." When he finally reached Brazil in late August 1941, he "felt like bending down and kissing the ground. Here was a free land." When Paris was liberated from the Nazis on August 24, 1944, one of the first battalions to reach the city's center had the axiomatic name of Aguirre's politics and life—"Gernika." He moved to New York and, while teaching at Columbia University, collaborated with the U.S. State

Department and intelligence services to form a Basque espionage network operating in Europe and Latin America. Basque nationalists felt certain that as soon as the Axis lost the war, Franco's days were numbered. But a bitter reality—principles and promises trumped by pragmatism—became apparent in 1951, when the United States reversed its position and sided with Franco. To Aguirre, this was the end of what the Statue of Liberty in New York and the Tree of Gernika stood for. At the age of fifty-six, he died in March 22, 1960, of a heart attack.

"He is already in his casket, but you can go see him," they told François Mauriac, the French Nobel Prize winner, in late March, 1960. Mauriac could utter only "broken words" in the presence of his friend Aguirre's corpse. Later he wrote, "The casket has a crystal peephole at the face's level. What a vision! . . . In this face, as if eaten away from inside, I cannot recognize the noble and frank face of Don José Antonio de Aguirre. . . . Who could have been the victim of a more unjust destiny than he?" Mauriac saw in Aguirre's face the horror that had destroyed its nobility, that still haunts his legacy—the bitter truth of the century. He wrote, "With the liberation [of Europe from fascism], José Antonio de Aguirre drank the chalice to the last dregs, when he understood that Franco would be respected and the apparent victory of the democracies covered up, concealed, at the very heart of the West, another very hidden victory: the one of the professional armies and policemen." Disguised as "free" and "democratic," or as "socialist," the cold warriors, led by Churchill, Truman, and Stalin, remained in charge, plotting the next Hiroshimas—only now with hydrogen bombs, thousands of times deadlier than the atomic ones. Mauriac observed in Aguirre the face of the century's unfinished agenda.

Among those who, bypassing the controls of Franco's police, attended the funeral on March 28, 1960, was Aita Patxi. The Basque president had been a thoroughly modern and cosmopolitan man; Aita Patxi was ignorant of politics and world affairs. Yet no one but Aita Patxi could have been a better witness to Aguirre's "passion and resurrection"—the title Aita Patxi gave to one of the chapters of his autobiography, written at Aguirre's request. Aguirre and Aita Patxi were united, not primarily by religious discourse or political ideology, but by the traumatic core of their religiosity and Basqueness within a modern and fascist Europe.

Aita
Patxi

"What a vision!" Mauriac had exclaimed. He saw in Aguirre's extinguished face the face of modernity's apocalyptic ending—not only the death of God, but the death of Democracy, Liberty, and Justice, values upon which Aguirre had wagered his life. If the Spanish Civil War "is like an internal miniature of the entire century," the events of Gernika/Bilbao are a miniature of the miniature—the inaugural quintessence of the horror that would soon expand to the Holocaust. Gernika was the symbol of the accursed twentieth century which, in its condensation of horror and promise, has been characterized by its passion for the real. Aita Patxi was there to uphold Aguirre's most intimate belief: "Oh Death, where is thy victory?" The Passion was over for Aguirre's generation. It was time for mine to take the relay.

The same day Aguirre died, Julen Madariaga—who as a child had been evacuated from Bilbao following Gernika's destruction—was in a Bilbao prison charged with propaganda activities in ETA. He was released in time to cross the border clandestinely to attend Aguirre's funeral. Aguirre's remains had been flown from Paris to Donibane Lohizune (Saint-Jean-de-Luz in French), and Madariaga kept a vigil at Aguirre's corpse. He was there to receive the torch. "Aguirre dies and ETA is born," his biographer Batista wrote. Madariaga had first met Aguirre in the French Basque Country where he had been sent to learn French and Aguirre went for summer vacations. "José Antonio treated me like a son," Madariaga told me.

Aguirre's discussion of "the Iberian Problem" had ended in a dark prophecy: if the Peninsular peoples continued to be subject to dictatorship, he observed, "a new era of violence will result." Just months before his death, Aguirre learned of ETA's birth through a letter originating in the same office at 7 Sendexa Street in Bilbao where he had discussed Gernika's Statute with Julen's grandfather, the Republican Ramón de Madariaga, in the early 1930s. Even after Gernika had been destroyed by bombs, Aguirre found reason for reassuring all who would listen that bombs and terror could not destroy the spirit of the Basque people. That "spirit" had been palpable in the nationalist leader Juan Ajuriaguerra's prisonmates, truckloads of whom, at daybreak, had gone to their execution singing "Eusko Gudariak Gara" (We Are Basque Soldiers). But before he died, the cruelest thought for Aguirre was Gernika once again in flames, but this time with no Steer, Lauaxeta, or Picasso to show the world the difference between a true and a false crusade. It was Madariaga's turn to prove Aguirre right or wrong. Both

Aurelio Arteta, *Portrait of the Madariaga Astigarraga Family* (1921). Bilbao's Museum of Fine Arts.

these Bilbaino men were adamantly nationalist, yet there was an abysmal gap between their worlds, beginning with religion. A torch had been passed, the fire was still burning. But were the crucible and sword the same?

When I visited Madariaga at his family home at 7 Sendexa Street, overlooking the Nervión River and close to Bilbao's city hall, he showed me his grandfather Ramón's barrister's wig with pride. Educated at the University of Madrid and the London School of Economics, Ramón was a liberal freethinker and atheist who, on Sunday mornings, would take his wife and six children to church while he stayed in the car with the chauffeur smoking a cigar. He was a federalist, one of the key writers of the Basque Statute that at the start of the 1936 Civil War granted substantial autonomy to the Basque Region. After the Civil War ended, he sought safety in southern France, was arrested, and had to pay a heavy fine for his release as soon as he returned. A few days later, at the end of December 1940, as he visited his expropriated 7 Sendexa

Street office, he dropped dead from a heart attack. It was in this house by the river, a ten-minute walk from the University of Deusto along Campo Volantín street, that the future ETA activists had their first meetings at the end of the 1950s.

Julen's father, Nicolás, was also a lawyer, educated at Salamanca and Cambridge. The philosopher Unamuno, a family friend, taught him Greek. Nicolás was involved with Basque Nationalist Action, the left-wing nonconfessional branch of Basque nationalism—his family's liberal tradition did not have to be anti-nationalist. The Madariagas were close friends of the Aguirres; Julen's uncle was married to Aguirre's sister. The families lived on the same street, the Madariagas at 7 Sendexa, the Aguirres at Number 15. They shared summers in Getxo until the Madariagas returned to Bilbao for the winter school months. The historic day when Aguirre went from Bilbao to Gernika to be sworn in under its sacred oak as the first president of the new Basque government, Julen's father, Nicolás, was sitting next to him in the back of the chauffeured car.

In his Sendexa office, Julen, himself a lawyer, showed me a copy of a family portrait by the painter Aurelio Arteta (now hanging in the Bilbao Museum of Fine Arts) that includes his grandparents and all his uncles and aunts. Arteta, the most important Basque painter of the prewar years, had become director of the Museum of Fine Arts and was one of the candidates for painting a mural for the Spanish Pavilion at the 1937 World's Trade Fair in Paris, a commission finally offered to Picasso that produced his *Guernica*. Everything seemed to turn upon Gernika—its symbolic tree, its ashes. In 1947, Julen was finally sent back by his parents to his Basque "promised land" to attend a boarding school and later study law at the Jesuit University of Deusto-Bilbao. True to his family's anglophilia, he spent the academic year 1960–61 studying international law at Cambridge.

The Spanish police had not yet discovered that Madariaga was living in Cambridge. On March 26, 1961, the police machine-gunned a car they thought Julen was driving and killed a Bizkaian industrialist, Javier Batarrita, instead. The Francoist vice-mayor of Bilbao at the time, Javier de Ybarra y Berge, gave his condolences to the victim's widow and children at the funeral. Ybarra was furious at the police, his sons told me years later as they recounted the tragic circumstances in which they became targets of a "family photograph" described below.

After the Batarrita incident, ETA members decided to start carrying pistols. It was a quarter of a century since the Basque nationalists had lost the Spanish Civil War. They thought historical nationalism was no longer valid and had no doubt what should be the new model—Israel. The Jewish state "was the appropriate antidote to Arana's racism, it was the nationalism of the universal country comprised of victims of the Holocaust. The book *The Revolt* (1951), by Menachem Begin [with the July 1946 Irgun's bomb attack blowing up the Hotel King David in Jerusalem as its centerpiece, killing 91 people and injuring 46] was the referential text for the initial ETA." If Gernika had been the first experimental step toward the Holocaust, if Basques and Jews were united by Hitler's genocidal savagery, why not replicate in Gernika's land the same historic success in creating their own state and recovering their native language? Like the Jews, most Basques lived in diaspora around the globe. Cultural universalism grounded by a singularity of native language was the premise for a new nationalism. If the Jews could do it, why not the Basques?

ETA gave Madariaga the assignment to establish links with Israel. The Basque Nationalist Party in exile had worked during and after World War II with the U.S. intelligence services and had some contacts with the Israeli Haganah and Mossad. Basques had helped many Jews escape the Nazis as well as purchase arms to fight the British. Madariaga approached Herut, the party that had replaced Irgun. In 1963 he sent a message to Menachen Begin asking for help in the "armed struggle for Euskadi's national liberation." Begin replied that he was in favor of their cause but could not provide military assistance because that would jeopardize Israel's relationship with de Gaulle's France. Then Madariaga looked to Algeria. He contacted the FLN and moved with his family to Algiers where they lived from March 1965 to October 1966. Two years later, Julen went to Cuba, that other showcase of national liberation.

ETA was no longer the "study group" of the 1950s. Armed struggle was what mattered now to these middle-class students. Hadn't Israel, Algeria, and Cuba liberated themselves with the power of blood and terror? But were these former Catholic altar boys prepared for real killing and dying? Madariaga believed there was no alternative to the use of violence when confronting the violent power of the state. The Cambridge-trained lawyer argued in terms of a law backed by force.

Any national independence movement would be deemed internationally "illegal," but "[w]e place Basque legality before Spanish or French legality. Not, however, with Platonic declarations . . . but with plastic explosives and machine guns, preceded and accompanied by tons of propaganda." In the meantime, the exiled war heroes of Basque nationalism were turned, in the eyes of the young militants, into vanquished replicas of their former selves with no fight left in them. The continuity between the old guard and the new was broken.

Madariaga had experienced four days and four nights of torture at the hands of the Spanish police when he was arrested in July 1961 after returning from Cambridge. ETA had derailed a military train on July 18, the commemorative day of the Francoist uprising—an "action" deliberately designed to prevent loss of life. But violent escalation was inevitable. At one point of internal crisis, Madariaga acted as the organization's temporary "leader"; he proposed that Txabi Etxebarrieta, a young economist from Bilbao considered the most brilliant student in his class, should lead ETA's 1966 general assembly.

The Tragic Subject: Etxebarrieta

Txabi Etxebarrieta is arguably the most influential writer and the most consequential figure in the history of ETA. In his writings for ETA's Fifth Assembly and for the volume of *Zutik*, ETA's official publication, that followed, he defined the armed group as "a Basque socialist movement of national liberation" and established its basic ideology, which would remain dominant for decades in the *abertzale* (patriotic) left. In the pamphlet he wrote calling on the working class to participate in the 1967 First of May celebrations, he began by bridging internationalism and nationalism: "'Stand up, the oppressed of the world' . . . thus begins the 'International.' 'Give and spread your fruit throughout the world' . . . proclaims Iparaguirre in his hymn to the Tree of Guernica."

But what is most remarkable in Etxebarrieta the writer is his poetry. Before he died at the age of twenty-three he had written five short books of poems—many of them love poems. In 1963 he had an intense love affair with Isabel, the sister of a classmate of his, that is reflected in his poems and letters, and which lasted from July to December. On October of that year, Etxebarrieta joined ETA. His older brother José Antonio was a top ideologue and a mentor to Txabi;

What Is Revolutionary Nationalism?
Tha National liberation of the Basque Country is the liberation of the People and the Basque man: it is the total negation of the current, oppressive reality. That total negation can only be carried out by Basque Working People through its situation as an exploited class. That's why the national struggle of the Basque Country is a socialist affirmation (revolutionary nationalism).

Nation
When the objective factors of ethnicity are developed, this takes consciousness of itself and becomes a nation. . . .

People
It is the oppressed part of the national community. In the current situation it is the whole of the Basque nation regarding the oppressive States: Spanish State and French State. These States are at the service of the Spanish and French oligarchies, including the oligarchy of Basque origin which is objectively foreign and oppressive.

Basque National Working Class
The entire Basque working class is nationally oppressed. . . .

that September he had contracted a grave illness that would kill him within a few years. Txabi not only replaced him in ETA's next general assembly, reading the report José Antonio had written, but nursed his brother's sores. Soon Txabi communicated his decision to Isabel, and his letters began to reflect the difficulties in their relationship. At one point, his letters become a repetition of strings of "I love you" followed by "forgive me." What did she have to forgive him for? One of his poems that very October was "Everything Is All Right," marked with the repeated uncertainty of "Perhaps . . .":

> Perhaps . . .
> I am cruel—for committing suicide . . .
> and for not leaving my blood to others, still unborn.

Even for an existentialist nihilist like himself, Txabi's passion for suicide was perhaps cruel. Why did he have to sacrifice himself by sacrificing Isabel? Did his motherland and his brother deserve that kind of love?

The year after he broke up with Isabel, the first six poems of Etxebarrieta's book of poems, entitled *En pie de pensamiento* (Standing in Thought), are devoted to "Bilbao." The book opens with this defining declaration:

> Bilbao is an act
> of pure existence.

Under the influence of Sartre, existentialism demanded a will to experience one's life without reference to a transcendent order. Section 2, "Motherland," begins with an epigraph from Blas de Otero: "Wretched whoever has a motherland and that motherland obsesses him as much as she obsesses me." Patriotism was both Etxebarrieta's fate and the curse that wouldn't allow him to enjoy a life with Isabel. Being the tragic subject was no longer a seductive intellectual possibility but the axiomatic decision for anyone joining the underground organization. Section 3, entitled "Circles," contains nine poems on nature and landscapes, the sea always in the background. The fourth and largest section, with fourteen love poems, is dedicated to "Your Body": "I'd like to be buried in you. / No longer to be." Two years later, already the leader of ETA, Etxebarrieta writes in one of his poems to her: "I don't know how to fill your absence." When he died he was carrying a gun, and in his wallet was a photograph of his impossible love, Isabel, by then married to someone else. Nothing else in Etxebarrieta's poetry comes close to the intensity of this decisive love, even while he was risking his life daily in ETA's armed clandestinity.

Immigrant Working Class

It is economically exploited by the oligarchy. . . . Those immigrants who get integrated into Euzkadi, who fit in the process of disalienation of the Basque Country, become part of this. . . .

What Is Revolutionary Nationalism For?

RN has the goal of the full development of the Basque people and Man, thus eliminating all the alienations that are suffered by the Basque Country, therefore taking charge of the part that makes us part of the International Working Class. . . .

How Is Revolutionary Nationalism Developed?

RN is . . . a total struggle against national oppression and, therefore, is a revolutionary struggle. This struggle is global, namely, it encompasses all the aspects of the Basque reality (cultural, social, economic, etc.) and therefore, before and above everything else, is a political struggle . . .

Quoted in Lorenzo Espinosa, *Txabi Etxebarrieta: Armado*, 239–44.

Isabel was Etxebarrieta's Ariadne, the ultimate enigma of a laby-rinthine love that indelibly wounded his Nietzchean subject. She was the riddle in those

> . . . equations that I never learnt how to solve:
> Like the desire that coming from your shoulders
> swept me away.

This was a poem from his 1966 book, *Turbias Potestades* (Turbid Authorities), with reference to "the turbid authorities of the bodies," in particular "the turbid sands of your womb,":

> Where the sea is the turbid breakwater of my love for you
> There where the light is without respite in your arms.

Etxebarrieta's previous book of poems ended with a poem entitled "Nevertheless" and dedicated "For you," in which only the infinite sea can be a substitute for her:

> To satiate myself with the sea
> full of waves and tides
> to the last corner of my body, by you
> abandoned.

She is so far away, and nevertheless so close in his desire,

> Because you are an inconceivable creature
> and you are at my fingertips, nevertheless.
> Unreachable.
> Your life is another world
> another country . . .

In his letters to Isabel, he'd like to tell her "everything Machado and Lorca said about the moon," while he cannot tire of repeating "I love you"—a love that he knows is timeless and stronger than even his impending death. After he broke with Isabel, it was the motherland, "*Patria*: Sea of the river of my blood," that Etxebarrieta can proclaim as his only certainty: "You are my only unequivocal feeling." But still, in the last poem of his final book written just months before his death, "You Made Me Live in Depth," an Etxebarrieta now fully surrendered to political action expresses his awareness that he would trade it all to simply be her lover.

From the time he was eleven until he was sixteen, "Javier Eche-varrieta" (in Spanish spelling) shared a school desk with the boy just before him in the alphabetical order, Germán Echevarría. They both wrote poetry and became intimate friends—"he is my friend-brother" Txabi said of him. When Txabi became a fugitive from the police and was forced to leave home, he handed his books of poems to Germán to keep. Years later, while in Moscow for business, Germán received news

> If I knew I'd die tonight
> I'd search for you madly;
> I'd raise you over my death
> to the country where my love for you
> has lived:
> To the state of the most sincere stars.
> (20/21.9.66)

(Lorenzo Espinosa, *Txabi Etxebarrieta: Poesía*, 113)
(Author's translation)

You Made Me Live in Depth

> With fury I would trade our lives
> for the enormous marching of bodies,
> where loving you would cover me
> like the sea covers itself, entirely.

(Lorenzo Espinosa, *Txabi Etxebarrieta: Poesía*, 120)
(Author's translsation)

of Isabel's death and wrote a poem conversing with Txabi, asking: "Was a word from her missing, a call from you, like the final centimeters while climbing a rope?"—the tightrope he had to walk between Isabel and ETA, the one by which he could climb or from which he could be hung.

Bust of Unamuno in the plaza of Bilbao's Casco Viejo bearing his name.

The Etxebarrietas lived on the fifth floor of an apartment house at the plaza Unamuno in the Casco Viejo. The plaza displayed the bronze head of Unamuno at the top of a column. From the balcony of the apartment Txabi and German would stare at Unamuno's bust and the roofs of Bilbao's old quarters.

In no other essay does Etxebarrieta's thinking shine as in his brilliant criticism of Unamuno in an essay entitled "Unamuno, Tomorrow (A Feeling Not Felt)," where he distances himself from the Unamunian tragic sense of life in favor of Sartrian existentialist nihilism. Etxebarrieta criticizes Bilbao's philosopher, whose influence on his own poetry is obvious, for being one of those who "displace their existential center" toward the future "and are not 'in themselves,' but come to live at the service of the hoped-for transcendence. Only the one who does not expect to be can be 'in himself' comfortably and fully, without any violence." And he continues accusing Unamuno of living in the "dative" case, toward an indirect third person or object or temporality— "the today in and for tomorrow, the now in and for later." Etxebarrieta claims that "one should live in a strictly human dimension," an attitude that "dispenses with totalitarian and global solutions" and dismisses Unamuno's tragic sense as "a romantic idea in the irrational sense of the term," because "there is a short step from irrationalism to fascism."

These were remarkable comments in a city and an organization that, led ideologically by Txillardegi and Madariaga, lived in the shadow of Unamuno's thinking. They were formulated by the nineteen-year-old Etxebarrieta in August 1964, the summer after he had broken with Isabel. Txillardegi, in his early essay on Unamuno, had extolled the thinker's "manliness" and "spiritualism," with his unwavering focus on death, and while using quotes from him such as "suffering is the road to consciousness" and "the struggle is what matters, not the victory"—his final confession was that "many of us have found ourselves thanks to him."

Etxebarrieta, however, was bluntly saying that there is no big transcendent Other for whom one should live in a "dative," third-person form of indirect subjectivity. He was aware of what decades later Terry Eagleton would say about Unamuno's work on the tragic sense

Txabi Etxebarrieta.

Isabel.

of life, that it was "laced with pseudo-profound banalities." Still, he could not live up to his breakthrough insight; he would be devoured by his own idealism and his passion for sacrifice—sacrifice being the mendacious act that "proves" the existence of the big Other. Caught between his passion for Isabel and for the motherland, Etxebarrieta surrenders to the Unamunian tragic sense of life.

In the summer of 1966, Etxebarrieta's nightly return home from his office at the Sarriko School of Economics was the inverse of George Steer's escape from Bilbao the night the city fell to the fascists when, everything lost, "there was moonlight" and the company "of the softly flowing river." Etxebarrieta describes how he would leave his office every night and "would walk down from Sarriko across the road to Deusto; then, through the Campo Volantín, by the river, I'd reach home by the city hall. The street lamps were on and on days of south wind I thought on the universe's perfect and intimate harmony. . . . The boats seemed to me the most beautiful things built by man's hand and when it was full moon I wanted to preserve, next to my most precious memories, those visions of an indescribable beauty." It was the poet's lull before the warrior's storm; in Unamuno's title for Bilbao's fratricidal Carlist Wars, it was "Peace in War." If Steer's "moonlight mirage" was the final image of Bilbao's total defeat, Etxebarrieta's moonlight mirage was the opening salvo of his friend Oteiza's "I return from death"—a return that would replicate for my generation a renewal of death.

By the end of 1966, having substituted for his brother in ETA's Fifth Assembly, a meeting that took place at the Jesuit convent of Getaria, Etxebarrieta had surrendered to those very tragic Unamunian traits of transcendence, romantic sense of life, and the utopian totality of living for the future. "We are for a radical and total change," he declared, while opposing any type of reformism. The revolution demanded the country's complete national and social liberation. Pathetic reformists were not only the Aguirres and Prietos of his parents' generation; so were the founders of ETA, such as Txillardegi (its main ideologue since the pre-ETA student group started in 1952) and his Socialist Group, whose program of mass action, working-class activism, and cultural struggle was voted down by ETA's Fifth Assembly as "petit bourgeois." Txillardegi had even studied Gandhi's tactics, pondering their applicability to ETA (his novel *Peru Leartzako* opens with an epigraph from Gandhi). Had ETA been able to see, as Žižek has argued, that Gandhi's radical political change was far more "violent" than the violent dictators of the century, my generation's political culture would have been drastically different. What Txillardegi's group opposed was turning ETA into a guerrilla group modeled after the Chinese or Cuban revolution. In the group's report, they pointed out that ETA as an "armed" organization was a joke, because "our militants have been arrested armed once and again, but our militants have never used the weapons." An example of this was what Madariaga told me: In 1966 he and several ETA members were arrested by the police in the mountains while trying to cross the border between Spain and France. They overpowered and disarmed the police, but they refused to kill them before running away. In July of 1970, after a botched bank robbery, an armed ETA member let herself be caught rather than killing the worker that was pursuing her, a decision that was welcomed by ETA's leadership at the time.

Etxebarrieta was about to change all of this. Txabi's main ideological influence was his brother José Antonio, whose thinking is reflected in a text he wrote at the end of the 1960s. The brothers embraced an all-out armed struggle as the centerpiece of the new ETA. Txabi was in fact plotting against the Spanish policeman Melitón Manzanas, an unforgettable man for Madariaga and others whom he had tortured, when he was killed. This was not going to be Benjamin's *divine violence* of breaking the link between law and violence, "lethal without spilling blood," but a physical violence of means/ends that was in the end not an act of radical change, but an act of reactive impotence. The Etxebarrietas criticized Aguirre for his "naïve simple-mindedness" in sacrificing an entire Basque generation for nothing, yet they couldn't see that they were putting ETA and the new generation onto the same path of reactive violence and martyrdom.

It wasn't for nothing that Etxebarrieta had long been obsessed with death, which he had repeatedly prophecized for himself. Already in his first letter to Isabel, and before they had fallen in love, he expressed his "anguish of living for nothing" and concluded that "I feel death among my fingers." There are repeated mentions of death as a self-fulfilling prophecy in his poetry. His father had died in 1957 when Etxebarrieta was thirteen; in 1965 he wrote three short stories about death, in one of which a boy, on his way home from school, feels in his entire body "the absolute certainty that he would die that night" and writes in his notebook that he "understood that it was extraordinary, that premonition" and "began walking waiting for death." When in the story the mother discovers her son dead after a heart attack, she reads in his notebook his farewell to her: "I know I am going to die in a few hours. I am astonished at how calm I feel. Goodbye, Mom, I am sorry to leave you even more alone than when my father left you. But I have been happy." In his last political text, written for the occasion of May Day, 1968, and in one of those clandestine cyclostiled pamphlets, Etxebarrieta made public his premonition: "Any day now we will have a dead body on the table."

His day of reckoning came on June 7 of that year, when he was stopped for a traffic violation. As the policeman José Pardines began checking his license plate, Etxebarrieta shot and killed him from behind. He and his ETA companion hid for a few hours in the apartment of an acquaintance. But an agitated Etxebarrieta recklessly decided to leave the hideout even if all roads were under police surveillance. He was stopped by police and killed on the spot; his companion escaped but was arrested the next day. His closest ETA friends believe to this day that he let himself be killed. One of his ETA comrades wrote after his death that he would say frequently, "the country needs me and I will offer myself for her." Another comrade, Mario Onaindia, wrote, "at bottom I always thought that he was obsessed with his own martyrdom and perhaps he shot Pardines just so that they could kill him."

When Etxebarrieta took over the ideological leadership of ETA at the Fifth Assembly, the faction led by Txillardergi abandoned the organization. Etxebarrieta's biographer Lorenzo Espinosa believes that no more than a meeting between the two leaders would have been enough to avoid the breakup. Etxebarrieta would end up repeating in real life the very subjective structure sketched by Txillardegi in his Leturia character—encounter and falling in love with a woman; the impossibility of an erotic relationship because of the high call of the motherland's Absolute; redemption of unconscious guilt through the patriotic love of self-immolation. Both Leturia's narrative and Etxebarrieta's life illustrate the struggle between the body as the site of death versus the body as the site of sex—a struggle that, as we shall see in book 3, would find a historic resolution in Yoyes.

ETA's new revolutionary discourse spoke of readiness to sacrifice one's life for the country. But on that day in June, the haunting issue for Etxebarrieta was how to face the policeman on the road whom he himself had murdered. He was the ETA leader who, a decade after its formation, had pushed the organization toward violence. It was by the force of his personality that the new ETA would start killing. Was this killing a revolutionary act or murder, reflecting Etxebarrieta acting out his own Nietzschean will? The ETA comrade with him in the car that day, Iñaki Sarasketa, stated decades later that this death could have been avoided, that Etxebarrieta was under the influence of *centraminas,* a drug widely used by students to combat stress and fatigue. Nothing would have been more ironic for Etxebarrieta than that history should record his killing of a policeman as a criminal murder. The one thing that could prove he was not a common killer was paying with his life for his commitment to the cause. Whether or not his obviously reckless behavior can be construed as "suicide," the political and ethical justification of this inaugural killing demanded that it be deemed a revolutionary self-immolation. If ETA's defining alternative, emblazoned as a logo in every pamphlet and publication, is *Askatasuna ala Hil* (Freedom or Death) or *Iraultza ala Hil* (Revolution or Death) then only death could "prove" one was truly for freedom and revolution. Etxebarrieta, who saw as no one else the romantic trap of Unamuno's "tragic sense of life," became the paradigmatic figure whose killing and death marked ironically the birth of ETA's tragic subject.

Fighting the heritage of the tragic subjectivity of the Bilbaino Unamuno, writing after the Bilbaino poet Otero, recruited by Madariaga, the Bilbaino founder of ETA, and captive to his Bilbaina girlfriend's image, the twenty-three-year-old Etxebarrieta had enacted the new ETA subject by killing and dying. ETA was transformed forever under the impact of his martyrdom. From its student origins to its violent re-foundation, ETA was a product of Bilbao. Out of a list of a hundred prominent ETA members during the years 1966–70, about 40 percent were from the Bilbao area.

In Etxebarrieta's essays, there is one writer quoted and invoked prominently—Feodor Dostoyevsky. If Nietzsche was the avatar of post-Christian atheism, Dostoyevsky was the prophet of my generation's deadly struggle between Christianity and faithlessness, crime and punishment, freedom and guilt. Etxebarrieta mentions each of the brothers Karamazov in his writings; he was impacted by rational Ivan's rebellion against God for the sake of a suffering humanity, combined with sensual Dmitry's hellish awareness that we are all responsible for everyone, all of this coexisting with novice Alyosha's mysticism and belief in resurrection. "Truly, truly, I say to you, unless a grain of wheat falls into the earth and dies, it remains alone; but if it dies, it bears much fruit" (John 12:24)—this was Dostoyevsky's epigraph for the novel, expressing his core belief in the human drama of death and transfiguration in the tradition of Dante's *Divine Comedy*, an epigraph that ruled Etxebarrieta's life. Dostoyevsky would not impose any final authorial resolution to this coexistence of the Christian spirit and atheism—a combination that defines my Bilbao generation as well, even if we had to oppose Francoism's Spanishness, capitalism, and Catholicism by becoming in principle Basquists, anticapitalists, and atheists. What was fiction in Dostoyevsky's novels—*The Brothers Karamazov* and the Grand Inquisitor, Raskolnikov in *Crime and Punishment*, the Underground Man in *Notes from Underground*—a century later became the vividly experienced reality of my generation. Two of the most influential writers of my generation, Ramon Saizarbitoria and Bernardo Atxaga, recognize Dostoyevsky's influence on their work. The nationalist Sabino Arana and the socialist Karl Marx would dominate our political discourse, but Nietzsche and Dostoyevsky were our true prophets.

The new ETA, erected on the memory of Etxebarrieta's murder/martyrdom, required vengeance from his orphaned comrades. They assassinated Manzanas. Killing was now a revolutionary demand. ETA was no longer able to distinguish with Benjamin between "mythic violence" and "divine violence." Žižek explains: "It is mythical violence that demands sacrifice, and holds power over bare life, whereas divine violence is non-sacrificial and expiatory . . . [it] serves no means, not even that of punishing the culprits and thus re-establishing the equilibrium of justice." ETA and its followers thought that the premeditated killing of a policeman, to be followed by hundreds of similar killings in the future, was nothing but the logical conclusion of the revolutionary embrace of violence. We turned Etxebarrieta into the paragon of revolutionary practice—we were unable to read and understand Benjamin's truth. This intellectual error, nourished by the Christian passion for sacrifice, would become foundational to my generation's political subject. It would take near half a century for us to confront the defeat of such mythic violence and fully awaken from its dream.

By then, Basque workers, students, and priests were staging protest after protest. All sorts of political groupings and workers' unions had formed clandestinely. ETA's actions became more and more prominent, leading to the mass strikes during the Christmas season of 1970 to protest the Burgos Trial in which six ETA militants were given death sentences. Sartre, whose intellectual authority was unparalleled on the left, who had long advocated revolutionary vio-

The six ETA militants condemned to death at the Burgos Trial: Top from left: Eduardo Uriarte, Unai Dorronsoro, Mario Onaindia. Bottom from left: Jokin Gorostidi, Xabier Izko, Xabier Larena.

lence and had even become "an apologist for political terrorism," hailed the condemned men as bearers of "the singular universality of the Basques which ETA justly opposes to the abstract centralism of the oppressors" and concluded that "against the fascist troops, Basques have no other way out but popular warfare. Independence or death—the same words that were said before in Cuba and in Algeria, are repeated now in Euskadi. The armed struggle for an independent and socialist Euskadi, that's the complete demand of the current situation. That or submission, which is impossible."

There was in Paris an alternate intellectual whose ideas of "freedom" and "revolution" differed markedly from those of Sartre and whose influence on my generation was sadly nonexistent: Jacques Lacan. For a generation for whom *ekintza* "action" was the ultimate fetish and the only truth, Lacan's thought that "an act always misunderstands itself" amounted to a joke. His idea that desire for a revolution amounted to the desire for a new master was simply unintelligible for us fighting fascism. A subject's claims to freedom look starkly different when seen from the Freudian perspective that the subject is determined by an unconscious. Lacan believed in freedom but only under the constraint of law and "spoke of the inability of any revolution to free the subject from his servitude" while "he took on for analysis a number of activists whom he prevented from embarking in armed struggle." The birth of Freudian psychoanalysis was for him related to the inevitable decline of paternal authority in modern societies. My Bilbao generation lacked such a stern father figure to tell us how romantically naive our ideas of freedom and revolution were.

Jean-Paul Sartre.

Etxebarrieta's walks through Campo Volantín, by the Nervión River, were over, but not those of his friend Germán, for whom Etxebarrieta's death was simply tragedy and no act of martyrdom deserving celebration, and who would long preserve Etxebarrieta's memory in his poetry:

> Even the trees of Campo Volantín
> appeared to have been uprooted by death.
> The river, like a shroud of shadows,
> with no longer any reflection of other lights and other nights.

By then, another poet/singer, Xabier Lete, echoing Brecht, sang at the top of his lungs denouncing their silence:

> *Ay*, poet; *ay*, poet,
> hard for you will be
> the day of freedom!

And singer Benito Lertxundi raised the unavoidable questions:

> How many are we?
> Four, one?
> Three, five, seven?
> What have we done?
> Nothing.
> What do we do now?
> Fight one another.
> What shall we do? Kill each other?
> Don't! Don't! Don't!

But who would resist by then the temptation of sacrifice? Israel had provided the world with a new model for revolutionary/terrorist violence, but what mattered most was a return to the old model of sacrifice: Isaac the son in the grip of Abraham the father, both caught on Mount Moriah in the throes of a higher Other's command, echoing words of surrender—"Greater love has no man than this, that he lay down his life for a friend" (John 15:13).

One of these young men was Mario Onaindia, who in the summer of 1967 had invited Etxebarrieta to give a lecture in his home town of Eibar. Onaindia's father had been recruited by the Basque army the day Gernika was bombarded, and his uncle had taken the young man to visit the mythical oak in front of which, bowing his head, he felt "deep emotion." But Etxebarrieta convinced Onaindia that it was no longer enough to be a nationalist like his father and uncle; a revolution was necessary, precisely to "take revenge on what happened to the father." Onaindia joined ETA.

Just days before Etxebarrieta's sacrifice, the events of Paris's May 1968 had become international news. One of the slogans in Paris's streets was "Revolution Ceases to Be the Moment It Becomes Necessary to Be Sacrificed for It." After Etxebarrieta, it was too late.

Jacques Lacan.

A Journey into Black Waters

In early April 1960, days after Aguirre's funeral, two of Aita Patxi's Passionist brothers knocked on the door of my house in Itziar. "They have come looking for you," my mother told me when I got home from school. "I don't *want* to go to the seminary!" I yelled at her. I was eleven years old. Thus began my religious nightmare.

I was born in Lastur, in a country house destined for ruin, with bulls raging in the basement stable. Ruins and rage—my birthplace inheritance. My parents were also from Lastur, a hamlet of a few dozen farmsteads, home to a breed of native bulls. The village doctor was too drunk to attend my mother while she gave birth to me at home. She had borne three daughters and four sons before me (including triplets), and all four boys had died. My father didn't dare come near me for months, fearing that I, a boy, would also die. Later came two sons and two daughters.

My father was a quarryman. Fifty-two weeks a year he left at dawn and returned late in the evening covered with dust. The Lastur of my parents seemed to come right out of the Middle Ages with its *baserria* farming subsistence economy and peasant mentality. In both its isolation and its association with the bulls that were used for entertainment during the annual fiestas in many towns, Lastur had the reputation of being the wildest place in the Basque countryside. I learned this as a student in Donostia-San Sebastián when, after seeing my rustic ways, twice a girl exclaimed, "You act like you are from Lastur!" "I am!" I replied. I was a barbarian in my own provincial capital.

The village doctor and hero of my birthplace was a folk healer of great repute. He was from a Lastur farm that for generations had produced the local doctor. In a state of drunkenness, he used all sorts of somewhat magical concoctions. On one occasion he saved my mother's life. His son became a famed *trikitrixa* diatonic accordionist, renamed by priests as "hell's bellows" because it inflamed sinful passions. With its combination of vibrant gaiety and deep melancholy, the *trikitrixa* was the music that colored the sentimental education of my parents' generation.

Lastur in the 1950s.

Lastur is also the place of the wound. A fifteenth-century woman from Lastur sang a funerary dirge for her sister Milia, who died while giving birth:

Zer ete da andra erdiaen zauria?
Sagar errea eta ardao gorria.
Alabaia, kontrario da Milia,
Azpian lur otza ta gainean arria.

What is the wound of a parturient woman?
Roasted apples and red wine.
But the opposite happened to you, Milia:
Cold ground underneath, a slab on top.

This is one of the earliest Basque songs and one created out of love for a dead sister and bitter hatred for the widowed husband who remarried immediately.

The marble quarry where my father worked closed a few months after I was born. My father's boss offered him a job in another quarry in the province of Navarre, and we moved there. But later my father was asked to return to Lastur when the old quarry reopened to produce stone for constructing the sanctuary of Arantzazu. We settled in nearby Itziar. The sculptor Oteiza, living in Bilbao at the time, had chosen Lastur marble for the pointed stones that were to form the tower of the Basilica of Arantzazu. Unbeknownst to me, my rocky relationship with "the *bilbaino* Oteiza" began there. The Lastur quarry's stone, dark and red, was appropriately called *sangre de toro* (bull's blood). For me, the meaning of the word *temple* is associated with that marble quarry deep in the mountain, its tall horizontal walls perforated with thousands of vertical holes that my father and his co-workers drilled amid clouds of dust and the high-pitched roar of machinery. In his dreams, my father would wake up at night drilling stone.

My grandfather was a hunter. In the company of his sons, my father included, he would spend days pursuing wildcats, foxes, hares, badgers. In nights of insomnia he used to hear the whistling of the legendary figure of Mateo Txistu—a priest-hunter condemned to eternal

"How to take grandfather's obsessive desire to the end, to the point of discovering its true nature?"

Zulaika, *Caza, símbolo y eros* (1992), 16.

wandering in the company of his barking dogs, in punishment for his excessive hunting lust. They were men blinded by their obsession for the hunt and, according to my mother, "wild" in their manners and passions. Yet they were also emotionally very vulnerable, easily tearful and inappropriately sentimental. The uncle who inherited my father's family farm died in his early forties "of sorrow," two weeks after the sudden death of his twelve-year-old son. That's how my father, who knew about that type of sorrow, explained the death to me. As I expressed surprise, he showed annoyance at my lack of understanding; he had tried to lift his brother's spirits, he said, by taking him to a nearby fair, but to no avail. For these men, who transferred the onslaught of their desire and grief into hunting, emotions were, as for Louise Bourgeois, their "demons"—"It is not the emotions themselves, it is the intensity of the emotions; they are much too much for me to handle." Emotion was chaos and danger; hunting was their flight from it.

My parents' generation believed in witchcraft and the evil eye. My father and mother both had personal experiences with this world—sightings of the witch Mari flying in the sky on a cart surrounded by fire, scary encounters with noisy nocturnal beings. Once, after I had given a lecture on mythology in the French Basque Country, I was introduced to a witch who told me in a state of alarm that an evil spell cast against my grandfather had been passed on to me and I was in serious danger. As I inquired about my grandfather, I was told that he, on the occasion of his brother's wedding—a celebration that in traditional society lasted for days and could turn into an orgy—had left three girls pregnant. He could only marry one of them, and he must have well deserved the evil eye. The witch performed an exorcism to rid me of my sensualist grandfather's evil inheritance. But at times I have felt that my grandfather's errant delirium was a mirror for my own compulsion to write, and that this book is my true exorcism.

Lastur was all about bulls, and Itziar was all about virgins. My father was carving and sending stones to Arantzazu. But it was Itziar's *Amabirjina* (Virgin Mother) that had a lasting effect on my emotional development. Since the twelfth century, Itziar's history as a pilgrimage destination centered upon the *Amabirjina* and Her church—the music, the bells, the flowers, the smells, the annual cycle of rituals, the festivities, the flow of pilgrims. It was also in that church where, from earliest childhood, we were subjected to the agonizing drama of sin and redemption—the hell, purgatory, and paradise we assumed to be ultimate reality.

The Virgin of Itziar.

When my daughter and son were born, I took them to the Virgin of Itziar for a private ceremony, praying that they would grow strong in knowledge and grace. And when my daughter was three months old, I also took her to the hills where Lastur's bulls roam and left her on the ground sleeping near them—so that she could replicate my infant experience with the bulls bellowing in the basement stable under my bedroom. My wife was not amused. Emotions can be demons that are much too much to handle.

The religious orders sought boys from this rural milieu for their convents and churches. That April, two monks in black habits and riding a Vespa motorcycle were determined to persuade me to go with them to the seminary. They had already convinced my mother with an offer she could not refuse: let your son come to the seminary for a few years in exchange for an education; he has twelve years to decide if he wants to become a priest. What remained unspoken, the driving factor in the deal, was their wager that in those twelve years they'd break my resistance, force me into the priesthood, and I'd remain with them forever.

The old spa turned Passionist seminary in Gabiria.

I pleaded with my mother not to make me go. But she knew the limitations of poverty and illiteracy from her Lastur education. A few weeks later, I was one of a hundred and twenty boys, aged ten to twelve, taken to an old spa turned Passionist seminary in the town of Gabiria. A week before I moved to Gabiria there was a fiesta in my village to celebrate the Grand Communion of the classmates about to turn twelve. One of the events consisted of dancing the traditional and choreographed *aurresku*. I was the lead dancer, and the entire village came to the plaza to watch us. The man who taught me to dance was Carlos, who years later would be killed by ETA and who would become one of the protagonists of my book on Basque violence.

"I was one of a hundred and twenty boys, aged ten to twelve, taken to the Passionist seminary of Gabiria" (Author is on second row, third from right).

After one year there, we moved to Euba, twenty minutes from Bilbao, where I spent the next five years studying. We were prepubescent captives, though not everyone was brought there against his will. Antón, for example, our academic wonder-boy, had been so eager to attend that he overcame three years of his mother's opposition to losing her only son to religion. He, like the rest of us, could get a secondary education only by surrendering to a seminary. And, also like most of us, he was from a Basque-speaking family. At the seminary, all of our education was in Spanish—or in Latin, the language we devoted most of our time to learning.

My father drove me to the seminary on his dark green Brio 81 Montesa motorcycle. I remember my small body against his, my cheek pressed sideways against his back, smelling his smell, holding with my two arms to his strength. That Montesa was the only transportation we could afford at the time; we had joyful rides on it to his workplace or for visits to relatives in the nearby towns. But this time was different.

As we said goodbye in the small plaza of the old spa, my father tried to reassure me that he'd be back soon. But I knew then that from this time on he'd be beyond reach. As I watched him disappear, the sound of the Montesa receding, he was perhaps remembering that summer morning half a lifetime earlier when he'd left me, at six years old, alone in the hills, pointing down the road and telling me to follow it to my aunt's farmstead, a long hour's walk away, where, against my will, I had to spend the summer helping with farm chores. When he returned home from work that evening, he was in a rage and said he'd never again let me be sent like that against my will. When I was twelve years old he abandoned me a second time in the seminary, and he knew exactly what I was feeling: Father, why have you forsaken me?

Once we entered the seminary, we weren't allowed to leave for a year; we could see our families only during a rare visit every few months. We weren't permitted to go home even for Christmas—something we learned only after our internment. With no radio or television, we were cut off from the outside world. The beds, lavatories, classrooms—everything was old, and each day we had to clean some part of the building, dressed in our grey overcoats wearing numbers to identify us. I was Number 53—a number that I see everywhere and remains "mine" to this day.

Defenseless, our childhood shattered and confined in a cloister, we were abandoned to friars whose only obsession was to eradicate sin and convert us to a God armed with heaven and hell. The psychological brutality of our quarantine soon left me ill, bedridden for days, and wondering "Why am I here?" I was being told I had to become a missionary, though my mother said I was only there to study. All the hundred and twenty boys slept in one large dormitory, our beds in rows three feet apart. Dozens of boys wet their beds each night, saturating the room with the smell of urine and humiliation. It was a systematic symbolic castration.

There was a hydroelectic dam adjacent to the seminary on the Eztanda River. It was in the reservoir behind the dam that I learned how to swim. People referred to Eztanda's medicinal properties as "black waters."

One of the two friars who came to our house looking for me that spring, Father Pruden, was a distant relative of mine. The other, Father Iñaki, would become my "spiritual director." Sick and depressed, I would tell him that I did not feel any "vocation." He would read this as "an excellent sign." Experience had taught him that traumatization is the first step in initiation. As in the military, a teenager's sense of self had to be shattered before a "vocation" could be implanted.

But Father Iñaki was not only the man responsible for holding me against my will and programming me with an outdated model of spirituality. He was also my friend and confidant who "understood" my agony, the good man of religious zeal whom I could be close to and identify with, even as I cursed my confinement. I was the hostage loving my captor, a Stockholm-syndrome product, the perfect initiatory catch-22. It was soon obvious that his goal of breaking my resistance would succeed.

One morning during Father Pruden's class, Father Iñaki stormed in and began screaming at him from the door, demanding that a boy be readmitted to the class. Father Pruden, my relative, the priest who had snatched me from my rural world, had been revealed as a pedophile who had molested scores of seminarians. One of the boys who had refused his order to undress was being punished by not being allowed in class. Father Pruden was soon removed from the seminary.

An older seminarian, Xabi, gave me some rare advice while we were both studying in Euba: "There are two important things: piano and literature." I began studying piano and taking exams at Bilbao's Arriaga conservatory; Bilbao at the time was for me nothing but piano and music. We hadn't seen each other for forty years when I met Xabi again in Bilbao. He, who was the best piano player in the seminary and later a church organist for decades, came to see me with a flute as a gift. It was the flute's lament that impressed him endlessly and which he saw as an echo of the body's language. Xabi imitated various "ay, ay, ay, ay" and

The former Passionist seminary of Euba, now turned into the Ikastola Lauaxeta.

66

modes of bemoaning, grieving, weeping, changing rhythms and tones of voice. Emotion and crying "are there," he observed, "they are something that you have to welcome." Every factory used to have its siren to call employers to work; Xabi heard a collective wailing in that "rainbow" of tonalities, from the lowest to the highest pitch. His father, an orphan from the time he was three, had also been a musician; he played the piano and sang—"he would play the violin weeping." He mentioned for me the rich folklore of songs dealing with sorrow and sobbing, including my mother's favorite lullaby, "The Little Baby Is Crying."

It was Mother who had struck the deal with the monks, one that could be linked to Franco's victory over the Republic—his regime would be supported by the Church in exchange for leaving all basic education in the hands of the religious orders. Franco's decisive international support came from the United States. A staple in our seminary diet was cheddar cheese, produced by American midwestern farmers, as part of the American food aid that Franco received in exchange for allowing the U.S. to establish military bases in Spain. We were exposed to American Cold War culture; how could you forget the gripping report of the Cuban Missile Crisis in October 1962? We were much aware that the unthinkable could happen any day. Similarly, the deaths of Marilyn Monroe, President Kennedy, Martin Luther King, Jr., and others had enormous media repercussions. While eating cheddar cheese and listening to Jesus Guridi's nostalgic Basque melodies, Aita Patxi, living at the time in Bilbao's San Felicísimo Convent, was our role model of sanctity.

The six years of seminary seclusion were followed by the religiously decisive one: the strictly monastic novitiate year of prayer and meditation. Sanctity was our only sport and aspiration. Jean Genet, the infamous transgressor and prince of French literature, saint and *canaille* at once, author of classics such as *The Miracle of the Rose*, wrote that "saint" is "the most beautiful word in the French language." "Though saintliness is my goal," he wrote, "I cannot tell what it is. . . . Like beauty—and poetry—with which I merge it, saintliness is singular . . . the word indicates the loftiest human attitude" But there was no aesthetic play to our search for sanctity. Our model of sanctity belonged strictly to the Middle Ages. It was inspired by the baroque spirituality of the Italian founder of the Passionists, saint Paul of the Cross, but our goal was to go back further to the Benedictine order of the eleventh century. We would get up in the middle of the night to sing at the choir. Self-flagellation was part of the daily routine. Despite the strict taboo on sex, the religious imagery and literature that surrounded our lives was highly eroticized. In his treatise on Genet, Sartre finds that the saint "challenges the human condition in its totality," but ultimately he finds "the outdated game of Saintliness" repellent. Our vow of chastity took place in the summer of 1967—the same Summer of Love that gathered a hundred thousand youths in San Francisco, smoking pot and practicing free love.

I moved to San Felicísimo with my seminarian friends in the summer of 1968. It was only half a mile from the University of Sarriko, where Etxebarrieta had studied economics and relaunched ETA. One Sunday evening, in the spring of 1969, we were startled in San Felicísimo by an unexpected visit from the Spanish police. They had come to arrest a monk whom they charged with cyclostyle-copying the propaganda pamphlets generated by Etxebarrieta's ETA. The monk, a professor who had taught me philosophy in Euba, would spend years in jail. In April of that year, Bilbao was shaken by the spectacular shoot-out and arrest of ETA commandos on Artekalle Street in the old part of town or Casco Viejo. One of those arrested was the ex-seminarian Mario Onaindia, who had been recruited to ETA by Etxebarrieta, himself educated in the religious school of the Escolapios. Another of my convent friends was arrested at one of the many political demonstrations in which as students we regularly participated. We found out later that earlier in the novitiate, and unknown to the rest of us, one of the novices was an active ETA member using the convent as a hideout. For many of us, Bilbao seemed to have only two alternatives: the seminary or ETA. At times they seemed to collapse into one.

On the Carnival morning when I visited San Felicísimo, the sanctuary was empty, but somewhere a congregation was singing. As I got closer, a mass was being celebrated at an adjacent chapel to which the recumbent body of San Felicísimo had been removed. The celebrant was most familiar to me—Father Iñaki. After mass, I went to greet him in the sacristy, expecting a warm embrace from him. He was rather taken aback by my unexpected presence, then he invited me to the palm-shaded patio and to lunch in the company of the other monks. This was the man who had taken me to the seminary against my will and who had witnessed my religious transformation and collapse. Despite our mutual affection, we felt at odds in each other's company. At one point he commented in jest to a friar passing by, "I am guilty for everything that went wrong in his life."

Iñaki might have been assaulted by the flashback of what happened that early morning in the choir when I had an anxiety attack while talking to him and fainted. For endless unconscious seconds my body kept shaking, Iñaki later told me, while a vision of fire opened in front of my eyes and I felt burning. As I recovered consciousness, Iñaki was holding me, his hands wet with my sweat. He took me to my cell where I spent days in bed to rest. Alone in my bed, exhausted and in a state of suffocation, unable to get up for days, I couldn't figure out what catastrophe had overtaken me. "I am a sick man," Dostoevsky's Underground Man begins his story; "However, I know nothing at all about my disease, and do not know for certain what ails me." I was will-less and cut off from the rest of the world, survival the only thing that mattered from then on. I looked into the mirror to see whether that face was still mine. I was a stranger to myself. Was I falling into madness? I had descended into Dante's Hell. Only Iñaki shared my secret.

Maldan behera (Downfall)

Aresti was for my Basque generation the quintessential postwar Bilbao poet. His *Harri eta Herri* (Stone and Country, 1964) became a milestone in Basque literature. He put himself and his writing squarely in Bilbao's inferno in a poem entitled "You Know Where I Am" and sung by the musical group Oskorri:

Eskribitzen badaustazu	If you want to write me
Ba dakizu non nagoan	You know where I am
Infernu labanagoan	In this most slippery hell
Deabruaren ahoan.	In the mouth of the devil.

Aresti's first major work was *Maldan behera* (Downfall), an initiation poem of descent into hell and final ascension that he completed in 1959. Over nineteen hundred verses, the poem is preceded by four "arguments" or epigraphs from Nietzsche and Christ. The poem parodies a Nietzsche-like prophet descending from the mountain to preach his gospel, tracing an allegoric voyage in which humankind evolves from the caves of prehistory to modern urban settings. The young poet's Dantean voyage is a recognition of the twilight and demise of the Gods, preceding the call for the city's revival. Aresti would make *oskorria* (red sky, twilight, dawn) his emblematic image, both crepuscular and revolutionary.

The writing of Dante's *Divine Comedy* was preceded by a visionary experience that he had in the Easter week of 1300, two months before Bilbao was founded on June 15 of that same year. Aresti's *Maldan behera* was written in Bilbao the same year ETA was born there, a pre-

Gabriel Aresti.

Blas de Otero.

figuration for my generation's descent into hell. Aresti follows Dante in his poetic voyage of descent into the underworld, like previously Homer's Odysseus or Virgil's Aeneas. As was the case with James Joyce or Marcel Proust or Samuel Beckett, Dante's "supreme fiction" granted Aresti the model of descent and ascent. The poem begins with "Untergang" (Downfall):

Egun honetan nire gogoak	Since my spirit today
Utzi nahi baitu mendia,	wants to leave the mountain,
MALDAN BEHERA GOA AGURO	DOWNHILL TUMBLES
NIRE GORPUTZ BILUZIA	THIS NAKED BODY OF MINE

The second part of the poem begins with a parallel quatrain, "Requiem," which is the antithesis of the initial *untergang*:

Nire arima hegalariak	Since my winged soul
Gozatu baitu zerua,	found heaven,
LURPEAN DATZA EHORTZIRIKAN	UNDERNEATH THE EARTH
NIRE GORPUTZ USTELDUA	LIES BURIED MY ROTTEN BODY

The strophe evokes Lauaxeta's shattering lines the morning he faced the firing squad: "Let my soul go to luminous heaven / my body to the dark earth." If the poet strives to hold the torch for an Ideal City, he must be ready, like Lauaxeta, to fight for change, accept persecution, die. "Maldan gora" (Ascent), the poem's final section in which Aresti dresses the poem's heroine in the image of Adam, concludes the classic initiatory cycle of Descent, Death, and Resurrection.

By abandoning the mountaintop, Aresti submitted himself to the essential tensions of his city: Christ and Zarathustra, Gernika and the working class, Euskara and Castilian. In order to transform himself and conceive a new culture for his city, he would be split asunder. His recurrent allusions to crucifixion, Nietzschean serpents and eagles, and tumbling descents from the mountain were the poet's obligatory steps in the cycle of eternal return, his confrontation with the end of the ancient world in his Bilbao. Aresti's inferno was the Bilbao of urban and ecological devastation of the postwar decades of military dictatorship, a city turned into a museum of horrors and social want, Dante's *città dolente.*

I met Aresti while I was a student at the University of Deusto. The few times we went for a drink, I was taken aback by his vulnerability—he the toughest and most luminous Basque writer. Always on edge, I was not surprised that he told his future biographer, Anjel Zelaieta, after their first casual encounter, "If you ever think of me, remember that you have known a wretched man who suffers a lot." By the time I met him, liver cirrhosis had irreparably damaged his health;

he blamed his illness not on alcohol but on the stress produced by Bilbao's political infighting. He died shortly afterward at age forty-one.

Aresti's close poet friend in Bilbao, writing in Spanish, was Blas de Otero. In "The Eternal," one of his poems from *Ancia* (1958), he describes the poet's world in postwar Bilbao:

A world like a mutilated tree

An uprooted generation.

Men whose single destiny

Is to prop up the ruins.

The ruins of Europe, Spain, and the Basque Country could not have been more staggering. The desolation lived by these poets is expressed in the embattled and harrowing wail of Otero's *Crecida* (Rising). This was Europe for Otero and Aresti. Spain was "Land / gnawed by war / unfortunate sad Spain / . . . / everyone should weep for you." Solitude and ruin, ruin and solitude. Words with the prefix *des* (less), which in Spanish signal loss and absence, appear in all of Otero's poems. Oteiza was at the time engaged in Bilbao in the *desocupación* (dis-occupation) of Euclidean forms.

Allusions to Bilbao are recurrent in Otero's poetry: "the glare of your factories"; "laborious city, psalm of factories"; "oh blast furnaces deep infernos in the fog." And always, "City where, far away, very far, you can hear *el mar* [the sea], *la mar* [the sea] of God, immense." He wrote, "So much Bilbao in my memory." And "Soy Bilbao de cuerpo entero" (I am Bilbao in all my body). The poem "Bilbao" describes his complex relationship with his city: "in truth you don't deserve my word, unless to insult you," yet at the same time "only you sustain my Gaze." If "Gernika is for Aresti a wound that can never be forgotten," so was Otero a child of Gernika.

In keeping with Dante's *Divine Comedy,* Aresti and Otero sought transcendence downward—by a conscious descent into hell. And what a descent Bilbao had endured in her ecology of place, politics, and culture! From this inferno, both Basque poets were committed to a single poetic mission: to give testimony to a fallen city while creating a new language traversed with truth and justice. If the poet's task is to invoke the "city" of belonging, a rooting tree, he must denounce corruption. Once he can bear the wound of the ruins of the fallen city, he is ready to destroy the mythology that, presenting itself as inevitable, limits re-creation. For this, he uses experience and allegory. After his personal descent into hell, the poet earns the right to sketch an imaginary city of the past and the future while demanding a just society.

Rising

With blood to my waist, sometimes
with blood to my lips
I move
forward
slowly, with blood to the edge of my
lips
. . . .
I move
forward, sinking my arms in blood,
some
times swallowing blood,
I move over Europe
as at the prow of a dismantled boat
that's bleeding
. . . .
I bring a rose in blood in my hands
bloodied. Because there is nothing
but blood,
and a horrendous thirst
screaming in the midst of the blood.

Otero, *Ángel fieramente humano*, 67-69.
(Author's translation)

Guernica

I return to you walking with open
arms
Bizkaia
tree that I carry and love from the
roots
and one day was ruined under the sky.

Otero, *Poemas Vascos*, 29
(Author's translation)

The writers and politicians of the Gernika generation experienced the recent past as trauma. The symptoms that plagued them presented a bodily archive; they experienced the losses and failures of the past as their own. Otero was interned repeatedly in psychiatric institutions, his "mind immersed in blackness." Aresti confided to his friend Juan San Martin that he feared he was going mad, admitting a "dreadful crisis of belief" and asking forgiveness from those he had offended. His friend, writer Jon Mirande, committed suicide on Christmas Eve. Oteiza, whom I regularly witnessed breaking into outbursts of rage or emotional sobbing, was arrested after shooting at the hospital in a bout of insanity the day his wife died. These incidents, "stranded objects" in Santner's use, were irrepressible sediments from the past, symptoms produced by what Bilbao represents. Bilbao was, for Otero, his "accursed city and one buried deep within my breast," that he suffered

>to breathlessness
>
>Bilbao: your skies, your houses
>
>black. And your hypocrisy.

Aresti's *Maldan behera* embodied both the Crucified and Dionysus. You could say of Aresti, as of Unamuno and of so many thousands of Bilbainos who abandoned religion in the 1960s, that he was Christian and atheist at the same time. This dual edge at the interface of Christianity and Dionysus, disciplined suffering and rebellious reaction, is a duality etched into the character of my generation. It is a traumatic cut that brought together, in their constitutive incompatibility, opposing realities in ethics, politics, art, and culture, and demanded the forging of a new subjectivity.

By the late 1960s, hundreds of youths had turned to political militancy; many of them ended up being tortured or exiled. The religious crisis became palpable as seminaries and convents were emptying. I was the organist in the large church of San Felicísimo when one Sunday morning, while leading the hymns of about two thousand parishioners mass after hourly mass, the thought hit me that I no longer believed in that music nor in anything else I was doing at the convent. Close by, under the altar, was the spooky reclining image of San Felicísimo, the church's "happiest" patron saint—"a recumbent wax figure, so real that it looked like a corpse, so rosy and brimming that it seemed a sleeping man happily exhausted," as Javier Viar described it. "His head reclined on a white pillow. The delicacy of his feminine face, over which the light glided smoothly, contradicted his masculine name. In his hands he held a yellow palm. There was nothing terrible in his appearance, except his absence and the cut that traversed his

The recumbent wax figure of San Felicísimo.

neck: from his thin lips, half-open, drops of blood were falling." That macabre San Felicísimo was the embalmed mask of the deadly morbidity that Nietzsche saw in our religious nihilism and which I could no longer deny.

By then I had spent a summer laminating metal at a large factory in Lamiako, ten kilometers away from Bilbao, and I had become immersed in the condition of the working classes of the Left Bank—Aresti's only religion. Come walk with me through the working class Bilbao's "lowest hell," one that "not even Dante could have / imagined," was Aresti's battle cry to my generation.

Hell Is Too Sweet

A trip through the Left Bank could be made in the company of the rock and punk music groups that would emerge in the area. A new musical current, known as *nova cançó* (the new Basque song), emerged in the 1960s with defiant songs such as Lourdes Iriondo's "Ez gaude konforme" (We Aren't Happy, 1967). Iriondo's song had the manifesto quality of The Who's "My Generation" (1965). The *nova cançó* songwriter/singers, influenced by American folk and Catalan protest songs, declared war on the romanticism of traditional Basque music. "We could in no way start now by singing the sad story of the white dove, for there are far sadder stories than that one. The white dove was long ago blackened by the smoke of the chimneys of our Basque industrial towns," explained Julen Lekuona, a priest turned singer. These new Basque singers would rather sing about racism, the Vietnam War, the murder of Martin Luther King, Jr., or the workers killed in Chicago or Bilbao.

By the late 1970s, the protest song, like much else of the earlier anti-Franco resistance, became dated. It was time now for rock 'n' roll and punk by groups with names like Garbage, Scurvy, Vomit, Belch, Fart, Scar, Cut, Delirium Tremens, R.I.P., Barricade, Police, The Dick Records. These heavy-metal groups, combining irreverent lyrics with rock's force, punk's anger, ska's gaiety, and reggae's warmth, became a social phenomenon. Years later, a vibrant hip-hop music emerged, influenced by international youth culture. "Bilbao, Shit, Rock and Roll," was the slogan of the group M.C.D. (Acronym for "Shit on God.") The trope "Tropical Euskadi" became popular. Drugs were everywhere.

A well-known group in Bilbao was Itoiz. Combining rock and pop, it played during the city's annual fiestas with great success. Lyrics were no longer as relevant as they had been for earlier songwriters.

Covers of records by Basque radical rock groups.

Still, ballads such as "Lau Teilatu" (Four Roofs), sung by its leader, Juan Carlos Pérez, with the bare accompaniment of a guitar and a flute, became very popular:

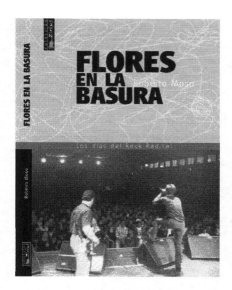

Flowers in the Dustbin, Moso's book cover.

Lau teilatu gainian	Four roofs above
ilargia erdian	the moon in between
eta zu goruntz begira,	and you looking skyward,
zure keia eskuetan	smoke in your hands
putzara batekin . . . putz!	blowing it with a blow!
Neregana etorriko da	It will come to me
ta berriz izango gara zoriontsu	and we will be happy again
edozein herriko jaixetan	in any of the town festivals.

Social protest was no longer in the forefront: "Where the radical rocker sees the police hitting a protester, Itoiz sees an old prostitute calling for the yellow taxi because she is cold and out of work." One of Itoiz's hits was "Marilyn"—the story of a Basque sheepherder who returns from the American West and installs on his farm a neon sign with her iconic image. Pérez was the son of a migrant peddler from Galicia, a handsome man who, with his big leather bags of clothes, used to visit homes in the rural countryside, mine included. At the height of its success, in 1987 Itoiz decided that it was time to dissolve the group. "Success did not satisfy me," Pérez confided.

Zarama (Garbage), from Bilbao's Left Bank, was also a prominent group influenced by the British rock band The Who. Another group, Negu Gorriak, performed a Basque version of The Who's "I Can't Explain." Zarama's first recorded song was the result of winning a music competition the youth organized in 1980 in my rural village of Itziar; soon ETA bombed the discoteque, built mostly by former ETA members and in which I also was involved during my fieldwork, because it was allegedly contaminated by foreign rock music and drugs; by 1984 ETA's political party was organizing concerts with rock and punk groups as a means to recruit sympathizers. Zarama's first song was a parody of Aresti's "I Will Defend My Father's House." When the leader of the group, Roberto Moso, wrote the story of Zarama, he entitled it *Flowers in the Dustbin*—a line from the Sex Pistols' song "God Save the Queen." "When you listen to the Sex Pistols," said Pete Townshend, "what immediately strikes you is that *this is actually happening*." Moso echoed the same electrifying reality when he wrote that in the midst of a chaotic concert he suddenly realized that "we were connecting brutally with the audience in a time when there were constant revolts in the streets. We were achieving the maximum aspiration of any artist who is worth his salt—to communicate sensations in all

I will escape
from my father's house
and if some poet wants it
let him go defend it.
Heads are burning
watching TV
at night on the streets
nothing but the shadows of dogs
and the old songs of drunks.
The poets are silent
nobody pays them any attention.

Zarama, *Bidea eratzen*
(Author's translation)

their intensity and in real time." Zarama was infected with the virus of Sex Pistol Johnny Rotten's scream, "No Future." What they liked about punk groups like the Sex Pistols, The Clash, or Ramones was that "they were straightforward, they made a music that was direct, blunt, sober, absolutely accessible. You didn't need to be a great musician or have expensive equipment to make it; you simply needed to have balls."

After one of Zarama's concerts, Moso met with Josu, like himself from Santurce, a town on the Left Bank. Josu was a teenager with long blond hair and a beard, carrying a guitar covered with stickers, among which stood out The Who's bull's-eye. Josu joined Zarama for three years before leaving the group to form Eskorbuto (Scurvy) in the company of Juanma and Paco. One of the most popular traditional Bilbao songs is "From Santurce to Bilbao." It describes the voyages of the past, now turned into folklore, made by women along the Nervión River carrying baskets of sardines on their heads. Eskorbuto, a group from Santurce, wrote a brutal parody of the traditional song, "We Are Rats in Bizkaia." One can find on YouTube other songs by Eskorbuto with titles like "Against Everything," "Hell Is Too Sweet," "Destroyed Brains," "Beyond the Cemetery," "I Search in the Garbage," and "In the Moon." When Moso goes to visit his father's tomb at the cemetery, he has to walk past those of Josu and Juanma, who were killed by heroin. The four members of another group called Cicatriz (Scar) also died of heroin or AIDS. They understood well, like their hero Johnny Rotten, Richard Huelsenbeck's words, "Life must hurt—there aren't enough cruelties." Far from the idolatry rock and folk heroes received on stage, the punks made thrown bottles and a rain of spit their canon. Eskorbuto's friends organized a concert in their honor; it was entitled "Train to Hell." At the cemetery, Moso hears the echoes of his friends singing:

> And they tortured me, and tortured me, and tortured me
> so that I would sing and should sing this song
> Satan, hell is too sweet
> Satan, hell is too sweet.

A Family Photograph in Winter City

But Bilbao's Nervión River has also a Right Bank. Neguri symbolizes its wealth. While Aresti was writing about his city's descent into hell and Etxebarrieta had entered ETA, Javier de Ybarra became Bilbao's Francoist mayor. He was the man who had been enraged when, in

RATS IN BIZKAIA

From Santurce to Bilbao,
I walk by all the riverbanks...
You will look at the sky and you will see
a great dirty cloud
don't think about it, don't doubt it
Altos Hornos of our city.
You will look at the house façades
full of shit, full of shit.
From Santurce to Bilbao,
I walk by all the riverbanks...
We are rats in Bizkaia.
We are contaminated rats
and we live in a town
that is a shipwreck, that is a
shipwreck, wreck, wreck.
The proud suspension bridge
underneath the great Nervión
where all the shit finds repose
stinking a nasty smell.
In its riverbanks how many people
struggle for survival.
From Santurce to Bilbao,
I walk by all the riverbanks...
We are rats in Bizkaia.
We are contaminated rats
and we live in a town
that is a shipwreck, that is a
shipwreck, wreck, wreck
wreck, shipwreck.

Eskorbuto, *Eskizofrenia.*
(Author's translation)

1961, police assumed they had found Julen Madariaga but mistakenly killed Javier Batarrita instead. From one of Bilbao's most influential families, Ybarra had been president of Bizkaia's Deputation (1947–50) and then mayor of Bilbao (1963–69); he left his duties as mayor to take charge of the multinational Babcock Wilcox, a large industry controlled by his family that was sliding into bankruptcy. He was also on the board of trustees of Bilbao's two major banks, the Bank of Bilbao and the Bank of Vizcaya, and president of Bilbao's main newspaper, *El Correo*—a critical tool through which he could exercise political control. Under Franco, he was a deputy for Bizkaia in the Spanish Parliament, and he was known as a polymath writer and author of a dozen books on Bizkaia's history and politics. He had eleven children and was a deeply religious man.

Ybarra embodied what was known as "Neguri's oligarchy." *Neguri* means "Winter City" in Euskara and was created as a district of Getxo at the beginning of the twentieth century, to serve as a permanent residence for Bilbao's affluent upper class. Its mansions and influence became a symbol for Bilbao's business elite, housing the handful of families who controlled half of all Bizkaian industrial output and most of its banking. Neguri made the Basque region wealthy by creating the strongest industrial center in Spain. By 1930, 25 percent of all Spanish banking, 60 percent of Spanish steel manufacturing and shipping, and 40 percent of investments in shipyards, engineering, and electrical firms were controlled by Neguri. But by the 1980s the industrial model had hit bottom, and the title of Antonio Menchaca's novel, *The Ashes of Splendor* (1987), captured what everyone already knew about the decadence of Neguri's society. Capitalism had entered a new phase. But it was the tragic fate of Ybarra himself that was going to symbolize Neguri's demise.

Neguri's business oligarchy ruled the Basque region during Franco's era. When the military rebelled against the Republic in 1936, Neguri abandoned its liberal tradition and sided with Franco. Neguri held both economic and political power, ruling Basque finance and industry, and frequently similar Spanish institutions as well; it was also involved directly in the politics of the dictatorship and controlled the media. In short, it was an oligarchy in its pure state.

An editorial in *El Correo* in February 1974 stated: "[t]he current [Francoist] regime is essentially Basque." It went on to argue that, since those who organized Franco's National Movement were Basque, and quite a few of the ministers governing under Franco were Basque, "those who oppress us are as Basque as are we ourselves." Bilbao was not only the birthplace of the contending forces of Basque national-ism and socialism, it was also where Basque and Spanish nationalisms would meet and give birth to two extreme forms: Spanish fascism and Basque terrorism.

As Bilbao's mayor during the second half of the sixties, Ybarra tackled grave urban issues, traffic and schooling in particular, in a city that grew from 297,942 in 1960 to 405,908 inhabitants in 1970. There was a chaotic growth "that provoked the greatest urbanization catas-trophe suffered by Bilbao." There was a lack of planning that turned the city into a series of disjointed neighborhoods, with the barrios of Santutxu, Begoña, Otxarkoaga, and Txurdinaga growing 240 percent. Ybarra traveled to New York to meet with U.S. majors with similar urban problems, those of Pittsburg and New Orleans in particular. One of the projects Ybarra promoted successfully was the creation of an autonomous university in Bilbao; even if Bilbao was the Spanish city with the third highest number of students, it lacked a public univer-sity for political reasons. But his grand project, one he would not see happen, was the creation of a new satellite city for 450,000 residents in the adjacent valley of Asua. For such vision of a "Greater Bilbao" that would join the city and its valleys, he pushed for the annexation of the towns of Loiu, Sondika, Derio, and Zamudio (towns that would disannex after the dictatorship). For Ybarra, "The important thing [was] the new city." For this he needed to attract investments from the central government, which he labeled "gifts from the State" and which he obtained in part because of his personal relationship with Franco and his ministers. He did attract investments for the water supply, access roads, city clean-up, and port improvements, but they were not enough for his grand "new city," which made a journalist label his ten-ure as "the City Hall of the projects." The new city would have to wait until the post-Franco period when the centuries-old fiscal autonomy of the Basque Treasury was restored.

On June 19, 1964, the political slogan "25 Years of Peace" was declared in Bilbao. It was the year Ybarra became mayor and Franco came with its entire cabinet to the city to celebrate. The previous day Franco visited the Basilica of Begoña, which he entered under the pallium and to the music of the national hymn. The commemorative events included the annual military parade and the open-air mass at the Elliptical Plaza, as well as the reception at the City Hall where Ybarra extolled the figure of the Caudillo. Ybarra had taken a very militant stance during the Spanish Civil War, in which forty-three members of his family had died fighting with Franco; in his youth he had been an ardent monarchist. God and Monarchy had been his two big Others, now embodied in Franco. By the end of the sixties Ybarra was immersed in the political contradictions of an anachronistic Francoism and the impossibility of exercising the fiscal rights traditionally enjoyed by Bilbao and which had been stolen by his protector Franco.

On May 20, 1977, eighteen months after Franco's death and less than a month before the first democratic elections in Spain, the unthinkable took place—Javier de Ybarra, the most public member of his family, was kidnapped by ETA and, after a month of failed negotiations, left dead near Mount Gorbea by the side of the road with a bullet in his head. Gorbea was one of Ybarra's favorite mountains for hiking; it is also the closest to a sacred mountain in the Basque nationalist imaginary because it was there that many soldiers died fighting against von Richthofen's Condor Legion. A popular song begins: "In Mount Gorbea, at the very top, there is a cross of love."

"In Mount Gorbea, at the very top, there is a cross of love."

Ybarra's son, also Javier, was writing a book on his father's murder and his family history while I was in Bilbao in 1999. Through a mutual friend, a historian researching the Ybarras' industrial history, I was introduced to Javier and his brother Borja one rainy November afternoon. I was unprepared for the story of their father's kidnapping that I was about to hear. ETA commandos, driving an ambulance and dressed as nurses, knocked at the door of their Neguri home at 8:30 a.m. Ybarra's housekeeper, Marcelina, expecting an emergency, went down and opened the door. Four hooded men demanded that she take them to Ybarra's bedroom. He was dressing for morning mass. The commandos woke the family and cut all telephone links. Borja had been awakened only a few minutes earlier by a hooded man with blue eyes. "Don't worry, nothing is going to happen," the man told him, machine gun in hand. When Borja saw his siblings Enrique, Ana, and Cosme still in their pajamas, and the housekeeper Marcelina, gardener Rogelio, and chauffeur Enrique herded into his room, he realized what was happening. He was twenty-three years old, and he noticed that the kidnappers were younger than he. When Borja began to protest, one of the commandos casually put a machine gun against his chest. "What? Is something the matter?" he asked.

Before the kidnappers left with their hostage, the commandos wanted a "family" photograph. Machine guns and cameras complement one another. It is the photographic flash that most matters for the next day's newspaper front pages. The father was brought to Borja's bedroom, dressed in the suit that he habitually wore to the Bank of Vizcaya, done up to the last button, except for the necktie, which the leader of the commandos would not permit him to wear. The family was framed by the window in the background. To their left were a large wardrobe and two beds flanking a small bedside table. Sensing that this might be the last time he'd touch his father, who was dressed in his usual alpaca suit with a white handkerchief in the breast pocket, Borja placed his arm on his father's shoulders for the photograph. In old photographs of Basque peasants, it was common for brothers to place their arms around each other's shoulders in a gesture of family solidarity, but this pose was unusual among Bilbao's elite. The father, surprised at Borja's protective impulse in that moment of ultimate danger, replied, "Don't worry. . . . The most these guys can do is shoot me, and in that case I will join your mother." It had been less than two years since Borja's mother, only fifty-four, had died of cancer. This was the decisive moment of the still photo, the final words, the indelible memory.

I interrupted Borja's story to ask about his last words to his father. He avoided the question twice and returned to the story of his youngest brother, fifteen-year-old Cosme, who had a poster of Che Guevara and a Basque flag on his wall, which prompted one of his hooded kidnappers to comment that he liked the bedroom. Borja noted that the *etarras* spoke Euskara, assuming that the Ybarras would not understand them. But at some point the housekeeper Marcelina, in her Euskara of Ibarrangelua, protested one of their disparaging comments about her employer, telling them they were utterly wrong, that he had always treated her well.

When I asked him a third time, Borja could not avoid returning to the last words he spoke in the presence of his father. He became silent for a few seconds, before recalling the indelible sentence: "Treat him well, he's a good man." That's what he had told them. Remembering that moment, Borja stammered, unable to continue, mute in front of the abyss he had reopened before him. Then his face collapsed into his hands in an uncontrollable sob, his entire body a wail that filled the room for endless minutes, leaving his wife, brother, friend, and me unable to react to his grief.

"Treat him well, he's a good man," summed up all that Borja knew about his father, all the affection and admiration he had felt for him since childhood. Even his political enemies recognized he was a "good man." His father's farewell to the family from captivity—"with immense affection your father blesses you and embraces you"—still leaves him bewildered, as do his other final messages: "I feel very strengthened spiritually, for I feel closer to God in adversity," and "Don't worry about me. I am in God's hands, I forgive those who kidnapped me and I ask forgiveness from those I might have offended, and I offer my life for the conversion of sinners." Twenty-three years after the terror of that farewell, the silence left in a father's wake and the absurd enigma of the patriotic faith that motivated that violent loss remain an abyss into which Borja can fall each day and at any moment.

The ransom negotiations between ETA and the Ybarra family went nowhere, and after a month in captivity Ybarra was killed. His cousin was the CEO of the Bank of Bilbao, but the billion pesetas that ETA demanded (about $16 million in 1977 money) was deemed excessive. The Bank of Bilbao and the Bank of Vizcaya offered less than $1 million each, but ETA insisted that the ransom they sought was from the entire Ybarra clan, not only from Javier (who was not as wealthy as other members of his family). Thus a victim's death was also decided by a board of trustees. When the president of the Bank of Vizcaya visited the Ybarra family, the dead man's sister refused to shake his hand—the banks created by the Ybarras had declined to save his life. As the former mayor of Bilbao and the visible head of the Ybarra clan, the most powerful industrial and financial family in Bilbao's history, Javier de Ybarra's influence amounted to nothing. His dead body was found with a cynical note from ETA: "Javier Ybarra Berge, R.I.P, is resting in THE LORD'S PEACE (according to him)."

In that last family photograph, Ybarra is the handcuffed, emasculated father. He is the one who, once sacrificed, is forever mourned, returning in the form of law—in the name of the Father. The ETA "sons" felt that they needed to kill him in order to regain the potency stolen from them for decades by a foreign dictatorial big Other, the Father who had reincarnated Franco. Ybarra's death signaled the death of a century of economic and political hegemony by Neguri's oligarchy—the end of the ashen "Winter City."

Ybarra's orphaned children felt betrayed by their own family; it had been a "sacrificial ritual, Abraham planning to immolate his son Isaac, on the way to Mount Moriah." Cosme, the son with the poster of Che and the Basque flag in his bedroom, never recovered from the shock. He entered a permanent depression and ended up a drug addict. "I am very sad, Borja. I want to die," he'd tell his brother. Taken to a detoxification center, he jumped from a bridge in an unsuccessful suicide attempt. Later he went to a gas station, asked for a can of gas, poured it over himself, lit a match, and set himself ablaze. A journalist from his father's newspaper, *El Correo,* mistook him for a black man when he arrived at the scene. Like other elite families of Bilbao, the Ybarras had long been charged with being *negreros* (African slave traders). It seemed that Cosme had assumed his condition as a "black" victim.

Upon hearing of Cosme's condition, Borja ran like a man possessed to the Cruces Hospital where his little brother lay in agony, hoping he'd arrive in time to repeat their father's words that morning: "Don't worry, Cosme, nothing is going to happen to you." He whispered those words again and again to his severely burned brother, now turned into an Egyptian mummy: "Nothing is going to happen to you, Cosme. You are going to die soon. But you are not going to be alone. You are going to be with Papa and Mama. They are waiting for you, Cosme. The priest has given you absolution. Don't worry, Cosme, you are going to be with Papa and Mama, you are going to be with Papa and Mama, you are going to be with Papa and Mama." Borja needed to feel that from then on Cosme would be forever in an imaginary dwelling with Papa and Mama, surrounded by childhood memories, souvenirs, photos. At the end, Cosme could not reply anything, but Borja desperately continued whispering into his ear, "Don't worry, Cosme, Papa and Mama are waiting for you"—as if to exorcise that final silence left by the departing father.

The Ybarras would always belong to their family house in Neguri with its main entrance facing the Avenue of Poplars, the back door facing the asphalt road overlooking the Gobelas River, the kitchen at the center, and Marse (their name for Marcelina) and their *aña* (wet nurse) Ciri as second mothers. In the garden there was a huge ailanthus, its immense trunk sheathed in gray bark with small longitudinal cracks, sinuous and white, its leaves forming rows of oval, pointed follicles and fragrant pale yellow flowers and red fruit. The ailanthus revealed its original Malayan etymology of "tree of the sky." Borja's mother had wanted to cut it down because it overshadowed the other trees in the garden, but his father had said no. To cut down that tree would have been sacrilege; watching his ailanthus be felled and cut into firewood would have been almost like watching his own death.

But that day would arrive for both man and tree. The same stormy day of Ybarra's death, the beautiful and luxuriant ailanthus was, astonishingly, uprooted and downed by an incredible wind. Not only had the lord of the house identified with the tree; it was as if the tree, unable to withstand the horror, was responding in kind by self-destruction. It was the tearing apart of the "tree of the sky"; as if echoing the earthquake and darkness that followed the agony and death at Golgotha, the garden was confronting the household's apocalypse.

As I listened to Borja's story, I was suddenly struck by a sense of déjà vu. Could these kidnappers have once been schoolmates and neighbors of mine? I had written about the kidnapping and killing of the industrialist Ángel Berazadi in my own village, and Ybarra's kidnappers had mentioned the name Berazadi in their letter to the public. In fact, Berazadi had been ETA's previous hostage in an action carried out by local teenagers. According to some reports, it was the same ETA leader who ordered the killings of both Berazadi and Ybarra. I left Borja's house in a daze and rushed to see my village friends—the same ex-ETA activists with whom I had built a discotheque and organized rock concerts, including the one in Vitoria-Gasteiz that we dedicated to John Lennon the day after his murder, he our ultimate hero whose "Imagine" had become our anthem, our new "L'Internationale." It was midnight when I found them in the street and told them the story I had just heard. I needed to see their reactions. Did they perhaps have anything to do with this second kidnapping? My friends had been in jail when Ybarra was taken and were unaware of how it had been carried out. But did they also belong in this family photograph?

My ex-ETA villagers had joined the organization through the mediation of Txiki, the son of Andalusian migrants. Later, Txiki was arrested in Barcelona in the company of Iñaki Pérez Beotegi, alias Wilson, a historic leader of ETA whom I knew from my days in London. Txiki was executed a few months later by a firing squad, fist raised and singing the Basque warriors' song "Eusko Gudariak." By then, there was no turning back for my friends. They ended up kidnapping and killing Berazadi. What always impressed me in the case of Berazadi were the effects of the weeks-long social intimacy between the kidnappers and their hostage. Berazadi had done the cooking and played the card game *mus* with his captors. They all planned, after the ordeal was over, to celebrate their forced conviviality together as friends with a banquet somewhere in southern France. In his father's case, Borja described one of the kidnappers as "the good one" who was friendly. Such familiarity between victims and executioners, Abraham and Isaac, each playing his ascribed role, is the most difficult thing to fathom—since in the end the murder ordered by the big Other had to be carried out. In Kierkegaard's apocryphal version of Abraham's story, Isaac loses his faith as he observes his father's idolatry. He knows that his father is not simply a madman or a vulgar murderer, but something far more complicated—a believer—and therefore a victim of his own belief, possessed by his *credo quia absurdum* without which he does not know how to live.

In Bob Dylan's rendering of Abraham's parable, God commands him on Mount Moriah to kill a son. Abraham protests that God must be putting him on. God insists that he is serious and that Abraham had better obey or else. Abraham asks where God wants him to kill the son. God answers, "on Highway 61." On Mount Gorbea, the big Other's command to ETA was to do the killing on the road to Bilbao.

Autobiography and Murder

But do I belong in this family photograph as well? The question haunted me as I listened to Borja's and Javier's story. Our fortuitous encounter on that rainy November evening was enough for them, children of the Neguri oligarchy, and me, son of peasants from Lastur, to feel that we had always known each other.

The issue of my complicity gained urgency when in 1999, and then again in 2006, I met in Bilbao with an old friend, Wilson, the historic leader of ETA arrested in Barcelona with his lieutenant Txiki in 1975. It took me back to my days in London, where I had ended up working as a porter in the old Charing Cross Hospital after leaving Bilbao. The high point of my summer there was the giant Isle of Wight music festival at the end of August. I took the train from London to Portsmouth and then the four-mile ferry ride to the island for three days and nights of music. The performers for an estimated audience of six hundred thousand fans included the entire pantheon of rockers. Most remarkable for me were Jimi Hendrix's Dylanesque "All

Along the Watchtower" (he died in a London hospital of an overdose two weeks later, followed soon by Janis Joplin), Cohen's mournful "Suzanne," Richie Havens's manic "Freedom," and The Who's vibrant rock opera *Tommy* (the deaf, dumb, and blind pinball wizard turned pop hero). I had lost God but was going to be saved by rock 'n' roll.

Religion and ETA were the two postwar traumatic sites for my Bilbao generation. As I was trying to escape them by leaving Bilbao for London, I was replacing the recollection of the convent's Gregorian music with the healing frenzy of a rock 'n' roll born in England out of the postwar trauma and echoing the violence of the Vietnam era. *Tommy* became an icon because "rock 'n' roll had essentially been born out of the turmoil of World War II." Like John Lennon or Keith Richards, The Who's leader, Pete Townshend, was acutely aware of living in an apocalyptic post-Hiroshima era: "My life began with a huge atomic bomb which . . . totally transmogrified the world, transformed it and distorted it . . . it is actually an apocalyptic world we live in, the rules have changed." While Townshend's *Tommy* was born in postwar bomb-damaged London, my Basque generation's *Tommy* was a child of Gernika, including the children of Civil War refugees in Stoneham Camp not far from London. *Guernica* is in fact an iconic reference for Townshend. We knew well that the autistic Tommy, shouting "See me, feel me, touch me, heal me," was, despite all its violence, about our most intimate "rebirth."

What I didn't know was how futile were my attempts at escaping from my country's political trauma. Summer and autumn went by in London, and it was December 1970 when, during my routine lunch break, I noticed a group of Basque migrants staging a hunger strike in Trafalgar Square, a hundred yards from the old Charing Cross Hospital where I worked. They were part of the worldwide protests against the Burgos military trial that would soon condemn six ETA members to death. It had been only six months since I thought I had escaped from Spain by taking the ferry from Bilbao to Southampton. The last thing I wanted was to be pursued by Basque politics. But the hunger strike lasted a month, and eventually I passed by the tent where my compatriots were camped across the street from the National Gallery. "You are Basque!" Juantxu, the ETA militant in hunger strike with Wilson, shouted at me. There was an iconic image of Juantxu bowing his head in front of the Tree of Gernika, taken from behind, and which with *Guernica* used to hang in many Basque homes. In London and other

Juantxu in front of the Tree of Gernika at the 1964 Day of the Motherland.

European capitals, multitudes joined the marches against the death sentences given to the ETA militants; the sentences were commuted to thirty years in prison.

Wilson and the London group of refugees asked me to teach them Euskara. Soon, twice a week I met with them in Wilson's apartment, which he shared with his Serbian girlfriend, Sarah; it was located, like my sister's apartment, on Shepherd's Bush Road in West London, the stomping ground of the musical group The Who. These were the months when I was utterly depressed and writing poetry for survival. Cultural activism or political militancy, writer or terrorist, there seemed to be no other alternative.

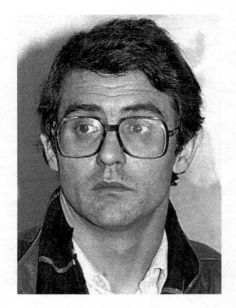

Iñaki Pérez Beotegui, "Wilson."

After I returned to the Basque Country the following summer, so did Wilson, and this time he suggested, to my alarm, that we rent an apartment together in Donostia-San Sebastián. I adamantly refused. I spent that summer working at my dad's marble quarry so that I could buy stereo equipment and listen to my London records. My younger brother Xalbador became my accomplice and we took turns to buy the latest releases. To our mother's embarrassment, we'd blast our rock 'n' roll through the balcony onto Itziar's only street. In one such occasion, in the middle 1970s, the Irish writer Paddy Woodworth happened to walk by the village during his first visit to the Basque Country and heard in the street at high pitch one of our favorites—Pink Floyd's "Wish You Were Here." It was music coming from the stereo I had bought with my dad's help. By then Xalbador was studying in Bilbao to become a marine pilot. It was also in Bilbao that he, never politically minded, was arrested and tortured when his Itziar friends were found to be ETA militants. When his heart gave out still in his thirties, I took his rock 'n' roll records, including Pink Floyd, and kept playing them for him.

I had said no to Wilson. Not that I disagreed with his anti-Francoist militancy; I simply didn't have what it takes to join the underground. These were the months when I was studying at the Jesuit University of Deusto's Donostia-San Sebastián campus. There I met Pertur, an outgoing student who organized cultural activities. He had been the guitar player of Los Amis, a group whose first record, composed by Pertur, was *La misa para los jóvenes* (Mass for the Youth)—religious songs that for years were played at the city's Jesuit church as well as by Vatican Radio. Pertur would soon belong to the leadership of ETA. He followed the generational pattern: religion, music, political militancy. With the prospect of a democracy following Franco's death, Pertur tried to channel ETA's forces from clandestine activism into the formation of a political party, when he disappeared in circumstances not yet known. His death was attributed by many to his own hardliner comrades who opposed him.

Wilson and I kept in touch. I remember one night in the spring of 1972 walking with him through Donostia-San Sebastián's main streets, talking about our days in London, unaware that the following morning his face would be on the front pages of all the Spanish newspapers as ETA's most wanted terrorist. Months later, I was having lunch at a student restaurant near Sarriko in Bilbao when I heard that the President of the Spanish government Admiral Carrero Blanco, Franco's anointed successor, had been catapulted over the nearby rooftops by an explosion after attending his daily mass. Wilson was one of the activists who plotted and carried out the assassination.

When he was arrested in July 1975 with Txiki, who was executed a few weeks later, it seemed that Wilson's execution was just months away. Days before his arrest, Wilson had crossed the border through the eastern Pyrenean town of Port Bou, a name that caught my attention when he told me this story. It was the town where Walter Benjamin found himself unable to cross the border into Spain while escaping the Nazis and had killed himself (I had visited his tomb on a pilgrimage). But for Wilson, Port Bou was not a literary reference but the place where he and his comrades, while crossing the border into Spain, had a shoot-out with Spanish police. "Mr. Ignacio," he had addressed himself, using his Spanish name, "this is the end of the story." But once again he survived. He always told me that he would not surrender, that he would die in a shoot-out. He bore the scars of fifteen bullets that had brushed his skin but without penetrating him. He was arrested later in Barcelona as a bullet hit him in a police confrontation and he fainted. He lived by luck.

On a Sunday afternoon in the summer of 1979, almost a decade after our initial encounter in a tent in Trafalgar Square, I was again face to face with Wilson in the coastal town of Zarautz. His date with the firing squad had been all but certain after months of solitary confinement. But Franco's death in November 1975 changed the course of events, and Wilson had been released in June 1977, part of a de facto amnesty. The media portrayed him as such a larger-than-life figure that, he confided, women regularly imagined him much taller and stronger that he was. I was an anthropology graduate student at Princeton University by then, writing my dissertation on Basque political violence. My career preference had been to study some African culture, but my mentor, an Africanist himself, prodded me back toward my own culture. I had been unwilling to collaborate with ETA in the past, yet unexpectedly, in the guise of anthropology, and perhaps because of an unconscious guilt produced by my unwillingness to join the underground anti-Francoist resistance, it was drawing me back once again. Suddenly, here I was, a graduate student, eager to seek contact with Wilson and write about the conflict that I had more than once fled. It was not primarily the country's cause for which I was willing to collaborate, but something more selfish and banal—writing a book that might establish my name.

My talking to ex-"terrorists" like Wilson did not present much of a problem. In my own village, former ETA members, barely in their twenties, were willing to discuss their surreal odyssey with me—from village camaraderie to ETA membership, from killing to arrest, torture, prison, the death of one of them, then release and renewed camaraderie. One of them, Agustin, after leaving jail had again joined the politico-military branch of ETA. His village friends visited him regularly at his hideout in southern France. I met with him there in their company.

My curiosity regarding Agustin's life was intense. He was a member of the organization's executive committee and willing to help with my anthropological project. Our meetings were obviously "illegal," but the issue for me at that time was the basic framework in which I would place the entire violent revolt. For the Spanish state, and after Franco for the Western media, it was all *terrorism*, a codeword that criminalized my Basque generation's political subject. As a student at a foreign university, I felt I could explore both sides without having to take a moral or political position. One consequence of the legal and moral *cordon sanitaire* against ETA's violence was the outlawing of the role of the witness. Any ethnography of "terrorism" was simply forbidden.

"But what do you want to prove?" my ETA interrogators asked me in the French hideout to which I had been summoned and then driven blindfolded. At issue were the extent of my contacts with them and potential participation in one of the organization's cells. I told them I had nothing to "prove." I certainly had no political agenda or commitment to the cause of an independent Basque Country. I simply wanted to know them before I wrote a book. And I was willing to assume all the risks of witnessing (which would make me an accomplice to terrorism). The most troublesome prospect was the possibility of committing murder. I would not obey if they ordered me to kill someone, I told them. Once you are "in," there is no separation between killers and nonkillers, they replied. I realized that if I joined them, my direct or indirect complicity in murder was possible, even likely, yet I persisted.

I had fallen into some sort of excessive witnessing that entailed the possibility of putting my own life and those of others at risk—a decision which, had it been accepted by ETA, would have pushed me into an unpredictable *passage à l'acte*. To my disappointment but soon to my relief, ETA's leadership decided that they did not want me around. They cited their concern about security; I could be from the CIA, although my Itziar friend's assurances obviated that. "Basically, we did not know what to do with you," one of the activists told me later. I concluded that the executioner did not want a witness. My "truth game" was over. The lesson I learned was the horror, not of some other person's evil but of my own capacity for complicity in murder.

I met Wilson in Bilbao one last time in the spring of 2006. He was having respiratory problems from his heavy smoking, and he'd be dead within two years. Wilson made fun of the ETA leader in the day's news for having endorsed the latest ceasefire. Although we had spent many hours together, I was aware that I would never penetrate the enigma of who he was. The more I questioned him about his former militancy and motivation, the more distant he became. He thought my desire to "explain" things was essentially silly—the crucial things in life, such as joining ETA or killing a man, which he had done more than once, spoke for themselves. The stated purpose of the rebellion to which he had surrendered his life was achieving an independent state for the preservation of Basque language and culture, but I had taught him Euskara for months in London and my impression was that he hardly learned anything from me and he didn't much care. What mattered was something else—and inquiring about it made no sense. I was asking questions at the symbolic level, as if joining a group such as ETA was primarily the result of a political calculation, when such decisions and events belonged rather to the *real* of a man besieged by repression and expecting death any day. He was right to find my incongruence annoying. "Didn't you want to get into ETA to write a book?" once he poked at me, looking sideways with his sarcastic smile. "Don't ask any futher. That's all you need to know."

The Ghost of Madness: Writing the Ruins

Reading and writing were for my generation what our parents didn't do. Reading and writing decided knowledge, and they could be a secret pleasure dome. Our most intimate subjectivity had been "scripted." It could be said that our catastrophe had all been literature.

Reading was a risky affair; our lives would be decided by our responses to texts turned into witnesses. We couldn't avoid the shattering experience of reading, compounded by that of writing—activities that turned into "a voluntary obliteration of the self. . . . Where a work had the duty of creating immortality, it now attains the right to kill, to become the murderer of its author." If reading as radical comittment had enslaved us within religious and political dogmas, in time reading became a double-edged sword that pointed out the avenue to liberation—an activity in which truth and fiction, far from mutually exclusive, were engendered simultaneously. My own religious subject was irreparably destroyed by the Blakean poem I wrote on the myth of paradise while I was dejected about my life. The ultimate challenge was to write one's *own* text, recreate one's *own* subjectivity—an activity that was not mere recollection but vital quest, frought with risk, a kind of exile.

But hadn't we become ghostlike figures dependent on literature for our life "experience"? Our parents' oral universe assumed that the word was spoken and heard—had a personal and social reality of its own. The writer's word, in contrast, is nothing but text, its relationship to the actual world speculative and noncommittal. Hadn't we returned to Plato's view of writing as a kind of shadow? The Socratic irony is that the culture of writing is at once more knowledgeable and more deceitful than the word—Socrates being the wisest among Greeks, the thinker who refused to write. In the old enmity between speech and writing, Socrates's complaint was that those who rely on writing will remember and experience things "by external signs instead of on their own interior resources." What mattered to Socrates was how to live.

As I was studying philosophy with the Jesuits at the University of Deusto, Joyce's *A Portrait of the Artist as a Young Man* fell into my hands. The world of Stephen Dedalus leaving aside the Jesuit vocation and accepting writing as the only calling was familiar to me. The character's name—Dedalus—referred to the Greek hero who was the architect of the labyrinth that housed the Minotaur—the labyrinth where the artist is trapped by religion, nation, and culture. Stephen allies the Cretan labyrinth with Dante's Christian hell while searching for a way out of the maze and undergoing a ritual of rebirth, the final result being that "Stephen has slain the Minotaur within himself." Literature and mythology were vital to create a new subject.

Reading and writing became for my generation a way to make sense of our descent into apostasy and its intellectual labyrinth. In Bilbao I found several people who had gone to the trouble of formally renouncing Catholicism by deleting their names from the Church's records in a determined act of committing "apostasy." Our de-conversion was the attempt to escape Hegel's "bad infinity" and a kind of inverse conversion—a breach with any stable definition of the self. For some of us, writing became an antidote to conversion and the most important part of living. The crucial conversion was to writing, that most decisive act in which the subject could engage. The interpretation of the world and of ourselves depended not on possessing a correct theory but on our own free wills emerging from the ruins of former selves. As with Sartre, our new atheism did not become a fixed position, but rather a process and a project.

In my own case, I tried at Deusto to mend with Wittgenstein's *Tractatus* the intellectual world that Nietzsche's *Zarathustra* had shattered. In his essay "Mysticism and Logic," Bertrand Russell contended that these are the two sources of knowledge (Blake's was the first kind, Frege's the second), but that only logic can guarantee truth. After returning to Bilbao from London, I studied philosophy. By then I was far more interested in Russell and Wittgenstein than Sartre and Heideger; I wrote my master's thesis on the ontology of the *Tractatus.* Still, there was an undercurrent that united Nietzsche and Wittgenstein, and that was their "antiphilosophy"—the belief that "Philosophy is not a theory, but an act" (4.112). The ontology of the *Tractatus* made one thing clear—the sovereignty of what cannot be spoken about. The entire edifice was built on an elaborate logical apparatus, but did logic and mathematics really matter, or was it all a means for voiding logical propositions before arriving at the mystical?

What was for Russell the greatest achievement of modern mathematics—Cantor's theorem of infinity—was for Wittgenstein emphatically "not a paradise" but "a cancerous growth," a quagmire of confusions. It was a season in hell. Wittgenstein attacked with fury the foundations of mathematics and the idol-worship of science; no other field was more responsible than mathematics for "so much sin" in misusing metaphysical expressions. Science, math—it was all ruin for the most influential philosophical mind of the century.

My generation had moved from transcendence and sacrament to what really mattered—the book. But the book was haunted by its own ghosts. The subtitle of Ray Monk's biography of Bertrand Russell is *The Ghost of Madness* (a life ruled by "a deep seated fear of madness" and condensed by the biographer as "tragedy"). As to my ultimate hero, Wittgenstein, the man torn "between saintliness and suicide," what most impressed Lacan about him was his capacity for madness and the "psychotic ferocity" of his philosophical operations; the task he set for himself was to show that philosophers, by producing an illusion of objectivity that relies on metalanguage, are in fact crooks, for there is no other language but desire, "There is no sense except the sense of desire. This is what one can say after having read Wittgensntein," concludes Lacan. Badiou repeated these charges when he concluded his study of Wittgenstein's work by openly linking the "terrible torsion" and the latent despair of the *Tractatus* ("a bit like [Rimbaud's] *A Season in Hell* written in the form of [Mallarmé's] *A Throw of the Dice*") to the psychoanalytic term *psychosis*—this meaning "the paranoid certitude of he who believes in saying the integral truth." What was difficult for me to fathom during my student years was the link between logical genius and madness in my two heroes. Facing this state of affairs in modern mathematics and the exact sciences led the poet and mathematician Mikel Lasa to write of "intellectual terrorism."

The ghost of madness, we saw earlier, also visited some of Bilbao's most representative artists and writers, but no one perhaps as much as Unamuno. He advocated furiously, and at times simultaneously, Basquism and anti-Basquism, socialism and antisocialism, nationalism and antinationalism, militarism and antimilitarism, Republicanism and fascism, Catholicism and atheism, becoming at once a hero and a traitor to them all. The most influential Spanish thinker of his times, his discourse could be frequently described as delirium. He would typically "try the impossible," as when he attempted to justify Franco's fascist military revolt as being compatible with the continuity of Republican legality. Unamuno's agonic subject, "a paradoxical form of being at once with everyone and against anyone," has all the traits of Lacan's "barred subject"—it exists only so long as it upholds its own impossibility. The source of such a hysterical subject is always an impossible totality in reference to which our lives will always be failures. Hence comes the passion for suffering, as if this were the final proof of our truth, in the vain hope that suffering will placate the tyranny of the big Other. He recognized Hegel as his main philosophical influence, but he never seems to have paid attention to his master's notion of "bad infinity."

The psychoanalytical premise that every subject is governed by some type of delirium, and that in the end "delirium is an interpretation," helps explain Unamuno's paradoxes and phobias. It also makes sense of his intense identification with Don Quixote, that "reasonable madman" whose comical figure could not escape him, yet his heroic madness was so sensible because there was never a more serious madman that Don Quixote. Unamuno interprets Don Quixote not as Divine Comedy but as Divine Tragedy. Unamuno's hystericized texts were a liberating force in a Spain dominated by the Church and the army. Unamuno spent the last two months of his life writing an essay on *The Tragic Resentment of Life,* a work that has been compared to T. S. Eliot's *The Waste Land*—"These fragments I have shored against my ruins."

But it wasn't philosophy alone that conjured up madness. As I was looking for potential informants for my anthropological studies, I met Maritxu Erlanz de Guler, a widow thirty-five years my senior and renowned as a "good witch" for her clairvoyance. As she opened the door of her apartment she gazed intently at me. "I can see your aura," she said. But what was she really perceiving?

Lacan developed a theory of *gaze* and *voice* as objects defined outside of perception—"We can all approach these two terms through perception but they are only really constituted when perception is not possible," observes Miller. Thus, "what he [Lacan] calls gaze is not something that is found in the eye or that comes out of the eye." Lacan's voice and gaze are grounded in the experience of psychosis. Miller adds on Lacan:

> If psychosis didn't exist, his thesis would not hold. It is in the experience of the psychotic that the voice that no one can understand, that the gaze that no one can see, find their existence. It is in the psychotic that Lacan finally introduces the theory of perception in order to detonate it, in order not to reduce the experience of the psychotic to supposedly normal experience.

Maritxu shared the ontology of the psychotic experience by which something shows "itself" and gazes at the subject—the frame is in my eye but I myself am in the frame. It was also the "illuminist" Rimbaud's experience when he wrote that "The Poet makes himself a *seer* by a long, gigantic and rational *derangement* of *all the senses*. All forms of love, suffering, and madness." In the scopic field, as different from the field of vision, the gaze forces the inscription of desire into the object; the counterpart of the psychotic is not the "normal" person but the subject of desire. Lacan stressed that the subject does not unify perception and that, regarding psychotic hallucinations, "it is not necessary to consider them as error or malady of the subject, but as exploitations of the structure itself of language." While exploiting the Lacanian objects of gaze and voice without falling into psychosis, Maritxu's world was also ruled by a theory of perception in which the *percipiens* was not external to the *perceptum*.

Maritxu's epistemology was largely Christian, much like Dante's figural thinking (the actual reality prefigures and demands another that it predicts). A widely read woman who had traveled extensively through Europe with her Swiss husband during the postwar years, Maritxu clothed her unconscious reality with tarot cards, palm readings, and other paraphernalia—the fetishes she used to *see* and produce self-fulfilling prophecies for her visitors—without ever accepting money or gifts. But then, with a gleam in her eye and a grin of disavowal, she'd add, "All this is a lie." Maritxu's intuitive powers dazzled many people and her figure became a legend; a park was named after her in Donostia-San Sebastián. With her savage love of life she put a spell on me as well. Our main topic of conversation was the nature of symbolism—or, rather, its *failures*. I was going to embark on the study of symbolism, and Maritxu became my Beatrice by telling me in advance that there are objects foreclosed from the symbolic, forewarning me of the impossibility of their being interpreted. This was the realm of what the Lacanians call the Real—the voice and gaze that do not belong to perception but desire. It was the bodily materiality of her world that was most remarkable—it all happened through her senses and was colored by the halo of a reality that emanated from the very objects that seemed to be speaking back to her.

Years later, reading Clarice Lispector, I had the uncanny feeling that she was describing Maritxu's world as well. Both Maritxu and Lispector were unsettling in that both could define themselves as "a monstrosity." For both, "the act of seeing [was] ineffable." Both were passionate about "the essence of numbers," when "everything takes the halo that's not imaginary: it comes from the splendor of the mathematical irradiation of things and from the memory of people." Both shared the awareness of time's simultaneity, the everyday evidence that "what will be already is," and that they could "manufacture the future." Maritxu wrote and patented symbolic formulas to read the future, a seemingly absurd mixture of numbers and letters inaccessible to anyone, and which she knew all along were a failure; she could say with Lispector, "in writing, I deal with the impossible. With the enigma of nature," because "a world wholly alive has a Hellish power." There was nothing "saintly" or "mystical" about the Maritxu I knew. Both Lispector and Maritxu were concerned with the closeness between madness and wisdom. Of Maritxu's symbolic "system," one could say what Freud said of Judge Schreber's paranoid "system"—that it was "not madness, but a desperate attempt to *escape* madness—the disintegration of the symbolic universe—through an ersatz universe of meaning." Yet both Lispector and Maritxu could also be overtaken at any moment by a "state of grace" beyond religiousness in which "the body is transformed into a gift," seemingly "achieving a higher plane of humanity. Or of inhumanity—the *it*," but in any case a state of grace that is "inherent" and "exists permanently: we are always saved." In the end it was all "an artifice through which there arises a very delicate reality that comes to exist within me: that transfiguration has happened to me." Maritxu's magic was to reproduce that metamorphosis in the countless anonymous visitors knocking at her door. Dante wrote for her: "I saw her there in all her glory crowned / by the reflections of eternal light."

A Pietà

In 1950, while in Bilbao, Oteiza was commissioned to work on the new Marian sanctuary of Arantzazu. He became the animating force behind the new modernist church project, which included a group of relevant artists. Oteiza sculpted fourteen Apostles in hollowed stone for the Arantzazu facade above the sanctuary's main entrance and flanked by two tall towers of pointed stones—stones, pointed or hollow, all extracted from the Lastur quarry where my father worked. In 1955, the Vatican censored Oteiza's statues, which looked as profane and aberrant as hanging carcasses. Donostia-San Sebastián's bishop called them "fourteen sacrificed pigs." Others described them as "aggressive and monstrous giants that chew with their teeth on the indolence of

Oteiza's *Apostles* in Arantzazu.

a conformist Christianity." The Apostles remained unfinished by the side of Arantzazu's road until 1969, when Oteiza, overcoming his initial resistance, was convinced to return to the work. As Oteiza and his wife, Itziar, moved to Arantzazu, they were joined by Blas de Otero and his wife, Sabina, who came from Bilbao and spent most of the summer with them.

By the early 1960s, Oteiza had become the dominant figure at the intersection of Basque art, culture, and politics. As such, he became a mentor to young ETA militants. Etxebarrieta sought Oteiza's advice, and they became friends. When, on June 7, 1968, Oteiza heard the news that Etxebarrieta had died in a confrontation with police, he knew what to erect high in the apse of the sanctuary—a pietà in memory of his friend and of ETA's generation. There is a pietà in Picasso's *Guernica*—the mother with a dead child kneeling at the far left, the head of the bull, with his horns in the shape of a moon and his ears like swords, hovering over her. Above the apse of the Basilica of Arantzazu up on rocky Mount Aloña, Oteiza added, carved in the gray marble stone my father sent him from Lastur's quarry, ETA's pietà—the everlasting prayer in stone of "the mother screaming to the heavens."

Lauaxeta's and Lorca's green moon of death, waiting for the firing squad at dawn, hovered over Gernika. In Arantzazu, as in Begoña, a pallid metallic crescent moon adorns the feet of the Virgin Mother's statue. It evokes for the believer the figure of the woman clothed with

Oteiza's *Pietà* in Arantzazu.

the sun and the moon under her feet mentioned in John's book of Revelation 12:1 and which found expression in Dante. In a pagan conception of the world going as back as Pythagoras, the moon traced a line in the universe below which humans were born; the ascent of the mind aimed at abandoning the sublunar realm of corruption and reaching the changeless region above, the Eden where all was immortal. Beatrice took Dante to the sphere above the moon.

Both Begoña and Arantzazu represent the strong Marian tradition in Basque popular religiosity in the footsteps of earlier "female" pagan divinities. During the first part of the twentieth century, the ethnographer Barandiarán recorded excerpts of a mythology centered around the flying witch-figure Mari, the moon being one of her standard images. On the basis of a text by the Roman geographer Strabo, anthropologist Julio Caro Baroja concluded that in prehistoric northern Spain, religion was female and based on the cult of the moon. He concluded that the "the current folkloric and linguistic data strongly support what Strabo's text implied"—namely, that Basques and other neighboring tribes in northern Spain practiced a "cult to an unnamed god during full moon nights." The archeological discoveries at Knossos centered on the cult of the Mother Goddess, represented by the figure of Ariadne, the daughter of the moon goddess Pasiphe. Caro Baroja's conclusion was that the pre-Christian Basque lunar culture echoed such discoveries.

1) In the past Basques adored the moon, whose current names are due most probably to a 'taboo' in naming it. 2) For them, the moon was the recipient of a secondary light ('argizagia'), or the light of the dead ('ilargia'). 3) The ideas of moon, death ('il') and month ('illa'), were linked in their minds. 4) They give the moon the title of grandmother ('amandre'), the same as they did the sun, which is considered in certain popular songs as being of female sex ('euzkiamandria'). 5) The Basque calendar is originally a lunar calendar, later accommodated to the agricultural tasks and to the Julian calendar. 6) The names of certain days of the week, and perhaps of the week itself, have their origin in subdivisions of the lunar month. 7) Besides vestiges of the cult to the moon, there are also those of a cult to the God of the sky, to the sun and to the earth.

In sum, the current folkloric and linguistic data strongly support what is implied by Strabo's text . . . As I believe and stated above, Strabo's references to the cult of an unnamed god during the nights of full moon by the Celtiberian peoples and their northern neighbors are intimately connected with these linguistic data.

Caro Baroja, *Los pueblos del norte de la peninsula ibérica*, 198–200.

Strabo's lunar descriptions were later repeated by writers such as Voltaire, with claims that Basques adored a female divinity and danced in the full moon. As I found in my own ethnographic work in Mendata, a town next to Gernika, Basque farmers still pay close attention to the waxing and full moon to sow their seeds and to the waning moon to harvest crops and cut wood. It is a common belief that the effects of the moon on animals and people are a fact of life, including the assumption that the menstrual blood of women ebbs and flows according to the lunar rhythm. The moon tells nature's story of transformation through birth, growth, fullness, decay, death, and rebirth.

During his Arantzazu period, Oteiza began in Bilbao a series of perforated "moons" as part of his large "experimental proposal," his hollow apostles an initial expression of his aesthetic of "*dis*-occupation." In sculptures such as *Earth and Moon*, *The Moon as Revolving Light,* and *Flotation (Lunar Sculpture)*, Oteiza, who would visit Crete in 1974 and who chose the red color of the palace of Knossos for his own museum in Alzuza, had no problem transporting the Minoan matriarchal culture to Mari and the Virgin Mother of Arantzazu.

His philosophical mentor, Unamuno had developed the theme of the moon's light while re-creating Velázquez's use of the contrast between light and darkness in his painting of Christ on the cross. He addressed the Crucified: "only your lunar light tells us in our night that the sun is alive." Unamuno, Bilbao's most influential thinker of the last century, has been described as a "man who philosophized, lived and poeticized *under the moon.*"

Someone who could not bear to see Oteiza's statues abandoned along Arantzazu's roadside because of the Vatican's censorship was his friend Gabriel Aresti. He devoted a thirty-six-page-long poem to Oteiza in his *Harri eta Herri*. But Aresti wanted nothing to do with the white moon of the Christian Madonnas and magical witches; his moon would be *red*:

> The moon in the sky
> has the appearance of a red orange
> a mirror of the blood
> spilled in this world.
> If we could live on the moon
> we would be more fortunate.

For Aresti, not only was the sky red, his signature *oskorria*, but even the moon was red, echoing the apocalyptic signs of Scripture: "The

Traditional image of the Virgin Mary.

I have to explain to him,
I have to make him understand
what it is that is,
because he has not arrived yet
to the bottom of the Basque soul,
to this lowest hell
where we are drowning.
We don't live here
comfortably.
We don't feel
A paradise.
Not even Dante could have
imagined
such a thing.
This is an immense quagmire.
Here even the souls of angels would be
soiled.

Aresti, *Obra Guztiak*, I, 552. Author's translation.

sun shall be turned into darkness, and the moon into blood" (Acts 2:15). With Arantzazu in the background, Aresti wrote to Oteiza, who by then was involved in high-spirited interpretations of "the Basque soul," explaining to him that if he wanted to get to the bottom of it he had to go down to Bilbao's hell. Oteiza, Aresti, and Otero, all three of them atheists and coming from Bilbao, found in "heavenly" Arantzazu a refuge to escape from their city.

Oteiza, *The Moon as Revolving Light*.

It was there, under Arantzazu's moon, that Oteiza erected a pietà for his friend Etxebarrieta. It was intended also for countless other victims—of ETA and by ETA. Etxebarrieta's ultimate tragedy had not been his own death, but his uncessary killing of the traffic policeman. As Aresti, the poet so close to Oteiza in Arantzazu, wrote, "the mothers of ETA activists suffer much when they kill their sons, but even more when their sons kill." The pietà had a special resonance for Julen Madariaga, the militant who turned Etxebarrieta into ETA's leader. Two decades after Etxebarrieta's death, Madariaga was once again arrested in southern France. By then fifty-six, Madariaga had distanced himself from and become severely critical of ETA's violence. But while in jail, one event would shake Madariaga "like nothing else before," he told me—the drowning in October 1988 of his twenty-month-old daughter, Iraia, in his house's swimming pool. The previous February, his three-year-old son had also died suddenly from meningitis. Madariaga was taken from the jail to his daughter's wake. As he entered the room, alone with Iraia's small exposed body, he was dazed: "I gathered myself in front of her body for a long time. A ubiquitous wave of irrepressible pity (enhanced by my impotence) overpowered me at the view of innocence in its pure state." Madariaga was the modern Basque "terrorist" par excellence, an internationally sought-after fugitive for much of his life, a man of war (he had named several of his eleven children, fathered with two women, for classical war heroes such as Ajax or Aeneas). He was historically the one most responsible for ETA's decision to adopt the violence that caused more than eight hundred deaths, while nearly three hundred of its own also died. In front of his dead child, the terrorist was a *pietà*.

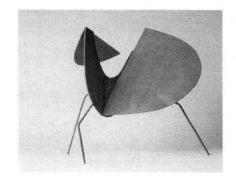

Oteiza, *Flotation (Lunar Sculpture)*.

In prison, Madariaga participated with the rest of his comrades in a hunger strike that lasted thirty-six days (he disagreed with the premise of the strike but accepted the majority's decision). After losing seventeen kilos and sensing death at his door, something unexpected happened to him, he told me. A profound serenity took hold of

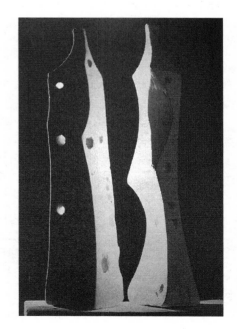

Oteiza, *Earth and Moon*.

him and there was no discomfort in his body, his mind was as clear as ever and he was at peace with himself—nothing any longer mattered. Everything had happened as ordained, he had completed his life's mission, his family would be well after he was gone, everything had a purpose. It was a moment of "mystical lucidity" for the man who had exchanged his father's and grandfather's barrister wigs for ETA's weapons, the quintessential fighter for whom there was at last nothing left to fight—*consummatum est* (all is finished).

Bilbao Dantesque: Painting a River Downstream

From Arantzazu's heaven all was *maldan behera* (down hill) for Aresti— the downstream of the Dantean rivers flowing to the ocean. After the fall of Bilbao, La Pasionaria, the revolutionary torch of mining Bilbao, communist Spain's Joan of Arc, felt that Bilbao's "rivers . . . are dyed in noble blood. The Ibaizabal, the Cadagua and the Nervión carry down the lifeless bodies of the sons of Biscay on their waters." Unamuno addressed Bilbao's mighty river thus:

> You are, Nervión, the history of the Town
> you her past and her future, you are
> memory always turning into hope
> and on your firm riverbed
> a fleeing flow.

"Nothing in the world is more magnificent than these mines," wrote Max Weber to his mother in 1887 after having seen the Nervión Valley. "The panorama of the mountains . . . rising above the sea and the Nervión Valley, smoking with a hundred chimneys, forms a spectacle that is simply so stunning as to become unforgettable." Weber's letter to his mother from Bilbao remarks on the internal contradictions of a modern business elite and rural communitarian institutions. Industrial capitalism as a global process had irrevocably transformed Bilbao's traditional social and urban structures. Weber mentions Ignatius of Loyola and expresses his fascination with Bilbao's work ethic—a knowledge that, according to several authors, goes against the grain of his famed "Protestant ethics" thesis. Over the course of a century, the glare of Altos Hornos' fiery molten iron had illuminated Bizkaia's nocturnal sky with pink and red colors visible from Bilbao and afar.

Bilbao, like every city, is the sum of its geography and history. Both factors have placed it at times at the vortex of Iberian affairs and

Altos Hornos (Tall Ovens) on the Nervión's left bank.

at others at their margin. Situated on the riverine narrow neck of an extensive estuary, while not quite coastal, Bilbao was a port before it was a city. For centuries, its sheltered waters and location near the Cantabrian Sea made the city an ideal transshipment point for Castilian wool destined for Western European textile manufacturers and for the import of an array of European products for the Spanish market. Bilbao is also adjacent to one of the world's richest iron-ore deposits, mineral wealth that was extolled by Pliny during Roman times but emerged most notably as the economy's driving force in the city's nineteenth-century industrial revolution.

It was by obtaining the rights to the Nervión's trade that Bilbao became the medieval town that excelled among the neighboring towns and later turned into a commercial powerhouse. The Nervión River had been the grand avenue to the open sea and Castile's window on Northern European trade. Before Bilbao's latest industrial boom was channeled through the Nervión, for centuries fishermen, whalers, sailors, shipbuilders, merchants, and other colonial adventurers and smugglers had been the characters who plied the Cantabrian Sea to return up the generous river and, upon seeing Her basilica up on the distant hill, sing "La Salve" to the Virgin of Begoña. Bilbainos had joined the ranks of Basque fishermen and whalers operating first in Cantabrian waters and later in the North Atlantic, including off Newfoundland. Bilbao created one of Spain's strongest merchant fleets. By the fifteenth century, and in direct competition with the Italian city-states, it was heavily engaged in commerce between Western Europe and the Mediterranean. In the sixteenth century, the Bilbao-to-Flanders run was one of Europe's most important trade routes. With the advent of the European Enlightenment, and given their proximity to France, the Basques were the vanguard of Iberian economic, scientific, and cultural developments. Bilbao was a principal center of this activity and became a progressive redoubt of Spanish liberalism.

During the last quarter of the nineteenth century, the mining and export of iron ore dominated Bilbao's economy. Between 1875 and 1900, 65 to 75 percent of Bilbao's iron went to Great Britain alone. Meanwhile, the city experienced a commercial and financial boom. The Banco de Bilbao was founded in 1857, and during that same decade a number of insurance companies were established. After 1890, Bilbao had its own stock exchange. During the last half of the nineteenth century, Bilbao's population increased from about 25,000 in 1876 to 230,000 in 1900. In 1876 the *ensanche*, or "enlargement," was approved, although it accommodated more of the social elite than the working class.

By century's end, the city was a serious steel-making center in its own right, producing no less than 20 percent of the world's steel. It culminated in 1902 with the creation of the mega-refinery Altos Hornos (Tall Furnaces) by a consortium of three independent refiners. Fortified by its steel industry, during the early twentieth century Bilbao attracted many ancillary heavy industries, particularly the modernized shipyards that came to line the banks of the estuary. This was the city whose products Franco would use to repay Hitler's favors.

The gritty industrial city that emerged in the late nineteenth century was made of miners, steelworkers, stevedores, and construction workers from the Left Bank sharing the urban space with the wealthy industrial elite and upper-middle-class bourgeoisie that inhabited the Right Bank. Nor were the workers in the main Basque. By 1887, 73 percent of the population of the adjacent town of Baracaldo was made up of immigrants from other parts of Spain, attracted by Bilbao's burgeoning industries. In Bilbao itself, immigrants constituted 38 percent of the population. The estuary became as much a political divide as a geographical one; Bilbao became the spawning ground of the Basque Country's first Socialist Association (1886). A new wave of migration took place in the mid-twentieth century. With 238,000 inhabitants in 1955, Bilbao received over 100,000 immigrants in the next decade. Between 1950 and 1970, the population of the Bilbao area doubled from 400,000 to 816,000. Its hills became shantytowns for working-class immigrants from other regions of Spain—shantytowns that Franco ordered demolished on one of his visits in August 1961 because he felt they reflected badly on his regime.

But the Nervión's river of life would eventually turn into a river of ruins. By 1997 the fire and the smoke were gone. Bilbainos could only watch the demise of the Left Bank as a spectacle of demolition and absence. Nostalgia took over the city. The black river, the abandoned ovens, the streets with derelict buildings, the fiery blast furnaces were a sight from the past, turned Dantesque ruin. Between 1975 and 1991, Bilbao's industrial wasteland lost 37 percent of its jobs. During the 1980s and early 1990s, unemployment was above 20 percent. Such devastation meant the loss of livelihood for tens of thousands of workers who decided to make a last stand in what became known as the Battle of Euskalduna—an epic three-month urban guerrilla battle between workers and police in Bilbao's streets. In September 1984, the Spanish government proposed a plan for restructuring the shipbuilding industry with substantial reductions that affected some 150,000 jobs, 40,000 of them in the Basque region. The workers called for a general strike in the shipbuilding sector, to be followed by another in the industrial sector, and later a general strike throughout Bizkaia. Beginning in early October 1984, workers launched an all-out resistance—including the raising of street barricades—that lasted until the end of December. They marched through the streets in mass protests, some consisting of as many as twenty thousand people. Two demonstrators died, and some one hundred were wounded in police confrontations. Among the badges worn by the protesters, one was paramount: Picasso's *Guernica* with a large word, *Euskalduna*, inscribed in its center.

The Deusto Bridge became a daily battleground. *"Zubia sutan"*— the bridge was on fire—is how old trade unionist Valentin Bengoa described the struggle, because he could see the bridge burning from his offices every morning. "Old Bilbao was on fire—the working class, the industrial region." It became "a symbol" for him. During the industrial period, Deusto's drawbridge had been the last link uniting the right and left riverbanks between Bilbao and the sea twelve miles away. Now even that bridge, the symbol that marked the continuity between the industrial Bilbao of the Altos Hornos and the new postindustrial Bilbao, was burning.

The workers' battle for Euskalduna ended in defeat; they yielded to the restructuring plans and accepted the government's preferred subsidies. "Our strength doesn't come from heavens like manna," the Euskalduna's Workers' Collective wrote in a book; "it is nothing but the sharp *sword* that gets tempered in the fire of the struggle, step by step, blow by blow . . . let us go forth to build a new society by breaking apart our *shackles*." This was the inner dialectic of the Shakespearean *bilboes* as both swords and shackles. But the fighting words only served to conceal the demise of Bilbao's militant working class. Bilbao's city planners were relieved that the struggle with the workers was over so that they could proceed to build, at the site where the Euskalduna shipyard had stood for a century, the new Euskalduna Music Hall and Convention Center.

The battle for Euskalduna.

The river "is the sea breathing through the city," people told me. The river is a deep, sinuous cut across the land, separating the lush valley into the Right Bank and Left Bank. The inner scission of both "margins" splitting land and city can only be transcended, at a distance, by the sea. The river conveys in measured form the fullness of the sea: "When we talk of plenitude," said the cloistered monk in Zenarruza, a man who gets up every morning at five to meditate until ten, "we are talking, in Bilbao's terms, of the river that every day goes up and down, up and down with the tide. There is a moment when the tide is full and that is the moment of plenitude. If you want to know plenitude, it has to do with the tide, with a vortex of attraction that is the moon. If there is a tide, there is plenitude. In monastic life, there is a tide that is God's plenitude made word." Txabi Etxebarrieta's main metaphor to describe his love for Isabel was also the "high tide"—"much like the tides get high with the full moon, so do I suddenly surrender to your memory in the midst of things." For Bilbainos, sea and river are one and the same water, respiration, distant proximity. When the river was uncrossed by bridges and maritime traffic had no impediment to reaching downtown, the sea itself reached the heart of the city. As new bridges were being built, one could hear people's complaints: "they are putting the sea farther and farther away from the city." Bilbao likes to keep the sea at some distance, yet close enough to breathe its salty air.

I visited Xabier, a painter and former Franciscan monk whose father had worked in a factory on the Left Bank. His grandfather had migrated to Portugalete to work for the legendary shipowner Ramón de la Sota; his grandmother became Sota's housekeeper. Xabier described for me vivid images of the Left Bank's landscapes, never illuminated by the sun. The beaches of summer belonged to bathers, never to workers. They were typically dense in browns, ochers, greens, and grays. Rain and storms gave a sense of obscurity. White seagulls contrasted with the gray chimneys. The river's panorama was one of work—like the "dunghill" boat that collected the slag, then went out to sea to open its guts and disgorge its filthy cargo, which would return to the beaches to be collected by poor people for fuel. There were tugboats towing great ships, a pilot boat, barges from Erandio and Santurce, boats offloading onto barges, new red-painted boats being launched in the marina. Dredgers, like monsters, scraped the alluvial refuse from the bowels of the river; a boat crossed the river—and sirens wailed and whistled in a sonorous language. At noon, the Altos Hornos siren sounded the hours, and about the same time the south wind would arise. Xabier remembered the breeze, when all the smells of Erandio's factories, along with the smoke of Altos Hornos and the soot that was everywhere, would enter his house and soil the blankets. Still, the Left Bank never seemed dirty to him—"it is dirty only when you see it from a distance."

Xabier couldn't talk of that imposing landscape without a strong emotional component. The cranes were like "prehistoric steel animals" in his childhood. "I have been a spectator of the river," he observed. "The landscape becomes symbolically internalized within you to the extent that you empathize with it affectively." Xabier could hardly find words: "The river is a marvel, it is a striking universe. . . . A sunset in this industrial world irradiates light that is otherworldly. True, not a pretty world. Erandio [his town] is a drama—with deteriorated houses, gray, dirty . . . and street demonstrations which even resulted in deaths." But Xabier still found the word "redemption" applied to it all, adding: "You hold to these forms because it is with them that you must reconstruct a surviving world."

Xabier Egaña, *The River of Bilbao*.

One of Xabier's enduring images is of workers exiting factories.
During the 1970s, Xabier became interested in ruins and began taking slides and painting from them. "I was searching for the broken,
the cracked image, the fissured, the not-yet dead but deteriorated,"
he summed up. Nostalgia for a bygone world overwhelms Xabier,
who experiences the modern steel works replacing Altos Hornos as
"something else." It had nothing to do with the landscape that he had
known for forty years. "The sky is gray, with dense clouds, and on top
the clouds of smoke from Altos Hornos." But it was the machinery
that dominated the landscape—Altos Hornos, the tall chimneys, then
the houses and the church of Portugalete, and Mount Serantes behind
them. "A worker who becomes unemployed experiences it all not only
as a personal tragedy but in its social dimension as well. It has an
emotional component. It was Dad who told me the stories about these
machines. When I saw that one of the Altos Hornos had been demolished, I had to leave, I couldn't look. I felt unable to confront a different landscape. I told myself, so what? I will keep the memories."
Xabier was sobbing by then, while he managed to add, "It wasn't a factory. It was a cosmos."

Bilbao's bookstores began to feature photography exhib-
its chronicling the destruction of the city's old factory buildings and
chimneys, enormous steel structures soaring from a devastated land-

scape of rusty phantoms that spoke of desertion and silence. The city's fiery sun had turned ashen—only to force its Dantean promise of transfiguration. The logic of capitalism required *producing* ruins as a precondition for reinvestment and renewal.

For a century, Bilbainos watching their black river were watching the flow of capital and dirt. Their senses could not avoid confronting the river's invasive presence; there was no way to evade its smells, although they learned to avert their gaze from its black flow. But not so Xabier. He is a prisoner of love among ruins—love of the lands, rivers, mountains, and cultures that nourished his generation.

I mentioned to Xabier what Frank Gehry said about Bilbao's "aesthetic of toughness." "All is in ruin, filled with memories, full of beauty, but that in itself doesn't take you very far," Xabier replied. Like so many of his generation, and while holding onto the ruins of a broken cosmos, the ex-Franciscan knows that the true learning has to come from this Theology of Hell. "Art must give content to the ruins," he concluded. "Art is the only means of converting death into life. A million ruins is a total ruin—a *holocaust*." Xabier is Paul Klee's *Angelus Novus*, Benjamin's angel of history watching the storm from Paradise. You are, Nervión, the history of the city, you are her past and her future, and on your firm riverbed you are a fleeing flow.

His eyes are staring, his mouth is open, his wings are spread. . . . His face is turned toward the past. Where we perceive a chain of events, he sees one single catastrophe which keeps piling wreckage upon wreckage and hurls it in front of his feet. The angel would like to stay, awaken the dead, and make whole what has been smashed. But a storm is blowing from Paradise.

Benjamin, *Illuminations*, 257-258.

Paul Klee, *Angelus Novus* (1920).

BOOK II
PURGATORY

Shackles and Swords: A Lover's Passion

Hamlet addresses Horatio:

> Sir, in my heart there was a kind of fighting,
> That would not let me sleep; methought I lay
> Worse than the mutines in the bilboes.

Bilbo refers both to *sword* and *shackle* in Shakespeare's old English; both were made with Bilbao's steel. According to the *Oxford English Dictionary*:

> *Bilbo* . . . from *Bilbao* in Spain. . . . A sword noted for the
> temper and elasticity of its blade.
> *Bilbo.* A long iron bar, furnished with sliding shackles to confine
> the ankles of prisoners, and a lock by which to fix one end of the
> bar to the floor or ground.

In history and temperament, Bilbao is all steel and iron, shackles and sword. The city's crucible, its Chillidean Anvil of Dreams, its purgatory of desire has to do with how to break the shackles with the sword—the past with the new, reaction with revolution, blindness with vision. As John Milton's Satan put it,

> The mind is its own place, and in itself
> Can make a Heaven of Hell, a Hell of Heaven.

Purgatory—the transitional place of passion and purgation between Hell and Heaven—is a sleepless place shackled by disturbing thoughts and emotions, like Hamlet's mind, like mutinous sailors tied restlessly to *bilboes.*

On the morning of April 8, 1991, Thomas Krens, the director of New York's Guggenheim Museum, landed at Bilbao's airport. He had reservations at the Hotel López de Haro, but first he was to be taken by helicopter to Vitoria-Gasteiz to meet Basque President José Antonio Ardanza. The Basques would treat him as if he were a head of state.

After a morning visit with the president, Krens and his hosts flew to Gernika, where they landed on the town's soccer field and went to lunch at the Baserri Maitea (Beloved Farm) restaurant in Bizkaia's pastoral countryside. Across the narrow valley was the prehistoric cave of Santimamiñe.

"In the beginning neither they nor we could understand why we were considering the possibility of a Guggenheim Museum in Bilbao," conceded Juan Luis Laskurain, the man in charge of the Basque treasury. The American visitor echoed this sentiment. But their initial incredulity soon gave way to considerations about the historic opportunities available to both parties. The Basques hammered on one message—"Bilbao is a strong, fundamentally healthy city" undergoing an economic crisis of historic proportions that would soon be overcome. It was building an underground metro system and expanding its harbor and airport. An urban renewal plan was in place. These projects, the hosts maintained, were not "castles in the sky" but harbingers of bigger things to come.

The visitor was not to be intimidated. "Why do you want a museum such as the Guggenheim in Bilbao?" he asked, adopting an air of indifference and vulnerability. "The country needs a challenge, and this is going to be it," the Basques replied. Krens was pleased. No other words could resonate better with Krens's own high-stakes agenda. He had started his stewardship of the Guggenheim by telling his staff after his first board of trustees meeting, "If I go down, I am not going by myself." Cost overruns at the Manhattan facility were triple the original budget, and he was desperate for cash. In the absence of an endowment, he was gambling with the museum's collections as a way to pay off debts. His auctioning off of three masterpieces and his purchase of the Panza Collection, mostly works on paper, had caused a scandal. The New York press was savaging him as having taken the Guggenheim to "the brink of absurdity." In Bilbao, Krens was in his element.

"They were seducing you," I interrupted him as he told me of being impressed with the Basques' sense of challenge. The word *seduction* touched a cord. "Clearly there was seduction," he admitted, before stating: "Seduction, that's my business. I am a professional *séducteur*." And continued with his theory of seduction, which "consists in getting people to want what you want without you asking for it. It's a transference of desire." It was all about Bilbao as *desire*—a lover's game.

One sentence, "I promise," summarizes the rhetoric of seduction. In literature, Don Juan embodies the perversion of promising,
whereby language is not about knowing but *doing*. A promise in itself
is only an act of speech, and even if the seducer has no intention of
keeping his word, strictly speaking he does not lie. I promise, you
believe; I place the bets, you pay; I'll be postmodern, you be modern—
such were the relations being shaped between Krens and his Basque
coconspirators. Appeals to "faith" and the need for a bold approach
became commonplace among Bilbao's editorialists. Everything had to
be risked for the future.

Thomas Krens.

    World cities are, for Krens, what women were for Don Juan—use-
ful accessories to satisfy his fantasies of power and conquest. Dozens
of cities were mentioned as potential "McGuggenheims," as the New
York press baptized them. Spain was not immune to Krens's offers.
"Bilbao? Are you crazy?" Krens replied when he first heard that Bilbao
was interested in a Guggenheim franchise. "I won't go to Bilbao unless
there are $15 million on the table before I sit down." During Krens's
visit with the Basque president, he was assured that such funds were
available. The $15 million, later increased to $20 million, became the
franchise fee. Seduction is a roundabout strategy, but the professional
seducteur's demands must be met directly and paid in advance.

    The Bilbao officials knew as well that the project was a gamble.
"It was like playing in a casino," the official in charge of Bilbao's planning conceded to me. The difference between Bilbao's first wave of
industrialization a century and a half earlier and its latest one could be
illustrated by the difference between a mine and a casino. The mines
were now long gone, and in late capitalism's postmodern culture other
intangibles were as essential—image, flagship, perception, challenge,
chance, media. It was time for Bilbao to believe again and to try the
casino model.

    "Money is not important," Krens told me. "The important thing
is now we know transnational museums are viable." He had invented
a new type of spectacular museum. It had required that the politics of
culture be permeated by the psychology of the auction house, at the
nexus between the museum and Wall Street, history and belief, aesthetics and gambling. It was the quantum leap in conceptual terms that
mattered. This historic novelty of a franchised museum signaled the
era in which a New York director was in charge of a branch museum
four thousand miles away.

Dressed as "strategic investment," the museum had been a wager. People who criticized the Guggenheim for being "expensive" didn't seem to realize that betting, wagering, casino gaming are never by definition expensive—they are always affordable if one has the opportunity and the will. The gambler's central premise is disregard for the reality of money. Whether you win or lose, money per se doesn't count; it is just a way of keeping score. What the new museum provided was the luxury of closeness to New York, the mecca of the international art community, defined as a whole by its proximity to the city's auction markets. Krens became a hero of the auction-based international art community. But the true auction house in New York is the stock market, so the Basque president traveled to Wall Street to hand over a check at Merrill Lynch's headquarters for the Guggenheim brand or franchise fee.

Richard Serra, the sculptor working with large, rugged, twisted planks, had never seen anything like Bilbao, where he, along with other five sculptors and architects, was exhibiting his work in 1983. As he went through the Left Bank's collapsing buildings, he was overwhelmed by Bilbao's toughness. The harsh aesthetic of postmodernism—"this whole 'degraded' landscape of schlock and kitsch"—permeated everywhere in obsolescent, postindustrial Bilbao, its blast furnaces no longer spouting fire and smoke. Bilbao was Dantesque—it was the dreamed-of landscape of Serra's cosmos of collapsing structures in rusty, contorted iron. He called his friend Frank Gehry in Santa Monica, California, to share this discovery.

It wasn't going to be the last time Gehry would hear about Bilbao. A decade later, Krens informed him of the city's wish for a branch of the Guggenheim. Could Gehry come to see Bilbao with Krens? The architect was reminded of Serra's enthusiasm years earlier—Bilbao, the tough city! A month after his first visit, Krens was back in Bilbao with Gehry. The architect looked down on Bilbao with his own eyes from Mount Artxanda, where the German Condor Legion had penetrated Bilbao's "iron ring" in June 1937. He fell in love with the city instantly. "This is my idea of heaven, a tough city surrounded by green hills," he exclaimed in ecstasies.

For Serra and Gehry, Bilbao was the ultimate expression of industrial capitalism's wasteland and ecological devastation. It was a city with no concessions to phony decorations or pretensions of false beauty, hard and ugly to the point of sublimity. As artists, they could bridge the frontier between ugliness and beauty, ashes and regeneration, staring at history to see paradise in hell. What could be more emblematic of the global postindustrial, postmodern world than a fabled basin of former world-class industries reduced to ruins, begging for demolition? It was the mythology of progress laid bare, stripped to its naked truth, reduced to allegory.

"Do you know how many treasuries there are in the European Union?" the Spanish king's brother-in-law, Carlos Zurita, asked Krens at the Bourbons' palace in Madrid, surrounded by royal portraits and fleurs-de-lis. It was the day after Krens's first visit to Bilbao. "You are likely to think there is one treasury for each of the twelve European governments [this was 1991]. There are sixteen. The twelve of the European nations, plus those of the Basque provinces of Araba, Bizkaia, Gipuzkoa, as well as Navarra." Krens was listening. This wasn't the earlier pitch by Basques trying to sell him on Basque enigmas and traditional laws—the ploy of the previous day in Gernika. On his flight from Bilbao to Madrid that morning, Krens was still skeptical of Bilbao as the site for his European franchise. But this was Spanish royalty telling him that Basques had the right to levy their own taxes and run their own treasury—taxpayers' money that was needed not only to finance the initial building but to subsidize it indefinitely, the only unknown being whether it would amount to about 70 percent or, if successful, perhaps 50 percent of the museum's annual budget of 12 million euros. As mayor Javier Ybarra learned during the later stages of Francoism, Basque fiscal autonomy was essential for carrying out the projects necessary for the new city. "So, can I trust the Basques?" asked Krens, who had been promised by the Basque president that all his financial requests could be met. "Absolutely," replied the king's brother-in-law. A month later, Krens was back in Bilbao. After a long list of European and Spanish cities had refused his advances, Krens was finally onto something.

On Krens's second trip to Bilbao, he and Gehry visited an old winery, the Alhóndiga—architect Ricardo Bastida's renowned building that Bilbao officials had chosen as the site of the future museum. It did not satisfy them. Krens and Gehry informed the Basques that a new iconic edifice was needed. Gehry left Bilbao the following morning. Krens stayed on. This was his challenge for the heroic museum, a testament to the exuberance of his passion.

Bilbao's Alhóndiga winery before the recent urban development.

Krens's hosts had organized an itinerary of sightseeing for the next day: Biarritz in the Basque French area, Donostia–San Sebastián, the Sanctuary of Loiola (Loyola in Spanish), then a return to Bilbao for dinner. Prior to dinner, Krens went jogging. This was his second day in a city about which he knew next to nothing. A hundred yards from the hotel, by the La Salve Bridge, he saw the dark river and a large empty space where the city docks used to be. An "epiphany" overpowered him, Krens later told me. The future museum had to be there or nowhere.

Seduction wasn't all that Krens needed to accomplish his goal. He also had to convince his New York board of trustees that establishing a new museum in Bilbao, renowned for its industrial decadence and Basque terrorism, was a sound idea, and there was resistance. Still, the $200 million promised by the Basques was not something to be dismissed. The sole condition imposed by the Guggenheim was absolute secrecy. The Basque public was not to be informed about the project, let alone consulted. In a society with a quarter of the labor force unemployed, each of the 2.2 million Basques was to pay $100 to bail out a private New York museum in a deal that was binding yet secret.

The *New York Times* carried a splendid cover article in its Sunday magazine by Herbert Muschamp, entitled the "Miracle in Bilbao." Not everyone was impressed by the miracle Krens was about to usher in.

The riverside between the bridges of Deusto and La Salve where the docks were before the
Guggenheim Bilbao was built.

Some two to three hundred local artists and writers denounced the
secret and one-sided terms of the deal, myself among them. Muchamp
called us "bean counters." He was right.

Krens scorned the thought that the seduction was not deliberate
on both sides. Bilbao knew well what it was doing, otherwise "why are
you going to allow the tiger to enter your bedroom?" he asked rhetori-
cally in his Manhattan office. Krens was just letting the tiger be a tiger.
"There were no premarital relations," one of the Bilbao negotiators
confessed to me, alluding to their ignorance of Krens's tactics. They
had been overtaken by a hunter's passion.

"The Guggenheim Bilbao is a combination of Egypt's Pyramids,
China's Forbidden City, and the Taj Mahal," Krens repeated in his
interviews. Only a lover, a man engulfed in his own desire, is unboth-
ered by such hyperbole. The analogy that best captures the magnifi-
cence of his heroic desire might only be the Taj Mahal—the archetypal
pleasure dome of a lover's exuberant folly. Only an amorous man could
display such a discourse of wonderment, passion, and optimism. Only
someone larger than life like Krens would accept such challenges. The
theatrics of Krens's self-aggrandizement were part of his play. History
progresses by scandal. But you couldn't disregard the intensity of his
desire, his love of risk, his dismissive attitude toward the conven-
tional art world—his *jouissance*. He was simply intoxicated by Bilbao.

Krens regaled me with an interview that opened my eyes to the performative and erotic dimensions of his exuberance, and I couldn't resist recounting it all as a "chronicle of a seduction." He considered my book a "betrayal." While celebrating his masterly seduction, my book was ironic about "the deal of the century" and skeptical of a *krensified* model of a translational franchise museum about to become a historical novelty in Bilbao.

But I was wrong. Krens's games of seduction were not what mattered most for the new city, nor was everything irony. What truly mattered, what was most real in the Hamletian dilemma of to be or not be, swords or shackles, was the force of Bilbao's desire and the decision to revive from its own ashes.

The Sword and the Wound: Virgins and Prostitutes

Thirty-two years before Krens and Gehry, another American, belonging to a far different world, preceded them in Bilbao—Ernest Hemingway. It was August 1959, the year Gabriel Aresti published his *Maldan behera*, and the days when a letter announcing the birth of ETA was sent to exiled President Aguirre in Paris. Two decades after Spanish Republican democracy had been defeated by Franco's fascist revolt, the American writer was visiting Bilbao to see the duel between two brothers-in-law, a *mano a mano* contest between bullfighters Antonio Ordóñez and José Miguel Dominguín. He took a room in the Hotel Carlton (a mile's walk along Iparraguirre Street and across Autonomía Avenue from the Vista Alegre), Aguirre's heroic Bastille, and kept his eyes on the Vista Alegre, the bullring that would exalt Ordóñez and doom Dominguín. The bullfight was the tragic ritual that had survived in Bilbao since the sixteenth century, having had four plazas in different locations. It was in the Vista Alegre that the death of the bull, the only event that mattered to Hemingway, would take place. All else was secondary, even the matador's life.

Hemingway was sixty and already an aged man, bothered by his weight, high blood pressure, back pain, cholesterol, blood sugar, hepatitis, and impotence. Alcoholism was an old and familiar problem. He was troubled by the death of his ex-wife and publisher, guilty over having abandoned his first two wives, and worried that his current marriage was falling apart. It was a summer of excess in which he followed the bullfighters from city to city, drinking heavily, flirting, and falling for a woman forty years younger than he. Commissioned by *Life* magazine, he was searching for another success like *The Old Man and the Sea*.

The final chapter of his last book and literary testament, *The Dangerous Summer*, describes the duel in Bilbao between Spain's two top matadors. It wasn't the first time Hemingway had attended the August *corridas;* in the decade before the Civil War, he frequented them. In the summer of 1960, his last visit to Bilbao, Hemingway wrote of the city's raw ugliness, and attributed to Ordóñez his own feelings—"Bilbao, a city that he loved." He went to visit Mundaka's cemetery, twenty miles away, where his friend, the Basque priest Andrés Untzain, was buried. He also wanted to watch jai alai, the pelota game he enjoyed.

Hemingway's real bullfight in Bilbao was with his own writing. The weakened old man, dosing himself heavily, was looking for a last chance—for his *suerte* (luck), a key word in *toreo*. By facing death through the killing of the bull, Hemingway confronted, as he put it, "the original moment of truth, or of reality." The bullfight was for him an antidote against the sentimentality, fear, and decadence of contemporary culture. He hated the *toreros* who tried to turn the art into trickery and spectacle. His writing about fascism had the same nightmare quality of the *corrida*, echoing the power of Picasso's painted allegories—both dealing with Spain's tragic labyrinth, a history of returning violence.

The bullring of Vista Alegre in Bilbao.

Pilar, a woman in her sixties, invited me to Bilbao's 2008 August bull-fighting *feria*. I had never attended a bullfight; although I had run in front of the bulls, the *corrida*'s bloody drama was emotionally alien to me. As we approached the bullring we met her friend Alex. "You are in the company of a strong woman," he told me, "and that is a very important thing. It is important that she transmits warmth."

I was ignorant of almost everything about the *corrida*, and Pilar was going to be my guide. "There are intense moments in bullfighting," she told me, where "the '*ay!*' is quite different." Hemingway had written of this "*ay!*": "There is no translation for this word and perhaps it is just a noise such as a man might make, involuntarily, feeling the nail go through his hands and into the wood." Pilar told me that she feels she is a "spectator" at a soccer match, but not at a *corrida*: "There is more diversion in soccer; more communion in bulls. I don't go to the bulls for diversion. There is more profundity with the bull." Once her own pregnant mother became so emotionally involved in a *corrida* that she suffered a miscarriage. I interviewed Alex to talk about bulls. "Bullfighting is lovemaking," Alex concluded his thoughts on tauromachy. Alex made me realize the extent to which the *corrida* presents a classic erotic model in traditional Bilbao. Alex, in his early sixties, is an accomplished author and a constitutional law professor, but his true passion is bulls. A chronicler of Bilbao's fiestas, Alex is the third Bilbao writer I interviewed who, unknown to me, had written a book about Bilbao and bullfighting. Why the fascination? "It is art," he replies, surrounded by books in his office. "It is rationality over instinct." And he invokes a matador's name I heard for the first time—José Tomás. "He has transformed me," Alex says with vehemence. He describes the bullfighter's return to the ring as a true "event." José Tomás does not allow his *corridas* to be broadcast on TV, Alex observes, as if to prove that his act is not spectacle but sacred performance. The *toreo* is not as goal-oriented as sports, and there is no enmity against anyone. There is for him nothing more magnificent than that beast, "the bull of moon and honey."

Tauromachy as erotic model has a long pedigree among writers and artists. Writing was tauromachy for Michel Leiris. After expanding on the *toreo* as "the great amatory metaphor," Alex surprises me with the complaint that women today are not as *toreadas* (bull-fought) as they should be. He describes for me the matador "dressed as a woman" with silk garments and ballet shoes. "The *toreo* is pure erotics; the *toreo* is an act of love, it is lovemaking." The good matador is not brusque, he continues; he has to *seduce* the bull, treat him well. He talks to the bull in endearing terms, "C'mon, pretty," "Let's go, *guapo*." Alex admits that bullfighting is an art in decline: "There is no longer the passion it once created." Alex's remark that women today are not "bull-fought" had a clear implication: the culture at the core of his subjectivity, the one that primordially entangles his erotic life with the amatory metaphor of the bull, is a culture in deep impasse.

Describing the matadors' relationship to women as one of taking chances as well, Hemingway underscored their saying that "*más cornadas dan las mujeres*" (women gore you more). The bullfighter as lover is trying to kill symbolically his erotic victim, but she replies with *cornadas* (acts of goring). The wound has been viewed as Hemingway's truth and "code." If a true writer is, for Leiris, someone ready to be gored, then Hemingway qualified.

The erotic experience modeled after the bullfight shares with the *corrida* the paradoxical premise of killing and dying for love. In theory, it is a naked duel to the death, even if in practice it is highly choreographed. As in hunting, this type of possessive passion entails the final atrocity of killing your beloved object. The violence is deemed to be just "a moment"—a sort of suspended point in time that is assumed to cause no actual pain for the victim. The sacrifice of the object of desire is essential in order for the event to make sense—"kill me if you love me," seems to be the interlocked imperative. Such "mockery of love and death" becomes the ultimate impasse of the macho erotic model. It is an instance of sexuality's intrinsic deadlock as "marked by an irreducible failure"—Lacan's view that the reality of desire is the impossibility of full enjoyment in sexual relations. Hemingway's writing is a good instance of the tendencies toward the hysterical impasses of such a macho erotic model.

When post-Franco democracy permitted local initiative, Bilbao reinvented the week-long annual fiestas of Aste Nagusia with an explosion of popular participation. Since the Corridas Generales, or bullfights, were the centerpieces of the fiestas—celebrated since the mid-nineteenth century and draped in Spanish flags during Franco's era—a relevant aspect of this recreation was the introduction of the bull in its popular forms, such as the morning *sokamuturra* (where a bull is let loose with a rope tied around his neck). These bulls were brought from where else but Lastur, my wild birthplace.

In the traditional culture animals belong to two categories: the wild ones, which are untouchable and normally invisible, which do not tolerate enclosures and are to be hunted, and the domesticated ones, which adapt to enclosures and human contact and become members of the social group. In the farming habitat the bull was somewhere in between wild and domesticated. In the farmsteads of Lastur, for example, including in those of my parents, bulls were kept at the stable during the winter season; it is in narrow roads or when they are with their calves, and particularly when trapped in a plaza, that buylls are dangerous. The bull is wild and yet it allows you to comptemplate its wildness and you can even keep it in the farm's stable. Hence the unending play procured by the bull in the village fiestas or in the corridas. The bull trapped in the plaza provides in traditional culture a case of the effects produced by enclosures on wild animals, while it becomes a paradigmatic metaphor for the effects of civilization on people as well. As the public identifies with the "metamorphosis" that transforms the relatively placid animal in its mountain habitat into the plaza's raging beast, it experiences what we could call *the minotaure effect*—the recognition of the duality that consists in being as once domesticated and wild, half man and half beast. In Dante's words:

> The way a bull breaks loose the very moment
> he knows he has been dealt the mortal blow,
> and cannot run but jumps and twists and turns,
> just so I saw the Minotaur perform.

I spent several autumns following wild boar hunters before writing an ethnograpahy on them; they described for me their passion as a kind of delirium (the legendary world of my grandfather's Mateo Txistu wandering endlessly in the company of his dogs), something that is "exactly like a dream" and on which they have "absolutely no control whatsoever." Emotion, intense and primordial, regularly accompanies the hunter. Hunting provides a complex semiotics in which the primary sensorial experiences of smells, sounds, visual traces, hand-clasps predominate, as they function at the level of preverbal animal communication. It is estimated that there are 77,000 hunting licenses in the Basque Country. What hunting as a hobby teaches these men is the premise that "freedom" defines the encounter with the hunt at the mountain whereas social ties characterize the domestic life of the city. Hunting produces a powerful subjective formation that conditions the hunter's perception, knowledge, symbolism, and emotional structure. It is a world of fantasy and desire in which, in Ortega y Gasset's words, "the orgiastic, Dionysian element . . . flows and boils." Delibes adds that "the hunter has more than a little of Don Juan." The play with and the killing of the bull partakes of such erotics of hunting in which the subject surrenders to the hybrid condition of the Minotaur in the labyrinth.

Am I a man or a woman? That ultimate hysterical question affects the bullfighter's identity. The bullfighter, dressed in a flashy *traje de luces* or "costume of lights," and wearing *zapatillas* (ballet-like shoes), projects a slim, almost feminine, sexless figure. Which sex is the matador? Is he a real macho, or is he a castrated impostor who represents what he is not?

Poster for Bigas Luna's *Bilbao* film.

    Am I *el* Bilbao or *la* Bilbao? Bilbao is also starkly androgynous. Its feminine side, *la* Bilbao (as she is frequently called), has an ancient pedigree. The city's first legitimate ruler and Lady of Bizkaia was a woman, María Díaz de Haro, as were the following three rulers. Bilbao also has her patroness—the Virgin of Begoña, the focal point of intense Marian devotion that persists to this day. Bilbainos refer to their city as *bocho*—a Basque term (*botxo/potxo*, meaning a *hole* or *pit* that invokes feminine imagery; a derivative, *potxor*, means *vagina*). Bilbao sits in a hollow nestled among softly rolling foothills more reminiscent of rounded hips and breasts than of mountain crags. In such a feminine valley emerged the masculine *el* Bilbao, a city that was all about mining and seafaring from the beginning, the quintessentially muscular city made of masses of grime-covered, sweat-soaked workers. The waters of *la ría* (river) or *el río* Nervión flow through and then out of the *bocho* and into the androgynous sea—referred to as *la mar* or *el mar*. *La ría*'s left and right banks are like the voluptuous legs of an earth goddess spreading ever further apart to eventually receive the sea. Both sides were reunited from the city's inception at the bridge of San Antón, which preceded the earliest development of the town. Thus the *bocho* and the river frame the imaginary of the Bilbainos. In Biga Lunas's film *Bilbao,* "Bilbao" is the name of a prostitute (since the nineteenth century, the city has hosted one of Spain's most famous red-light districts), whereas Unamuno, the city's most famous writer, speaks of the feminized *la* Bilbao as "maternal Bilbao," "mother" and "sea" being two key symbols, constantly mixed and identified, in his work.

The matador's "mockery of love and death" is echoed in other prevalent erotic models essential to an ethnography of desire in Bilbao.

Prostituion is one of them. "There is complete transparency in the game of seduction," the ex-prostitute Joanna told me, "until you conquer him with a final *estocada* and to bed." She was describing the resistance of a client who goes to a nightclub to have a drink and look voyeuristically at the girls. She seductively promises him great pleasure, while the future client keeps struggling against her lure. Will she kill his resistance softly, give him the final stab wound? Women can not only give you *cornadas* but fatal *estocadas* as well. Or will she rescue him, perhaps, from his impotence?

Men's impotence, according to Freud, derives from what he deemed "the most prevalent form of degradation of erotic life"— prostituted sex. It is the split between the idealized sexless woman and the whore that is, for Freud, the source of the neurotic's erotic impasse. It is mostly married men who, impotent with their wives, need prostitutes for sexual arousal and enjoyment.

Bilbao has been known as one of the most glamorous *plazas* for prostitution in all of Spain. The city's vibrant red-light district on San Francisco and Las Cortes streets, in Old Bilbao, a ten-minute walk from Vista Alegre through Plaza Zabalburu and across the bridge of Cantalojas, was popularly known as La Palanca (The Lever), in reference to its mining history—the neighborhoods of miners, migrants, and prostitutes. It was in Old Bilbao that Bertholt Brecht imagined "that old Bilbao moon" shining green. During Francoism, La Palanca's cabarets, music, and lively street life made it *the* place of erotic transgression in a city known for its rigid morality. Political and sexual repression complemented each other during the dictatorship—resisting one was resisting the other. These were the times when you had to cross the border to France to see Marlon Brando and Maria Schneider in *The Last Tango in Paris*. The popularity and growth of La Palanca in a bourgeois city controlled by the military and the Church did not countermand the sexual politics of the dictatorship. Rather, the transgression was an integral part of the status quo.

But as nightclubs, massage centers, singles bars, and prostitution apartments expanded throughout the city, La Palanca became an isolated and marginal space, a prime space for urban gentrification. The traditional model of prostitution, with the pimp as a central figure, gave way to more privatized and normalized contexts. In the past, prostitutes were permanent residents of La Palanca and part of the economic and social fabric of the barrio. Now they are immigrants

The man almost always feels his sexual activity hampered by his respect for the woman and only develops full sexual potency when he finds himself in the presence of a lower type of sexual object; and this gain is partly conditioned by the circumstance that his sexual aims include those of perverse sexual components, which he does not like to gratify with a woman he respects.

Freud, "The Most Prevalent Form of Degradation in Erotic Life," 210.

who stay for short periods and send money back home. The heroin junkie who supported herself through prostitution appeared in the 1980s. As La Palanca fell into the stigma of urban decline and danger, what used to be "normal" street sex and brothel lore became wild and marginalized. Its anomaly implied the normalization of more urban forms of prostitution announced every morning by the daily newspaper. Bilbainos now speak of La Palanca with nostalgia, remembering it as "the academy for erotic initiation," as "romantic prostitution," or as "vaudeville theater." It was the place where everyone could go on fiesta days, bachelors' parties, or for variety shows. It was the erotic complement to the deep Bilbao of religion, banks, and soccer. It was the site of initiation into sex without the dangers of drugs and AIDS, of eroticism turned into urban spectacle, of the glamour of cabarets and nightclubs as social transgression.

Moulin Rouge and Marilyn," two nightclubs at La Palanca.

Psychoanalysts differentiate between the old rule of desire governed by the Oedipal father who protects the group by forbidding excessive pleasure and the post-Oedipal rule without such protection against enjoyment. In the new order, society commands *jouissance* (consumption, seduction, fetishization) as a civic duty. If you don't enjoy the new products of late capitalism—gadgets, information, architecture, travel—you are undermining the economy and halting cultural progress. Whereas prostitution was formerly "permitted" as a lesser unavoidable evil, nowadays the conservative daily *El Correo*, under the banner of "relax," advertises a varied sample of several hundred prostitutes, photos included, à la carte. Similarly, pornography, once deemed something to hide, is currently so much a part of Bilbao that telephone installation entails a package of TV channels, several of which provide hard-core pornography on a nightly basis. In the old regime of desire, the benevolent-impotent fatherly Other was there to ensure that transgression and *jouissance* took place; in the new order, the father has dissolved into the capitalist moneymaking machine and the cause of alarm is no longer that "Big Brother is watching, but the possibility that Big Brother is not watching."

In the Freudian neurotic split, the counterpoint to the prostituted sexual object is the idealized sexless woman. Historically, La Palanca was filled not only with brothels but also with convents of nuns ministering to prostitutes. It was the battle between flesh and spirit. There we find the religious order of Mater Misericordiae, whose main mission is the care of prostitutes. A century ago, Blessed Rafaela de Ybarra, a member of Javier de Ybarra's elite family, became a nun and led a saintly life by helping prostitutes. Before the mining industrialization, there were already several convents and churches in Old Bilbao.

The religious model of the sexless woman is the Virgin Mother of Begoña. To reach her basilica from La Palanca you must walk down San Francisco Street to Atxuri; from there it takes about ten minutes to Plaza Unamuno in Casco Viejo, and then you must go up the 311 stairs and 46 landings that separate the plaza from the church on the hill. The Virgin of Begoña is the primary iconic figure of Bilbao's history. No significant event takes place in the city without a visit to Her basilica. Even in the current period of decline in religious attendance, the Basilica of Begoña is never without devout parishioners. Walking up the stairs from Plaza Unamuno to the basilica is a ritual that Bilbainos feel is central to their tradition.

The cult of the Virgin of Begoña goes back to Bilbao's founding in 1300. Mañaricua writes that her devotion emerged in the early Middle Ages among men "exhausted from fighting, with their swords dripping blood and their souls spouting hatred." She is also the patroness of fishermen and sailors, "a seafaring Virgin." The sailor far from home experiences continuous risks at sea and develops an intense attachment to the Virgin Mother's distant figure. The catch-22 of this erotic model has elements of medieval courtly love in which the Lady operates as a mirror upon which the vassal projects his idealized wishes. What matters is "the inaccessibility of the object"—the vassal turns what is an impossibility into a prohibition, the object of desire being the same condition that forbids its obtainment.

Over time, the cult of the Virgin of Begoña and the site of Her basilica became a political problem, as it was used as a fortress from and for which battles were fought between traditionalists and liberals. The entire Marian religious complex, its very erotic structure of motherly sublimation and filial sacrifice, its distant projection and actual abstinence, became a cultural deadlock with dramatic consequences. Two very different sensibilities at odds turned into an endemic battle—the traditional Marian ethos that sought pilgrimage, repentance, and religious fervor as the best guarantee of peace and unity in the population; and the liberals who identified that tradition as religious fundamentalism and Carlist insurrection. The erotic models had become political.

Virgin of Begoña.

The Dominatrix

Wedding in Begoña is a painting produced by Francisco de Mendieta in 1607. With a large figure of the Virgin of Begoña's statue in the background, a pregnant bride and her groom stand before a priest, surrounded by a dozen barely visible men and forty-five prominent women wearing the notorious horn-shaped headdresses. *The Swearing of the Fueros of Vizcaya by Fernando el Católico*, a work by the same artist from 1609, is another emblematic historic painting of the period with a similar composition. In reproduction, it is much on display in Basque official buildings. The tableau depicts Bizkaia's two governors kissing the hand of the Catholic King upon his swearing under the Oak of Gernika to uphold Bizkaia's old laws. But what is striking about the painting is the structure of the composition: two horizontal rows of people presented frontally, the men below, the women with their horn-shaped headdresses above.

What do these horn-shaped headdresses mean? Given their shapes and the husbands' reported displeasure with such feminine adornment, as well as certain formal prohibitions against women entering a church with them, writers have pointed out their phallic connotation. In Mena's painting, there is also a large horn-shaped crescent moon at the feet of the Virgin's image and over her dress—the moon and the headdress replicating the shape of the horn. The virginity of Andra Mari's image thus contrasts with the strong sexual connotation of the actual "phallic" women depicted in the painting.

The vassalage toward both the idealized and the castrating woman was brought home in an interview I had with Ines, a Bilbao performance artist working as a dominatrix in a European city. "I learned to be a dominatrix from my own Basque traditional nationalist family," Ines surprised me at the outset. "I didn't discover my current world [of being a dominatrix], I *recognized* it. I said to myself: 'I know this. It's in my education.' Being a Basque woman imprints character—you are tough, suffering." Armed with whips and other paraphernalia, dressed in an all-black leather outfit, Ines had turned the sexual persona she observed since childhood into a well-paid S/M performance.

Ines is also a writer, and when I reminded her that in one of her texts she describes Basque women as "phallic," Ines was all fired up: "The way a Basque woman speaks, particularly after a certain age, is

Miss Martiartu's sequence, by Juan Carlos Eguillor.

castrating. Look at the way we talk to men: 'Come on, Joe, look at you, you don't know how to dress, *I* have to dress you.' Men don't say anything. Not that those stereotypes are exclusively Basque, of course." Don't many Basque men consider their women to be superpowerful? I asked. "Here the Madonna complex is very, very exaggerated. There is the prostitute and the Madonna. The Virgin of Begoña. My mother would take us to the basilica and light candles for us. There is no sensuality here, we don't hook up. Basque sensuality concentrates on food. Observe what they are talking about when you see two people together—it is always about food. If they'd talk about sex as they do about food, oh my God. Sex has been internalized as religion or as politics. For a Basque woman to openly use her weapons of seduction is frowned upon."

Asked about her work as a dominatrix, Ines explained that "it is a psychodrama that has a visual aspect and a sexual one. But as Foucault says, it is not a sexuality centered in the genitalia. Many Basque men like to be at the feet of a woman. Men from other ethnic groups also, of course, but Basque men in particular enjoy it. It fits them." What about pornography in Bilbao? "We have a shame-filled acceptance of pornography. It is accepted reluctantly, like sex. It's true, we don't like sex. We accept it because we can't avoid it. We accept sexual desire, but underneath, if we were given a choice, we would prefer to masturbate and be done with it. We have this prejudice that sex is like wasting time."

Ines showed me photos of her performances. In one, she was wearing a large black rubber penis. "This photo creates blisters," she said. "I don't know what a woman with a dick has. She becomes like an epiphany of what woman is *not*. She is not a woman, she is not a man— she is really the Other. That is why this performance is such a success among men, men who I am sure are not homosexuals; if they were, they'd prefer men with the dick, not women. To be penetrated not by a man but by a woman—this is a persona that attracts men. I think it also has to do with the luxury that you can park for a while the anxiety of being a man. As we know well, the anxiety of masculinity is there. If a woman puts pants on, her femininity is not in danger. But if a man puts on a skirt! Masculinity is a very fragile identity construction. It breaks down with anything, is a heavy burden." If, in former times, Bilbao women represented their phalluses in the shape of a headdress, Ines prefers to display it on her website as a rubber penis. Both forms confirm Lacan's view that while men *have* a phallus, women *are* the phallus.

Franciso de Mendieta, *Wedding in Begoña* (1607).

Ines informed me of what she calls her "commandments": "Never trust a woman who doesn't wear makeup." Another: "Normality does not exist." A third: "The most important word in your vocabulary is No." As I mention Mari, the legendary flying witch from Anboto, who is "nourished by the no," Ines remembered her grandmother, who "used to throw combs to Mari of Anboto, saying: 'Take it, ugly Mari, and comb your hair.' We Basques are all about what we deny. Everything we conceal is what we are." And she went on interpreting her "no": "Why do they pay me? They pay me *not* to do things; not to give, but to deny. This is not about bunging a little girl. Dominatrixes are usually grown women who have a life, who know how to say no. Saying no is part of my will; I don't do what they want me to do. It is a symbiosis: I don't do anything that will not have a positive result."

The woman who sacrifices herself unconditionally for her family is a prominent archetype among Basques. But Ines suggested an opposing allure—"the woman who gives nothing but demands the impossible. To get *no* for an answer is immensely erotic." Commenting on the relationship between the femme fatale and negation, she added: "By

Horned Bilbao by Juan Carlos Eguillor.

Francisco de Mendieta, *The Swearing of the Fueros of Bizcaya by Fernando el Católico* (1609).

saying no, I am denying his sexuality. By saying no, I am nonaccessible. It is symbolic castration."

The male masochistic dream of a woman is summed up by Deleuze in three words: "cold-maternal-severe," where cruelty is intimately related to the Ideal, and where a woman has already won when the man submits to masochism. Like Baudelaire and Sacher-Masoch, the masochist hails "the tyranny and cruelty that constitute woman's essence and her beauty." The guilty masochist asks to be beaten, but for what crime? Deleuze suggests that "the formula of masochism is the humiliated father." The masochist experiences the symbolic order (of religion, patriotism, the family) as a maternal order: it is the Mother who requires the Son's sacrifice. In this cultural configuration, which is constitutive of my generation's subjectivity, masculinity is embodied in the role of the son, whereas femininity is projected into the role of the mother. A relevant case of the absence of the father and the omnipresent presence of the *woman-mother* can be seen in the life and literary work of Unamuno, a key influence on the initial ETA, many of whose female characters display a "furious hunger for maternity," compensated with the *boy-man* who finds refuge in his mother's bosom.

I was mesmerized by Ines. There was no secret to my fascination: I knew that practice of self-transformative whipping from my own past religious experience. Ines was bringing me back to my turbulent novitiate with the Passionists. While she was talking, images of metal cilices with inwardly pointing spikes and whips to discipline the body flooded my memory. It all happened in that monastery. Before going to bed, for fifteen minutes, we novices would take the bundle of cords with knots on their ends and whip our naked shoulders, back, and buttocks. The whips hung on the walls of our cells, reddened with our blood, an obscene punishment for our body's wretched erotic desires. With its combination of mysticism, eroticism, and perversion, that theater of flagellation was a self-inflicted torture to attain mastery and truth—it was blood in exchange for sanctity. But was it also arousal and erotic pleasure? Following the masochistic rule by which the satisfaction of desire requires a previous punishment, the ironic result was that it could result in "the opposite of what might be expected (thus whipping, far from punishing or preventing an erection, provokes and ensures it). It is a demonstration of the law's absurdity." Comedy was central to our sacrificial fervor.

What we did as spiritual exercise was for Ines erotic exercise. In both cases, it was the same disciplinary exercise—flagellation for self-transformation. It was all the same duty for knowledge and enjoyment, the one that had pushed us into the religious life and her into performance art—because "sadomasochism's punitive hierarchical structure is ultimately a religious longing for order, marked by ceremonies of penance and absolution." I understood her cause—a mastered body, free for herself and her clients. In her practice, Ines was the equivalent of the all-important figure of "master of novices" in the convent. The point was to experience Bataille's definition that "eroticism . . . is assenting to life up to the point of death." At the novitiate, we dreamed of becoming missionaries in faraway lands, a vocation intimately associated with martyrdom among the infidels. Anything sexual was far from our lives and consciousness, yet we were being introduced into the pleasures of eroticism by means of our religious passion. While we were exposed to eroticized images of saints, our religious instruction had to do essentially with *how to desire*. It was the naked law of the sword: "Do not think that I have come to bring peace on earth; I have not come to bring peace, but a sword. . . . He who loves father or mother more than me is not worthy of me" (Matthew 10:34–37). The *bilbo* (sword) was there to cut us apart from any family or erotic love and to slice our sexual being in two—the same wounding sword from which we had to gain pleasure and healing.

Ines brought to my attention in the starkest terms what is at stake in the historic opposition between Christianity and sexuality. As Freud underlined, the transition from animal instincts to eroticism proper is the primary step from biology to metaphysics. Sexuality becomes "evil" for Christianity, not because of its debased nature "but precisely because sexuality competes with pure spirituality as the primordial meta-physical activity." Ines concluded with her own axiom: "Good sex must be one thing: an epiphany."

In the Name of the Father

"We men of the postwar generation don't exist," I remember my father saying to me as Franco's regime ended. I did not yet grasp what he really meant. In the early 1930s, my father had been taken by his parents to Alonsotegi, a town five miles from downtown Bilbao on the Left Bank, to learn Castilian Spanish and basic math. His transition from rural to urban worldviews, peasant to industrial, Basque to Spanish, was as radical as anything I had to endure later. A blast furnace, a train, a movie—how could he explain these Bilbao realities to the people at home on his farm? When he married, he took my mother for a honeymoon to Bilbao—that old Bilbao moon.

On one of his visits to Bilbao in 1969 to see me in the convent, he took me on his new red Impala Montesa motorcycle (he still could not afford a car) to Alonsotegi. But it was not until 1999 when, invited by a university colleague from Alonsotegi, that I returned to the town and came to appreciate the voyage to the prewar Bilbao he had made a generation prior to mine. As I imagined him in that setting—the shy, stuttering farm boy from Lastur trying to learn Spanish, whose entire world had suddenly turned into nothing but an anachronism—his presence overpowered me. I pictured him in that grim mining landscape with the polluted river, the meandering road in the narrow valley, the empty church, the ruined farm. I became protective of him as never before; my colleague remarked the paleness in my face. Aresti's

...ne came back to haunt me, "I will defend my father's house"—the quarryman's house of stone and dust.

As a boy I would occasionally visit my dad's quarry and he would throw a bucket of water to clean the stone from the mantle of dust and show me the secret colorful canvas underneath—the vivid greens, the tender pinks, the soft greys since ever engraved in the marble. But the reds stood out as the most notable color, that *bull's blood* as it was named, as if I shouldn't be overly taken by the harmonious beauty of the marble's paintings, oblivious of the trauma printed in the stone. After all, it was above that quarry that he, helped by his coworkers, had planted a huge fifteen feet tall, ten feet wide marble cross—a religious promise he had made for either the healing or dying of his sick daughter, four years younger than me, who was born with an incurable condition and who was in constant pain during the seven years she lived.

My father with the marble cross that he built.

It was in Alonsotegi that I understood the "nonexistence" of the men of my father's generation. I couldn't forget how he had driven me there in his motorcycle in 1969, the year I had been deeply impacted by *The Brothers Karamazov*, with its central myth of parricide, a shock only comparable to Nietzsche's Zarathustra. I identified intensely with the turbulent Dmitry, the son whose regeneration came about through the murder of the father. In Freud's psychoanalytic myth of the primal horde, parricide sets in motion taboos against murder and incest; moral law returns in his name once the father has been murdered. Furthermore, Freud links the primal myth with the structure of Christianity, where "the original sin was one against God the Father"—a myth that, adds Lacan, "is the myth of a time for which God is dead." But God had always been dead for Freud, "He has never been the father except in the mythology of the son"—in the commandment to love him. Psychoanalytically the father function has to do with castration (in the son's rivalry for the mother's love) and with the origin of the superego. When asked about his name, this God/Father responds in the Exodus, "I am who I am"—His name is The Name, and it is in the Name-of-the-Father, turned superego after his death and by assuming his voice, that the subject speaks and acts. The first thing that the believer must do in the Name-of-the-Father is of course the sacrifice of Isaac—so that the bond between father and son becomes binding forever. With the Karamazov parricide Dostoyevsky was putting his finger on the core drama of my generation's killing of

Marble quarries in Lastur.

the Christian Father as well as the cultural killing of our vanquished fathers—a parricide that filled us with an unconscious guilt that could only be redeemed by our intense masochistic passion for religious and political self-sacrifice.

The death of Franco marked the end of the patriarchal politics of the military dictatorship and a transition to democracy that brought great expectations for solving the Basque political conundrum. The "messy democracy" also brought tolerance and new laws for divorce, abortion, and freedoms that until then had been suppressed.

In the absence of political parties and basic democratic rights, other forms of association, besides soccer and sports in general, had flourished during Franco's era. Prominent among these were the *cuadrilla* peer group and the males-only culinary club or *txoko*. A town of thirty thousand inhabitants such as Eibar could have well over eighty gourmet societies, each with about one hundred members. "Yes, we come here to get away from our women," men in a Bilbao *txoko* conceded. Displaced at home, in need of male bonding, men routinely go to their eating clubs to cook for themselves. With the new democratic freedoms and economic gains, women's participation in the workforce became the norm and couples were now confronted with the realities of new family patterns. Gender relations were no longer under the restrictive regime of the dictatorship. "The crisis of masculinity" began to be discussed in public forums.

The attitude of Jasone, a businesswoman and an outspoken feminist who is an opinion-maker through her radio and television appearances, is typical of Bilbao professional women: "Men/women relationships are always power relations. If we women win, the relationship does not work." Any talk about the alleged power of women over men among the Basques she dismissed out of hand as "nothing but machismo." In fact, Jasone thinks that the couple is no longer needed to have children: "In order to procreate you don't need marriage, there is now artificial insemination, which is becoming relatively common." She indicated to me a nearby sperm bank not far from the Gran Vía. I visited it, and Patxi, the director, instructed me about artificial insemination being available to anyone. It is lesbian couples who seek it most, he told me. He had helped in about three hundred cases of assisted reproduction (it was the year 2006), which was about 10 percent of all Bilbao's cases. "We have changed very rapidly. We have suddenly become very secular," he observed, adding that the Catholic Church was the only "loser" in the process. Patxi is a convinced Marxist who abides by the motto "being creates my consciousness." Unlike most professionals in Bilbao, Patxi speaks Basque, a tool that opens doors to him, he noted. He celebrates the drastic changes in sexual practices. "Marriages are now for the most part secular. Divorce has become common. This is a modern society." Twelve out of a thousand women abort, Patxi remarked—the average for European countries.

In this post-Franco transitional period of deep anxieties regarding the redrawing of traditional gender roles, a new cultural discourse became a sensation—"Basque Matriarchalism." In a nutshell, this was the proposition that women dominate the Basque household and, more relevantly, the Basque unconscious. The idea was formulated by Andrés Ortiz-Osés, a philosopher teaching hermeneutics at the University of Deusto in Bilbao. He was from the neighboring region of Aragón, had a Basque-Navarrese mother, and, having become a priest, had studied theology and later Heideggerian hermeneutics at the Innsbruck University Institute in Austria.

Cover of the book on Basque matriarchalism by Andrés Ortiz-Osés and Franz-Karl Mayr.

Ortiz-Osés's matriarchal configuration had a distinguished tradition in European thought, dating back to the work of Johann Jakob Bachofen and fueled by the epochal archeological findings of Arthur Evans at Knossos. Basque anthropology echoed the European fixation with lunar mythologies. Combining evidence from Basque social customs and traditional mythology with notions of archetypal symbolism, Ortiz-Osés concluded that Basque society was originally, and still is, unconsciously matriarchal in nature. Cultural anthropologists protested that, *pace* Bachoffen, such "matriarchy" existed nowhere. If anything, feminists argued, Basque society is staunchly "patriarchal." Feminist theologians added that the traditional reading of the Bible was hopelessly patriarchal.

The Minoan archeological discoveries that found expression in Picasso's *Minotauromachies* and *Guernica* impacted Freud as well, but more particularly the group of Jungian psychoanalysts who resided in Zurich—including Karl Kerenyi. Ortiz-Osés also became a member of the Zurich Eranos group in the 1970s. While Kerenyi combined Jung, Nietzsche, and Minoan culture, Ortiz-Osés incorporated Jung, Oteiza, European hermeneutical philosophy, and Basque anthropology. He wrote of "The World as Labyrinth: Knossos" as "a place of recirculation and rebirth: in the Labyrinth of Crete the sun or the hero dies in order to be resuscitated in the dark night of the minotaur's forces. . . . [The labyrinth's] symbolism is essentially lunar, Genesiac and matriarchal, for it represents a place of initiation and transmutation." In this view, shared by Oteiza, the transition from the matriarchal state to the patriarchal, from the lunar to the solar, was the great divide in the history of civilization. Obviously the Basques were, for Ortiz-Osés and for most of his readers, under the aegis of "that old Bilbao moon."

When I visited Ortiz-Osés at the Jesuit University of Deusto-Bilbao, he had just retired after thirty-three years teaching hermeneutics and metaphysics. I had been among the anthropologists who had criticized his archetypal approaches to Basque culture, yet I admired his writing and insightful symbolic interpretations. The story he was about to tell me would change my view of him and his work. He was five years old when, a decade after the Spanish Civil War, he witnessed the murder of his father by a *maquis* (member of a resistance movement against Franco). "It was five in the afternoon and I had just arrived at my family's shop from school," he began. "Now, this is terrible, what I am going to tell you. Suddenly I hear terrible noises, gunshots and screams inside, while I am still at the door. I enter and see my father tumbling, holding his stomach. It reminds me of Goya's painting *The Third of May* [1808], the man at the center in white. Ay! I see my father trying to walk up the stairs followed by my screaming mother and uncle. They took him to Huesca for surgery, but it was too late." I was unprepared for his confession that his life and theories were marked by this traumatic childhood event. "Death is real, resurrection is symbolic," Ortiz-Osés summed up. "I have seen death in my arms. This produced in me asthma, existential anguish, I became sickly. But in the process I was inoculated against death, I became strong. The death of my father and my mother made me go beyond death. Death is an opening. I support euthanasia. Suicide should be a 'normal' thing. Death is liberation."

As he finished his story, Ortiz-Osés remembered why I was in his office—to discuss his anthropological theories—and observed in reference to his childhood trauma: "This is behind my matriarchalism, my interpretation of violence, and all my discourses. The need to remake myself again, to interpret myself." He had just presented a book of aphorisms at the Center of Aragonese Studies in Huesca in a building that was the former clinic in which the doctor had performed surgery on his mortally wounded father. "Afterward, I wrote an aphorism: *There where the father dies, the son resuscitates.*" He continued: "After my father's death, Mother became my refuge. Religious symbolism saved me. Otherwise I would have been a savage, a madman, or maybe committed suicide. . . . In my search for my mother I found refuge in ritual and symbolism, and decided to become a priest. That search is the origins of my later theories of matriarchalism."

At the end of the interview, Andrés gave me a dozen of his books, one of them his autobiography. In a revealing paragraph of radical self-exposure, he sums up the genesis of his subjective core. It was in his house's chapel, when he was still a child, that "the reunion, the alchemy, the sacrament took place." He was going to be a real father, he confesses, but the religious vocation turned him into a "symbolic" one—"the loss of the (external) father coincides with the loss of the (internal) father or paternity." What is extraordinary in Ortiz-Osés is the acknowledgment and willing acceptance of symbolic castration—in line with Lacan's views that truth, in its "weakness," accepts castration. The popularity of his ideas in the 1980s must have derived in part from the readers' projection of such a "loss of paternity" in the male subject and the realization that there is a strong unconscious identification with the mother figure among Basque men.

The fathers of my Bilbao generation had lost the war against fascism. At the time of the transition, it was not uncommon to hear about the "absence" of an entire generation of Basque men from politics. Where had they been during Franco's forty years? The nationalist political father figure was embodied by the Basque Nationalist Party; they were the Aguirres, Irujos, and Leizaolas, the war heroes so lauded by Steer, Bowers, Mauriac, and pro-Republicans worldwide. Yet for the new generation of young militants in the 1960s, these men were nothing but a bunch of Christian democrats, politically irrelevant in their Parisian exile—they were the impotent father who had sold his soul to bourgeois placidity. José Antonio Etxebarrieta, reflecting on the "impasse without exit" in which Aguirre's generation had fallen in their gradualist and law-abiding approach to politics, characterized

Tito Echevarría and his son Mikelats exiled at the Isle of Yeu (1976), a rare photo of an ETA man holding the hand of his son.

their struggle as a "crisis of adolescence"—they had not even reached adulthood.

The Etxebarrieta brothers were partly right: Aguirre believed he was the embodiment of Providence to save his people and was subject to the big Others not only of religion and his nationalist ideology, but also to the interests of America's Cold War politics. This led him, who was the most pragmatic of Basque politicians, to deny the changes happening in the international arena. Aguirre was for his generation the charismatic father whose authority rested on representing his people but who ended up as a stand-in for the interests of the United States or Europe. The man of integrity and unconditional surrender to the cause of his people was forced to be an impotent father, a substitute for powers external to his country.

The fierce alternative to democratic nationalism was ETA. Its members were those who "had the balls" to fight the armed revolt, casting a shadow of castration over those who did not have them. And who were these armed young turks? If anything, the *etarras* were not fathers. I never saw the photo of an *etarra* as a family man; the very image of an ETA man as a father holding his child's hand was hardly imaginable. For the most part, the ETA men were quasi-adolescents who combined having their first sexual experience with aiming a gun. ETA had no father. Killing the father was the initiation requirement for becoming a revolutionary and avenging the motherland's prostration.

Matriarchy served as the screen upon which the father's absence could be projected. Caught in the dilemma of underground armed struggle or political irrelevance, Ortiz-Osés was pointing out what many Basque men felt—they were powerless, fatherless, helpless in shaping their society's direction. Viewed through a matriarchal screen, fatherhood meant one thing—impotence. Father, why have you forsaken us?

A Broken Sphere

Half a mile along the riverside from where Ortiz-Osés expounded his matriarchal ideas in Deusto's university, and walking in front of the Guggenheim Museum, in front of City Hall there is a large sculpture by Oteiza. Oteiza and Ortiz-Osés admired each other's work. During the 1950s, beginning in Bilbao, Oteiza had developed a series of deconstructive works as part of a larger project he named *Experimental Proposal*. In 2002, one of the sculptures of that series—*Ovoid Variant of the Dis-Occupation of the Sphere*, 1958—was reproduced in large scale and placed in front of the city hall. Made up of fragmented circular plates of heavy steel uneasily held together in a broken sphere, the work captures the shattered image of the modern world and the newly emerging city. Oteiza identified strongly with Russian constructivists such as Malevich, who affirmed the Bolshevik Revolution, and with European avant-garde figures such as Mallarmé, who stated, "Destruction was my Beatrice."

In the 1950s, Oteiza and Chillida, both raised in Donostia-San Sebastián, were the two Basque sculptors who gained international recognition and became dominant figures in the Basque and Spanish art worlds. These two artists are the most prominent in Bilbao's museums and streets, with each having about twenty works in the city. Still, they did not emerge from a vacuum.

Soon after completing his Experimental Proposal, and having won the prize for Best International Sculptor in the 1957 São Paulo Biennale, Oteiza decided to stop sculpting and end his career as an artist. "I was left without a statue, but I was premiering life," he said. From then on, his existence would be a holiday, he added. Sculpture having been his lifelong occupation, Oteiza had reached a dreadful impasse from which there seemed to be no exit. At the height of his career, he was caught between capitalizing on his international success or surrendering it. His act of self-cancellation enacted a defeated hero's end. "From this *encierro* I infinitely want to escape," he had exclaimed, applying to himself the image of the bullfighter standing at the center of the plaza. It was an attempt to escape all that he saw as distortion and decadence in the art world. Oteiza would return again and again to the figure of the Minotaur with which he obsessively identified. The Minotaur was born in Lascaux, Oteiza argued, on the basis of the shamanlike figure dying in a ritual fight with a bison, and Lascaux being for him somehow associated with Basque prehistory.

Oteiza insisted all along that his giving up sculpture was a sort of overcoming of art, but it would be perhaps more appropriate and productive to see it as his ultimate *failure*—a failure that was also a sign of his artistic integrity. His trajectory as an artist had been nourished by the perspectival opposition between Basque art

Oteiza, *Ovoid Variant of the Dis-Occupation of the Sphere*, 1958.

(preeminently prehistoric) and contemporary avant-garde; when he interpreted the Neolithic cromlechs in the Basque hills as being *the same* as his own conclusive deconstruction—a zero of form that he replicated in the statue in honor of Father Donostia—the creative tension between the two poles vanished and he was left without the statue. What Žižek wrote of the greatest musical composers—that "failure is a sign that the composer is dealing with the *Real* of musical matter. It is only the 'light' *kitsch* composers who can pass from one smooth triumph to the next"—could be applied to Oteiza; having embraced his own failure and deadlock as his ultimate truth, he detested artists who were constantly triumphing.

In a lecture given in 1961 to explain his abandonment of art, Oteiza mentioned Samuel Beckett's latest writings as a development parallel to his. Like Oteiza, the young Beckett who wrote *Proust* (1931) had engaged "in the not uncommon process of finding in art a surrogate for the faith which had been abandoned or lost," and had led himself by the mid-1950s to a complete impasse, writing *Endgame* (1957)—"I'm horribly tired and stupefied but not yet stupefied enough. To write is impossible but not yet impossible enough." Beckett had concluded *The Unnamable* with the words, "I must go on, I can't go on, I'll go on." Next he wrote *Texts for Nothing*, where the tension between "I can't go on" and "I must go on," and the temptation to abandon the imperative to write, become unbearable. Beckett's modernist belief was "that failure is the inevitable outcome of all attempts at artistic creation." Beckett wrote *for nothing*, meaning that "writing has nothing more to assert. This text tells us of a situation, namely, Beckett's at the end of the 1950s: what he had written until this point could not *go on any further*."

Beckett had compared James Joyce's writing to Dante's in that both dwelled on "the purgatorial aspects of human existence." Dante's work, says Beckett, "is conical and consequently implies culmination. Mr Joyce's is spherical and excludes culmination. . . . Sin is an impediment to movement up the cone, and condition of movement round the sphere." In Dante's Hell the sinners go nowhere, whereas in the Purgatory the sinners desire and move with a purpose. In his *Experimental Proposal*, the labyrinthine Oteiza had engaged himself in the deconstruction of the basic Euclidean forms, including the cone and the sphere, in an ultimate effort at overcoming transcendental absolute forms. But at the conclusion of his proposal, Oteiza was left without a statue and could not go any further. Beckett, however, did go on. How did he effect a breakthrough? In Badiou's conviction, Beckett passed "through a veritable intellectual and artistic mutation, and more precisely through a modification in his *orientation of thought*"—one that "opens up to chance." Oteiza, unlike Beckett, decided not to go on sculpting. He took a chance and "moved to the city" by engaging himself in urbanism, film, and poetry. Oteiza's artistic mutation as sculptor/architect would have to wait for Gehry in Bilbao.

By the effect of his artistic "ending," Oteiza de facto turned himself into a *posthumous* artist. He was no longer alive as an artist, yet he still had more than forty years for all sorts of "conspiracies" on the "cultural and artistic front"—including his involvement with ETA activists. His endgame was a sort of desertion, a desperate attempt at escaping from the enclosures of the bullring. Rebellious, paradoxical, authoritarian, oracular, armed with the symbolic capital of having died or killed himself as an artist, Oteiza's uncompromising stance on matters of cultural politics plunged him into one controversy after another, not to mention confrontations with public officials. Having rejected selling his work on the international market, all his sculptures were piled in the basement of his house. Although his influence on the Basque artistic scene was unparalleled, he judged his life to be, I heard him say many times, "a clean sheet of nothing but failures." He was the intransigent and difficult man, the angry and disturbed artist full of unresolved contradictions, deliberately *against* everything in the art market, always proclaiming the rights of art not to abdicate in favor of what is fashionable. He embodied Edward Said's figure of late style as *negativity*—"where one would expect serenity and maturity, one instead finds a bristling, difficult, and unyielding—perhaps even inhuman—challenge."

Then unexpectedly, in 1987, Bilbao's mayor, José María Gorordo, asked Oteiza to conceive a massive cultural and artistic project for the city. He gathered his favorite architects and enthusiastically immersed himself in the initiative that became the *Cubo* (Cube) to be installed in the Alhóndiga Winery. "It looks like I might have a blot on my clean sheet of failures," Oteiza confided sarcastically. But no chance. Gorordo was forced to resign, and Oteiza's project was abandoned. Many Bilbainos were not happy; they had collected over seventy

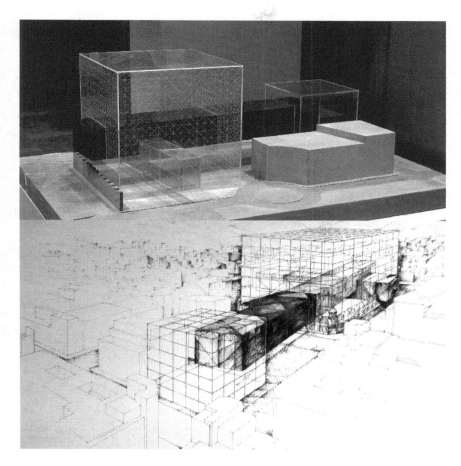

Drawing and maquette for the Alhóndiga project in Bilbao, also known as the Cube.

thousand signatures in support of the *Cubo*. Within weeks, another museum project was knocking at the door of Bizkaia's foral treasury—the Guggenheim Museum.

Years later, I visited Oteiza, the former artist turned by then into "a figure of lateness itself, an untimely, scandalous, even catastrophic commentator on the present." As I told him that I was writing about the Guggenheim, he cut me short: "Forget about writing and quit fooling around. Kill them. I will pay you." I was startled by the fury of the ninety-year-old artist, by then in complete self-exile, opposed to anything acceptable. Both Gehry and Krens had told me of their great admiration for his work and asked me whether I could convince him to sell some of it to the Bilbao Guggenheim. He refused. His obsessive call to "murder them," repeated for any visitor, was too much to bear. "Hate has overtaken me," he confessed bitterly. "I'm writing an essay entitled, 'I'm already an assassin.'" This was the period during which the *New York Times* was writing about Bilbao as a "Cinderella story." Fairy tales need murderous monsters. For global museums to succeed showing international art of universal value, there must be local primitives opposing them. But Oteiza was also the aesthete who, for half a century, had preached to the Basques the Gospel of the Artistic Avant-Garde. "For me Oteiza is like Le Corbusier, like Picasso," Gehry said, and Serra added, "Oteiza is the greatest sculptor alive." Oteiza's aesthetics are modernist to the core, art as heroic quest for truth and transformation—a literal substitute for sacramental religion. Bordering on madness, Oteiza could not perceive that the Bilbao Guggenheim could also be seen as deferred action, a sort of historical revenge via Gehry and Serra, for his own broken sphere and rage.

It was March of 1983, and Bilbao's Museum of Fine Arts announced the inauguration of the exhibit *Correspondences 5 Architects/5 Sculptors*. Gehry, Emilio Ambasz, Peter Eisenman, Ventura-Raush-Scott Brown, and Léon Krier were the architects; Chillida, Serra, Joel Shapiro, Matthew Simmonds, and Mario Merz were the sculptors. The young Bilbao sculptor Txomin Badiola approached Serra for an interview; later, Serra agreed to give a lecture at the School of Fine Arts. As they approached the school's final stony climb, Badiola's rickety car gave out, and Serra and his illustrious company had to step out and push the car upward until they reached their destination. The school's main hall was packed with hundreds of art students. During the presentation, Serra was shown a few slides depicting art works to comment on, among which was one entitled *Empty Box* by Oteiza. Serra was surprised that he didn't know this work. He asked when it had been done, and he was even more surprised to learn that it was created as early as the 1950s. After the lecture, Serra wanted to know more about the sculptor: "How is it possible that I don't know this artist?"

The visit of the internationally renowned Serra had an enormous impact on the young group of Bilbao artists and students who were at the time conducting a guerrilla warfare with the city's museum. Serra was clearly on their side. But the other effect produced by Serra was the renewed acknowledgment of Oteiza's significance. The young artists working at the School of Fine Arts had been the beneficiaries of Oteiza's commando-style storming and "taking" of the school on November 6, 1979—an act that forced the school to open up to local artists. Minimalism, conceptual art, installations, art as discourse, social sculpture, and so on were in fashion at the time, and so were the interests of these artists—anything but the "essentialism" and "localism" of a Basque art that had made Oteiza a father figure. The new generation of young Basque artists began a process to "rescue" Oteiza to their project. This led to Oteiza's 1988 grand retrospective exhibited in Madrid, Barcelona, and Bilbao, curated by Badiola. "In no way did we feel Oteiza's disciples, nor influenced by him," Badiola writes of his group of young sculptors. "Our strategy consisted in appropriating some of his expressive modes . . . or icons, such as the 'box,' recreating Oteizian pieces but subject to new or bastard linguistic plots that exploited Oteiza's sculptures' counter-discursive aspects; that is, his vitality in the management of error, of exception, of the imbalance of his works." Nor was Oteiza enthusiastic about their appropriation of his figure and work, their "copying, mixing, falsifying, destroying and recomposing." He rebuked them: "I don't know what you are doing still in the world of art. Contemporary art is finished, what you call art is nothing but popular entertainment destined for the art market; the real tasks are outside of art."

Years later, in 1994, Badiola and Ángel Bados conducted a four-month-long influential workshop at Donostia-San Sebastián's experimental art center, Arteleku, directed by Santi Eraso, for a group of young artists. Badiola summarized the results of the workshop in a text entitled *Arreglárselas sin el padre* (Getting on Without the Father). It was the Lacanian axiom that the Father's big Other position was vacant. Oteiza's figure was no longer valid for them. Yet, prompted by Serra—who in 2003 wrote that "the space conquered in these [Oteiza's] works has no precedent. They transmit a particular immensity that derives from their totality"—and despite much Bloomian "anxiety of influence," the young artists needed to re-create Oteiza as "a key reference" who, in his formal overabundance and political transgression, could be tailor-made to their artistic predicament. Much as Bilbao's "atheist" Christians did with religion, or the post-ETA former activists did with revolutionary politics, the post-Oteizian younger generation of artists had to show fidelity to the Thing by first sacrificing it.

Easy Rider: From Sacrament to Spectacle

Art is sacrament—this axiom condenses Oteiza's key theoretical novelty in a book he completed in Bilbao in 1952. *Writing is tauromachy* is the equivalent summary of Hemingway's work, the foreign writer who ironically commanded Bilbao's largest international audience. Yet, at the turn of the 1950s, both men were in a life-or-death crisis. Their culture of sacrifice and sacrament had entered a blind alley. Oteiza quit sculpting in 1959. Hemingway committed suicide in 1960.

In postmodern times, when everything is deemed simulacra, irony, spectacle, and emotionless pastiche, Oteiza and Hemingway stand apart. These two old Minotaurs confronted the deadlock of an entire culture of sacrifice and sacrament—in religion, art, politics, erotics, marriage—a crisis that remains a defining cultural complex in contemporary Bilbao. The impasses that forced them to quit their work must have derived from the contradictions between sensuousness and reason, between the avant-garde's abolition of the autonomy of art and its integration into the praxis of life—not allowing, in the absence of a Beckett-like transformation of thought, any other exit but suicide or hysteria.

The move from sacrament to spectacle had been a long time coming. In 1960, in the last chapter of his last book, Hemingway had invited his American public to "go to Bilbao" if they wanted to see terrorized bullfighters. Thirty-seven years later, there was a new call from the American arts to go to Bilbao. Architecture critic Herbert Muschamp summoned the reading public from the cover of the *New York Times Sunday Magazine*: "Have you been in Bilbao? . . . If you want to look into the heart of American art today, you are going to need a passport. You will have to pack your bags, leave the U.S. and find your way to Bilbao."

Throughout his many years of writing about the *corrida*, Hemingway fought a life-or-death struggle against the "decadence" of the art of bullfighting, summed up in one dreadful word: *spectacle*. Tourists and women—less eager to partake in and unable to endure the ritual killing of the magnificent beast with green eyes—should perhaps look at the *corrida* as spectacle from the distant gallery, he suggested. A retreat into spectacle was for Hemingway the death of the real event.

Every page he wrote on the art of the matador was an exorcism against such "trickery."

But forget about Hemingway's "generation of the bull," as Zambrano called those who fought against fascism, "because of their sense of sacrifice," and forget Bilbao's Unamunian tragic sense of life. Spectacle is the real event for Krens and spectacle is what Bilbao wanted by now despite the presence of ETA in the streets—the ETA that would welcome the museum's grand opening, presided over by the King of Spain, with a bomb in a flowerpot that killed a Basque policeman. If armed ETA was established on the killing/martyrdom of Etxebarrieta by the road in 1968, Krens brought to Bilbao in the spring of 2000 performed images of the 1969 film *Easy Rider* (in which the two bike riders and antihero heroin traders Peter Fonda and Dennis Hopper are killed on the road by a redneck) by riding bikes with Gehry through the city in the company of Hopper, Jeremy Irons, Lauren Hutton, and Lawrence Fishburn—while the museum held the hugely successful exhibit "The Art of the Motorcycle." This had to be post-tragic Bilbao. Krens was going to be the new monster-slaying Theseus that Bilbao had long awaited.

"Can we do business with this man?" the treasurer Laskurain remembers asking himself when he first saw the tall figure in the raincoat descend from the plane with a laptop computer hanging off his shoulder. Krens had replaced Thomas Messer at the helm of the Guggenheim, which was lagging behind the other great New York museums. What the Guggenheim needed was someone who could do for it what Thomas Hoving had done for the Metropolitan—someone interested above all in "masterpiece theater" and spectacle, obsessed with publicity, who bragged that "almost everything I thought of or looked at, I tried to bend into a business." Both Hoving and Krens were risk-takers and megalomaniacs. By turning the museum into an exhibition factory, the only thing that mattered was the mega-show. Both spent much of their energy in franchising and marketing. And they both engaged in questionable auction dealings that left their institutions chronically strapped for money. While Hoving dealt through auction houses to purchase works of art, Krens went even further and sold three of the museum's masterpieces at Sotheby's. But the $35.4 million he raised by selling Chagall's *Anniversaire*, Modigliani's *Garcon à la veste bleu*, and Kandinsky's 1914 *Fugue* were far short of covering the costs of Krens's projects.

Members of the Guggenheim Motorcycle Club in Bilbao: among others, Dennis Hopper, Lauren Hutton, Thomas Krens and Jeremy Irons.

Ernest Hemingway.

Jorge Oteiza.

The night he invited me for an interview, Krens was obsessed with a painting that was his ultimate object of desire. His entire Bilbao Guggenheim project, he said repeatedly, was in essence "making a heroic museum for a heroic painting." That painting was none other than *Guernica*. Krens laid down the details of his planned transfer of Picasso's painting to Bilbao from Madrid's Reina Sofía Museum. "If the *Guernica* comes to Bilbao," Krens predicted for me, "it will pay all of the museum's costs in two years." The best art of the century in the best architecture of the times, all made possible by his heroic museum. If the destiny of *Guernica*—which the Museum of Modern Art in New York had been required to return to Spain after Franco's death, *the* painting of the century—was going to be in his Guggenheim franchise in Bilbao, then an ecstatic Krens knew he was rewriting contemporary art history.

Krens wanted a *Guernica* tailor-made to his size and character. It was true that in *Guernica* Picasso had conflated the Minotaur, the *corrida,* and the Crucifixion. The painting was Picasso's life, in his eyes the most important thing he ever did. It had been an emblem against European fascism. In the nationalist demonstrations of the 1970s and the workers' struggles of the 1980s, such as "the Battle of Euskalduna," Bilbao's streets had been filled with thousands of demonstrators and strikers displaying badges with the *Guernica* image. But someone had to tell the Basques the truth—the painting was now a relic of itself, its proper mission now being to serve as a tourist magnet for Krens's Bilbao Guggenheim. It was no longer the painting that had electrified the world in the Spanish Republic's pavilion at the Paris World Fair. Upon its return to Spain four decades later, to the Casón del Buen Retiro in Madrid, the explosive work appeared sedated, having lost its capacity to shock. In the words of one commentator, "*Guernica*'s presence in the Casón had transformed [it]. . . into a morgue; a place of pilgrimage." Another added: "Here it is now, in the Neolithic Casón, just like a primitive cave painting trapped in intensive care." If Gernika's original Basque imaginary has no more iconic place than Santimamiñe's prehistoric cave, Picasso's *Guernica* had become a dated drawing in another primitive cave. Krens wanted to change all that. After all, wasn't the great irony that, as the Nazis were entering Paris and when Picasso offered the painting to President Aguirre (the very work that would later become their endless object of desire), the Basques showed no interest in it? It was no longer enough "the loss" of

Gernika; *Guernica* had to represent now "the loss of loss." The sacrament had to partake of the spectacle.

Oteiza and Hemingway's Bilbao legacy had reached a dead end. I had the opportunity to experience the sacramental impasse during my own wedding ceremony, which I shared with Oteiza's fiftieth wedding anniversary. It was by chance that in the early 1980s I happened to be a neighbor of the Oteizas in the town of Zarautz. We became friends but we had a falling out because his antagonist, Chillida, had designed the cover for one of my books. I was sure our relationship was over, but his wife, Itziar, intervened, and a few months later I visited them with my girlfriend. That Sunday morning, Oteiza was in a terrible mood. As he tried to toast some bread to go with oysters, smoke began to come out of the toaster and Oteiza almost threw it against the wall. Our falling out had not been patched up yet, and our exchanges were chilly. But later at lunch, unexpectedly, the conversation veered toward their upcoming fiftieth wedding anniversary. When I mentioned that my girlfriend was pregnant and we were also getting married, Oteiza replied, "Let's do it together!" He'd call the Arantzazu poet and Franciscan monk Vitoriano Gandiaga to be the celebrant, and insisted that the matter was closed. His anger at me had suddenly evaporated, a joint wedding suddenly a kind of reconciliation and recommitment. That's how one Saturday noon, on May 14, 1988, my soon-to-be wife and I found ourselves in my childhood Romanesque church, a spacious void sculpture with a groin vault and columns reminiscent of Bourgeois's *Maman* spider, sitting next to Oteiza and Itziar. On their golden wedding anniversary, the four of us were to take our marriage vows together. There was a small problem, however—everyone, including Gandiaga, knew that Oteiza and I were nonbelievers. At the moment of the "I do" vows, each time Gandiaga began to recite "Do you . . .?" Oteiza would interrupt him before he completed the question with his "Me yes! Me yes! Me yes!" to the amusement of the congregation. For my wife and me, the occasion was not humorous. I worried that the village parishioners would think I was taking religion lightly and be offended. Some of my academic friends were miffed at my "religious" wedding. Was I, an atheist, turning the sacrament into spectacle? Compelled to explain myself, I wrote a one-page justification that I distributed among the congregation.

"The sacrament is perverse," Gonzalo, a longtime Bilbaino friend, told me. I had agreed with him after my descent into apostasy.

Oteiza, *Unconscious Figures* (1966).

Between 65 and 70 percent of all Basques are now married in secular services. But there I was in my village church, forty years old and tying the knot in a religious ceremony. I had long despised the Unamuno/ Oteiza theatrical agony of "I am not a believer in my head but I am a believer with my heart." Yet I was caught in a similar impasse, torn between conscious atheism and unconscious religiosity. It seemed that Oteiza had won me over once again. Ideological agnosticism was the easy part; the risky thing, the real, was how to handle, prisoner of love, the Kierkegaardian *eternity* of marriage. I kept telling my wife and myself, "If this crazy man and his wife can sustain marriage for fifty years, so can we."

Sensing that her death was near, Itziar, a Bilbaina woman of unusual grace and fortitude whom Oteiza met and married in Buenos Aires, repeatedly voiced her worry to me: "As soon as I die, he [Oteiza] is such a madman he will be arrested." And she was right. The very day she died, in a bout of insanity Oteiza blamed the nurses for her death and began shooting up the hospital with his pistol. He was arrested but then released by the governor of Navarre (who had recently negotiated with Oteiza for the donation of all his work to the province in exchange for establishing a museum for it). Upon Itziar's death, Oteiza, who had been far from an exemplary husband and whose fits of anger and dejection had made her last years most difficult, published his "Elegy to Itziar":

Image of Itziar Carreño on the cover of Oteiza's book of poems.

> I've never had
> another life but hers
> the only thing I have
> is my wife
>   and she is dead.

In the poem, he called her "Itziar-Eurydice"—the beloved wife of Orpheus who, upon Eurydice's death, sang so mournfully that the gods wept and told him to retrieve her from the underworld.

Increasingly, Oteiza became a figure of scandal and derision. In his last years he would self-pityingly complain, "I did not deserve to die like this, like a mangy dog." He knew he had become a target of ridicule—he had become *trash,* as Lacan defined the saint and the psychoanalyst.

The last time I went to see him, Begoña, his caregiver, shooed me away, saying he was having a siesta. I begged her to let me see him for just thirty minutes. He was waiting for me at seven p.m. As I entered his apartment, I knew from his ferocious eyes that the ninety-two-year-old Minotaur was not vanquished yet. We greeted each other with the slaps and blows and obscenities we always exchanged, while he protected his head with his left arm. Five hours later, past midnight, there we were still, in endless laughter, the man in his nineties pleading with Begoña to let the party go on just a little longer, unable to say goodbye. She had served us dinner—wine and whisky had flowed freely—and we were smoking those forbidden cigars that he kept by the boxfuls. As so often before, our laughter sprang from his abandon and total excess, his unique gift to his friends. Whenever I'd phoned him from afar, he was all about lament, failure, and absence. The very mention of Itziar would make him weep—he had recorded both of them saying the Rosary together and he'd replay it and pray with her every night. But face-to-face, while complaining about everything, cursing politics, mocking death, our meeting was frenzied laughter and happiness.

"Here's me, a happy fool," he laughed at himself. "Happiness is not only about laughing freely. It's also about being thankful. But happiness can't be demanded. I live off of that innocence—that's what really saves me. If it weren't for that, I'd feel guilty . . ." Then he made fun of me: "I feel sorry for serious sages like you."

He was the man damned again and again, the man with ridiculous pistols on the table, the ever-conspiratorial, absurdly theatrical warrior, the apocalyptic man of "it's all over" from whose follies, rages, and laughter I had learned the most. "Ninety-two! I'll be damned! Ninety-two years! Sons of bitches! They've snuck up on me from behind! Screw me!" he shouted in self-deriding celebration. The artist always in need of healing found salvation in the excess of laughter, his final creation. His laughter went hand-in-hand with his *amor fati*: "If I'm an idiot, it's because the gods exist. I love them. I love everything, even misfortune—it's a sign that you're alive. If you don't feel your misfortune, what *can* you feel?"

Besieged by absences, voids, and all kinds of empty forms, he was a radically vulnerable man. It wouldn't be a meeting with Oteiza if there weren't a "conspiracy" involved. "Where are the others? We lack the feeling and intelligence to live these moments as important poetic ones, and we're not making the most of them," he'd tell me. He worried about me: "If you keep wasting your time for a long time, all the efforts ultimately disappear." Wondering what was to be done, he spoke of Saint Ignatius who "had the balls to know how to choose."

At one point, Oteiza, the implacable aesthete, lowered his head to calmly issue his verdict: "I have the feeling that we've lost. We have been defeated in everything." His confession of *consummatum est* followed: "Culture's finished, art's finished, everything's finished. Everything has been fulfilled. How hard it has been." His identification with the man from Nazareth on the Hill of Golgotha left him silent. It was as if the only thing that mattered was to certify the ruin of everything he and his generation had attempted; as if the only gesture that could reveal the truth of his aesthetic *void,* impermeable to any idol, was to undo at the end of his life everything he had built around his figure.

He lit another cigar. "Death—it'll come any day now. Dammit!" His "everything is finished," said calmly, with the peace and freedom of someone who no longer had anything to lose, sounded ominous. He began singing an old song I didn't recognize. After the laughter, he sighed, "I'm glad I'll die soon." And the laughter continued, as if echoing the ballet he wrote for his apostles in Arantzazu, those "fourteen sacrificed pigs":

     I ANDROCANTO and continue
             continue continue
     I continue the ballet
     one one
             onetwothree
     now different onetwo onetwo
             onetwothree
                    fourfivesix
     dearly beloved enemies
             peace and well-being.

Euskadi Fantôme

Champagne, kept years for the occasion, was uncorked on November 1975 when the news announced that Generalissimo Franco was dead. Expectations for long-forbidden political, cultural, and sexual freedoms filled the streets with excitement. It was the transition from *dictadura* to democracy, and a new era was about to dawn with an explosion of artistic and ethnographic surrealism. Every aspect of culture and politics was a reality deeply in question. The hyperpoliticized Euskadi turned into a carnivalesque *Euskadi fantôme* ripe for parody and trangressive humor—"Transgression does not negate an interdiction. It transcends and completes it," wrote Marcel Mauss.

A cover of the comic magazine *Euskadi Sioux* by Vicente Ameztoy.

New comic magazines made their appearance on the stands, including *Euskadi Sioux* (1979). The idea that the Basque Country was Indian territory—Sioux Country—resonated with the anthropologization of the Basques as the descendants of the Cro-Magnons and the last Indians of Europe. Turning Basques into figures in an ethnographic museum allowed for endless parody. On one of the magazine's provocative covers, Vicente Ameztoy painted the image of a hooded girl with large, white teeth, on a background of flowers and green pastures, the Basque *lauburu* swastika hanging from her neck, a *makila* (traditional walking stick) in her hand, one of her breasts pointing forward and the other in profile and outside her T-shirt. The lead article was on "municipal erections"—after so many on "municipal elections." Freed from the shackles of four decades of dictatorship, everything could be turned into carnival.

Cover of a punk fanzine.

Fanzines (from "fan-magazines") became fashionable, and dozens of free radio stations emerged in Basque towns. Cartoonist Eguillor created his fanzine *Bilbao la muerte* (Bilbao, death) with images of Marilyn Monroe. "Humor," Eguillor wrote, "must be first of all a revenge against reality . . . humor can only spring from a hopeless hope . . . close to suicide, let us say." Ameztoy painted *poxpolinas* (girls dressed in traditional Basque costumes), with the Left Bank's blast furnaces in the background, and their typically green and red colors morphed into grays. Not only Oteiza's ovoidal sphere was broken; Ruper Ordorika was also singing Bernardo Atxaga's lyrics, "Hautsi da Anphora" (The Amphora Has Broken). Atxaga and several other writers formed in Bilbao a group calling themselves *Pott Banda* (Pott Band)—based on the colloquial term *pott egin* (becoming exhausted and giving up). Between 1978 and 1980 they published in Bilbao six issues of a satirical magazine also entitled *Pott*, combining news and literary criticism, poetry and short narrations, outright farce and frontal attacks against the cultural and political establishments.

Juan Carlos Eguillor, *Bilbao, death* (1982), with images of Marilyn Monroe.

It was also time to parody the sacred cows of Basque art. Andrés Nagel made sculptures with names such as *Metaphysical Box* (a favorite Oteiza title), his metaphysical box being an iron cage of raging tigers, a forewarning, perhaps, of the soon-to-arrive bedroom tiger Krens in Bilbao. Nagel also produced figureheads doing one-hand stands on cardboard boxes, surrealistic pop sculptures he named "levitations" (a title by Chillida). Other artists followed suit. "I want nothing to do with Oteiza," Jon, a prominent young Bilbao artist whose own favorite artist is Andy Warhol, told me when I asked him about the old sculptor. Most other young artists would say the same. Beginning with architecture, a new postmodern sensibility was corroding the formal seriousness of modernist aesthetics. Pop and kitsch were fashionable. It was time for the ironic, the parodic, the sinister, the obscene. Humor became de rigueur, humor being "the operation of a triumphant ego, the art of deflecting and disavowing the superego, with all its masochistic consequences."

In 1995, Arantzazu—where Oteiza had left his imprint with the statuary of the apostles—provided the opening scene for Bilbaoan filmmaker Alex de la Iglesia's *El Día de la Bestia* (The Day of the Beast). Far from sublime spirituality, the film narrates the outrageous story of a Basque priest who knows *when* the apocalypse is going to happen but not exactly *where*. He makes a pact with Satan, whose favors he repays by committing as many sins as possible. The other two main characters are a metal salesman, who dies at the hands of a laughing Satan, and the host of a television show dealing with the occult. Another movie that same year, Daniel Calparsoro's *Salto al Vacío* (Jump into the Void), filmed among the ruins of Bilbao's Left Bank, tells of drugs, violence, and sexual impotence. The protagonist has the word *void* shaved onto her head—the one word that sums up Oteiza's and Chillida's aesthetics. In the 1990s, Basque television turned Oteiza into one of its satirical spitting-image caricatures. What had been so recently deadly serious was turning into a culture of kitsch, camp, parody, best represented by the popularity of the rock band Orquesta Mondragón (named after the town with a madhouse), whose first record was entitled *Muñeca Hinchable* (Inflatable Doll) and had songs such as "Put a Dead Man in Your Engine." For the new sensibility of post-everything, the former images of struggles for identity and freedom seemed to belong to a naïve past. Yesterday's passions were baroque; today's frivolous. When the Generalissimo was alive, everyone knew there was no freedom. After his death, a *March for Freedom* brought together a hundred thousand people in the Basque Country. But soon people were left wondering what happened to that desire for a freedom that seemed so at hand. The word *desencanto* (disenchantment) summed up the new political mood of a generation that in its youth had been addicted to utopian thinking.

Pott Tropikala (1980), the cover page of one of the issues published by the Pott Banda.

Poster for the film by Alex de la Iglesia, *The Day of the Beast* (1995).

The Spanish army represented the *dictadura*'s iron grip. In the biography of young boys of my generation, the dreaded fourteen months of military service stood as a period of mindless disruption and unmitigated waste of time—a humiliating initiation ritual into the "manhood" of military culture. By the 1990s, the Spanish army could no longer impose mandatory service. It became instead a fixture in Bilbao's streets, a source of antimilitary parodies by actors dressed as soldiers pretending to take over the city for the amusement of bystanders.

ETA's violence was the one thing that could not be rendered as comedy. That had to wait until September of 2003 when Oscar Terol created the Basque TV comedy *Vaya semanita* (What a Little Week). Suddenly audiences could laugh about the troubles of a southern Spanish immigrant with two sons—a Basque policeman and an ETA member. One of Terol's successes was his sarcastic treatment of "Basque matriarchy" and other similarly hot anthropological topics. Terol's bottom line: "Here woman rules, period." The life of a Basque man, concludes Terol's humor, consists of "planning the escape from his particular Alcatraz, his mother." Hence the relevance of the ubiquitous *cuadrilla* peer group as "an itinerant institution that gives shelter and protects its members," soccer and women its two themes of conversation. "There is no humor without trauma," Terol told me.

Urban Processions

When Frank Gehry presented his Bilbao architectural project in the city's stock market, a project that would take 80 percent of Basque monies for museums, the one thing the urban planners had not anticipated was that the formally dressed people in attendance would have to cross a picket line of unemployed workers shouting "Thieves!" "Scoundrels!" "Fewer museums and more jobs!" With the city's 25 percent unemployment rate, the shouts were part of the aesthetics of the "tough Bilbao" so lauded by Gehry.

I wanted to know who these unemployed people were. In the spring of 1999, I began attending the Assembly of the Unemployed, housed in a shabby fifteen-by-fifteen-foot basement on Prim Street in Bilbao's Casco Viejo. Every morning at nine a.m., some one hundred jobless people would meet to gather information, update their records, and organize marches demanding work. They were the *para-dos*—the word *parar* (to stop, to come to an end) reflecting the fact that their lives were at a standstill. On the bulletin board of the Assembly's office a number caught my attention: Bilbao's jobless were 28,606 (out of a total population of 358,000). They had no jobs, no careers, no means to support their families. Every morning began with taking attendance and reordering work requests—every day each person present climbed up a notch on the waiting list; the top applicant became eligible for the next menial job that came along (generally for a month or two and at minimum wage).

Once we went by train to a construction site in Durango, twenty miles away. The boss in charge would not take on another workman, no matter how temporary, and called the police. For over an hour, surrounded by officers, more than a hundred men and women begged for one single job. The situation was becoming more and more tense. Some young men respectfully tried to reason with the boss. A young woman with colorful dyed hair and a pearl in her nose pleaded with him, addressing him affectionately, "You are a big head, darling." A young man wearing the cap of the Athletic soccer team kept repeating: "We aren't delinquents. We have the right to work." The police stood by patiently, aware that the encounter was nothing but the impotent airing of grievances by desperate people.

I felt like an intruder. Before getting on the train that day, to my embarrassment, one of the women demanded a vote to see whether they wanted me with them. They voted in favor. Then, in the middle of the confrontation at the work site, which I was tape-recording, they used me to pressure the foreman, saying the journalist with them would report his harshness. No matter. On the way back to Bilbao, Beethoven's Fifth was playing over the train's music system and I pretended to be absorbed, too ashamed to even start a conversation. I knew how they felt—the scum of society, bordering on illegality, with no unions or lawyers to defend them, no charities to help, the "losers" nobody wanted around. They were barely organized, the mystique of "class solidarity" too much of a luxury for them, only the most basic human dignity held them together. Anything they might tell me would be superfluous, an anecdote of their obscene reality. I imagined them returning to their families, apologizing for their failures with downcast eyes and mouthing their routine, "It's not fair, hombre." At one point I broke my silence and asked the young man next to me what his situation was. His reply came fast, "You don't need to be a rocket scientist to know the conditions of my life." I couldn't believe I'd asked that question. I was an impostor, a "writer" worth nothing, scared that they might ask how much I earned as a university professor.

Another morning, our column of the unemployed walked the Ribera, passing the Guggenheim and the University of Deusto until we reached a new construction site next to the Deusto Bridge. There was no work, and an air of hopelessness was palpable. At a striptease club next to the construction site, a poster announced that Robert Carlyle, who had acted in the British comedy film *The Full Monty* (which portrayed unemployed steelworkers who form a striptease act and are willing to strip all the way in order to make enough money to support their families), would be in Bilbao the following week for the latest James Bond film, starring Pierce Brosnan. For days, Brosnan's visit was the talk of the town. Crowds of Bilbainos followed each step of Agent 007, from the airport to the hotel to filming the street jump in front of the Guggenheim Museum (which became the opening sequence of *The World Is Not Enough*).

The visit to the construction site over, I took the direction of the Gran Vía, through the pedestrian undercarriage of the Deusto Bridge, the site of the fiercest street confrontations during the Battle for Euskalduna—the working class's last stand in 1984. Walking next to me across the bridge was Jon, an intelligent and likeable man in his early forties, a participant in the procession of the jobless. He had many years of experience as a waiter, but age was becoming his enemy since younger waiters were preferred for jobs. He worked at the Sociedad Bilbaína—for a century the meeting place for Bilbao's industrial elite, located next to the city's stock market. It is an Anglo-influenced architectural jewel with a great library, international dailies, a gymnasium, and a first-class restaurant. He was only called to work occasionally on a meal-by-meal basis, so he came every morning to the Assembly meetings. He told me that 80 percent of the Assembly members had families to support. At one time, more than a thousand came, but now many felt too ashamed to do so. Once he was arrested for walking onto a construction site. Society was divided for him between those who work and those who want to work. He said that being jobless, though, was not the lowest fate; being a beggar or a gypsy was worse. While five hundred pesetas got me a daily cup of coffee and two newspapers, for Jon they meant three rolls of bread and two liters of milk. Only on Sundays could he afford a newspaper. Earning enough to feed his family—a wife and three kids, thirteen to eighteen—was a challenge. He hadn't been able to pay his rent for eight years. The Basque government wasn't collecting the monthly 20,000 pesetas ($110) from the twenty-five neighbors in public housing who were unable to pay, but it didn't dare evict them—it would have been bad publicity.

"When money doesn't enter through the door, love escapes through the window," Jon quipped. He and his wife had once separated for three years. His commitment to family was attested by his daily search for the five thousand pesetas, his pride evident when he talked of his oldest daughter, who paid for her own studies and would attend college the following year. He had worked in various parts of Spain. Once a man fell in love with him. Another time, a customer gave him a car as a gift. This is the man who for years couldn't find a job in the new mecca for tourism, the service-oriented Bilbao.

As we walked along the Deusto Bridge, we looked at Gehry's building before us in the full power of its voluptuous forms. I asked Jon whether he had ever visited the museum. He hadn't. I invited him to come inside with me. He had something more important to do—a job-related interview. I passed the floral sculpture *Puppy*, descended the long flight of stone steps, and walked into the museum. A Robert Rauschenberg retrospective was being featured in the Fish Gallery. The first thing I noticed was a BMW turned into an art object. Robert Rauschenberg's great uninterrupted collage, the thousand-foot-long work-in-progress that he began in 1981 and continued to work on between other projects, was impressive. Ahead was Serra's massive *Snake*. Krens had told me that he'd begged Gehry, "Frank, build an entrance that will make people fall on their knees as they enter." I didn't feel like falling on my knees.

In the afternoon, as I was driving past the museum through Campo Volantín, I recognized someone in the street—the drunkard who, during our morning procession and from across the street, had greeted the jobless with shouts and his arms raised as we walked silently. Leaving his El Corte Inglés plastic bag on the ground, he had come into the middle of the road with his cheers, holding up traffic while angry drivers were honking. For a minute, the somber column of the *parados* turned into a raucous parade, until they removed him from the road. He had been our only supporter during the thirty minutes or so we had walked through Bilbao's streets. Later in the afternoon, there he was again, standing in the Bilbao rain. He was next to the La Salve headquarters of the Guardia Civil, infamous during my student years as a torture chamber.

When I stopped to greet him, he replied in Basque with a *bai!* (yes!). "Are you Basque?" I asked. "I'm Galician," he said. "I've lived here thirty years," and pointed to a shanty on the hill right behind. Bent forward and red-faced, he added, "I'm a quarryman. I've spent my years at the marble quarries of Markina." "Markina?" I was taken aback. "My father too was a quarryman and sometimes worked in Markina's marble quarries," I replied, hoping, unrealistically, that he might have known my father as they both worked in the same quarry. Like the Galician migrant quarryman, my father had also been forced to migrate to Bilbao's Left Bank before he began work in the quarry in Lastur. "I was born in a large stone house, as long as from here to there," he continued, drawing my attention to the size of the Civil Guard quarters. "I'm a loser," he said. Then, as if wanting to give me some reward for talking to him, he added, "But I'm happy enough." He told me that he was sixty-five. My car was blocking the traffic, someone honked, and I moved on. I would never see him again. The image of his hands raised in the middle of the road cheering on the *parados* remained with me. He made my father's absence unbearable.

That spring there were in Bilbao other kinds of urban processions as well—those of the Holy Week in celebration of Christ's Passion and in which thousands of Ku Klux Klan–like hooded "penitents," dressed in dark cassocks, many barefoot, slowly and rhythmically moved through the city to the tune of electrifying cornets. At the center of the procession, on men's shoulders, were the baroque lifelike sculptures of the Nazarene dressed in purple, the Virgin of Sorrows in black, and other icons. Local TV and the general public packed the sidewalks as each night of the Passion Week the hooded icon bearers took a different route. In an era of mass desertion from the Church, many agnostics still take part in the Holy Week processions, often after months of rehearsals. Under the anonymity of the cassocks and hoods, riveted by the convulsive music of cornets echoing at night in the city streets, thousands of Bilbainos are exposed to the satisfaction of this penitential theater for sins they are unable to admit. For these curious onlookers, the street passion is one more event of ethnographic surrealism, a religious thrill anyone can afford in an era when religion has become an affordable indulgence, a feel-good experience that does not commit you to change your life.

One Holy Monday, I joined the crowds as one of the most popular processions passed through Old Bilbao's red-light street, La Palanca. For an hour we waited, listening to the distant hair-raising music echoing in the night, evoking Christ's agonic Passion, coming closer and closer. As the center of the procession reached us, the Nazarene's effigy stopped in front of a brothel and one of the "scarlet women" sang a *saeta* to him. That night there was a haunting full moon—the old Bilbao moon, which Brecht located right there in one of the nightclubs of that Old Bilbao district, the beer hall where for a dollar you could have music and boundless pleasure. And you could hear in the memory of my generation Antonio Machado's "La Saeta," a song popularized by Joan Manuel Serrat:

Oh, you are not my song!
I cannot sing, nor do I want to
To this Jesus of the wood
But to the one who walked on the sea!

The Actor's Labyrinth

I was in a bar on San Francisco street with my wife when there was a bustle when there was a bustle of movement and shouts from the crowd, and an old rowdy man appeared. He was all bent over, smoking, dressed in a ragged raincoat, talking to himself while drinking, eating a banana, throwing up. It was Ander performing *Ardoaz* (On Wine) at the corner of a bar, acting out the life of Ignatius, an alcoholic who remembers his childhood, whores, dreams. The audience was electrified. In a repetition of André Breton's simplest surrealist act, Ander/Ignatius took out a toy pistol and began firing into the crowd. "It's so beautiful the ruin. . . . Poetry, poetry." Ander was reciting the Spanish poet Leopoldo María Panero's words and telling the story of Ignatius's love for a prostitute. When he left the bar I was sweating, exhausted, stunned.

I met with Ander some days later. He was preparing a play on Panero at the madhouse in Mondragón where the poet had been confined after a mental breakdown. Our conversation centered on madness and around his favorite authors—Artaud, Holderlin, Brecht, Nietzsche. Two years earlier, he had temporarily stopped performing after both his eighty-year-old teacher and a twenty-five-year-old friend had committed suicide. The theory and experience of chaos are paramount to him. The very day the Guggenheim Museum opened, Ander inaugurated a theater group, "Workshop of Imaginary Theater," in a Bilbao locale by the name of Mina Espazioa. In Spanish *mina* means "mine, quarry" and in Basque *mina* is "pain." "Everything is like a howl, a howl that emerges from the void, from nothing, from a zero feeling," Ander wrote at the time in one of the group's pamphlets. As a child, Ander had to confront his mother's mental illness, and acting was his way of maintaining sanity, of "curing" his relationship with her. He had studied drama in Madrid for years and continued expanding his skills while visiting faraway cultures. He positions himself within a central metaphor of the Western tradition—the Minotaur in the labyrinth, saved only by Ariadne: "In each action, in each either/or, it is the Minotaur looking at us," Ander wrote.

Some time later, I introduced Ander to Oteiza in a bar. If for the sculptor art was "sacrament," for Ander, following Stanislavski's theory, acting is total identification with the character. We ate lunch and drank, and a riotous Oteiza felt free to speak his mind. After Oteiza's death in 2003, Ander was asked to contribute to a DVD in his honor. His performance was based on the words he had taped from Oteiza at that lunch, including his curses and mad rants, as well as his excremental theology—the idea that God was hidden inside a big pile of shit: "what a lesson in humility, a tremendous creator that He is, and He emerged from a grain of corn inside a pile of shit." In Oteiza's poetry as well, the word *shit* stands out, as it did in his daily hysterical outbursts, at times comparing his own abjection—his being a "mangy dog"—with that of a trashy saint. Ander's work in honor of Oteiza was censored. Ander's Workshop of Imaginary Theater was invited to perform in Chicago, Miami, Teheran, New Mexico, Rosario, Cairo, but he failed to attract invitations at home in Bilbao. After a decade of existence,

And it is not an escape, nor evasion, nor a dream,
but the only true life.
And I do what is possible,
and I hold again the cup as if it were the neck of life
and I tell someone that this might be the life of the gods:

. . . .

It is so beautiful the ruin, so deep
I know all its colors,
and it is like a symphony, the music of ending.

Leopoldo María Panero, "La canción del croupier de Mississipi."

the group disbanded and Ander left Bilbao to continue performing in other places.

Bilbao is for Ander far more than a city surface newly raised and fashioned by the glamorous spectacle of star architects. It is also the elaborate maze of kilometers of impressive underground sewer tunnels channeling waste to Galindo's filtering plants to produce at the end of the process *cookies* of distilled refuse. He must act out the destitute subject—the chaos of the mad city and its underbelly's excremental reminder.

Happy End in Mahagonny Paradise

It was the night of January 15, 2005, when the rock group Doctor Deseo (Doctor Desire) gave a memorable concert at Bilbao's Arriaga Theater, later released as a CD and DVD with the title *Metamorphosis*. Ander, the actor/shaman, dressed in rags and wearing dark glasses, introduced the group, commanding, "Doctor, Doctor! Look at me! Metamorphosis is my virtue, my perdition! Doctor, Doctor! This is my gift, my pulse, my blood, and my caress! Here is your Desire!" Then, led by their exuberant singer/songwriter, Francis Díez, the group jumped to the stage to deliver music pulsating with Bilbao's urban life. Soon they were playing "¡Abrázame!" (Embrace me!), Francis's gritty voice overpowering the theater with words he had been told by a rock singer after their farewell concert and before killing himself: "Embrace me! Embrace me! And don't tell me anything."

The following spring, Doctor Deseo presented its following album, *Detrás de los espejos rotos* (Behind the Broken Mirrors), in Kafe Antzokia. There he was, Francis, like a mountain climber, hanging from a rope against the wall at the second floor and singing while letting himself swing and descend on top of the audience:

How difficult to maintain the course!

. . .

and I don't know whether to continue
or whether I prefer the shipwreck
any night now, my love,
I am going to collapse.

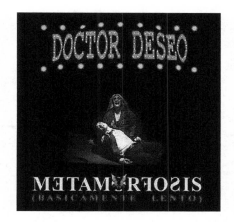

Cover of the CD *Metamorphosis* by Doctor Deseo (2005).

Embrace Me

When the cup of dreams is empty
and a thousand stinging bees in my
guts rob me of my nights
don't leave me alone, for I am now so
small
and when I awake from the nightmare
nothing changes, all remains the
same.
Embrace me! Embrace me!
and don't tell me anything
for this sadness doesn't leave me
and this fear pains me even more.

Doctor Deseo, "Abrázame."
(Author's translation)

You knew with Doctor Deseo that, whatever else, *this is actually happening*. It was music to move and change the audience. Later, Doctor Deseo sang "La Luna Lunera, El Amor Mata" (Moony Moon, Love Kills): "Let's go somewhere else, my darling, / where love will not kill us." The message could not be lost: Let's enjoy life fully, let's take desire to the end, let's change our lives.

Doctor Deseo's "Moony Moon" echoed The Doors's "Alabama Song," written by Brecht and Weill in parallel to "Bilbao Song," both sung by Lotte Lenya: "Oh, moon of Alabama / We now must say goodbye." The "Alabama Song" was part of Brecht-Weill's *Rise and Fall of the City of Mahagonny* (1930), a three-act drama about the emergence and decline of a "paradise city" in the middle of the desert, a prophecy of Las Vegas perhaps, and a protest against rampant capitalism. Lenya performs the character of the prostitute Jenny. A bacchanal follows after a rule is passed that the townspeople should do as they please, and, despite the efforts of Halleluiah Lillian of the Salvation Army to convert the sinners, Mahagonny goes to its doom.

The "Bilbao Song" belonged to another Brecht-Weill musical of the same period, *Happy End* (1929). The song praises the locale of "That Old Bilbao Moon" in Old Bilbao's red-light quarters:

That old Bilbao moon

Oh, how did it go? . . .

It's been too long ago.

I am not sure you would have liked it. But

It was the most beautiful!

It was the most beautiful!

It was the most beautiful!

In the world!

This was Brecht singing to Bilbao years before the German Condor Legion would destroy Gernika and capture Bilbao in the spring of 1937. In Brecht-Weill's song, while vocalizing three times "Bilbao," and two lines later again three times "*Krach und Wonne*" (noise and pleasure), the voice keeps dropping, as it does in "Alabama Song," "like a drunk whose legs buckle under him as he staggers forward," before the final release arrives for both songs of the "arching tune shaking off the churlishness of the verse"—"Oh! Moon of Alabama"; "That Old Bilbao Moon. It was fantastic!"

The collaboration between Brecht and Weill was guided by the politicized concept of emotional "estrangement" required by an epic theater that appealed less to the spectator's feelings (as in the Wagnerian operas) and more to critical reasoning—and which called for assimilating more popular styles such as jazz and cabaret. It was music for a postwar Germany that "had constructed out of America a fabulous, visionary domain, partly concocted out of reality, mostly built in fantasy." It was the dream of the American dollar against the collapse of the postwar German mark that Brecht-Weill were ferociously satirizing—a dream taking place in the fantasy land of "Mahagonny paradise," where the opening lines of "Bilbao Song" belong:

> Bill's beer hall in Bilbao, Bilbao, Bilbao
> Was the most fantastic place I've ever known
> For just a dollar you get all you wanted
> all you wanted, all you wanted
> of whatever kind of joy you call your own.

In Act 1 of the farcical gangster comedy *Happy End,* Bill's beer hall in Bilbao was replicated in Chicago where it is the meeting place for the city's criminal gang. Brecht situated his parodic reenactments of the fantasy world of capitalism in the geography of real or imagined American cities—Chicago, Alabama, Mississippi, Mahagonny—plus in one European city—Bilbao. Bilbao was the city about whose Nervión Valley Max Weber had written that, with smoking chimneys, it created an unforgettable spectacle, the city that gave rise to "the most modern of capitalisms." It was the city of capitalist dreams par excellence—dreams that by the late twentieth century had turned into devastation and which were once again revived when Thomas Krens arrived knocking at Bilbao's treasury and promising a museum that would open the doors to Wall Street.

Brecht was a key reference in the Bilbao of the 1960s for writers such as Aresti and Etxebarrieta, who with his friend Ignacio Amestoy staged one of Brecht's plays at the University of Sarriko. Brecht's song echoed in the "Bilbao-Song" by Germán Echevarría, Etxebarrieta's poet friend, written after a memorable concert by Ute Lemper in Bilbao:

> Bertholt Brecht wasn't here. A sailor
> had a love here, in Bilbao. It was
> during a night. A woman. Her voice. No one else

was like hers . . .

Bilbao . . . the old moon reflected
on the river, nude dawn
that flows into the Abra already lost.

Kurt Weill's song. The broken voice
—Bilbao-Berlin tied by the song—
of Ute Lemper with makeup in black.

Mikel Laboa produced a record with Brecht's lyrics in 1969. One of the songs was entitled "Against Seduction":

Do not be seduced.
There is no return.
A new day is dawning.
It brings a cold breeze.
There will be no other morning.

Laboa used guttural screams in several of his songs to evoke his own childhood trauma during the war. Another title from Brecht that Laboa sang was "Nocturnal Shelter," with lyrics that begin by reciting the story of a man who shelters New York homeless, then adds, "The world cannot be changed like that."

In 1962, Bob Dylan was still a newcomer in New York when he found himself in the audience of a small theater listening to Lotte Lenya sing "Pirate Jenny" at the revue *Brecht on Brecht*. It is a wild song about prostitute Jenny fantasizing revenge on her clients. Dylan was mesmerized. Intrigued by the impact of the "nasty song, sung by an evil fiend," he began taking the song apart—"it was the form, the free verse association, the structure and disregard for the known certainty of melodic patterns to make it seriously matter, give it its cutting edge." That song was "like the Picasso painting *Guernica*." Dylan realized that "I hadn't done anything yet," and began searching for his own song "totally influenced by 'Pirate Jenny.'" Brecht and Weill blew new life into Dylan's songwriting. On the cover of *Bringing It All Back Home* he was holding a Lotte Lenya album. "The times they are a-changing" was a direct quote from Brecht.

Dylan's own influence would soon be pervasive among Basque songwriters. On July 12, 2006, Laboa, who composed several "Gernika" songs, and Dylan shared the stage to give a concert in Donostia-San Sebastián. They didn't exchange a word between themselves, but the

Concert by Laboa and Dylan in Donostia-San Sebastián, July of 2006.

combination of the two masters of song spoke with unique intensity to my generation—they'd made sure that our *happy end* wouldn't be a Mahagonny paradise built just on fantasy.

The *moon*—"the moon of Alabama," "that old Bilbao moon"—was for Brecht the ultimate image of that desired American fantasia, the dream of the fabulous riches and green pastures of capitalism. In Brecht's practice of "estrangement" and de-romantization, of shaking people from the sleeping "illusions" of theater and opera, the moon represented everything he wanted to exorcise—it was the ultimate literary emblem in the history of European romanticism, the mirage that had to be suspended to get close to the reality of life. Doctor Deseo added "Moony Moon" for Bilbao's nightlife, echoing with Morrison's "Alabama Song," and "Embrace me!" echoing Morrison's "When the Music's Over." If The Doors saw themselves as "riders in the storm" in the stream of art maudit that went back to Blake and Baudelaire, Rimbaud and Nietzsche and Buñuel, for Doctor Deseo and their audience all that mattered was the stormy edge of Bilbao, the attempt to survive a city immersed in the night of communal alcohol and drugs and orgiastic abandon. Embrace me, embrace me, and don't tell me anything. Not from priests, or politicians, or academics—Bilbao's nightlife dwellers could hear a truth that carried conviction only from groups like the metamorphic Doctor Deseo or singers like Laboa and Dylan: you must pursue your desire to the end, you must change your life.

Streets of Love

In one of my walks through La Palanca I heard about Martha, a middle-aged woman who helped the neighborhood's junkies and prostitutes. I met her at the AIDS Center on Bailén Street, and she gave me some literature on drugs, prostitution, and neighborhood associations. "Read it and then we talk," she said, before returning to the prostitutes who had come for free condoms. I had already discussed prostitution and drugs with various priests, nuns, social workers, and psychologists. Martha, with her defiant directness, was different. I voiced something I'd just heard in another welfare center about helping prostitutes get off the street. She looked at me icily: "It's their work. I have no objections." Value judgments, moral superiority, pity, pastoral care were not part of her approach. She was mortified when the leader of the neighborhood gypsies in a public meeting called her Mother Theresa, referring to her efforts in the community in the 1980s and 1990s when entire families of gypsies were wiped out by heroin.

For years, Martha and a nun had been the only people allowed to enter the *chutaderos* (from *chutar,* to shoot-up heroin) or *picaderos* (from the *picador* who in a *corrida* "pricks" the bull with a pike). These were derelict houses on Las Cortes Street, without light or running water, where an acrid odor seemed to ooze from the walls—places of intolerable stench where all the junkies did was pee, shit, fuck, and shoot heroin. Martha visited these *chutaderos* every evening. During her nightly walks through the barrio, she sometimes found moribund junkies for whom she was the only last-minute recourse. She would try to take them to a hospital. At times they would resist, and she might find them dead the next morning. Several junkies died in her arms. Some cases were clearly suicides, as when addicts who had overdosed refused the injection that could save their lives. "I've seen too much," she remarked almost absentmindedly.

The pietà image of Martha holding a dead junkie in her arms captured my imagination. I decided to go through the *Arkupe* (arcade) of the former Naja docks now turned *picadero*, a place where junkies lay on mattresses while shooting up. I'd heard stories about them attacking people with an AIDS-contaminated syringe. As I was walking by him, a junkie jumped up from the floor toward me. I froze, afraid. But he only asked for tobacco and after giving him what I was smoking, I left in a hurry. Who did I think I was kidding? I was not Martha. I had taken for granted that there was nothing I could do to help them; Martha's attitude couldn't be more different: helping them live and die was the only thing that mattered.

When I returned to Bilbao a year later, I wanted to see Martha. I was told she had stopped going to Bailén's AIDS Center and had fallen into a severe depression. One day, during a street demonstration, someone touched me on the shoulder and it was her. She had lost weight; her pallid face added beauty to her black eyes. "I don't feel well," she said by way of introduction. "I have collapsed psychologically." The vacant look in her eyes was disquieting. She gave me her phone number. Twice we made appointments, but she didn't show up. A third try, and we met briefly for coffee. Her traumatized body had shut down, she told me; for a while she couldn't get out of bed or eat without the help of her sons and friends. What she had seen and experienced had taken its toll.

Finally Martha told me her story. Her father had been an anarchist. At fifteen, she told him she wanted to be a nun: "A nun?" he had replied. "I'd rather you be a whore than a nun!" Martha later discovered that her father knew what he was talking about—his own mother had been a whore. Her father had been taken "from the street" and raised by the family of Martha's mother. That's how he had met Martha's mother, fallen in love, and married her. A militant anarchist, after the Civil War he had to flee Franco's regime, and they ended up in Paris. They sent their four children to Spanish schools and the children would visit their parents once a year in Paris. Her father continued to be a bon vivant, and her mother remained religious. While Martha's mother might have liked her to be a nun, her father had a higher opinion of whores. Everything about Martha was sort of excessive. She, who wanted to be a nun at fifteen, joined ETA in Paris when she was seventeen. She had two sons in her early twenties but had been living with a woman partner for many years. She began helping prostitutes in La Palanca after two Italian prostitutes at a conference organized by Bilbao feminists spoke of overcoming the stigma of their occupation and seeing it as legitimate work.

Martha is worldly, educated, a leftist, psychoanalyzed. But none of that mattered in her depression. No portrait of the city could be complete without including the perspective of her twisted body and her obstinate commitment to destitute people. No, her love was not an infantilism that returns to the spiritual for solace but, as Luce Irigaray put it, a "revelation."

About a hundred meters from the place Martha worked is the office of Doctors of the World where I met Cristina, a physician who in the company of other volunteers works pro bono twenty hours a week helping immigrants, the unemployed, and people without papers. Her husband had recently died of cancer. The day I visited her office, several doctors and nurses in cheerful moods were doing their work. These medical professionals on the forefront of globalization don't talk of virtual cities and architectural wonders. Their care for immigrants (there are in Bilbao over thirty thousand of them from about several dozens of nationalities) makes them live in a transnational world. The "battle for Euskalduna" marked the demise of the work-

What does it mean that the word is made flesh? Why does its prophecy have such a wide influence? . . . Can the legalism, the sentence, even the ressentiment of Christianity claim to take credit for the enthusiasm and exuberance of that creation? . . . In a language that of course goes beyond and stops short of any grammar or reason. Cryptic, or mystic, in its language.

Luce Irigaray, *Marine Lover: Of Friedrich Nietzsche*, 179.

The arcades of the Naja.

ing class in Bilbao; the void left by the category "workers" is being filled among left-wing militants by "immigrants" and "those without papers." I asked them naively why they volunteered to work with migrants and poor people. "Because we enjoy doing it!"

On the other side of the river, facing the offices of Doctors of the World and the *picaderos* of La Naja, was the Center for Caritas. I went there to see José, the Capuchin friar who was helping the junkies and their families. He told me about how they face death, and he read me samples of their farewell letters to their loved ones. We also talked about his life as a monk, his community, his celibacy. Soon after my meeting with José, City Hall closed the Naja *picaderos* because it gave a poor image to a city of architectural miracles. Later they closed the Center for Caritas as well. Heroin junkies were the city's vagabond lepers. A tourist walking along the Gran Vía would feel a chill in their presence. As I listened to José's horror stories, I saw the man who I perhaps might have become had I not failed in my religious career. His life, ruled by the premise that "whatever you did for one of these least brothers of mine, you did for me," was a direct challenge to mine—my writing was worthwhile only if it had the intensity of his wager.

Closing the circle traced by Martha, Cristina, and José, and returning to San Francisco Street, we arrive at the Posada de los Abrazos

(Shelter of the Embraces), a refuge for drug addicts and the mentally ill. There I met Anna, who is a sociologist and writer, as well as a political refugee who first left Colombia and then Guatemala under death threats because of her human rights activism. Her brother, nephew, and several brothers-in-law were killed for their political involvement with the FARC guerrillas; another brother was in jail; a third in exile after twelve years in prison where he lost his sight, a leg, and a hand from torture. Anna herself was tortured and raped by the military. "In Colombia I believed a better world was possible, the dream of social equality was possible, and since I could not find it there, I tried in other places, Peru, Ecuador, Guatemala, El Salvador . . . and now this Posada, a small piece of hope. It is not letting the hope of history die. I am not allowed to work in my own country, so this country allows me to build a network in search of a better world." Anna, who had come to Bilbao in 2000 after having spent time digging mass graves in Guatemala, was acting as witness for the wretched of the earth, placing Bilbao on the map of a borderless world replete with migrants and refugees.

Anna's view of her "friends," the *posaderos,* whose recovery depends on the almost impossible decisions, actions, and changes in circumstances they must make to overcome addictions and traumas, is anything but sentimental. "Sometimes we work with the language of tenderness," she explained, "sometimes with the language of rage. Sometimes we just look at each other. Sometimes we question each other from our own experiences. I always tell them something about my own life. There are times when they are very nervous, sad, and then we calm them by embracing them. At times, when they are crying, we put our arms around each other: 'Hug me, get close to me, give me what you have, let us share the pain.'" "We tell each other that life is tough," Anna explained, "something to be worked at, and we all are working at it together. When they are having a relapse, when they are taking drugs, we bring them to the room and talk. 'What's the matter? Why are you shooting up again? What hurts?'"

Anna is not only helping the people at her shelter but also herself—her work allows her to pursue her internationalist dream. As she put it, "In Bilbao I have recovered my resistance identity. I am a survivor." Anna studied the theology of liberation. As a teenager she wanted to be a nun and spent a year with the mothers. She was influenced by the Colombian guerrilla priest and sociologist Camilo Torres, and she knows the work of liberation theologians such as

Leonardo Boff and Jon Sobrino. "My coming to Bilbao has been a reencounter with my necessity to *be*. In Sweden I had citizenship but was looked upon as someone from the Third World. Here I have links with workers, the unions, social movements, feminist groups; I went to the university; I feel at home. Bilbao has been a sort of resurrection for me. I became again what I was in Colombia. . . . Christian life is commitment to life itself."

I interrupted Anna: "What would you say, to those of us who don't have much faith that society can be fixed in this manner?" "If I lose my faith," she answered with an edge in her voice, "if I lose my capacity for social commitment, life is not worth anything. If I lose my belief in the resistance, that a different world is possible, I lose my identity. Since I was a child, faith has meant that we can build something different, we can *be* something else, understand life from some other vital premises." Anna's *embracing* provides her with an embodiment of utopia. She is attuned to what desperate people know—that perhaps an embrace can heal them. Embracing is a means to *sacarme el dolor* (to take the pain out of me), so that dreaming and healing are not just abstractions but embodied.

Agurtzane was a nineteen-year-old homeless girl who'd sit against the wall of a bank on the Gran Vía, across from the El Corte Inglés department store, shyly smiling and holding out her begging pan. She was known as *La Niña* (The Baby Girl), one of several beggars whose presence you couldn't avoid on any day along Bilbao's Gran Vía.

One day, against all street rules, I invited her for a drink in a nearby bar. She was surprised but came along. Her mother had died three years earlier and she had no family. "I need to do this to live," she said. I asked her what she thought about as she sat there. "I think about what I will do in the future, what I would like to be. I dream. . . ." "Aren't you embarrassed to beg?" "At the beginning it was humiliating, but you get used to it. Just because I'm on the street doesn't mean I'm worthless." Sometimes people give her a bill with comments like "You remind me of my daughter." Very occasionally a passerby hands her an envelope with several hundred euros. They give without wanting to know anything about her. At Christmas time in particular that isn't unusual. She wondered if "maybe it was because they'd made a promise, or had a wish, or a priest told them to do something generous to get rid of some guilt." Otherwise, it was the same people who handed her help. One man gave her something each time he passed with a *"Hola, guapa"* (Hello, pretty), and she'd give to him in return a *"Hola, campeón"* (Hello, champion). She wasn't supposed to talk, and she rarely did. "Money is the devil of this century," she said at one point.

Amid the busy pedestrian traffic on the Gran Vía, the sitting figure of La Niña creates a different space in which her living statue casts a presence outside society's ordinary rules and expectations. Passersby can look at her and wonder who she is, even give her a coin—while she remains an enigma with a smile, a silent and distant someone pedestrians can't avoid. Throwing a coin at her is like giving alms for a religious icon, or like throwing a coin into a fountain for good luck. Such nonreciprocity marks the elsewhere of an uncanny space ruled by the gift's logic of arbitrary donation. In the midst of the Gran Vía's capitalism, La Niña marks the existence of an *elsewhere*.

"Here Comes Everybody"

Go out any evening in Bilbao and you will find the streets overflowing with an avalanche of people wandering from bar to bar, greeting each other, bantering, making plans, showing off, watching, hooking up. Everyone is expected to be on the street—joining a *cuadrilla* or simply drinking and eating, sharing a presence. Parade through the Gran Vía, Casco Viejo, or elsewhere in the city and you will be immersed in a constant urban spectacle of people shopping, banking, or bar-hopping. Bilbao is not only about the one hundred and fifty years of ruthless industrial capitalism; it is also, more intimately, all about primordial communities of affect, intense social bonding, the soccer team, and the Joycean "Here Comes Everybody" of street enjoyment. Bilbao is first of all this society of collective desire and consumption.

I was asked to give a lecture on "affordable luxury" at the Architecture School. The concept of *affordable* luxury was new to me, but I soon realized that it struck at the heart of Bilbao's culture. Wealthy Bilbao is known for its *bilbainadas*—grandiose projects mocked for their extravagance and whose underlying premise appears to be the

People shopping at the Gran Vía.

Bilbainos at the Main Plaza of the Casco Viejo.

Getting out to the street from the underground metro.

Drinking in the street.

need for squandering wealth and public display. The *bilbainada* is a too-muchness that, except in Bilbao, is unaffordable. It is the city's alter-ego behavior, the extravagant antidote to the frustrations of an understated, modest lifestyle. Going for the Guggenheim Museum was for many a typical *bilbainada*. What for an outsider seems a braggard's exhibitionism is for Bilbainos ritual consumption.

As the saying goes, "The only virtue that is lacking for Bilbainos to be perfect is modesty." It goes with such grandiosity that there can be nothing greater in life than being from Bilbao. A typical joke goes: "Jeez, Patxi, the truth is that we from Bilbao are amazing, right?" "What the hell are you talking about, aren't you from Cuenca?" "C'mon, Patxi, I'm sorry, but those of us from Bilbao, we are born wherever it pleases our *cojones*." The Bilbao ready to conquer the world is reflected in the joke of the father counseling his son who is going to study abroad: "You know, son, when you meet people abroad you must show good manners and don't ask anyone where they are from." "Holy shit, Dad, why shouldn't I ask anyone where they're from?" "Well, because if they're from Bilbao, they will let you know, and if they are not, you don't want to embarrass them."

Everything in Bilbao appears to be "affordable luxury," but the notion led me to Zara in particular—the flagship store of the international fashion company Inditex that has become ubiquitous in the Gran Vía and elsewhere. "You want to know about current Bilbao? Forget the Guggenheim. Look at the Zara girls," Blanca, a successful business woman in her forties, told me. "In our generation, smart girls would go to the university for a career, to study art, or find a man. Nowadays, the smart and pretty ones go to work for Zara." She listed eight Zara shops in Bilbao and added as many others belonging to the same company with different names. Being a Zara girl was the coolest thing, Blanca commented; that's where you can best find the fetishistic quality of current Bilbao's bourgeois culture.

Zara's formula for success is simple: sell for a hundred dollars what Gucci and Armani sell for a thousand—not the same thing, but close enough so any difference can be ignored. Zara's copy is not only cheaper, it may also be more hip. Who wants a handbag worth four hundred euros when you can have a copy for fifty and then spend the balance on other more worthwhile things, such as traveling? Expensive "authenticity" smacks of the old-fashioned. Luxury should be now affordable to anyone—so long as one redefines luxury and restates the goals of desire.

Shopping at Zara in the Gran Vía.

I visited Antonia, a woman in her sixties in charge of a luxurious boutique next to the Hotel Carlton. "The Basque woman's fashion is nothing strident," she observed. Despite the excess of the *bilbainada*, even the aristocracy of Bilbao's business elite shunned the ostentatiousness of luxury. She recalled the figure of Cristóbal Balenciaga, the renowned Basque fashion designer installed in Paris who dressed not only the world's elite but Neguri's upper class as well. His primary quality was "sobriety," yet his fashion was also feminine and ultramodern. Dark suits are preferred in Bilbao. People show off only at weddings. "Before, fashion used to be a 'women's thing.' Now it's a powerful industry," she added. Youth follows international fashion in movies, TV, music. Fashion is becoming "faster," more industrial— "Here we have a *calm fashion*," Antonia concluded.

Balenciaga's invocaton was not accidental. Before moving to Paris and becoming "the master of us all," he used to exhibit his new clothes in Bilbao in the early 1930s while staying at the Hotel Carlton—when Hemingway was there to watch Vista Alegre's *corridas* and before Aguirre turned it into the headquarters to defend Bilbao from fascism. Balenciaga left for London and Paris in 1936, a victim of Donostia-San Sebastián's falling to Franco's army; Franco's wife had been Balenciaga's client since 1933. In the Paris where Balenciaga reigned as the grand maestro of haute couture (for Coco Chanel, he was the *only*

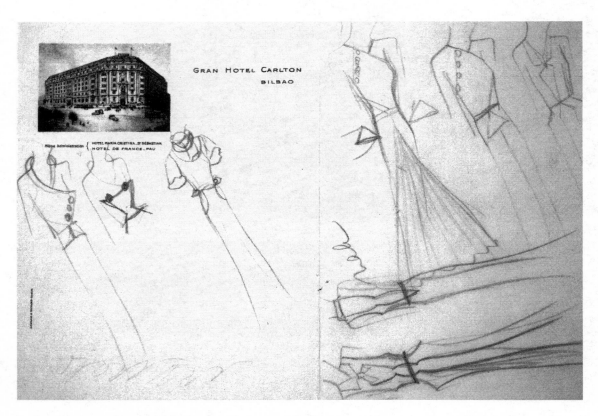

"In Bilbao, Balenciaga had a loyal following of well-to-do customers who bought his dresses every season. These sketches, drawn on Hotel Carlton stationery in 1932, show that he stayed at the Bilbao hotel, were he probably hosted one of his much-awaited fashion shows" (Arzalluz, *Cristóbal Balenciaga*, 120).

"Some of Cristóbal Balenciaga's designs incorporated other elements of traditional Basque costume, such as the *azpiko gona*, a long gathered wool underskirt, generally red, decorated with horizontal bands. This was the inspiration for Balenciaga's spectacular 1949 dress featured on the cover of the December issue of *Harper's Bazaar*." (Arzalluz, *Cristóbal Balenciaga*, 230).

couturier, for Christian Dior the conductor of the designers' orchestra), Walter Benjamin was writing in the late 1930s about the "metaphysics of fashion" for his unfinished opus on the Arcades—his study of "Modernity, the time of Hell." In its denial of death and decay, fashion is for Benjamin the modern "measure of time" in the new relationship between subject and object produced by the phantasmagoria of commodities. The master of ceremonies of this Parisian modernity consumed by the raging bonfire of vanities was the monklike high priest of fashion from Getaria, living a reclusive life and praying daily in a nearby church. No wonder he felt empty and wretched. As Roland Barthes put it, "the idea of fashion is antipathetic to the idea of sainthood." When his longtime lover, Wladzio d'Attainville, died suddenly in 1948, in his grief Balenciaga decided to enter a monastery. Everyone begged him not to until he was persuaded to continue working; his next collection was one of "mourning, all black, sad beyond belief." His models were ordered to walk down the salon's catwalk like robots, remote rather than appealing, with no smile or eye contact. Never fulfilled in his work, unable to reach perfection, his "pessimism" was noted by writers. He could be overtaken by terrible rage. In the only interview he ever granted, and only after his retirement, Balenciaga told Prudence Glynn, "Nobody knows what a hard métier it is, how killing is the work. Under all this luxury and glamour. Now, *c'est la vie d'un chien* [it's a dog's life]." He also told her that when the Germans took over France, Hitler wanted to transfer the capital of fashion to Berlin. "I said [to the Germans] he might as well take all the bullfighters to Berlin and try to train all the bullfighters there." While living the life of a dog, he was the bullfighter of haute couture, risking his art and his soul in the Paris plaza of high fashion.

Balenciaga's only redemption was the absolute formal purity of his work, even while luxury was the hallmark of his materials—velvet, lace, damask, tulle, satins. He abided by "the great rule that elimination is the secret of chic"—a rule he had lived by since 1938, a decade before Oteiza was engaged in Bilbao in his negative aesthetics of the *dis*-occupation of Euclidean forms. Such elimination of unnecessary detail made Balenciaga's work "simplicity dramatically presented." With Balenciaga, "the black is so black that it hits you like a blow." It became a cliché to insist on the pure "sculptural" form of his dresses; the couturier was not a decorator but a builder. He preferred structure and volume over decoration; his ambition in the 1950s was "to develop lines gradually" from year to year in a "quite clear progression from one to the next" and to "create classical, timeless models." Balenciaga, like Hemingway, found aesthetic inspiration in the *corrida* (which he didn't like) as he paid attention to "the boleros of the toreadors" and "derived much pleasure from . . . the *traje de luces*." Much of Balenciaga's creation was nourished by the tension between Spanish/Basque traditional designs and European high modernism.

In the end, just as Oteiza's formal abstraction and Hemingway's sacrificial realism concluded in impasse, Balenciaga found himself in a *desfase* (gap) and decided to retire in 1968. By the end of the 1960s, the industry of the exclusive production of high fashion had undergone drastic changes. The rigorous sculptural lines of Balenciaga's art beyond ornament were becoming dated by the 1960s. "A woman, she is not a cube, she is curves," a former Balenciaga model, who set up her own boutiques, complained in September of 1967 in the magazine *Elle.* Oteiza liked to quote Cézanne: "that man you see there is not a man, it is a cylinder." Balenciaga saw and turned a woman into a "cube." Much like Warhol and Koons rebelled against abstract modernist masters such as Oteiza and Chillida, so did the younger generation of fashion designers rebel against Balenciaga. Couture no longer depended on an elite cosmopolitan private clientele; the commercial notion of "confection" or mass production for department stores and wholsesale buyers took over. This was the era of ready-to-wear *prêt-à-porter* designs produced by commercial firms.

Zara, the ubiquitous brand in Bilbao, represents Joyce's catholic principle of the "Here Comes Everybody" of fashion. As I visited luxurious boutique shops at the Elliptical Plaza to find out the difference between "affordable" and nonaffordable luxury, Miren, the owner of one such boutique of children's clothing, who can sell a dress for two- to three-year-olds for 1,200 to 1,500 euros, made it explicit: "Luxury is for privileged people. 'Luxury' is one thing, and 'affordable' another. Luxury is neither necessary nor affordable. You must have all sorts of things, but we always say, 'that was a luxury,' meaning it was not absolutely necessary." Currently there is less luxury than in the past, Miren observed, and added, "Zara has nothing to do with our business—with luxury shops. The Zara people come here to the sales. In large cities you have luxury shops in one quarter, and Zara shops in another, but not here in Bilbao." She says Zara has "cheapened" the city because "people who go to Zara are without culture, people who delude themselves into thinking that Zara equals Gucci, who believe something they buy for fifteen to twenty euros is the same as something that cost you six hundred in a luxury shop." What bothers Miren is the "lie" implied in wearing a "fake." Ana, a classy bourgeois woman in her sixties, agreed with Miren: "I am against so much Zara. Now you see the Gran Vía filled with lower-class people from the Left Bank coming to Zara. It is clothing to use and throw away. Zara is making every city the same by putting its shops in the downtowns and driving out local businesses. They are distorting fashion."

The secret of Zara's success is the relationship between quality, price, and service—quick service at a low price that responds to immediate demand. "Say you put out the color pink as fashionable and it doesn't sell—we change it immediately," María, a Zara girl, told me. She had worked in both Gucci and Zara. What is also fashionable is to have something "authentic" from Gucci, say a belt, and the rest Zara. At the end of July, Zara changes fashion for the fall and winter; at the end of January for the spring and summer. You can have jeans worth forty-five euros, but also nineteen euros. María is a supervisor in charge of hiring girls for Zara: "You have to make them fall in love with the shop, like I did," she remarked. When deciding fashion, they look first at what women want, then at children, and finally men. Zara girls are in part like mannequins for their products by wearing themselves the clothes they sell. Just as all boys want to be soccer players, girls want to be Zara girls. María earns three times more than her mother, Begoña, who has been working in the El Corte Inglés department store for thirty-six years.

"El Corte Inglés was the Zara of thirty years ago when it began in May of 1969," Begoña told me. It is a grand warehouse where you have everything, not only clothes as in Zara. It presented a stiff competition for the shops of Casco Viejo. "Some thought it would not work, but the public took to it wonderfully." El Corte Inglés was open from 9:00 to 1:30 and from 3:00 to 7:30, so "you could not be here if you were married." She fought with her husband because of that. "During my generation we wanted what we had been lacking: perfumes, jewelry, lingerie. . . . We waited for the sales. Nowadays youth doesn't come as often; they spend [their money] on leisure, in traveling, free time."

"Calm fashion" is how Antonia defined Bilbao's style. But under the calm there is raging passion stoked by the luxurious fetish object—affordable or not. Silvia runs Loewe, a classy boutique shop at the Elliptical Plaza where she sells leather and animal skins that "are never cold." Besides their "warmth," Silvia mentioned the "fetishistic" and "erotic" quality of leather objects, such as high heels. She displays shoes and purses made of snake skin. Her handbags have a 160-year history. One of them was selling for 2,200 euros. People come in just to ask about the price and ponder the object, she told me. In the summer of 2013 Loewe closed its doors and moved to El Corte Inglés. Louis Vuitton, installed at the Gran Vía in November of 2008, also closed in April of 2014 to be replaced by Starbucks.

"Luxury doesn't work very well in Bilbao," said the spokersperson for jewelry store Suaréz at the Gran Vía. But affordable luxury does, a notion that, we could add, extends to the very notion of "culture" in postmodernity. It's the ability to imitate that matters—the turning of a fake into the canon. Failure in authenticity is precisely the success. The Zara model that turns worthlessness into value (objects in whose value we no longer *believe* but are the new objects of desire) exemplifies the impasses and promises of postmodern consumerist culture. It recalls the former *Vogue* editor Diana Vreeland's words: "Give 'em what they never knew they wanted."

A new culture of leisure is replacing the traditional work ethic of Bilbao's capitalist entrepreneurialism. I interviewed Rubén, a researcher of leisure patterns, who provided me with numbers: in the grandparents' generation, 58 percent of people found satisfaction in working, and 16 percent in leisure activities; in the parents' generation, 41 percent found satisfaction in work, and 44 percent in leisure; in their children and grandchildren's generation, 70 percent find satisfaction in leisure and only 19 percent in work. Such a shift is perhaps the best index of the emergence of a post-Oedipal society in which the big Others of religion, politics, and culture are receding in favor of a permissive society where leisure is the dominant value.

Urbanites once romanticized traditional lifestyles and landscapes of farmers and fishermen. But nowadays the old *baserriak* (farms) have been turned into chalets and residential houses where vacationers find refuge from urban life. In Bilbao's coastal ports, hundreds of recreational boats have displaced fishing boats. The remaining commercial fishermen are now mostly from sub-Saharan Africa. Affordable luxury has replaced romanticism. Changes in luxury's affordability lead to others in ideology and forms of desire. Occasionally one reads in a newspaper that one-third of Bilbainos, or some 36,500 households and 90,000 persons, live "at the limit" of poverty (defined at below 900 euros per month). Whether or not they have the money, they have bought into the ideology of affordable luxury. The European debt crisis that has affected Spain and the Basque Country after 2007 has put a question mark on the continuity of such a lifestyle. The frontier between what is necessary and what is superfluous, authentic and fake, what we really believe in and what we don't, affects not only fashion and consumerism but the most fundamental aspects of culture, politics, and identity. A new structure of desire is being called for.

Bilbao's new urban spectacle rests on the premise of a new economy, the postindustrial "city of services," with Zamudio's Technology Park becoming the infrastructural support for the new industries' technological innovation and architecture its new cultural imperative. What wrapping paper is to a boutique object, architecture is to a city's aura. It is an aura that can make miracles in real estate: three years after the Guggenheim opened, the value of the apartments around it had risen 74 percent. The ritual of packaging is central to the sale of the object. In boutiques, a purchase is first wrapped with silk paper, then put inside a paper bag, then placed within a shiny larger plastic bag displaying, in big letters, the boutique's name. This culture of layered wrapping and packaging, like Chinese boxes or Russian dolls, is an allegory of the newly diffused postmodern self—boundaries between interiors and exteriors.

Oteiza and Balenciaga had to wait for Gehry to see their ovoid variants and sculptural designs take on the wrapped and voluptuous shapes of architectural dress. If Balenciaga could create a new silhouette for the female body by dressing it as pure geometric form, Gehry would turn *la Bilbao* into a new canon of fashion and beauty by wrapping her in architecture. Almost a hundred cities would contact New York requesting from the Guggenheim "another Bilbao." Bilbao was now the canon, the desired city.

San Mamés stadium during a game.

Play It Again, Joe

Beyond the street life, shopping, fashion, urban consumption, and architectural spectacle, there is one arena of play that particularly transfixes the city by generating collective passion and enjoyment—soccer in San Mamés, at the end of the Indautxu neighborhood, a twelve-minute's walk from the central Elliptical Plaza through Licenciaado Poza. Currently Bilbao is all for soccer, imported from Great Britain during the period of industrialization at the end of the nineteenth century. But there is also pelota, a handball game played in the fronton court—the traditional recreational space in every Basque town, including Bilbao in the past. A variant of pelota known worldwide is jai alai. The fronton traditionally and the soccer stadium currently are the dominant playfields that teach citizens forms of action and subjectivity—a quality space inside of which imagination and desire move and project themselves back and forth with the ball. The cosmos is renewed again and again by Chance while the subject confronts the ball, as if it were Mallarmé's throw of the dice, and is once again constituted in a timeless game.

In such fields of triumph or defeat, of chance overflowing in a purgatory of desire, the players are heroes idolized by the fans. One such hero was Telmo Zarra, the greatest Bilbao Athletic Club soccer player ever. He scored 337 goals in the 1940s and early 1950s. He died a legendary figure on February 23, 2006. The day after his death, the front page of *El Correo* carried the photo of the two captains of the team, Julen Guerrero and Joseba Etxeberria, placing a flower wreath in front of Zarra's bust at the Lezama Athletic's training ground. Several pages described the players' moving homage.

Two days later, on Sunday afternoon, San Mamés Stadium was filled to capacity as the crowd paid its respects before the Athletic-Villarreal game—a historic moment turned once again into a life-or-death test. If the team failed, it implied the unthinkable—Athletic's almost inevitable descent from first to second division. There was only one way to pay real homage to Zarra that day—to win. The players had sworn to winning. Before the game, the crowd's prolonged ovation gave tribute to Zarra's widow. A minute of impressive silence followed; the public, eyes downcast, stood as one in Zarra's memory. The air was heavy with the overwhelming memories of Athletic's past greatness, each second pulsating with the emotion of forty thousand fans bound together by that solemnity of feeling and the palpable concern for the team's ultimate fate. The fans had been exhorted to fill every seat, since a single empty place seemed an offense to Zarra's memory. The club's entire history was at stake.

During the first forty minutes, the game was scoreless, with Villarreal creating the best scoring opportunities. Then suddenly, San Mamés erupted in a frenzy—Athletic's forward, Aduriz, scored a goal and we jumped to our feet, arms extended and screaming "GOOOOL!!!" The players embraced each other. The team captain, Etxeberria, raised his fist to an ecstatic public. The miracle was happening—Athletic was going to be saved. Zarra's legacy was being reenacted. His tradition of greatness would survive. San Mamés overflowed with relief.

The only problem—there were still fifty minutes left to play. Two minutes later Villarreal scored its goal. It was the apocalypse. While their players celebrated, there was dead silence in the stadium—disbelief and denial. Was it a goal, was it a goal? people kept asking, refusing to believe what had happened. Soon the ball was in the middle of the field again. A few minutes later, the referee signaled half-time. We fans remained silent, anxious for the second half to begin. When it did, an emboldened Athletic attacked with determination but was unable to produce a goal. Time was running out when suddenly Aduriz stood alone before the Villareal goalkeeper. The magic was about to happen again! But he missed. "Wooooo," we roared in desolation, followed immediately by shouts of "Athleeeeeeeeetic! Athleeeeetic!" It was an act of exorcism, a pitiful invocation, an agonic prayer to the gods unconcerned that Athletic might lose. If only that great opportunity had been converted into a goal! We still had to continue believing in the miracle that would honor Zarra, uphold history, and save the Athletic.

Athletic redoubled its attacks. Could it be possible? Minute by minute, time was running out until the ninety minutes were up. The referee added four minutes of overtime. There was still hope for the impossible salvation goal. Minute ninety-three, and a penalty was awarded in Athletic's favor! Elated, we jumped to our feet—penalty shots are almost certain goals. Orbaiz, who two weeks earlier had scored on a similar penalty, was going to shoot. The anticipation was excruciating. The referee whistled. Orbaiz advanced, stroked the ball low and to the right, and their goalkeeper, Viera, stopped it! Wails filled the stadium; a feeling of pity spread for the player who had missed the kick, depriving the city of its victory celebration. Rhythmical and agonizing shouts—"Athleeeetic!!! Athleeeetic!!!"— echoed through San Mamés. A minute later, the referee signaled the end. It was the stuff of tragedy.

There was a coda. The players, crushed by not winning and facing a historic category descent, moved to the center of the field to applaud the public, which replied with a standing ovation! The players were applauding their fans for their faith in the team, begging them to remain loyal, asking forgiveness. The fans were reciprocating with a pledge of unconditional support, signaling the players not to give up.

The *Correo*'s headline on Monday, under the photo of a dejected Orbaiz lying on the field with his head in his hands, read: "Suffering and sadness." A second headline: "Frustration takes hold of San Mamés." And a third, lamenting "I'm sorry," under a photo of Orbaiz unable to stand up, supported by his teammate Iraola, his arms in the form of a cross.

After the game, we vacated the stadium in orderly fashion and walked away in silence. Too much had happened. As if in search of some "normality," it was time to remind ourselves that "it is all a game," time to erase the traces of intense emotion, elation, hysteria, tears evident on peoples' faces. The previous Sunday, in another climactic moment when Athletic scored in Santander in the final moments and gained the points it desperately needed, many fans, asked how they had reacted, replied simply, "I began to cry." But this time, leaving San Mamés without the crucial victory, it was time to return, somehow, to ordinary life. It was Carnival in Bilbao that Sunday. But the true carnival of emotion and desire had already taken place. All else was afterthought.

The following day, a multitude of soccer fans packed the sanctuary of the Virgin of Begoña to say goodbye to Zarra. The eulogies stressed the man's goodness, humility, religiosity, gentle touch, courage, and determination. Everywhere he was presented as the embodiment of Athletic's values. A minute of silence for him had been observed during all of that Sunday's games in every stadium in Spain. Players of mythical stature who had played against him, including Gento and Amancio, attended the Begoña ceremony. At its conclusion, an homage was paid to Zarra outside the basilica. His grandson held the vessel containing his ashes, surrounded by his widow and the authorities; a dancer performed a traditional *aurresku* for him; somebody shouted "*Gora, Telmo!*" (Long live Telmo!), and we all echoed "*Gora!*"

But there still was one written homage that, among many others, took precedence in honoring Zarra's memory—that of the legendary goalkeeper José Ángel Iribar, perhaps the one Athletic player who comes closest to Zarra's stature. In a column entitled "Zarra's Greatest Goal," Iribar described a game in Valencia, in which the teams were tied, and Zarra broke free with the ball to reach the goal posts unimpeded, prepared to score easily. But instead of firing at the net, which was his task as player, he deliberately cast the ball away! He'd realized that Valencia's goalkeeper was lying on the field injured, and he decided to pay respect to him by not scoring. In another game away from home, also tied, he had done the same, to the chagrin of his teammates who became furious at him. In both cases, Zarra later scored another goal and Athletic won. *Everything* in soccer is about that final GOOOOL!!! But it seems there was something, for Zarra, even more important. It took a genius like him to be beyond all the rules of the game and have the authority to transgress all the expectations. He was the maker of the magic of the final goal, and he was the one who could forsake it as well. In a crazy act of self-elimination, Zarra gave up the power to make the goal, win, and bring his audience's intense anticipation to an ecstatic end. That goal was the conclusion of desire, the *exceptional point* that gave sense and satisfaction to the entire play. But incredibly Zarra decided against scoring.

Desire had rules even higher than victory—seemed to be Zarra's lesson. There was the preference for desisting in the effort to score. Zarra had become the Balenciaga of soccer who could fashion art by elimination. This was formal excess to the point of transgressive self-cancellation, its classical ritual context being the potlatch-like *need* for loss. It was that "*loss of meaning* that Zen calls a *satori*" or enlightenment. It was as if Zarra was abiding by Beckett's discovery: "the wisdom of all the sages . . . consists not in the satisfaction but in the ablation of desire." Zarra had enacted the essential lesson for my post-ETA generation—you must first lose to win, liberation may require the loss of meaning of what seemed most important. In his desistance and indifference to losing, his going beyond desire, Zarra had achieved his "greatest goal"—the glory of scoring, deliberately, the *non*-goal.

It was the end of July 2006 and the hour had arrived to leave Bilbao after half a year of immersion in its day-to-day affairs: eating and drinking in its bars, walking its streets, talking to and interviewing the people, reimagining a new city. I put my suitcases in the car Josu had lent me and took the A-8 highway in the direction to Donostia-San Sebastián. I pressed the button on Josu's stereo system and his CD with Mozart's Coronation Mass began to play. From the highway I could see the city down in the valley; the intense nework of relationships, obligations, fantasies weaved during the last months was being dissolved as I was leaving Bilbao. Suddenly the majestic Gloria in C major changed register and proceeded to the section *qui tollis peccata mundi* in minor key. I got a lump in my throat and felt unable to breath. It was one of those "stranded objects," emotional sediments from my past that I could not control. It was perhaps the liberation Dante and Joyce must have felt when leaving the Purgatory of the city.

Brecht's final command in his "Bilbao Song" could only be: *Hey Joe, play that old song they always played.* Bilbao—city of shackles and swords. *Villa invicta*, reborn from Gernika's ashes and the ruins of the Left Bank. City that, dethroning the supremacy of Capital, shouts: "Desire is the Real!" *Finnegans Wake.* Here Comes Everybody.

Play it again, Joe.

"The word is out that miracles still occur. . ." And in Bilbao, that miracle has been Frank Gehry's Guggenheim, seen here through the lens of Louise Bourgeois's *Maman*.

BOOK III
PARADISE

"The Word Is Out That Miracles Still Occur . . ."

". . . and that a major one is happening here," proclaimed the cover of the *New York Times Magazine.* "'Have you been to Bilbao?' In architectural circles, the question has acquired the status of a shibboleth. Have you seen the light? Have you seen the future?"

If you want to see the light, go to Bilbao's downtown axis, the Gran Vía, and walk to its center, the Elliptical Plaza. From there, head toward the Nervión River through Alameda Rekalde or Iparraguirre, where Frank Gehry's creation, its curbed forms draped in titanium, appear like a magnet at the waterside, emerging sixteen meters below the level of the rest of the city. Look at the orthogonal, blue, Fritz Lang's *Metropolis*-inspired limestone blocks, lending gravity to the building's dizzying shapes—the 24,000 square meters of sinuous glass curtain walls, the titanium and stone forms fully integrated into the city's urban design, the complex curves designed with the aid of computers, the towering rooftop shaped like a blossoming rose. As you approach Gehry's cathedral and leave behind Jeff Koons's enormous floral sculpture *Puppy*, walk down a broad ramp of stone stairs descending to the entrance. Pass the main entrance and enter the radiant atrium, fifty-five meters high, looking out on the river, and you will be immersed in streams of light glinting through the metal flower skylight at the rooftop. From the atrium, which brings together the three levels of exhibition galleries, you can reach the canopy-covered terrace. A flight of stairs will take you up the sculptural atrium tower where hanging walkways connect the nineteen galleries. The main gallery, directly across from the atrium, is the Fish Gallery, a space 30 meters wide by 130 meters long that slides beneath the La Salve Bridge and ends at the tower, as if embracing it. It is here you enter the maze of Serra's permanent exhibit of torqued steel constructions. Be careful. You must still return to the atrium and let yourself inhabit this pleasure dome, the translucent building on the river. This is the miracle in Bilbao.

But what *is* the event of the Bilbao Guggenheim? At its most obvious, everyone knows it is the flagship building of the city's ambitious 1-billion-euro urban renewal plan focused on improvement of the port and new transportation facilities—Foster's sleek subway and the expansion of the airport by Calatrava. This plan is concentrated on the Abandoibarra riverfront and includes the office tower by Cesar Pelli, the Euskalduna Conference and Concert Hall by Federico Soriano and Dolores Palacios, the Araka Isozaki Towers, the Sheraton Hotel by Ricardo Legorreta, the University of Deusto Library by Rafael Moneo, and the University of the Basque Country Auditorium by Álvaro Siza.

As impressive as these projects are, they don't fully capture the force of architectural evangelist Herbert Muschamp's proclamation, "Miracle in Bilbao!" To understand what he meant one has to return to that rainy evening in Bilbao when Muschamp, while writing notes in his hotel, looked out the window and saw a woman alone, "wearing a long, white dress with matching white pumps, and . . . a pearlescent handbag." He wondered, "Was her date late? Had she been stood up?" Then he found the answer—"When I looked back a bit later, she was gone. And I asked myself, Why can't a building capture a moment like that? . . . I realized that the reason I'd had that thought was that I'd just come from such a building. And that the building I just came from was *the reincarnation of Marilyn Monroe*." The word is out that miracles still occur . . .

Marilyn Monroe reincarnated! A new Ariadne, a new Virgin of Begoña! Something extraordinary had taken place in Bilbao, having to do with architecture and writing, and which forced the spectator to see beyond what was there in front of the eyes. Muschamp noted that both Marilyn and Gehry had reclined on the same couch while consulting the same analyst. The building, like the analytical couch, allowed for all sorts of free associations: "It's a bird, it's a plane, it's Superman. It's a ship, an artichoke, the miracle of the rose." But it is the embodiment of the building as Marilyn that really mattered to Muschamp: "what twins the actress and the building is that both of them stand for an American style of freedom . . . voluptuous, emotional, intuitive and exhibitionist." He was visualizing the iconic image of Marilyn in *The Seven Year Itch* when she lets her skirt fly up in the air. There are countless depictions of Marilyn in films, plays, television, dance, and opera, and in the more than five hundred books written about her. But her

Marilyn Monroe statue in Chicago based on the iconic scene from *The Seven Year Itch* (1955). Photo by David Brent

über-mythical dimensions had to wait until Gehry's Bilbao creation for her *temple* to be erected. "The miraculous occurrence," concluded Muschamp, "is the extravagant optimism that enters the outlook of those who have made the pilgrimage." The eyes have been transfixed; the building is also a woman; the spectator has been transformed in its most intimate architecture.

"You are, Nervión, the history of the Town / you her past and her future / you are memory always turning into hope," wrote Unamuno. But he couldn't imagine a future in which his river would become the guardian of a new sanctuary on the very site where sailors sang a *Salve* of thanks to the Virgin Mother of Begoña—the last and first spot from where they saw her basilica on the hill as they sailed down and up the river. Marilyn also wrote of a river in one of her poems. Gehry's Marilynesque building at La Salve Bridge would enshrine again what Begoña had been throughout the centuries—the embodiment of "maternal Bilbao."

The rebirth of Eros—this is what Freud called for in the midst of the suicidal European militarism between the two world wars. This rebirth was what Marilyn represented in the McCarthyist years of the 1950s when she became the symbol of American freedom, a "combination of sensuality and spirituality . . . a revolt against the puritan mores associated with the anti-Communist movement." This was the period in which the atomic bomb had become a national fetish on the basis of which a massive "radioactive nation-building" was taking place. The bomb produced not only a new apocalyptic imaginary but reorganized the human senses—people were exposed to nuclear tests to measure the impact of the nuclear bomb on their bodies. As much as technological, the effects were cultural and sensorial. It was also in Nevada, where a test site for the army's nuclear experiments was located, that *The Misfits*, starring Marilyn, written by Arthur Miller and directed by John Huston, was filmed. Nevada, wrote Miller, "became a mirror to me, but one in which nothing was reflected but a vast sky." It was filmed in the Nevada desert near the southern shore of that paradise,

> . . . past Reno, Pyramid Lake's
> blue Altar, pure water in Nevada sands'
> brown wasteland scratched by tires.

Marilyn refuses to be a metaphor, a male projection, a symbolic proxy for some manly Absolute. She is the real deal—in body and figure. She was the "gift of life" for men around her, wrote Miller. As Dean MacCannell put it, above all, "Marilyn Monroe Was Not a Man." "Being

I'm looking for my lover.
It's good they told me what
the moon was when I was a child.
That silent river which stirs
and swells itself with whatever passes
over it
wind, rain, great ships.
I love the river—never unmoored
by anything.
It's quiet now.
And the silence is alone
except for the thunderous rumbling of
things unknown
distant drums very present
but for the piercing of screams. . . .

Marilyn Monroe, *Fragments: Poems, Intimate Notes, Letters*, 72-73.

with her, people want not to die," Miller said. The "openly sexual" Marilyn is "sheer cultural terrorism" for a Puritan culture fixated on military power. The potential she represents in her iconic forms "is more powerful than the atomic bombs that were being tested in the Nevada desert precisely coincident with her career." MacCannell links the time-space of Marilyn's figure to Klee/Benjamin's "Angel of History." Her gift is "to raise the possibility of a purely feminine figure operating at the level of history itself, a powerful feminine figure which submerges in its plenitude all the positive and negative attributes of 'femininity.'" She can be seen as "a kind of breakdown" in the relation between the sexes and her wager is to be, in her trangression against both men and women, the promise of a new kind of "intersubjective imagination" between them and a new sensorial alignment.

Marilyn Monroe and Arthur Miller.

As Ken Russell would portray her in his 1975 hallucinatory movie, *Tommy*, Marilyn is the miracle-working sacred icon that will heal the sensory deprivation of the deaf, mute, and blind protagonist of The Who's 1969 rock opera. Marilyn's erotic grace and the rebirth of the autistic Tommy were, in Pete Townshend's words, nothing but his hero's restoration of "the use of his senses." At the church devoted to Marilyn, the frenzied priest flashes her image and Pete Townshend and Eric Clapton play "Eyesight to the Blind"—"She has got the power to heal you, never fear." It was the effect of Beatrice on Dante who, "confounded by my blindness" and, after pleading with her to "restore my eyes that were the gates," finds in Paradise that "Beatrice drove out every speck / clouding my vision with her splendid eyes / whose radiance spread a thousand miles and more."

But how would Marilyn have felt in the land of *Guernica* and in her Bilbao temple? Remember Gernika—the site of the trauma—and remember the outsized Thomas Krens wanting nothing but "a heroic museum for a heroic painting." Gehry thought of designing a special space in his building, labeled "the chapel," with the sole purpose of housing *Guernica*. It was in Bayreuth where Hitler, inflamed with Wagner's music, decided "Operation Magic Fire" in support of Franco, setting in motion his Condor Legion toward Gernika. As in memory of that fateful ring of fire of the Nibelung, Yves Klein's *Fire Fountain* was installed on the museum's river side, a fire wall of five geysers parallel to the building and emerging from the water that surrounds the eastern flank.

Marilyn must have known about *Guernica*, for she was a committed leftist who in 1956 risked her Hollywood career by standing next to Miller the day before they got married, when he was subpoenaed by the House Un-American Activities Committee. Miller was guilty only regarding the Spanish Civil War: "I have always been, since my student days, in the thirties, a partisan of Republican Spain. I am quite proud of it," he told the committee. Two of Miller's classmates died in the Spanish war fighting the fascists, and Miller carried the burden of his own decision not to fight in Spain "like a kind of sinfulness." Miller and Marilyn sided with the Republican loss, a tragedy whose emblem was *Guernica*. The defender of Gernika, Aguirre, had made his marriage vows and had sworn to surrender his life for the Republic by kneeling in front of the icon of the Virgin of Begoña. Miller had proclaimed his loyalty to the Spanish Republic in the presence of Marilyn, his muse and his soon-to-be wife.

"The word is out that miracles still occur. Have you been to Bilbao? Have you seen the light? Have you seen the future? It is the miracle of the rose! It is the reincarnation of Marilyn Monroe!" Muschamp is well aware that only fools can write like this about their projected visions—unless there is an obvious literary model for his "miracle of the rose": Jean Genet's hallucinatory novel the *Miracle of the Rose*. The presence of Genet in Muschamp was made obvious the previous year in another *New York Times* review he wrote of the Macy's Flower Show, forty truckloads of flowers that became a "true miracle on 34th Street," "a vision of paradise" that evokes Bataille's ideas of excess, but is above all an Eden "that might have been dreamed up by Jean Genet." For Muschamp the magic of the flower show is such that all you need is a new scent or scarf from Macy's for you to be "transformed into a lily, an orchid, a bird of paradise." It is Genet who authorizes Muschamp to enter such an enchanted garden in New York as well as to render the rose-shaped roof of Gehry's Bilbao building into a miracle.

In a massive study of Genet's work, Sartre provides the keys to his artistic and existential biography, and by extension to Muschamp's appropriation of his aesthetics. Sartre finds that the art of the impostor and aspiring saint Genet consists in rejecting history by transforming it into mythical categories. Turned prostitute, his erotic objects are pure symbols, he prefers the gesture to the flesh—like the fetishist who is more interested in a woman's shoes than in the woman

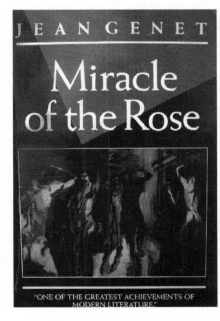

Cover of the book by Jean Genet.

199

herself. Events and people become archetypes. Theft is for him "a religious ceremony," "a transfiguration"—the thief/writer raises to a sacred temporality, time becomes liturgical, reality is achieved by repetition as in the archaic societies. As time disappears and the transition to timelessness is marked by the narrative substitution of the present for the past tense, "an event is nothing other than a transubstantiation," and "a *miracle* has taken place." These are poetic miracles effected by the magnifying aestheticism of the power of language; in such linguistic alchemy naming changes being. Sartre characterizes this as "Platonic idealism." A word becomes magically an idea by identifying with a category and sharing its entire history, and thus "reproducing what might be called a sacred Platonic drama." All is needed for this linguistic alchemy to work, so that "each creature is the word incarnate," is "the magical action of analogy." One of those terms procuring a "miracle" of transubstantiation is a rose—"I even tried, me too, to be a rose!" exclaims one of Genet's characters. "Harcamone is a rose," Genet writes about the murderer protagonist of his novel. For the Genet who wrote from prison "there is a close relationship between flowers and convicts"; the poet's alchemy turns the metaphor into the *real*, as when Lispector writes that "[a]n intimate and intense relationship was established between myself and the flower," and she can say from her most real experience that "[t]he rose is the feminine flower that gives of itself all," that "[i]ts perfume is an insane mystery" and that "the rose isn't *it*. It is *she.*" For Genet and Lispector, their perception can only be described as "the miracle of the rose."

The "Platonist" premises underlying such philosophy of concept, turning the analogy of naming into being, makes Sartre compare Genet's thinking to the "thinking of the medieval clerk." For this Genet who "was cast into an artificial medieval world," there is a great model of medieval Platonism whose work is based on poetic analogy: Dante, considered rightly "Plato's poet." Whether Harcamone is a rose, a building reincarnates Marilyn, or Beatrice is Dante's guide, "it is art," concludes Sartre, "art alone which [in these writers as in Plato] links truth to the myth."

Platonism is pivotal in the intellectual history of my generation—to grasp the paradises we lost as well as to regain the paradises that will always be with us, either through art or through contemporary thought. Dante provides a supreme illustration of Platonism in literary history, as do many other great contemporary writers. One can adopt a skeptical position toward such Platonic visions, as I also did in the past. But how can we ignore the poetic value of Dante's use of Beatrice to prop his literary work? Dante's magical result was the transfiguration of Beatrice into the inspiration of his masterpiece: "The whole of Dante's work suggests that Beatrice remained the liberating force of his lyrical powers, because she had formerly presented to his gaze that excruciating beauty possessed by some bodies which promise more than a body can hold and something other than a body can give." Dante's poetic genius makes Beatrice a living being, whose radiant and direct reality fills the space of his writing. Dante loved Beatrice, yet her primary influence over him had to do not with sexual desire but with her power of inspiration for his work, even long after she was dead. Beatrice *qua* woman existed, yet the revelation of Beatrice *qua* muse was the poet's creation. Baudelaire told his muse Marie, "You are the part of myself that a spiritual essence has shaped." How we conceptualize Beatrice's role in Dante's creation—how we view the bridge between eros and art—has relevance for Muschamp's bold assertion that Marilyn was an inspiration behind Gehry's masterpiece.

Beatrice Addressing Dante, William Blake (1824–1827).

Such Dantean transfigurations have to do with mimetic realism. They are instances of "the astounding paradox of what is called Dante's realism"—that he saw images of the essential beings of real personages eternally fixed. In his classic study, Erich Auerbach views this as a case of "figural thinking," whereby earthly events are fulfilled in a celestial world. But in Dante the earthly figure retains all its *real* historical traits (rather than symbolic personification). Daringly, postmodern Muschamp treats Marilyn not as symbol or allegory, but as a historical figure. As Beatrice was the true reality in Dante's figural thinking, Marilyn also, observes MacCanell, "insisted that she be read—as a *figure.*"

Dante's religious heresy was identifying "the incarnate body of Christ in Beatrice," bridging nature and grace, the Goddess and the real woman. Gehry's architectural heresy is, for Muschamp, the transfiguration of a building into the embodiment of Marilyn. Like Beatrice for Dante, Marilyn's life "signifies not only itself but at the same time another, which it predicts and confirms, without prejudice to the power of its concrete reality here and now." The link between the two worlds is not logical or chronological but takes place within a larger aesthetic horizon, also illustrated by Genet's work. Dante's poetic metaphors are not ornament but lead to the concrete, and his horrific metamorphoses, like those provoked by Gehry's architecture, are not ancient fables but enter "into present reality, for in every living man a metamorphosis may lie hidden." Far from being the artist's illusions of remote beauty, Beatrice and Marilyn may become real figures that are a revelation of the powers of the artist, replicated in the reader or the viewer—"Here revealed truth and its poetic form are one." Both Dante and Gehry express an awakening. Their work has the character of conjuration; they are testimony to the reality of artistic mimesis with reference to the actuality of events. Both go beyond human tragedy, which postulates a happy beginning and an unhappy ending, to reverse it into their opposite, human comedy.

The only thing Muschamp overlooked is that it was Bilbao herself—her portentous river, her apocalypse in Gernika, her ruins on the Left Bank, her "miracles" engraved in the Bilbaoans' bodies—that made Gehry's building thaumaturgical. The Cinderella narrative of Gehry's "Lourdes" required that it be placed in a distanced and dangerous jungle amid unsophisticated natives. But Gehry, for whom the relationship with the client is most decisive for his work, had a far different perception. Bilbao was his "idea of paradise," he'd repeat in his interviews. "Why did you fall in love with Bilbao?" I asked him. "Let me tell you why," he answered, then excused himself to return with his wife. "Here is why, because she is from Bilbao." As they saw my surprise, they explained that her Panamanian parents were originally from Santander, an hour to the west of Bilbao. Gehry was saying that his love for his wife, his true Beatrice, was also his love for Bilbao, giving shape to his masterpiece.

Amid the ruins of Bilbao, overwhelmed by her toughness, Gehry felt most at home. His Marilyn Monroe was not Brecht/Weill's *Happy End* in some American dreamscape Mahagonny city. His building, his Bilbao song, would be the embodiment of a city's trauma, a building that shouts: let us mock the wound of history; let us make an architecture that recreates a whale, a galleon, a mermaid; let us build a temple that reincarnates Marilyn Monroe!—a new twenty-first century goddess for a city resurrected.

Maialen's Bilbao Song

It is December 13, 2009, the twelfth anniversary of the signing of the Bilbao Guggenheim contract, and some fifteen thousand people are gathered in the new center to listen to the *bertsolariak*, the Basque troubadours. The exhibition center had opened in April 2004, on the ruins of Altos Hornos, five miles from downtown Bilbao. From ten in the morning to eight in the evening, an enraptured audience of fans immerse themselves in the improvised songs of the oral poets. With no musical instrument but their voices, they sing impromptu *bertso* strophes that follow strict patterns of rhythm and rhyme. If you want deep song, this is the event.

Audience listening to the *bertsolariak* at the BEC.

The only criterion for poetic meaning is to create it. Each time the *bertsolari* is asked to improvise a *bertso* for an audience, an abyss of silence and emptiness opens during the long seconds that precede the singing. Every listener feels the tremor of what is at stake—how will the singer break the silence, how will she fill the void of language and images with language and images alone? The ten to fifteen seconds the bertsolari requires to begin—deep in thought, looking into the distance, microphone in hand, shifting from foot to foot, sniffing the air—become an eternity. Finally the solitary voice rises slowly and the audience breathes again; the universe is once more *created* from chance, verbal play, miraculous homophonies, and a bombastic destruction of language.

Unai Iturriaga improvised this strophe, explaining "the abyss" of the bertsolari's risky art each time he faces the microphone:

Unai Iturriaga singing.

Amildegi bat zeure oinetan	An abyss opens before you
bertso berri bakoitzean	when you sing a new bertso
handiagoa, sakonagoa	larger and deeper it grows with each breath
den uste hori lantzean	in your mind, ever more profound
inoiz sentituarazen zaitu	sometimes, just sometimes,
bazeunde legez etxean	it makes you feel right at home
inoiz pentsatu izan duzuna	and other times you wonder
zer ote da erortzean	"and if I were to fall, where would I roam?"
eta berriro plazara joanda	when you step back onto the square
bihotzetik kantatzean	ready to sing with all your heart
salto egiteko gogo horrexek	that same feeling of great despair
mantentzen zaitu ertzean.	makes you sit tight fighting the bite.

The bertsolari's truth consists in piercing a hole in the grammatical, narrative, and rational sense of language. Manuel de Lekuona expressed this best when he argued that the "rapid movement of images" in a bertso is obtained by elisions and the absence of rhetorical links. Maialen Lujanbio was asked impromptu to sing on "fire." After linking fire to prehistory, invention, passion, danger, and cooking, she produced the final punch of the strophe out of the blue: "fire is the flame that sparkles / when two people gaze at each other."

The bertsolari brings us again to Joyce's "Here Comes Everybody" of his *Finnegans Wake*, where instead of the sentence we have the sounddance. In this story of resurrection, Finnegan is thought dead, but as the mourners at his wake start drinking and pour whiskey over his corpse, he rises to join them in the celebration. Joyce turned such comedy into the regenerating power of the cycle of life, "wake" representing both death and awakening. Bertso singing typically takes place in lavish commensality and drinking, bringing together wine and resurrection. In the bertsolari's body, voice, and emotion, the community knows and is, understands and makes anew. We do it, like Joyce, by the principle that *the soul of everyelsebody rolled into its oleseleself*. The bertso singer does it by breaking ordinary language's everyday meaning; the trick is to smash literal meaning by homonymy, rhyme, and rhythm. Rhyme shows that meaning depends not on actual references of the word but also on mere sound. The meanings of two words could not be more separate than *fandango* (a dance) and Berango (a town), or *katea* (chain) and *batea* (together) but in a bertso like Aresti's their associations become explosive:

Apur dezagun katea	Let us break the chain
kanta dezagun batea	let us together sing
hau da fandango	this is fandango
biba Berango!	long live Berango!

Sounds interact, creating poetic forces that give birth to a new world of meaning in which *freedom*, *song*, *dance*, and *people* scream raucously. You must first destroy language to turn everything into song and poetry. *In the buginning is the woid, in the muddle is the sounddance*. Words have lost their referential meaning, they have become mute, their silence turned into arbitrarily linked sonorous words.

The bertsolari proves with each song that fantasy is the origin of language. Truth derives from verbal play—imaginative *mis*understanding. If you want to know the truth, look at the "lies" I am telling you, look how we don't know anything, and yet what else can we do but sing and laugh and be touched by happenstance? In the bertso song there is no way to distinguish thought, imagination, emotion, and body. It all comes down to the tone of voice, the modulations of melody, the gestures of the body, the facial emotions—followed by applause and then once again the return to the abysmal silence.

But how does rhetorical ellipsis achieve this endless imagination, thought, emotion? As Lekuona reminded us, by *subtraction*. By dismissing relations of grammar, logic, rhetoric, chronology, and lexicon, the "truth" of the song emerges out of language's excess. The premise that no bertso can be repeated, that each improvised bertso is heard for the first and last time, is linked to the infinity of the linguistic situation that allows for endless permutations in each bertso— the limits of the formal strictures are such that meaning continuously transits through them. Every word, line, rhyme, and strophe is a throw of the dice. The bertsolari is Mallarmé's oral counterpart, his method one of cancellations, vanishing points, foreclosures. It is a statement that there has been a *moment of truth*—that something has actually taken place.

The bertsolari is a continuous ricorso; the final "point" at the end of the bertso is what must be present in the singer's mind at the beginning. In the bertsolari's improvisation, time is *eliminated*, as in Giambattista Vico's new science where an ending discloses a new beginning. In this universe of words bursting with new meaning, the bodies of the audience can barely endure the impact of such excess. As emotion takes hold and a drama unfolds on every face, one can see in their eyes a determination that the truth they are hearing remains timeless; as their mouths begin to mimic those glorious words sung for the first and last time, some try to guess the punch line . . . until finally, when the bertso succeeds, it reaches the concluding climax and there is release and everyone falls into applause, marveling over the event that has just happened—*hori dek bota, hori!* (Wow, what unloading!) The listeners have been shaken, electrified, transfigured. It is the resurrection of the bodies.

I learned to love the bertso songs in my childhood from my father, who would sing them quietly in the corner of the kitchen from a book. My illiterate father probably never entered a library or a bookshop, but he collected the bertso books from fairs and door-to-door booksellers—texts that had been written or dictated by some bertsolari, perhaps transcribed after they had been sung in a plaza. He kept the books on top of the big Philips radio in the kitchen, and in his spare time he would sing them for hours in his low monotonous voice. The humorous *bertsoak* would bring laughter in him; the elegiac ones would provoke tears. Despite his occasional commentaries on the songs, nobody paid much attention to his low-key singing. After one series of strophes was over, he might change the melody to one that was more fitting to the next topic and continue singing, mostly for himself. Rarely, on the occasion of some special fiesta, he would improvise a song in public (he was a mediocre bertsolari).

My father sang bertsoak for sheer pleasure, but later, as I became a writer, I began to realize that his song was also a catharsis and a window to his most intimate world. Belonging to a culture in which his basic communication and identity hinged on the word, he used it sparingly and mindfully. He preferred silence to excessive talk, aware of situations in which speech was undesirable. My father never talked to me about his grief of having lost five of his children; he just sang bertsoak at the kitchen table, laughing and shedding tears.

The day of bertso singing in the Bilbao Exhibition Center was the culmination of a once-every-four-years *txapelketa* (championship). On this occasion, something historic took place: of the eight singers who reached the grand finale, including the former champion and exceptional singer Andoni Egaña, one was a woman—and she was proclaimed the *txapeldun* (literally the beret holder, the champion). As Maialen sang her acceptance bertso to a rapturous audience while wearing the beret on her head, the other seven singers—beretless male bertsolariak who had just embraced her—stood behind her with their arms over each other's shoulders in a display of solidarity.

But there was a second message that could not be avoided regarding the *txapela*—a type of headwear that traditionally is worn by men. Figures such as Picasso, Hemingway, and Oteiza used to wear this Basque beret—flat, wide, without a peak, the surrounding section folded inside, a single seamless piece, made of natural wool. The Bilbao socialist Prieto claimed that such a "symbol of Basque social equality" was consubstantial to his personality; he was the first to wear one in the Spanish parliament. Even so, modern urban men rarely wear it; cartoonist Egillor and others depict Bilbao's country bump-

Maialen Lujanbio singing her last song with the *txapela*.

kins with the txapela. So, when Maialen Lujambio won the bertsolari championship and put the beret on her head, it was a new moment. For the men in the audience, it was implicitly a kind of symbolic castration as that most masculine of symbols was suddenly and solemnly claimed by a young woman, signaling that the time for a new feminine subjectivity had arrived.

You could hardly imagine which other young woman performer had worn a black txapela years earlier—it was Marilyn Monroe in *Gentlemen Prefer Blondes.* You can also see her wearing it in photographs of her 1954 trip to Japan and Korea with Joe DiMaggio. Coco Chanel, who opened her shop in Biarritz in 1915 and had many Basque girls working for her, worked in Hollywood in the early 1930s. She made berets fashionable. Marilyn's beret passed mostly unnoticed among Basques, but now Maialen seemed to be reincarnating Marilyn. Both were women wearing a txapela, one an actress in Hollywood, the other a bertsolari in Bilbao's native plaza. The narcissistic fetish of manly clothing no longer belonged to men alone. Rising from the ashes of Altos Hornos and traditional masculinity, a cultural revolution, prefigured by Marilyn, was being inaugurated by Maialen's song.

Placing the beret on her head, Maialen sang a final strophe, concluding with these lines:

Marilyn Monroe and Jane Russell in *Gentlemen Prefer Blondes* (1953).

Gure bidea ez da erreza	Our road is not an easy one
beti legez, juizioz, trabaz.	besieged by obstacles, trials, and laws.
Euskal Herriko lau ertzetara	This evening we return
itzuliko gara gabaz.	to the four corners of the Basque Country.
Eta hemen bildu dan indarra	And with the energy, passion and
grina eta poz taupadaz	heartbeats of joy gathered here
herria sortzen segi dezagun	let us keep re-creating our country
euskaratik ta euskaraz	from Euskara and in Euskara.

Overtaken by emotion, people rose to their feet as if in slow motion, applause their only relief from the historic moment. Earlier that week, the audience had been angered by the *Egunkaria* trial (the closure of the only Basque-language newspaper by a Spanish judge alleging unproven and later dismissed links to ETA). Lujanbio's strophe was a proclamation: the Basque Country is an *event* taking place here in this song and in our native language. The bertso did not invoke a closed history or anachronistic identity, but only the passion to create a new world out of this embodied and unfinished song. The new Basque Country, she was singing, if it is ever to be, must be configured from this shared song emerging from the ruins of Altos Hornos and the ruins of an Euskara mostly unspoken in Bilbao, and by this community of transformed imaginations. It was an affirmation that the rebirth of Euskara (a language representing a rare case of revival from near extinction) is a defining dimension of the reborn Bilbao—thanks to the power of a naked song that kept fifteen thousand spectators (and many more watching the televised event) absorbed for hours. For those listening to Maialen, it was the most decisive aspect of "the miracle in Bilbao."

The Snake, the Spider, and the Rose

We are back from the bertsolari festival and once again at Bilbao's new epicenter in Abandoibarra, inside Gehry's museum. Let us walk across the translucent atrium and go deep into the gallery under the La Salve Bridge. There you are in the Minotaur's labyrinth, with *The Snake* at its center. Enter Serra's eight twelve-by-fourteen-foot sculptures, *The Matter of Time*, each 44 to 276 tons of torqued steel, and allow yourself to feel and wonder what space you are in. Follow their irregular, narrow, meandering pathways, leading to more enclo-

Richard Serra, *Snake* (1994–1997).

sures and dead ends. The further you go into each of these sculptures, the more you will be aware of the claustrophobic tension created by the rising torqued megastructures and their unstable equilibrium, the more you will feel the weight and the threat of collapsing steel walls over your head. You are on your own, deep in the Minotaur's secret gallery.

And where is Ariadne, the mistress of the labyrinth, the one who helped Theseus defeat the Minotaur by unwinding her thread through the maze? She is just outside, between the museum and the river, standing in the form of Louise Bourgeois's gigantic thirty-foot *Maman* and offering you her endless web. The sculpture creates a building that invites you to walk under the spider's eight steely legs standing as columns. Will Bourgeois's spiderwoman, endlessly weaving her web, liberate Serra's Minotaur from his torqued labyrinth? Bourgeois and Serra, Ariadne and the Minotaur, the Spider and the Sword—this is the mythical drama at the heart of Marilyn's temple.

Bourgeois, the creator of the *Woman House* series—sculptures of hips, vaginas, legs, and split torsos in which heads become houses— said, "My body *is* my sculpture." Bourgeois named her spider Maman. Go inside the sculpture and you are inside her body—"a woman weaving a man." Aresti, in the tradition of masculine *el* Bilbao, is best known for his line "I will defend my *father's house*," a title replicated by Chillida in Gernika with his massive "Our Father's House." *La* Bilbao had to wait until Bourgeois's spider to have a *mother's* house—a mother who weaves and protects the city within her *body/house,* but a house that is not natural but presents conflicts to woman. In both the sculptural *Maman* and the architectural "Marilyn," the female is a resurgence of *la Bilbao*'s aesthetics—Bilbao as a woman, a *bocho,* traversed by *la ría,* ending in *la mar.* The mascot that presides over Bilbao's annual festivities is the figure of *Marijaia,* from Mari and *jaia* (fiesta)— a gigantic and colorfully dressed female with arms extended, which is carried through the streets as the patroness of the fiestas until she marks their ending by being ritually burnt.

Frank Gehry designed a rose on his Bilbao museum's rooftop, and Muschamp described Gehry's reincarnation of Marilyn, via Genet, as the "miracle of the rose." The rose was Marilyn's favorite flower; Joe DiMaggio had a huge heart of red roses made for her crypt, and each week during the twenty-five years he outlived her, he brought roses

Marijaia, the mascot of Bilbao's annual festivities.

Louise Bourgeois, *Maman* (1999), the thirty-foot tall spider standing between the Guggenheim Museum and the river.

to her grave. Miller called her "a flower of iron," and his name for Marilyn's character in *The Misfits* was *Roslyn*.

George Steer found rose petals scattered beneath the old oak the day after Gernika was bombed and burned to the ground. When Picasso heard of Steer's report, he painted, in *Guernica,* a rose sprouting from the dead soldier's broken sword. Before his *Hiroshima, Mon Amour,* Alain Resnais made, with Robert Hessens, the film *Guernica* (1950), illustrated by Picasso's painting and based on a poem by Paul Eluard that had accompanied Picasso's *Guernica* at the 1937 World's Fair, including this line: "Women and children have the same red roses in their eyes." The Bilbao poets Lauaxeta ("Let the smell of the roses be for the cowards"), Otero ("I bring a rose in blood in my hands / bloodied"), and Figuera ("How are you? Very well, thank you. And that rose? That rose?") put roses in the tragedies of Spain and Europe. As if in homage to Gernika and Bilbao's bloodied roses, Gehry added a flower of titanium to Marilyn's temple.

In Dante's poem, the image of a gigantic white rose dominates the final cantos of *Paradise*. It proclaims the fulfillment of the poet's quest, for "the rose embodies the chief spiritual implications of the poem as a whole." Dante took advantage of medieval religious and literary traditions such as the rose attributed to the Virgin Mary as the counterpart to the rose of woman's carnal love celebrated by poets. Dante used the rose to fully reconcile both loves on the grounds of his own love for Beatrice. The rose is "the flower of Beatrice, but of Beatrice exalted in eternal glory beyond the mortal woman Dante had known." The Dantesque vision of the Empyrean as a white rose, like the Gehryesque architecture of the titanium rose, *is* for the artist the true reality—the rose as the expression of a love that was at the beginning and end of the journey's ordeal. Such visions of Dante, or Blake, are grounded on an apocalyptic theory of perception in which the object is not mere symbol or allegory. It is the thing that is more than the thing itself.

"Bilbao has the aesthetics of reality," was Gehry's mantra, as if in the postmodern world of fantasy and desire elusive reality is the only thing that matters. Critics such as John Richardson characterized Krens's museum franchises—Bilbao's in particular—as "shades of Disneyland." As he traveled between Los Angeles and Bilbao, Gehry knew better than anyone the differences between the two places. Both

The *rose* at the roof of the Guggenheim Bilbao Museum.

designs—the Disney Concert Hall and the Guggenheim Bilbao—are formally close, yet Bilbao's *toughness* guaranteed that Gehry would not fall into the trap of a Disneyfied architecture. Gehry's "idea of heaven" was the opportunity for his imaginative metallic flower to transfigure the abandoned docklands of a derelict city. Gehry's axiom is: Bilbao is about *the real*. To which Muschamp, Gehry's Saint Paul, added: so real that it is the reincarnation of Marilyn.

At the center of modern philosophy is Hegel's reversal of crucifixion to redemption with the metaphor of the Rose on the Cross. The Cross is reality, and its reversal, resurrection, is the Rose. Resurrection "is nothing but 'the universalization of the crucifixion.'" The conclusion for an apocalyptic Christian worldview is that, "in Hegel and Blake alike, crucifixion and resurrection are finally and ultimately identical." It is "this beautiful Rose of joy" that Dante placed in paradise and Gehry at the top of his Bilbao architecture. Marilyn's flowers and Gehry's rose, like Hegel's thought and Dante's poem, all say: the Cross *is* the Rose.

The Architecture of Labyrinths

"If we willed and dared an architecture according to the kind of souls *we* possess," wrote Nietzsche, "the labyrinth would have to be our model!" There is no other secret to the extraordinary success of Gehry's masterpiece in Bilbao: this is not the architecture of hierarchy and ascent, as in the sublime beauty of Gothic cathedrals, nor is it the architecture of structure and power, as in the formal beauty of the modernist cube; as you look at his ghost ship run aground by the river in all its elliptical, torqued, and ovoid shapes, its forms bent into daring torsions, you see the architecture of labyrinth. The 24,000 square meters of sinuous computer-designed glass, titanium, and stone create a mathematical infinity of complex curves. The building-turned-icon of world architecture reveals the new Bilbao. Its curled and twisted architectural forms are the city's aesthetic crucible, the glorious "shipwreck" containing and shaping the viewers' subjective landscape.

There at the center of the labyrinth dwells the Minotaur—the profoundly ambiguous center that is denied by the maze. The architecture of premodern thought, up to Descartes, led "us into the labyrinth of the infinite. Freedom is such a labyrinth; so is space; so is God." In an 1887 notebook, Nietzsche, that prisoner of love, lamented, "Oh Ariadne, you are yourself the labyrinth from which one does not emerge again." Labyrinthine souls call not for harmonious Greek temples but for the antiarchitecture of ruins and torsions.

Bilbao's Casco Viejo: premodern circular structure around the cathedral of Santiago.

214

None of Serra's torqued ellipses and Gehry's torsions are alien to Bilbao; they fit with the city's tradition of elliptical plazas, and ovoid sculptures. A primary model of labyrinthine architecture can be found in Bilbao's circular bullring. Oteiza had observed that "the circularity of the bullring, if occupied by chance, becomes LABYRINTH." But it is the form of an ellipse, not a circle, that epitomizes modern Bilbao's urban geography. At the center of the nineteenth-century industrial city, at the middle of the Gran Vía, Plaza Moyúa, also known as the Elliptical Plaza, is the axis of downtown business, the geographic center of Bilbao's urban grid. On March 18, 2011, Plaza Euskadi, another ovoid-shaped 6,600-square-meter space—linking twentieth-century industrial Bilbao with postindustrial Abandoibarra's new urban center, a replica of the Elliptical Plaza in shape and dimensions—was inaugurated.

The original layout of medieval Bilbao, the Casco Viejo, could only be *centered* and self-enclosed, with the Church of Santiago as the pivot around which the "seven streets" branched out. This was the integrated architectonics of Dante's world organized around centered Gothic cathedrals. When Bilbao's *ensanche* (enlargement) was designed for the new industrial city of the second half of the nineteenth century, the focal point, at the precise midpoint of the Gran Vía, took the form of an ellipse—it was the torsion produced by the dimension of the Gran Vía in relation to the other radial streets that forced the ellipse. The Arriaga Theater, the city's greatest building at the end

Elliptical layout at the Hotel Carlton in Plaza Moyúa.

Elliptical plaza Moyúa at the center of the Gran Vía.

of the nineteenth century, had a circular design. But by the 1920s, the large glass-covered hall of the Hotel Carlton at the elliptical plaza was oval-shaped. The elliptical form suggests that circularity had lost its grip upon the planners' and architects' imaginations. "The layout of a city," wrote Le Corbusier, "determines the physical and mental condition of its residents."

Copernicus's disciple Johannes Kepler discovered that the movements of the planets were not circular but elliptical, revolving around not one but two foci. This discovery marked the transition from the "closed world" to "the infinite universe." What elliptical plazas do, urbanistically, to centered spaces is the equivalent of what, in the 1950s, the sculptors Oteiza and Chillida did to circular stele. These funerary discs iconically represent a pre-Copernican world controlled by the premises of circularity, enclosure, an irradiating center, and the formal requirement of an internal void. Oteiza's ambition at that time consisted of decomposing basic Euclidean forms, his large broken ovoid sphere in front of Bilbao's city hall being his conclusive statement. Such deconstruction signals the historic transition from the finitist aesthetic space of premodern semantics to the infinite world of modern cosmology and mathematics. It *repeats* the funerary stela from its "third" dimension by breaking its biplanar field into a third plane, turning the bi-dimensional irradiation into a multidimensional one, the centered circle into a fragmented, uncentered, elliptical, open sphere. The space of premodern aesthetics and subjectivity had been shattered.

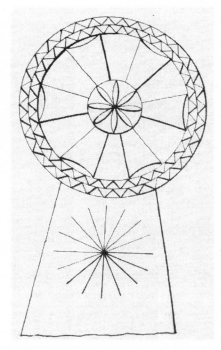

Traditional funerary stela.

In the fall of 2002, Oteiza sent a gift to Gehry as a token of friendship—an iron sculpture, a foot and a half by a foot and a half, entitled *Expansion (Disoccupation of the Sphere)* which represented two ellipses expanding in horizontal and vertical directions. Gehry looked at it in silence. Everything was in that form. "What a beauty," he finally murmured—it was the elliptical code, infinity's revolutionary form, binding both artists. It was Gehry's torsions that gave new life to Oteiza's hyperboloid. It was Gehry who had to sacrifice Oteiza's modernist *Cubo* in Bilbao's Alhóndiga to preserve fidelity to the city's truest elliptical tradition.

Oteiza, *Expansion (Disoccupation of the Sphere)* (1958).

Freudian psychoanalysis, that new "Copernican revolution" in thought, insisted on the "elliptical" nature of the decentered subject's speech. Lacan commented on "the emergence of the ellipse as being not unworthy of the locus from which the so-called higher truths take their name. The revolution is no less important for concerning only the 'celestial revolutions.'" The new spatial infinity had profound cosmological and subjective implications. Gehry's torsions are for architecture what "symptomal torsions" are for psychoanalysis—*symptoms* that inscribe the excess and lack of an event that never ceases to haunt us. The points of lack and failure—lapses and compulsive acts in psychoanalysis, economic crises in Marxism—turn out to be structural necessities. If the Gothic cathedral was a sort of architectural bible for the believer in Dante's centered and orderly cosmos, Gehry's cathedral presents a visual canon for the modern subject. The psychoanalytic premise is that the relationship between the subject and the object is one of "torsion," not a matter of straight lines or complete reversals but elliptical, slanted by perspectival illusions, where "the true . . . is never reached except by twisted pathways." Torsion is the topological figure appropriate to the dialectics between the *bilbo-shackle* and the *bilbo-sword*, the clash between chains and desire. It is a form of appearance, a curvature of being that is materialist in the end, not the idealistic fact of lack requiring transcendence.

Gehry's architecture in Bilbao forces a double-edged sword—the place and the force, the symbolic and the real. Nothing new can come except from the ruination of the past by the present, the creation of new law through the destruction of an old one. Two matrices of a single process. To understand Bilbao's transfigurations, one must go beyond the primacy of the symbolic to the tenacity of the real seen from the perspective of what has been lost, the desire by which the subject is split. The space with no window and doors, where oppositions dissipate, where one doesn't know whether he is inside or outside—that is the labyrinth.

Gehry compares his work to *sujitzu*—that is, turning to your advantage the forces coming at you. He broke with the well-established architectural plan and made it labyrinthine. If Bataille linked the origin of the modern museum with the guillotine, in Bilbao its origin is Gernika's massacre and the ruins of the Left Bank. The cathedral, the palace, the monument, the tomb—these are architecture's prisons, Bataille argued. They are authoritarian, a city's superego, an ostentatious spectacle. They transform individual subjectivities, as in Bentham's panopticon. They function as the escape fantasy for people's desires. Gehry's architecture, too, works on the viewer's perception and subjectivity. But Gehry's building is "not founded on a fantasy of controlling history, culture, or nature," but

Chillida's first abstract sculpture was *Ilarik*—a funerary stela deconstructed by turning its biplanar structure into a three-dimensional form. Close to *Ilarik* in San Sebastián is his three-piece *Comb of the Wind*, its powerful iron tentacles in elliptical shapes constituting the supreme expression of my generation's struggle with "the wind of freedom." Chillida's later *Homage to the Horizon* in Gijón is also an ellipse—"the horizon is not circular, it is elliptical," he explained. The text that accompanied Oteiza's winning submission to the São Paulo Biennale, the "experimental proposal" that summed up his artistic project, ended with a note on "funerary stele."

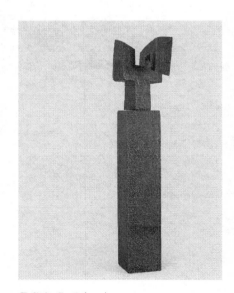

Chillida, *Ilarik* (1951).

Richard Serra, *The Matter of Time* (1994-2005).

The torsions in Gehry's architecture.

Frank Gehry, Marqués de Riscal winery (2006).

rather "acknowledges the absence or lack at the heart of the symbol and in the human subject" and "confronts this originary wound."

The monster that Gehry slays in Bilbao is authoritarian architecture as the mirror image of the triumphant We. Beginning with his own house, Gehry is "the architect who has most challenged the structures of sexual and social oppression within the profession itself." In Gehry's work, architecture as a formative force in shaping human subjectivity does not result in a prison. The thin layer of titanium that covers the building is paperlike; the glass stands for lightness and transparency. This is deconstructed architecture with no skeleton— "architecture without the grid." This architecture of multiplicities and movement, one that "reinvents location through dislocation," appears as a "formalism of formlessness," in which form gets dissolved and can hardly be grasped. It is "a shipwreck," Gehry himself said, by which he meant: we haven't conquered anything, we have simply run aground; this is not a point of arrival, it is a point of departure.

It is in Gehry's later work, fifty miles from Bilbao—the Marqués-de-Riscal Building in Elciego, a historic cellar by bilbaino wine-makers—where the ectoplasmic quality of the architecture fully takes over and form appears to collapse into formlessness. If what mattered was the undoing of the bullring's enclosures and the Minotaur's labyrinth, here we witness the self-immolation of architecture—as if Gehry had heard the biblical command: "Destroy this temple and I will raise it again in three days" (John 2:19). No temple, only the resurrected body.

Painting Paradise

From the collapsing forms at Gehry's Riscal Winery in Elciego, twelve miles northwest to Labastida is the Remelluri Winery and its necropolis that dates back to the tenth century. Its grapes have been cared for by monks since the earliest Middle Ages, and there is an ancient chapel whose walls were painted in the 1990s by Vicente Ameztoy. If Gehry's building externalizes the symptomal contorsions of modern art, Ameztoy's paintings are the work of a man who, before death, saw the world through the torsions of a body ravaged by disease. A painter of great formal purity and exuberant surrealism, his work depicted oneiric themes in Basque landscapes, human figures with vegetable heads evocative of the Renaissance Italian painter Arcimboldo.

Vicente Ameztoy, *San Esteban* (1993-2000), at the chapel of the Remelluri Winery.

Ameztoy was caught up in all the cultural and political cross-currents during the turbulent years of armed resistance to late Francoism and the carnivalesque culture that ensued. He enjoyed rock and punk music, groups such as Orquesta Mondragón and singers like Lou Reed. In his abandon, he fully experienced Allan Ginsberg's "Howl": "I saw the best minds of my generation destroyed by madness." His art depicted the ecological degradation of his period. Next to his town, an ETA man was arrested and tortured to death at the hands of the police; under the cover of night, Ameztoy unburied the corpse at the cemetery to photograph it and release the gruesome images.

In the early 1990s, his health ruined by a previous heroin addiction, Ameztoy was asked to paint the chapel in Remelluri. His guide during this period was Piero della Francesca, whose *Resurrection* was for Aldous Huxley the best painting ever. He painted a *Paradise* and six large paintings of saints that were both a self-portrait and an arresting testament. Nothing moved him, he once told me, like the devoted visitor praying to the images he had painted and kissing the fingertips that had touched them. An agnostic, Ameztoy found that his paintings had become sacred icons with healing powers. He titled the catalog of his Remelluri paintings *Sacred-Profane.*

Ameztoy's Remelluri sanctoral images are farewell portraits of people he loved—the Augustinian *sero te amavi,* late I learned to love thee. In their beatitude, these paintings produce fright. They are Blake's disturbing marriage of heaven and hell. It is monstrous love's redemption. Painter of profane illuminations, creator of art so subtle, its colors charged with enthusiasm, with the simplest yet most sophisticated eyes, Ameztoy is the man of innocence and experience. While the world of art was celebrating Gehry, Ameztoy was a recluse for years in his Remelluri Chapel. Unlike Gehry's glamorous architecture nearby, Ameztoy's paintings are almost as unseen and unknown as undiscovered works from the catacombs—the work of an artist in self-exile, in the lateness of his life and art, with no space for self-delusion, in deliberate contradiction with his own former parodies of religious themes, unyielding in his rejection of any art that does not favor reality. Adorno's words apply to him: "In the history of art late works are the catastrophes." For my generation, these paintings are, in their martyrdom, in their terror and rapturous bliss, the equivalent of Blake's drawings in his final years of Dante's ascent from the Inferno to Paradise.

Santa Eulalia, one of Ameztoy's paintings, shows us a deer and wild boar in the distant background, snow-covered tombs in the woods, and a red-haired young woman with bare breasts, bare feet, and singular beauty—she is the daughter looking to the heavens with mournful melancholy. She looks to her father, the painter, while a timeless white dove protects her. Another painting, *San Esteban,* shows a bloodied stone in a clutched hand, the assassin's projectile as if caressed by the blue of the lavender, with a geometric chasuble of diminutive liturgical drawings torn apart at the level of the saint's heart. There lies San Esteban, stoned to death—why have you forsaken me? His eyes are raised in pitiful lament, Ecce Homo, as if asking his torturers, what have I done to deserve this?

A third painting, *San Vicente,* is a self-portrait in which the martyr is levitating over a burning pyre under the arc of a cluster of green grapes, his body transfigured into grass and moss, rising among purple vines with yellow foliage, while one can hear Mozarabic music and smell thyme. With a golden palm in his left hand, a raven in front, a glorious cluster of mature grapes hanging from his raised right arm, he contemplates it all, blesses it. A slit-open body reveals a triptych of white stars in an intensely blue sky, and the statue of a Romanesque Virgin—a body turned into a reliquary, suspended on the distant landscape, *et incarnatus est.* Oh, no, don't take this cup from me, this cup of Remelluri wine, filled with grapes of wrath and love; raise it and drink it for me, do this in my memory.

San Vicente, painter and martyr, ora pro nobis.

The Last Supper

While a painter who knew and practiced tradition and classicism, Ameztoy loved pop art. He painted magazine covers and postcards and collected all sorts of fetish objects. In postmodern Bilbao, foregrounding the museum's architecture, Jeff Koons's floral *Puppy* is the new canon of art—*the* postcard/souvenir for the tourists. If "Guggy" is the emblem of the new Bilbao, *Puppy* is its chosen complement, the emblem of the emblem. As you approach Guggy's esplanade, you will be greeted by *Puppy*'s fifty thousand pansies (if in fall and winter) or its combination of forty-five thousand begonias, petunias, and Chinese carnations of red, orange, and white (if in spring and summer). If Guggy is the "miracle of the rose," *Puppy* is the transubstantiation of thousands of living pansies, begonias, petunias, and carnations into art and postcard/souvenir. Before you walk down the flight of stairs to the main entrance, you must stand next to the fifteen-foot-tall terrier with a smile and ask someone to take a photograph of you.

Jeff Koons is known as "the spiritual son" of Andy Warhol. When I asked young artists in Bilbao about their primary influences, Warhol's name was prominent. In October 1999, two years after its opening, the Guggenheim Bilbao exhibited "Andy Warhol: The Factory." Following Muschamp's description of the building as "the reincarnation of Marilyn Monroe," the images of Warhol's *Marilyn Diptych* became particularly revelatory of Bilbao's new art reality. Days after her suicide, Warhol created his *Gold Marilyn Monroe* as a memorial act of mourning—"Saint Marilyn of the Sorrows."

Andy Warhol, *Golden Marilyn Monroe* (1962).

Puppy is "a very spiritual piece," Koons claims. In Bilbao's two most prominent past artists, Oteiza and Chillida, the spiritual was linked to the abstract and the ideal—a view radically subverted in pop art. Warhol and Koons criticized abstraction and formalist spiritualism as hypocritical. Koons's key axiom, "Abstraction and luxury are the guard dogs of the upper class," is a revolt against abstraction, hierarchy, and the spiritual ideal. He fought those guard dogs with his own floral *Puppy*. The spiritual art that Koons wanted was closer to the paternalistic kitsch of the large statue of the Sacred Heart on Bilbao's Gran Vía. Many of my generation saw *Puppy* as sentimentalist kitsch—a provocation. We accepted it as irony—keeping in mind Kierkegaard's saying that irony is modernity's baptism by fire.

What Warhol and Koons brought to Bilbao in the form of Pop Art was the Joycean Catholicism of "Here Comes Everybody." Rather than the hermetic world of modernism and the artist's self-discovery, what matters to them is the reception of art by the general public in the platitude of everyday experience. Kitsch takes high forms of art and popularizes them. Koons has been described as the artist of the present Age of Money. He created ensembles having to do with the American middle-class lifestyle—*Equilibrium, Luxury and Degradation,* and *Banality.* He was the Warholian artist chosen to accompany the planting in Bilbao of an American museum that reflects the influence of American power and lifestyle. Koons knew Picasso's *Guernica* from his three-year job at the MoMA Museum when he guided visitors to

Jeff Koons, *Puppy* (1992–1997).

the painting. But it was time to liberate art from esoteric contexts. His *Puppy*, so beloved in Bilbao, confronts the public with the question of what it is in art that sustains us.

The work that made Warhol famous was *Campbell's Soup*—the all-American canned food he'd eaten daily as a boy. Before he died from a routine surgery, Warhol had been engaged in a series of over one hundred *Last Supper* works inspired by Leonardo da Vinci's great mural. Warhol's work was again about food, this time as a symbol of spiritual life. The Pope of Pop Art, Warhol was famous for the dissolute and partying lifestyle of his studio, known as The Factory. But unknown to the general public, he was also a practicing Catholic who visited and prayed at Saint Vincent Ferrer's Church on Lexington Avenue and regularly served soup to the hungry and the homeless in city shelters. Religiosity in Warhol's work has attracted the attention of art critics who have pointed out that, through his work, Warhol was seeking a *transubstantiated culture*. The search for the trans-

Andy Warhol, *The Last Supper (Wise Potato Chips)* (1986).

formation of the ordinary wasn't the result of a religious turn but, argues Danto, "a zone of transfiguration" in which "Warhol underwent an artistic change deep enough to bear comparison with a religious conversion." The result was his subsequent interest in the vernacular and everyday as realities transubstantiated into art. Art was but surface and camouflage—but what else were the sacramental changes of bread and wine in his Catholic practice? If art had the power to transform an ordinary object into sculpture, Warhol was not that far from the basic perspective by Oteiza, whose aesthetics was in the antipodes of pop art, of "art as sacrament."

"What was the novelty in Christ's teaching?" the Jesuit Valentín Bengoa asked me one day, concerned about the radical secularization implied by the Gospels, then answering himself: *"A dinner, an open table—the Eucharist. Nothing else."* The interest in sacraments is an interest in community, he added. Where Oteiza faced a sacramental impasse after his pre-Columbian stone as "Eucharist," Warhol signaled a breakthrough with his Campbell's Soup as Eucharist. Religion ended, this Agape, the *Last Supper,* was what most mattered spiritually to Arrupe's Jesuit group, much as it did to Warhol artistically.

Ignacio Amestoy is a Bilbaoan playwright living in Madrid for decades and who during his student years became close friends with the ETA leader Txabi Etxebarrieta. In 2011 he staged a play entitled *The Last Supper,* about a writer living on a farm and close to death who suddenly receives a call and a visit from his ETA prodigal son who left home twelve years earlier. The ETA man in the play had an older brother who was his mentor and introduced him to the organization, who had flat feet and died of some illness—facts that replicate the life of Etxebarrieta and his older brother. The ETA son tells his father that he has been diagnosed with cancer and has only two months to live, and that he has returned home to beg his father to kill him. The father had gone hunting that morning and shot four wood pigeons, anticipating the supper with his lost son. They decide to have their last supper together and reconcile before they plot their joint suicide in a planned car accident.

The father tells his son that he is writing a play entitled "The Death of the Father." The son suggests he write one on "The Death of the Son." While they muse about the meaning of "tragedy" and the interlocked fates of father and son, the father intimates to the son that it was his older brother who had become his real father while he, the father, was "only a spectator." He was the impotent Basque father, a loser, an anachronistic intellectual, who had been planning his suicide even before his son's unexpected visit. At one point, the son calls him *Aita* (Dad), a name the father then repeats in disbelief. The father realizes that he doesn't know who his son is, a son who is armed and of whom he is afraid, who comes as if "from a foreign land . . . like Oedipus." The son becomes enraged with his father's charges and confessions. The deadlock between father and son is in the end between the symbolic and the real: "You have believed in the word, in literature, in theater, and I haven't," the son tells the father. "You haven't believed in violence as a transformative force, and I have. You had your utopia [literature, liberal democracy], I had mine."

But father and son must reconcile, and this can only be done at the last supper's table, eating and drinking together without rancor. There is repeated mention in the play of "a family secret," which is the father's making of *txakoli,* a tart white wine, following a generations-old home tradition. The playwright father is bent on what can bond them, wine—"Dionysus, Bacchus, the father of tragedy and of tolerance." The third part of the play, "The Sacrifice," is under the sign of Dionysus, as is Euripides's last work, *The Bacchae,* a work that does not end in reconciliation and that Nietzsche thought signaled the end of tragedy. Only the Dionysian god of excess can turn the impossible encounter of father and son into the closest embrace. But there is no final harmonious closure, only a desperate celebration before the suicide pact goes into effect.

In Dante's *Vita Nuova* there are three figures: Beatrice, the poet, and Love. In Amestoy's play the three figures are: the son, the playwright, and Love. Dante sought to reconcile the conflict of his times between the courtly love of woman and the Christian love of God. Amestoy seeks to reconcile the impasse between the pagan love of the senses and the sacramental love of the land. Amestoy's theory is that the drama of our generation's political love, pivoting among brothers and in relation to the *mother*land, can find perhaps a solution in the figure of the emasculated father. For what could be a greater bond than the one of ordidnary love between father and son—without the sacrifice of Isaac and in the company of Dionysus? At one point, as the father asks for more txakoli, the ETA son raises his glass and utters ls from the Last Supper, his Eucharist of wine, words that nobody could understand with the pathos of the father: "This is my blood . . ."

The Passion for the Real

To visit the site where much of it all seemingly began—ETA's founding revolutionary dream, Bengoa's commitment to social justice—all you have to do is walk down a few steps from *Puppy* toward Abandoibarra's riverside by the northern flank of the museum, cross the river over the Arrupe footbridge, and you are at the Jesuit University of Deusto almost in front of the Guggenheim. Arrupe's followers belong to this university, including Bengoa, the Jesuit concerned with the radical secularization of Christianity who had found a way to combine his religious and social callings by a lifelong dedication to the workers' unions ELA (Euskal Langileen Alkartasuna, Union of Basque Workers). He was "the brain" behind ELA, its general secretary told me when I visited its general headquarters in Bilbao in 1999. "ELA was organized as an alternative to ETA," Bengoa told me as we sat down for what would be the first of our several conversations, always in Euskara. He talked quietly, almost whispering. A self-effacing man, Bengoa is the prototype of the highly educated Jesuit with an iron will and total dedication to a cause whose real influence was inversely proportional to his public anonymity.

Bilbao is the city known for its tradition of workers' solidarity and activism, which often led to general strikes. ELA was founded in Bilbao in 1911, under the name "Solidarity of Basque Workers," as the nationalist alternative to the Socialists' UGT or General Union of Workers. Its cooperative movement served as a model for José María Arizmendiarrieta, founder of the world-renowned Mondragón industrial cooperatives. Bengoa joined the Jesuits the same day World War II was declared; he was sixteen and, even as a Jesuit, he would carry with him his father's passion for organized labor. After being ordained, Bengoa was destined to Loyola. Being a Jesuit gave him institutional cover for his subversive work of channeling activism toward trade unions and instructing Catholic youths in Marxist doctrines. Bengoa's task was "team formation." Thanks to his efforts, by 1966 there were sixty people "liberated" to work for ELA—ready to leave their regu-

Valentín Bengoa.

lar jobs and work clandestinely without pay. He sent them to Bilbao's industrial Left Bank, the heart of the militant working class. After the dictatorship was over, in 1976, a de facto refoundation of ELA transpired and Bengoa's influence was pivotal. Each new member had to pay membership dues; militancy demanded that the dues be collected in person, hand to hand, not transferred from bank accounts. The weekly newsletter was also distributed by hand. Currently ELA has over a hundred thousand dues-paying affiliated workers and is the strongest workers' union in the Basque Country.

"We never doubted where the headquarters should be," Bengoa said. "For us, Bilbao's Left Bank was a sacred place. That was where the world of the workers was brewing. The Reds were there. The class struggle was there. And it was where the initial sixty ELA 'liberated' people went in 1966 *a la buena de Dios* [just with God's help]." Someone else we know would also soon be on the Left Bank—Txabi Etxebarrieta. Leading a group of about twenty ETA militants, he was in charge of the links between his organization's "working class front" and the labor union Comisiones Obreras.

"So you were sending to Bilbao's Left Bank the labor activists you had formed in rural areas as if they were *missionaries*—to unionize and change the lives of the workers there?" I asked him. "Yes," he replied calmly.

"So you were doing what Saint Ignatius did with the Jesuit Order, but with labor unionists?" He smiled coyly while admitting the saint's influence. "All I did was help organize. My only task was formation. The studies after lunch were always subservient to the militancy. For us, trade unionism is not an affiliation, it is *a way of being*."

"You mean that the labor unionist first has to *work on himself* to become this 'fool'? Isn't that Jesuitic?" "Yes, yes, if you think about it, that's what it is," replied Bengoa, whose influence upon the labor unionists of ELA was nothing if not ideological and subjective.

Bengoa wanted me to know what nourished his militant passion, and he spoke to me about a group of Salvadoran Jesuits he'd visited and with whom he'd kept in close contact. Among them was Ignacio Ellacuría, the Bilbaoan Jesuit who in November 1989 was murdered with four other Jesuits and their two maids by a Salvadoran death squad supported by the United States. Ellacuría was the rector of the Centro-American University in El Salvador and a prominent public intellectual engaged in negotiations between the government and the guerrillas. For Ellacuría, Jesus was not an abstract son of God but "the Liberator," the title of one of the books by Jon Sobrino—another Bilbaoan Jesuit who spent sixteen years with Ellacuría and was only by chance absent when his companions were massacred.

There was another name to which Bengoa attached particular relevance—Father Miguel Elizondo, the man responsible for the crucial decisions that had changed his and other Jesuits' lives. All of them, including Oscar Romero, Ignacio Ellacuría, Jon Sobrino, Fernando Cardenal, and a group of influential liberation theologians, all of whom had made month-long spiritual exercises with Elizondo. As he spoke of Elizondo's close ties to Arrupe—the witness of Hiroshima who opened the way for "liberation theology" in the Church—Bengoa noted one critical event of particular significance: Elizondo's "epistemological break," a conversion experience that came to affect the people under his influence as well. "The epistemological break had to do with justice for the poor, but not as an ideological issue—in *reality* itself," Bengoa told me, underlining each word. Such a "paradigm change" did not remain at a personal level alone; in the late 1970s it became the institutional doctrine of the religious order. What happened was that a group of Jesuits "led by Elizondo and Ellacuría, forced the entire province of Central America to make a decision: having made the Ignatian spiritual exercises, they proposed to introduce the epistemological break at an institutional level. The entire province placed itself in that line of thought, even if some were opposed."

I pressed Bengoa on the consequences of the "break." He replied, "Elizondo confronted the struggle of the poor as part of a general approach. Until then, entering this world—engaging the poor, injustice—was a kind of moral imperative, but one that was separable from faith as such; you could fail, confess your sins, and keep your faith. But in the new thinking, justice is an *integral* part of faith. In other words, the only God that exists is the God of Christ, and the God that appears in Christ is poor, an idiot—the God of the poor, the God of life. There is no other God. And if you want to get by with such a God, you have to act in terms of that option, that kind of faith." In Bengoa's personal experience, his visit to his Jesuit friends in El Salvador was no less consequential; he embraced their radical posture and, upon returning from the trip, tore up his previous theology notebooks and got rid of his books. "I had to throw it all away," he said. "This was the epistemological break."

Bengoa was telling me all of this in Bilbao, a city about which he harbored no illusion that the loss of religious faith had been precipitous in recent years—in a country where 75 percent of the citizens identify themselves as Catholic but fewer than 20 percent are practitioners. A new phenomenon has emerged in places like Bilbao—"two-thirds of the youths between fifteen and twenty-four years are atheists, indifferent or agnostics." According to a recent report, one-third of the people between fifteen and twenty-nine declare themselves to be a Catholic, but only 4 percent of them are practicing Catholics. It is no longer the institutional religion that is abandoned but the very structure of religious belief and sentiment. But it wasn't this that concerned Bengoa—only the "epistemological break."

"If helping the poor is the only obligation, what would you say to an atheist who agrees with such a break?" I asked. "The Gospels are disturbing to me in this respect," he replied. "What does Christ teach? He breaks with the temple, with the priests, with the rituals." He was looking at me inquisitively, as if afraid that his words might scandalize me, before stating that Christ's only mandate was a *dinner* at a table for everyone: "Religion as a set of sacred times, sacred places, sacred persons, rites—none of that is of value. That is why the first Christians were *atheists* for the pagans—they were not religious. Their lives consisted of having dinners, of writing and reading each other's letters. I see more and more people in that vein, and I am quite happy with that approach." It appeared to me that Bengoa was embracing some form of atheism. It was perhaps the "atheism" of Blake, the radical Christian visionary who committed the blasphemy of "identifying the biblical God as Satan," and which "is in part a radical and prophetic reaction to a non-redemptive God of power and judgment who stands apart from the kenotic movement of the Incarnation." Like Blake, Arrupe's radical followers were caught in the paradox that they were "most deeply Christian when [their] language is most anti-Christian, [their] vision becomes most real when it is seemingly most blasphemous or atheistic." While electrified by the presence of the divine, these men and women embodied the radical perspective of authors for whom, like love itself, "Christianity is, at its deepest core, already atheist." All that is left is the collective work of love without any protection from the big Other. The extreme wager one is confronted with in the Bilbao of these "atheist" Christians, much like in the Bilbao of the writers and artists of the postwar period, is that the atheist subject has to "believe" after the disappearance of the big Other and engage in religious, artistic, political action without any ultimate guarantee of anything. This is the crazy subjective standpoint by which "not only is *Christianity . . . the only truly consistent atheism*, it is also that *atheists are the only true believers*." And the only true prayer is, as Unamuno wrote, "The Prayer of an Atheist": "Listen to my prayer You, God who does not exist, and in your nothingness accept these my grievances."

Bengoa would waste no time in telling me, from his working-class consciousness and without any spiritualization of the struggle, his version of where reality stands: "The class struggle is as acute as ever, even if Capitalism has changed. Now it is the financial sector that gets all the profits and the productive sector, including the owners, are the victims. *Capital is in paradise*—it does not even need labor to enrich itself. The states no longer have the power to regulate international capital. The markets command and the governments administer." What is needed, he told me, is a radicalization of the notion of the working class in transnational terms and beyond the notion of mere labor. The only terrible thing he finds about capitalism is that it limits the number of guests at the table. In a Bilbao directly affected by immigration and the exclusion of non-Europeans from the Last Supper, he is the voice of a generation that, knowing that the economic problem is no longer the production but the consumption and distribution of wealth, will continue to be haunted by the belief in the universal of Socialism.

In the spring of 2006, Bengoa alerted me that the liberation theologian Jon Sobrino was coming to Bilbao on one of his visits home from El Salvador and was going to speak in Loyola. As I arrived there with my wife members of the audience were overflowing into the street outside. Sobrino began with a question: "How can you be a Christian today in the developed world?" before answering himself: "To be Christian we have to be honest with *reality*. But our tendency is to be blind to what is around us, to ignore reality. Bishop Romero and Ellacuría were true realists," men who understood and lived by the belief that "*you* [the poor] are Christ crucified." Sobrino reminded us that each day twenty-five thousand people die of hunger. He referred to the poverty in Africa as a shoah. He directly linked African poverty to First World countries' subsidies that render African products uncompetitive in their own homes—"our wealth requires their poverty," he summed up. He denounced Europe's immigration policies that lead to thousands of people dying as they try to enter from Africa. "What the European Union cares about is an economically strong Europe; human rights and all the rest are simply children's bedtime stories." About democracy, he said, "Just look at what the United States did in South America to defend it." The sermon continued: "What is to be done? We must side with the poor. God is not impartial. Let us get rid of the idea that being a Christian is easy; it is joyous but not easy." He expressed his sense of "bewilderment" returning to his native Basque Country from El Salvador and seeing the bounty in the supermarkets, the modern highways, and "the architecture of prosperity."

"What is to be done?" he returned again to the Leninist question before presenting us with a stark alternative: "One road begins with poverty and opprobrium and leads to life; the other with prosperity and arrogance and leads to death." The Church's official doctrine—"there is no salvation outside the Church"—had changed to "there is no salvation outside the world." But the liberation theologians' position was even more extreme—"there is no salvation outside the poor." The only antidote to the current world order, Sobrino concluded, is a "civilization of poverty." There was nothing new in his preaching. What was extraordinary was his saying it, backed with the testimony of his Salvadoran Jesuit companions martyred for sharing those ideas.

Bengoa had one more request for me—that I meet with Elizondo, his hero. He arranged our encounter in the Passionist convent of Euba, where Elizondo had come to direct spiritual exercises and where I'd spent five years of my adolescence as a seminarian seeking sanctity. Bengoa accompanied me to the meeting. I was fascinated by these two men, radicalized by their inner experience. I knew Elizondo was a close friend of Arrupe, the man I so much admired, and I wanted to know more about him. Elizondo recounted the Assembly that elected Arrupe as leader of the Order, and how during breakfast on that election day they sat next to each other in silence. He described Arrupe as a "deeply spiritual" and "driven man." He remembered Arrupe's first words after the election: "First, we must be open to listen to the world and to youth in particular; second, given the challenges we have to confront, we have to be more Ignatian than Ignatius himself." Elizondo added with emphasis: "One of Arrupe's traits was his *freedom* vis-à-vis the institutional Church. He had to pay dearly for this."

After Arrupe's election, the two men had a meeting of lasting consequence. Elizondo would be responsible for molding the subjectivity of the Jesuits at their most critical moment of decision—the final year in the Jesuit formation. Arrupe liberalized its structure, which had been too similar to the reclusive novitiate. Then Elizondo made a startling admission of what dawned on him as the result of that encounter with Arrupe: *"The philosophy I had studied, the theology I had studied, the Christology I had studied, the morality I had studied . . . all of it had collapsed, all of it had to be demolished.* What I experienced one day is that Jesus Christ had been taken hostage by these forms of conceiving the religious life." He suddenly understood the need to reformulate what had become religious deadlock for the current times in the urgency of having to "form" the subjectivity of future missionaries: "I was forced to remake my theology and my ecclesiastics. I went asking for aid from those I thought could help me." One of them was the great Uruguayan liberation theologian Juan Luis Segundo, who didn't mince words: "Sacraments, as they are lived today, are invariably aseptic, deceitful signs of a celestial grace that does not enter history." Elizondo summed it up for me: "Jesus Christ took religion away from sacred places, sacred persons, sacred times. He carried it into life. Where should you live the Eucharist if not in someone's house? He said the charade is over." After the epistemological break, for these religious Bolsheviks everything had to be demolished. It was all commanded by their passion for the real.

It was not only art, architecture, literature, culture, and politics that had been caught in an endgame. Arrupe, Elizondo, and Bengoa were saying that this was *the end of religion* as they had known it. Their language of "ruins" and "collapse" could not be more graphic. "We have confused faith with structures, faith with religion . . . we must liberate faith," Elizondo continued. "This is what Arrupe has done: to concentrate on the nucleus of faith, the consciousness that God intervenes and acts. For me, Arrupe is a man who has truly lived a personal faith of the most *real* presence of an active God." I asked Elizondo how such an experience becomes concrete. "It becomes concrete in our lives as God communicates gratuitously with us, manifests Himself within us. That's the nucleus of the faith, not the obligation to go to mass, to take the sacraments and other practices."

I wanted to know about Arrupe's influence on the theology of liberation. "Arrupe created the climate in which we can confront a radical change in behavior, a way of being of complete liberty. The Episcopal Conference of Medellín in 1968 revolutionized the structures of the Christian faith, provoked the epistemological break. Ellacuría, immediately aware of the transcendence of this break for Central America, called me. I had just come from Argentina to Medellín to be in charge of 'the third probation.' After talking with Arrupe I decided to place the center, with its fifteen students, in a super-marginalized area of Medellín, where we stayed for two years without water and electricity. We continued there another twelve years without television or telephone. Arrupe visited us and cheered us on."

Elizondo was forming future missionaries in the tradition of his Jesuit congregation and in that of many thousands of missionaries produced by the Basque region. But what kind of "religion" were they going to proselytize? The work of the towering theologian Karl Rahner, with whom Ellacuría had studied after instruction from Elizondo, was the backdrop of their thinking. Rahner, who had worked with Heidegger, brought a philosophical foundation to a new theology in the attempt to reconcile modern subjectivity and the experience of faith. For Ellacuría, however, grounded in the political reality of Latin America and in the tradition of the apocalyptic Christianity that seeks a radical transformation of the world, the merely interpretive philosophy he had learned at the feet of his masters Rahner and Xabier Zubiri was insufficient. True, it was crucial to examine the transcendental a priori structures of knowledge, but in Ellacuría's writings, thought must contribute to the transformation of the world as the realization of God's kingdom *in history*.

The war in El Salvador, which had already taken more than seventy-five thousand lives, was a dramatic aspect of the reality that Ellacuría's group thought must be transformed. This was *the passion for the real* that Ellacuría had to theorize about. Its initial premise was an "epistemological break" with the received forms of religion and morality. The symbol had to be broken in order for an ethics of the real to emerge. This is the ethics that many of our generation recognize in the words of Bikila, a historic leader of ETA and of the Basque internationalist left: "Even if I consider myself an atheist, after knowing some followers of the Theology of Liberation I cannot but have deep respect for some forms of religion."

One of the guerrillas who fought in the mountains of El Salvador was Laura, a woman I met in Bilbao in 2006 through a mutual friend. She had been a hero of my older sisters when Laura was a leader in the Catholic Action *Herri Gaztedi* (People's Youth) rural movement of the middle 1960s. Later she spent three years in jail as an ETA activist during the early 1970s and, after a period in Bilbao studying economics, decided to join the Central American revolution. These were the days when ETA was torn between its nationalist and internationalist souls. Laura flew to Caracas, Venezuela, where she became involved with Paco, an ETA activist. Laura and Paco's own epistemological break occurred when they decided to act out their internationalism—a break for which they'd pay dearly when they joined the guerrillas in Nicaragua and El Salvador. Paco was injured in the mountains of Chalatanengo in north El Salvador and lost his leg—his amputation above the knee was carried out with a Swiss knife while under enemy fire. Laura came from Nicaragua to take care of him. This was not left-wing internationalism to be talked about in a Bilbao café. They were in the mountains of Oscar Romero's El Salvador fighting a U.S.-backed army. Paco died in combat two years later, unwilling to surrender while returning fire to a troop of Salvadoran soldiers led by a U.S. commander; later, the guerrillas found his body, riddled with bullets and beheaded. Days later, Laura and two of her companions buried him there. With their fists raised, they sang "Eusko Gudariak" and "The Internationale," then Laura gathered some wildflowers and placed them over his grave. "I am a happy man," he had written in a letter, "I don't belong to anyone . . . only to this [Salvadoran] country, only to the [Basque] country where I was born." It was the passion for the real.

Laura kept fighting for eleven years, frequently shaking with terror under fire from U.S. helicopters. Laura's job, a machine-gun hanging from her shoulder, was to protect and take care of the wounded left behind. She saw hundreds die—including a seventeen-year-old boy who begged her to keep him alive and who still haunts her memory. During the evenings, she taught the illiterate young guerrillas how to read and write, as well as basic instruction on health, sexuality, and general culture—the very same kind of work she did during her Catholic Action years in the rural Basque Country during Franco's dictatorship. Later, I found in a book how crucial Laura, "an extraordinary woman," had been in her leadership role of organizing mountain hospitals, staying with the wounded while under fire, rushing escapes. An unassuming woman who felt uncomfortable talking about herself, she epitomizes my Bilbao generation. I found myself avoiding eye contact with her, as if protecting myself from her excess, the monstrosity of her radical love. "We only did what we had to do," she said by way of conclusion. It was the passion for the real.

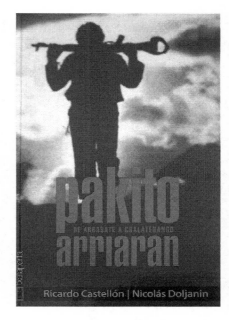

Cover of the book on Pakito Arriaran.

The Monstrosity of Love

Anthropologist Mari Luz Esteban conducted in-depth interviews with twelve women, mostly from Bilbao, on the role of erotic love in their lives. Their stories reveal the centrality of love as their key subjective experience, both in terms of expectations and impasses. Love is what is most present in their conversations and what structures their lives. They openly admit all along that "love is a trap, a delusion." As Jone put it, "Love is the only moment of madness we have, the moment we fall in love. Nobody goes mad for a job, or for a trip to some island." Berta, fifty-four, talks of being "blind" for love to the point of falling for someone who warned her in advance that he was alcoholic— "how stupid of me!" It is the puzzlement, as Leire, forty and who likes "canailles," put it: "I have asked myself frequently: why do I fall in love with this person? What does this person have to make me this carried away? And I don't know it, because after all they are ordinary people."

Rosa observes that there is "a point of mystery in desire: why does my body react like that to some persons and not to others?"

Jone, after recognizing that love is everything, adds immediately, "I have always been scared of love, generally I have been closed. . . . It has not been easy for me to fall in love. . . . I have been very scared of suffering." Eider, twenty-one, for whom also "love is very important," comments, "Love is a delusion. Everybody says it, right? I believe love is the greatest lie they have sold to us women . . . they have taught us the wrong way of living it, at times as if it were a form of masochism." Loli adds, "It is fundamental to point out how many negative things for women are justified in the name of love."

Faced with the deadlocks of love, the life of the couple becomes an *atadura* (binding), says Berta, and the *desamor* (lack of love), while dreaded, is also experienced, in Rosa's words, as "very liberating when you get out of the fix." The ambivalence takes at times the form of uncertainty as to whether one is really in love, whether it is a relationship of dependence that echoes the relationship with the mother, or whether one "believes" in love, while there is the awareness of power relations in which "we women are oppressed." It is the hysterical impasse by which the lover is uncertain whether her love is genuine or simply an echo of his desire for her. Even seductiveness, whether a woman should shave her legs and be more attractive for him, becomes a sort of imposed "blackmail"—does he really want me or my looks?

Love becomes for these women a unique field of knowledge. Besieged by the overpowering feelings of happiness and excruciating impasses produced by being in love, they are forced to search in themselves for what is most real. When the situation becomes unbearable, the breakthroughs demand resorting to *desamor*, to forgiveness, to friendship, to forms of "sexual fluidity" beyond the monogamous, or to a new understanding of what love is. Some, like Pilar, fifty-seven, find maturity in the difference between the state of "searching for love" and the state of enjoying the love one already has. Most of them are acutely aware of their men's "emotional illiteracy," and that, as Amaia, sixty-five, put it, "the changes have been very abrupt for them. . . they notice it much more perhaps."

A dominant theme in all the interviews is the difficulty in sorting out "romanticism" from "pragmatism," "fantasy" from "reality." Like no other issue, love provokes an acute awareness of the force of fantasy and its traps in the subject's everyday life. The result is the unending effort to find an answer to the enigma, the truth beyond the tragicomedy and the trauma, of what the *real* of love is.

Lucía and Fernando told me their love story one evening in March of 2006 while we were walking together through Bilbao's streets. I had known Fernando since the early 1980s when he was a student at the Basque university where I was teaching. A large painting that Fernando gave me as gift, splashed with his own blood, hangs on my wall. Lucía makes her living as an architect. I had known them as a couple since they began dating. They were an unlikely couple, she a student from an upper-middle-class family, he a struggling artist. They met at a party that lasted most of the night in the home of a mutual friend. He remained silent all night, and by the time the party was over Fernando's enigmatic "terrible sadness" had intrigued Lucía. They became involved. A month later, Lucía discovered that Fernando was a heroin junky. By then she was in love, but he was not. He kept trying to put her off, saying, "What are you doing here with me? I am the history of an error."

Lucía had just broken up with her previous boyfriend after her pregnancy ended in abortion. Could Fernando be her redemption? He kept telling her, "I'm wretched. I can't give you anything good. What do you want from me? You don't know what you're getting into." Why the attraction? Lucía answered, "His utter darkness. I began to think I could get him over his addiction. He had no hope, but I did. He was someone on the edge that I saw as beautiful, and through him I glimpsed my own redemption." Fernando's body took complete hold of her erotic passion, and she realized that nothing mattered like the vibrancy of that love. It was the Blakean perception of sex as "the deepest epiphany of the Divine Man."

Months earlier, in a routine hospital check, Fernando had found out in New York, where he was spending a year on a grant for promising artists, that he was HIV-positive. He took it as a death sentence. He tried to kill himself four times with an overdose. In one attempt he took forty sleeping pills plus 1.5 grams of heroin. Three days later, his sister found him in his studio unconscious but still alive.

"You have three months to find out whether to go to the cemetery or start a new life," Lucía challenged Fernando at one point. "Leave me alone," he replied, adding: "If you want me to leave, I will." Once she snatched the needle from his arm as he was shooting up, taunting him, "If you're an artist, why do you want to destroy yourself?" He had lost his capacity to paint, write, even talk. Heroin gave him great euphoria, relief, but also total solitude. She begged him to go to "Project Man," a rehab center. He laughed at her. They decided to go on a detoxification trip through Spain. "In the end, you want to get out, you want life," she explained, "It's like a bullfighter who loves life in the midst of danger." Fernando couldn't endure going cold turkey. He banged his head against the walls and windows, wept and screamed in spasms like an epileptic. She photographed his spasmodic convulsions.

Finally Fernando agreed to try "Project Man." Lucía began to hope he was changing. He stuck with the program for three years. They invited me to his graduation ceremony at the rehab center. His old father was there. He had, with the rest of his own and Lucía's family, forgiven Fernando for the anguish he had caused them.

But after he left "Project Man," Fernando relapsed into heroin use a few times and Lucía was shaken. She couldn't change him after all. Fernando found work with another artist. He and Lucía moved into an apartment together. Their relationship deteriorated, and they divided their apartment in two. He began to bring other women home. Lucía concluded that he not only didn't love her but was actually seeking ways to hurt her. After two years of hell, she demanded that he leave.

Had her love been a fantasy? Lucía wondered at her failure. The affair had been deeply revitalizing and most real, and yet she had to admit that it all had to do in some fundamental way with fantasy coloring her desire and her perception. It was as if her desire had played a cruel trick on her. Her entire universe had been distorted by the power of an attraction that had created so much enjoyment and pain. Had the power of that unconscious fantasy gotten Lucía closer to or more distanced from real life? Hadn't she fallen into the paradox of the superego whereby the commandment to enjoy had itself become a duty that distances the subject from its freedom? The collapse of that relationship, an erotic love that she felt she could not avoid, left her lost and depressed.

For years, Fernando refused to treat himself for his HIV condition. Again on his own after leaving Lucía's apartment, he collapsed. He decided to pay a farewell visit to her. She found him at the bottom of her stairs, cadaverous, unable to climb up. "I saw him dead," Lucía observed. By then, Lucía had another boyfriend. But when she saw Fernando "dead" on her stairs, she found herself unable to accept it. She sat down with him. "Why don't you take the medication?" she asked. "If you look at me differently, I'll take whatever medicine you want," he replied. Lucía had been "over" him for months, but she found herself once again in an abysmal situation with him. She realized that his request that she look at him, and not at her boyfriend, was blackmail and told him so. And yet she could not help herself. Her boyfriend, her family, her friends no longer mattered. "He was visualizing for me his own death. Suddenly the only thing that mattered was that he did not die." Yes, she'd take him back, there was no question about it. Lacan's formula described best Fernando's love: "Love is giving what you do not have to someone who does not want it." She sat there on the steps talking with him for an hour, then drove him to the hospital. It was *l'amour fou,* the monstrosity of a love incapable to be reduced to common sense.

"I could not understand myself at all. I didn't give a crap about being reasonable," Lucía remarked, almost absentmindedly, faced with the senselessness of her own love. Attractive, professional, accustomed to a bourgeois lifestyle, Lucía was an enigma to herself. I asked her about her boyfriend. "They are different loves, incompatible. For my boyfriend, what I did was a betrayal, something I did out of impotence. But I had to help Fernando. I told him he'd have no trouble finding another girlfriend. I loved him but not at the expense of Fernando's death. I had no choice." Lucía's father was furious at her Good Samaritan deed: "That's motherly love. You are not his mother. How can you do that?" "I don't care. He is dying," was her only reply. "Was it forgiveness?" I asked. "It didn't feel like forgiveness," Lucía answered. "The urgent thing was life. It was something prior to forgiveness."

When Fernando was released from the hospital, he met a healer who gave him medicinal plants and pushed him into accepting a healthy lifestyle. He seemed a changed and happy man. They started living together again but were no longer lovers. They had gone through the kind of Hegelian "negation of negation" by which both "lost the loss itself. . . . In a way . . . [they lost] desire itself, its object-cause."

"Fernando gave me back life," Lucía concluded. "I've become free and no longer depend on him. But I love him and he gives me enormous happiness. I feel I won the big prize in the lottery. This is his resurrection and my resurrection." Their incompatibilities were all too obvious and they couldn't be bridged by a sexual relationship or mutual sublimation, yet their de-sublimated love radiated a sort of jubilant fidelity to their initial encounter. Having embraced the *lack*

intrinsic to their relationship, and leaving aside the fallacious plenitude of a fusional love, Lucía and Fernando were proof that "Love fits
through desire like a camel through the eye of a needle."

Years later, on my answering machine, I received a message from a
bewildered Lucía with the news that Fernando had died. His fragile
body had given up after a pneumonia infection. Weeks later I met with
in a café with a distraught Lucía whose face I could barely recognize.
She could do nothing but repeat compulsively every detail of those
days in which his body, in acute pain, ravaged by his former addiction, with blisters on his lips and fingers, riddled with allergies, had
gone into a state of exhaustion and breathlessness. She had been with
him every hour during the month of his final agony, and yet she was
in disbelief that he could die. She begged Fernando's sisters to reconcile with him before he died, which they did, and yet she felt suddenly
paralyzed and angry against God for His utter betrayal of her hopes
that Fernando would survive. She wished her apartment was not on the
second floor but the seventeenth so she could jump from the window
in revenge against Him. She told me of the hours she spent kissing and
embracing Fernando's dead body. Her violent onslaught of love and
grief reminded one of the sacrilegious correspondence between love's
apocalypse and Hiroshima's explosion in Alain Resnais's film, written
by Marguerite Duras. "Hiroshima. That's your name," the anonymous
French woman tells her anonymous Japanese lover. In the café filled
with people, Lucía couldn't stop sobbing. In the brutality of her love,
Lucía could repeat Heloise's words to Abelard, "I have . . . kept nothing for myself." Instead, she kept murmuring, her face in her hands:
"I didn't love him enough, I didn't love him enough, I didn't love him
enough."

Poster for the film *Hiroshima, Mon Amour*, based
on a script by Duras.

Forgiveness

Lucía felt her pardon—her taking back Fernando—was a life-or-death
imperative, almost an involuntary act. And yet granting or denying
pardon is the most gratuitous of acts, the hardest to justify, closer to
madness than reason, because nothing is more inexplicable than forgiveness. I've heard many stories of pardon in Bilbao. One that stands
out is that of the Bilbao intellectual Rafael Sánchez Mazas during
the Spanish Civil War. He went to Rome in 1922 as a reporter for the

242

Spanish newspaper *ABC* and ended up identifying with the Italian fascist movement. He became an advisor to José Antonio Primo de Rivera with whom in 1933 he co-founded the Spanish Falange, later co-opted by Franco. He also co-wrote the Falange's anthem—the Civil War's battle song "Cara al sol" (Facing the sun) that I, like most children during Francoism, had to sing in school, extending the right arm in the air with a straightened hand in fascist salute, under the inspection of a military man turned teacher:

Volverán banderas victoriosas	Victorious flags will return
al paso alegre de la paz	at the happy step of peace
y traerán prendidas cinco rosas	and they will bring five roses
las flechas de mi haz.	the arrows of my quiver.

We were singing to the roses turned incendiary arrows over Gernika.

Even though Sánchez Mazas emerged from the war a winner (an alley at Bilbao's Casilda park bears his name), one event marked his life and became the subject of a best-selling novel and later a film. His friend José María Areilza, Bilbao's first mayor after Franco's victory on June 1937, refers to it in his memoir—the moment when Sánchez Mazas was "miraculously saved from the firing squad in Catalonia." While he was trying to escape from Spain in 1937, Sánchez Mazas was arrested in Barcelona. Months later, he was taken to a forest where he was to be shot by a Republican firing squad, along with another fifty or so prisoners. At the last moment, Sánchez Mazas somehow managed to spring from the group and run into the forest. In the ensuing manhunt, he was found under some bushes by a *miliciano* (Republican soldier). The soldier looked at him and, incredibly, decided not to report him, sparing his life—the Spanish expression is *perdonar la vida* (to *forgive* someone's life). It was not a supernatural intervention but the irrational freedom of the miliciano that "miraculously saved" Sánchez Mazas who, days later, rejoined the fascists' anti-Republican army.

The miliciano was one of those men whom Sánchez Mazas's comrade Areilza had described in his writings as "infrahuman," "barbarian," the epitome of "criminal madness." Yet he was the embodiment of the figure of the soldier capable of heroic acts, when "heroism is properly the act of the infinite at work in human actions"—not the old heroism of the individual warrior given to a religious type of sacrifice, whose passive form is Christian pacifism, but the heroism of the democratic and collective soldier whose "victory over death . . . is both anonymous and nonreligious." What must have been puzzling and unsettling for the privileged minds of Areilza and Sánchez Mazas was the miliciano's incomprehensible act of forgiveness.

Even if in a traditional context we associate forgiveness with religion, this was no religious deed; the Reds, if anything, were anti-religious. This was an act with no explanation. The Red who had suddenly and gratuitously forgiven Sánchez Mazas's life acted in a way beyond all modern categories. In Vladimir Jankélévitch's words, "To understand, we say, is to forgive, or at the very least, to understand is to excuse. But if we can forgive without understanding, we can just as well understand without forgiving, which proves that to understand is one thing and to forgive is another." The soldier had simply preferred not to kill the *enemy* hidden in the bushes. Thinking about it, he might have wondered whether, if their situation had been reversed, his enemy might not have killed him. But something in him remembered that, were it just up to him, it was better not to kill a wretched man cowering in the bushes, and remembering that made him forget all he had been taught and ordered to do by the army, the State, the Church, and the law.

Had either Sánchez Mazas or Areilza been in the miliciano's situation, they might well have reached the "rational" and honorable conclusion of disposing of the fugitive's life, simply resorting to the military code. Political Philosophy (the State's duty to kill enemies deserving of the firing squad) and High Civilization ("infrahuman beings, representatives of the primitive barbarian savagery") demanded as much. Forgiveness requires that the enemy and his actions be met *as if* they had never happened. But there in the woods, beyond Christianity and politics, the miliciano had come to understand Nietzsche's frightening conclusion, the anathema to the core axiom of all modern states, expressed in the folly of the slogan "Enemies, there is no enemy!" The critical consequence of the unilateral subjective decision, whereby the enemy no longer exists, is that killing or dying for such a figure no longer makes sense.

Bilbao's Catholic tradition emphasizes the central role of forgiveness in religious and personal experience, yet it is a contested premise that spills over into notions of justice and politics. Forgiveness has no reasons, because "reasons for forgiveness abolish the raison d'être of forgiveness." There is no "right to forgiveness," just as there is no "right to grace." Forgiveness profoundly changes the one who gives it as much as the one accepting the gift. "Forgiveness inaugurates a *vita nuova*," even though one can never know in advance the reaction of the forgiven. Sánchez Mazas went back to fighting and the miliciano's insensate act preserved an enemy determined to crush his benefactor. It is the scandal of forgiveness.

Such asymmetry of forgiveness, motivated neither by reward, honor, sublimity, nor reason, is for Jankélévitch madness. Yet it is a madness of incalculable consequence, for it suspends the existing order. The radicalness of total and definitive forgiveness lies not in some inner state of guilt, repentance, or spirituality, but in the fact that it is dialogic—a free and uncontrollable relation between two persons. Forgiveness is the last hope of the desolate lover begging, with Jacques Brel, "ne me quitte pas" (don't leave me). The act is total because it makes of past events a tabula rasa. This is why, for Kierkegaard, melancholy is sin—"the sin of doubting the forgiveness of sins." Forgiveness "resuscitates dead people."

In the era of the Holocaust, forgiveness poses a moral paradox. In the encounter between Colonel von Richthofen and Aita Patxi in Ermua and Gernika, was it valid for Aita Patxi to raise his cross of forgiveness for the dying soldiers with the sacramental words, imperious and final, *ego te absolvo a peccatis tuis*, forgiving at the same time the Nazis who were bombing them from the sky?

After the fall of Bilbao, Aguirre asked his followers to harbor no feelings of hatred or revenge against the victorious fascists. These were the days when Aguirre's neighbor, the Francoist Areilza, became mayor. For years, the two men had ridden from the same station on the same daily train, met every Sunday at their parish church. During Holy Week or Corpus Christi, they had borne together the pallium, Aguirre the lead pole on the left, Areilza the one on the right. After the procession, they would meet in the sacristy, friendly Christian neighbors despite their political differences.

As its new mayor Areilza spoke harsh words that would define his legacy: "Bilbao is a city redeemed by blood. . . . Let it be clear: Bilbao conquered by arms. Nothing of pacts and posthumous thanks. The law of war, hard, virile, inexorable." While Areilza was haranguing the public, the political commissars were executing their vanquished enemies. Could there be forgiveness? Areilza was talking of winners and losers, of heroic soldiers and sewer rats. It was the highly "educated" man—son of a legendary doctor portrayed as a hero in Vicente Blasco Ibáñez's liberal novel *El intruso*—who would become, as mayor

Seix Barral Los Tres Mundos *Ensayo*

Vladimir Jankélévitch
El perdón

Cover of the book on forgiveness by Vladimir Jankélévitch.

of Bilbao, the man cheering for Franco's "liberation" and praising Hitler.

But in time, even "victorious" Areilza distanced himself from the dictator and began to work to change the regime. In his memoirs, he paid tribute to Aguirre. While in the heat of the war Areilza's words about Aguirre had been pitiless and unforgiving, in his autobiography Areilza praised him. Recognizing that "the nationalist error was an error of excessive love," Areilza recalled the moment when, after the fall of Bilbao, Aguirre in public had warned, "Damned be whoever harbors in his heart a feeling of revenge." Areilza must have wished that as Bilbao's mayor he could have said the same. He visited and found Aguirre's grave in Donibane Lohizune "simple and moving," adding that such nobility "honors the memory of a man." The vanquished man had won over the victorious one.

Can the century of Gernika be forgiven? Doesn't forgiveness itself—a law beyond the law that takes place in a history beyond history, the only thing that remains heterogeneous to law and politics—turn into an impossibility? Sánchez Mazas wrote the introduction to one of the books by Javier de Ybarra, the captive who forgave the ETA killers who would not *forgive* him his life. Recently, as ETA declared a definitive ceasefire and began to dismantle, some jailed members of the organization asked to meet with their victims face to face (after decades served in captivity and outside of any judicial process) to beg forgiveness.

The orders of justice and forgiveness are two opposing poles of the conditional and unconditional. For Aita Patxi and Aguirre, the only crime against the spirit of Christianity would have been the denial of the power to forgive; for Blake forgiveness was Christianity's only novelty. Twenty-five years after the event, Oteiza marked with two sculptures the sites where Etxebarrieta and the policeman Pardines were killed, the two foundational killings that began ETA's cycle of violence—an act that called for reconciliation. And yet, when forgiveness confronts the realities of the violent foundation of the nation-states, one that is *outside the law*, forgiveness becomes an obscenity, as it would imply the victor's final imposition of dominance on the subjugated people. In political terms, the dilemma is: if sovereignty, then no forgiveness. The only escape from this twenty-first-century dilemma is the affirmation of a world in which sovereignty is not denied but overruled by a higher universality of law and politics. We can only dream with Derrida of "a forgiveness without power: *unconditional but without sovereignty*."

Jai Alai in New York

While Areilza's fellow party members were mayors in Bilbao in the early 1940s, the nationalist Aguirre and his old antagonist/friend, the socialist Prieto, would meet in New York's Jai Alai, Valentín Aguirre's restaurant and port of entry for Basque refugees. Prieto had come there from Mexico for treatment of the degeneration of his cornea. Sometimes, in addition to Manu Sota and Jon Bilbao, the noted scholars Américo Castro and Fernando de los Ríos would join the party. Valentín Aguirre would invite them for squid in its black ink and Marqués de Murrieta, the wine both Prieto and Aguirre preferred. A recurrent theme in these evening meetings was—what else?—*Bilbao*. Both men were planning a public Basque university in Bilbao, though it would have to wait decades until it materialized. One of their prewar projects had been the construction of a tunnel under Mount Artxanda to open the adjacent valley to future development. Prieto gave impetus to the idea, but it was Aguirre's government that began work in 1936, after the war broke out. Months later, during the fall of Bilbao, Robert Capa photographed people taking refuge in the tunnel from von Richthofen's aircraft.

Restaurant Jai Alai, managed by Valentín Aguirre in New York.

Aguirre and Prieto had represented the two dominant Basque political parties, socialism and nationalism, caught in a historic standoff to this day. Prieto was nationalism's nemesis in Bilbao. What most mattered for Prieto was his city, Bilbao. Although opposed to any talk of "independence," Prieto's ideology embraced a national affirmation of the Basque Country within a federal Spanish state. He served a militant nationalism of his own, based on the notion that Spain needs "to be saved among all of us." He argued against the monarchy that he despised and helped to exile, because "there is already no other power beyond the state than the one represented by the public power." Like Aguirre's fervent Basque nationalism, Prieto displayed "an ardent and patriotic regenerationist faith in Spain." Aguirre's support for Basque independence and Prieto's visceral opposition to it constitute, in a nutshell, the unbridgeable antagonism within Basque politics— one that, from Aguirre's perspective, came down to the antagonism between Basque and Spanish nationalisms. Both men were from Bilbao, both accepted the legacy of Gernika, both recognized the existence of a Basque national entity—and yet each man's ultimate national frame implied the exclusion of the other's. It would be in exile that the two men would come to terms with the failure of their antagonism.

While he served as minister of public works for the Spanish Republic in Madrid, in 1933 Prieto had developed, along with architect Ricardo Bastida, a series of urban plans. There was only one problem— Prieto was an atheist socialist, Bastida a fervent Catholic. Religious faith being central to Bastida's life, he found a solution of sorts to their unlikely collaboration—Bastida gave the salary he received from Madrid to charity so that God would grant his friend religious faith. When Prieto learned of his partner's action, he was moved to confess, "What a tragedy it is for me not to have religious faith." When Prieto's forty-six-year-old son died in Mexico and someone wanted to remove the crucifix on his coffin, atheist Prieto remembered Bastida and ordered that it remain there to honor his friendship. Bastida went to Mexico to console his grieving friend and offer him a crucifix he had designed; he became ill on the trip and died soon afterward. Prieto wrote a farewell piece for Bastida entitled, "To my most beloved friend." Religion had also separated Prieto and Aguirre. Yet the three Bilbainos, so apart in ideological terms, were bonded by friendship and civic responsibility. Gehry's and Guggenheim's late-century Bilbao was the deferred action of a plan designed seventy years earlier in Bilbao and New York by these three men's passion for their city. Aguirre's odyssey after the war was narrated in a book entitled *From Gernika to New York via Berlin*

After Prieto's cornea transplant failed in 1945, for days he was blind in the dark solitude of a New York hospital. In his imagination there was only one place to flee: Bilbao. Bilbao was his dreamscape—his *paradise*. He revisited in detail the projects he had shared with Bastida and Aguirre and tried to improve them in the maps of his imagination. "Every single night I think of Bilbao, of my Bilbao," he wrote. He was captive of a "Bilbao, city of iron, that forged chains of affection I could never break," his only paradise lost. The following year, while lecturing in Mexico, Prieto detailed his plans for the ambitious transportation hub that would transform Bilbao's infrastructure—a city a few thousand miles away and a plan not to be realized until half a century later. It was not until the late 1990s that James Stirling and Michael Wilford would design a transportation hub for the new Bilbao, which remains unbuilt.

If Bilbao was the candle in the night of an exiled Prieto, his city of lights, politics was all darkness. "My failure is total," Prieto wrote in a November 1950 letter of resignation to the executive committee of his Socialist Party. Washington had decided to support Franco, and Prieto saw his party as the "victim of an illusion." As a socialist, he was embarrassed that of all the European countries that voted against Franco in the United Nations General Assembly, not one was socialist. Prieto suffered heart failure three times the following spring. Aguirre held on to his pro-American dream until 1958, when finally he had to accept reality. He died of a heart attack in March 1960. Both were vanquished men, their hearts heavy and ready to explode, yet unwilling to bow to the betrayals of history.

When Prieto heard of his political antagonist Aguirre's death, he wrote of "a wound I will never be able to close." He eulogized Aguirre's "innate goodness" and the "magical force" of his "unshakable optimism." He praised Aguirre's work as "inspired by the deepest personal conviction," and claimed that nobody in any party, including his own, combined Aguirre's "exceptional qualities." But what is haunting is that Prieto started his eulogy by linking Aguirre's death with his own son's, in a clear expression of a father/son relationship—"because José Antonio was a few weeks older than my son, dead—with the same illness!—twelve years ago. They shared the same draft, they served in the military during the same period, and they even played together in a reserve [soccer] team of the Athletic Club." The loss of his son had left a grieving Prieto unable to function. Aguirre, worried that Prieto might abandon politics altogether, had urged him not to give up. What Aguirre could not have imagined was that his own death would be a reenactment of that filial one for Prieto. They were father and son, accepting the cross of history for the sake of their city. Prieto died two years later.

The exiled Prieto and Aguirre, broken men drinking together in New York's Jai Alai Restaurant, were stricken with the pathos of their singular political complicity. Half a century later, they remain a historic challenge to the Basque political deadlock still rumbling in Bilbao and Madrid. Despite his staunch nationalism, Aguirre, considered by some as "a sort of *prietista avant la lettre,*" displayed in exile extraordinary statesmanship—to the point that he was proposed to head the presidency of the Spanish Republican government-in-exile to carry out "the project of a co-federal [Spanish] State." Without equivocation, he recognized that "today we know that the Spanish problem cannot be resolved without our collaboration. Ah! But neither can the Basque problem be solved without resolving at once the Spanish problem." This co-dependency between the Basque and Spanish problems, so in contrast to his party-line Basque "separatism," caused even Aguirre's closest collaborators to think he was betraying the cause.

How did Prieto and Aguirre overcome their conflict? They had to accept that their antagonism could not admit a mediation—that, in sharp contrast to friendship or love, the enemy defines politics—while at the same time concede the *failure* of their antagonism. The only way each could be faithful to his own political truth and overcome its impasse was to include the other's perspective—they had to "bite the bullet" and see the validity of the other's truth. They saw the limits of their own oversimplifications when they divided their political space into two antagonistic fields, rather than situating one another in pluralist democratic space. Beyond a religious or secular view and beyond the big Others of the Nation and the State, Aguirre and Prieto forged a new type of political relation in which previous oppositions were not dissolved in a plurality but articulated differently in a Gramscian type of hegemonic interdependencies. Similar to Zarra's *nongoal* that dissolved the rules of the game, Aguirre and Prieto's recognition of their failures promised to transform the coordinates of what was politically possible.

As these leaders died and ETA emerged as the new political power, my generation had to confront all over again the unsolved political labyrinth regarding "the Basque problem." For the Basque resistance, an independent state with full sovereignty became the ultimate political desire. Hegel had claimed that the proper subject of historical narratives is the State, an abstraction made concrete in the conflict between desire and law. ETA's sacrifice has been for my generation the starkest proof of such an ultimate imperative. It had been easy to agree on the foundational idea behind ETA—"freedom"—yet its derivations into "independence," "sovereignty" or "nation-state" were far more contested. Influential authors such as Manuel Castells and Michael Keating wrote persuasively about the decline of the nation-state and about living in a "post-sovereign" era. European nation-states had delegated many of their basic historic competences to supra-state or sub-state institutions. Yet this "residual state," described in a series of reports in *El País* with the moon metaphor as "the waning state," is also the one that holds on to the fetish of its indissoluble sovereignty.

A theoretical mapping of what Aguirre and Prieto achieved can be articulated in terms of the changes they provoked in the hegemonic relations of their political system. The new articulation of political relations could at once, beyond the typical operation of populism, embrace what it opposes—that is, in Gramscian terms, a new hegemonic structure was needed to create a different and more expansive system of equivalences that started by recognizing that the terms of their antagonisms were not fixed in past history or present political convenience. They took their antagonisms not as final limits but as frontiers through which they found a larger political field in which more autonomy meant simultaneously more hegemonic interaction. What defines antagonism is that "the presence of the 'Other' prevents me from being totally myself" Laclau and Mouffe, *Hegemony*, 125..

Many of my generation are split between the Left's tradition of considering the creation of "ethnic states" as the initial step toward disaster and the national liberation tradition that sees a stagnant Spanish state that buttresses its centrist agenda with the legality of an untouchable democratic constitution. The Catalan intellectual Xavier Rubert de Ventós raised the question, "Does the State exist after the Nation-State?" The issue emerges as to what is more mythical and "ethnic," the current Spanish state with its claims to unity, universality, and "manifest destiny," or an alternative state that, Rubert advocates, is "constituted by a historic conglomerate of flows and functions," a system of a more direct and efficient redistribution of recourses and inclusive of any religion, morality, or worldview respectful of minimal rules.

Whether one advocates for "independence," "co-sovereignty," "federalism," or "autonomy," the solution to the continuing Basque political impasse requires the repetition in ideological and subjective terms of the complicity forged in exile by Aguirre and Prieto. Most likely they would have agreed with Edward Said who proposed, as a solution to the Israeli/Palestinian problem, to form a bi-national state in which both countries "are parts, rather than antagonists, of each other's history and underlying reality." But this requires a clear distinction between "state" and "nation," and a willingness from the central state to share sovereignty with the peripheral nations. It is in the end a matter of political will, where politics embodies, beyond party calculations, society's full desire, a truth forced by history and realized in a common cause that treats all people as equal beyond ethnic essentialisms. "A man can be destroyed but not defeated," Hemingway wrote of Santiago in *The Old Man and the Sea*. The shared truth of Aguirre and Prieto, the indispensable men of Basque politics, was crushed but not defeated. The dream of the new political order they foresaw is for Basque nationalists and socialists still an unfulfilled prophecy.

It was February 24 when Gemma Martínez and José Gabriel Rubí were in Paris having arrived from Bilbao to attend a meeting of the OECD (Organization for Economic Co-Operation and Development) at its Conference Center at the Rue de Andres Pascale, close to its headquarters at the Château de la Muette. As in other instances in Brussels, Martínez and Rubí were representing the Deputation of Bizkaia, where they work as technical experts in taxation, and by extention they

A crucial consequence of antagonism is that it provokes a misreading by which "the two antagonistic poles differ in the very way in which they define or perceive the difference that separates them." (Žižek, "Da Capo senza Fine," in *Butler et al. Contingency*, 215). A bipolar field gives rise to the "popular subject position" and is far different from a multipolar hegemonic field, ruled by the "democratic subject position." (Laclau and Mouffe, *Hegemony*, 131). What Aguirre and Prieto achieved was the transformation of their respective Basque and Spanish "popular" subject positions into truly "democratic" ones by erasing the nullifying presence and the mutual misreadings essential to the antagonistic Other. But we could say that they went even further in recognizing that democracy per se might not be enough to reconstitute a valid hegemonic project and that, besides the "democratic equivalence," what is needed is "the construction of a new 'common sense' which changes the identity of the different groups." Laclau and Mouffe, *Hegemony*, 183.

The current Basque political impasse calls for such "common sense" Prieto and Aguirre displayed.

were also representing the autonomous Basque Treasury. The right for Basque institutions to represent themselves in international fora had been won in 2002 by the then President Juan José Ibarretxe and Vice President Idoia Zenarruzabeitia from the Spanish government of José María Aznar in exchange for obtaining the support of the Basques for passing the state budget; it was later in 2010 that the State's commitment to such participation was made effective during José Luis Rodríguez Zapatero's government, again in exchange for Basque support at the Spanish House of Representatives to pass the state budget. Martínez and Rubí were part of the Spanish delegation, which included two more members representing the common territory of Spain. "Espagne" was located between "Danemark" and "Etats-Unis." The meeting was concerned with coordinating the fiscal policies of the various countries to avoid harmful tax practices; since the Basque territories have their own fiscal autonomy, Spain needed the commitment of the Basques to secure that it would not be blacklisted as uncooperative. Nothing else embodies sovereign entitlement as does tax policy, and OECD's task consists in coordinating the policies of its diverse member states.

Martínez and Rubí are essentially "technicians" and do not hold any political office. But at the OECD meeting they represented Basque self-government as expressed by its fiscal institutions that go back to the nineteenth century to an era previous to political parties, including the nationalist party. They represented internationally the *real* of Basque sovereignty, in its association with Spain but different from Spain, in a complicity of mutual dependence. OECD's assembly was a case of Rubert's argument that currently the only possible state is a conglomerate of flows and functions, that is, a state *after* the Nation-State. And what remains of the big Other of the Nation-State? It remains its potent symbolism, with all the unsolvable antagonisms that pained Prieto and Aguirre. But for both Spain and the Basque Country, the most real aspect of their sovereignty was being expressed in the committments that their four "technical" representatives were forced to accept at the OECD, one of the fora in which the actual sovereignty of the states in the current world is decided.

The Paris meeting was taking place the year in which Catalonia had planned to hold a referendum on independence or, in case this is declared unconstitutional, of having plebiscitary elections—after the central government refused to grant a fiscal regime similar to the one in the Basque Country. Suddenly, the Catalan society, known for its moderation as an autonomous region, has become in its majority independentist—an option that was quite minoritarian until recently. In the words of Antoni Segura, "Catalonia has passed from being a pro-autonomist region to becoming a pro-independence one without passing through the nationalist phase." In short, Catalans are not looking for the big Other of a Nation-State that will embody their national essences and their universal destiny, they are looking basically for a taxation system they can control from Barcelona and which will take into account their country's real needs.

But it is hard not to believe in the big Other. There might be much evidence to show that the Nation-State no longer operates within its former military, economic, and cultural parameters, but how can one stop believing in it and desiring it so much? And furthermore: Will the Nation-State ever find out that it no longer has the kind of sovereignty it used to have? One imagines Prieto and Aguirre attending the OECD meeting in representation of the Spanish and Basque treasuries and, while having squid in its black ink and Marqués de Murrieta, asking themselves at dinner: what is here the real of today and what the imaginary of yesterday? The real, says Aguirre, is that we share this table each one paying what is his due, and then helping those who have nothing out of our Christian or socialist convictions. To which Prieto replies: the imaginary are those giants we fought so hard against and that now happen to be windmills. It was jai alai in Paris.

A Red Dawn Is Breaking

"We remain hardly half a dozen," Prieto noted of his bilbaino militant friends, "We are volcanic mountains, with snow at the top and fire in our entrails. They have blown us out on the outside, but we are still burning from the inside." This revolutionary fire for a new red dawn was shared at one point by his former friend Unamuno and would be reignited in the spirits of other bilbainos such as Otero and Aresti.

Unamuno is the name for agnostic post-Christian thought in Bilbao. He was the Sophoclean hero who became one of Spain's key intellectuals during the first half of the twentieth century. The climax of his life was marked by his confrontation with the military at the University of Salamanca on October 1936. It was preceded in July by his delirious reaction to the news that Franco's troops had taken Salamanca when he went out to the street yelling "Long Live Spain, soldiers!" and calling them to go after the Republic's president Azaña. Days later, hearing of Republican officials—former comrades—being executed, Unamuno wrote of Prieto to the effect that hell was his destined place. As the fascists turned his bellicose discourse into their own ("the army is the only fundamental thing of value in Spain"), Unamuno realized that he had made a monumental blunder once again. Unamuno's name was erased from the Bilbao street that carried it and his awards annulled. Weeks later, in the main hall of the University of Salamanca, where he was the rector, in a solemn act to celebrate the Spanish Day of the Race and in which he was representing Franco, he confronted Franco's co-legionaire and close ally, General Millán-Astray, in a Socratic act of suicidal heroism—"You will win, but you will not convince!" "Death to intelligence!" shouted back the general's followers.

Unamuno surrounded by fascists at the University of Salamanca.

Unamuno was removed from his post. A hystericized Unamuno was and wasn't with the fascist army led by Franco, as before he was and wasn't with the turbulent Republic. He was visited during those dramatic days by the Greek novelist Nikos Kazantzakis, to whom he declared, "Despairing is he who knows very well that he has nothing to hold onto, that he doesn't believe in anything, and since he doesn't believe in anything he is overtaken by fury." Weeks later, Unamuno died of a heart attack.

Unamuno was condemned by the very Francoist Spain he tried to save. The Vatican put his writings in the Index of forbidden books, and Bilbao's bishop issued a letter of condemnation of Unamuno's works to be read in all of Bizkaia's churches. Unamuno was beyond Christianity, yet he combined modern atheism with existentialist religiosity, and his writings allowed my agnostic generation to retain humanistic and spiritual values. With his attempts at "conversion" and his tormented struggle with God, he embodied the fate of a Christian subject in a post-Christian world. In order to be a true writer in Bilbao, he had to assume a hysterical subject.

In his theatrical search for lost faith, Unamuno knew that "faith is passive, feminine, the daughter of grace; not active, masculine, and a product of arbitrary choice," and yet he dedicated an entire chapter to "the virility of faith"—he had to be manly and a fighter to the point of intimately identifying with the chivalrous Don Quixote, whose life was meaningless without the idealized figure of Dulcinea. Unlike Beatrice for Dante or Marilyn for Muschamp/Gehry, who were women from real life subject to actual passions, Dulcinea was Quixote/Unamuno's illusion of a female beauty that could only be idealized, never desublimated. Unamuno's struggle, much like Loyola's, is for a culture apart from real women that overvalues the good fight. His is a premodern heroism in which the subject risks everything for a Cause—except the Cause itself. Unamuno, in line with his quixotism and tragic sense of life, had a posthumous child he failed to anticipate—ETA, whose founders were fervently Unamunian.

Unamuno will surrender everything except the agonic struggle. Unamuno hasn't reached the modern ethical "feminine" stand in which the "exception" is itself sacrificed—not only the institutional structures but the specific forms of a religious experience—so that one's fundamental values can be redefined. Through Unamuno, many of my generation could replicate the experience that "the modern atheist thinks he knows that God is dead; what he doesn't know is that, unconsciously, he continues to believe in God." This is best illustrated with the joke of the man who goes to see the psychoanalyst because he believes he is the kernel of a grain; the analyst convinces him he is not; he goes out and soon returns terrified because he has seen a chicken outside; "but you know you are not a grain but a man," the analyst tells him; "yes I know," he replies, "but does the chicken know?" Unamuno knows that God doesn't exist, but does his God know He doesn't exist? Hence his obsession with and terror of God. This relationship toward the big Other (I don't believe in Him but I will worship Him) makes Unamuno the most religious of thinkers. The problem with his tragic sense of life or his agonic Christianity is his inability to see the comic side and the humor underlying them.

The Danish philosopher was Unamuno's spiritual teacher but he never learnt Kierkegaard's concept of irony, which was the topic of his doctoral dissertation and a key condition to his personality and his modern thought. Unamuno was too much of a searching and wishing individual to be ironical, for true irony consists in "situating one's pain at the precise point where others situate their desire. The inability to possess one's beloved is never irony. But the ability to possess her all too easily, so that she begs and pleads to become one's own—and *then* to be unable to possess her. That is irony." Socrates was the first ironist in history, and his death was provoked by "the ironic nothingness" of his moral stance. Unamuno saw his life in tragic terms, when in fact, as best expressed in the confrontation that preceded his death, it was deeply ironic: at that, his final public event, when he was representing the Caudillo Franco, whose wife was seated next to him and saved him from being lynched, he was the intellectual that embodied what his antagonist Millán-Astray was fighting for, and *then,* when the mutinous army led by Franco wanted to belong to him, he was "unable to possess" them. It was such "ironic nothingness" that provoked his ultimate despair and death.

Having lost the Christian god, Unamuno could not stop lamenting a lost eternity and romanticizing finitude. Anything but to celebrate the end of the big Other as the "good news" that opens the possibility of new freedom—that first one has to succumb and be duped by the big Other in order to discover the truth concealed in the illusion, that "being abandoned by God is the most God can give us." He couldn't bear to hear the message of his forsaken Christ—the resurrection of the humiliated body has *already* taken place in a new subjectivity.

Another type of writing, radically different from Unamumo's, emerged in Bilbao during the dictator's long rule. Gabriel Aresti was its main author. He wrote these verses, in the manner of the traditional bertsolari, as self-presentation; they became popular as Laboa sung them:

Poeta naizen ezkero,   Since I am a poet,
ez dut zerurik espero.   I don't expect paradise.
Bederatzi kopla ditut,   I have nine songs,
lau zuhur eta bost ero.   four wise and five fool.

Aresti did not take refuge in a prestigious university or glorify the superiority of Spanish or Greek while calling for a "pious death" of his native Basque. Neither did he buttress his work with the authoritarian claim to a universalism that, while extolling European civilization, was blind to its very particular interests. He remained unyielding in Bilbao's inferno. He undertook the poet's radical task of proclaiming an ideal city by espousing Dante's imagery of descent into hell and while attempting to resurrect his native culture and dying language. In his "Eleventh Rebellious Sonnet" he chastises Bilbao as "City raised against my Basque Country." The sonnet defines his city by playing the moon/sun dichotomy:

Here Bilbao. A sleeping city, life
harshly conquered in apathy.
A moon beam comes through, instantly
we forget we are children of the sun.

Like Dante and Blake, Vico and Joyce before him, Aresti provoked scandals and formulated prophecies in order to transform his city. His claim was that poetry, always a particular subjectivity, is the ultimate foundation of truth and knowledge. Aresti's event, and the greatest gift a language can receive from a poet, was his true re-creation of the native Euskara he learned as an adult, a work based on its best poetic bertsolari tradition and inspired by contemporary literature. He was the essential writer who taught us that aesthetic vision alone is not enough; that, beyond the Basque imaginary, Christian symbolism, and capitalist fetishism, there is the question of justice. His was not a dramatic search for lost faith à la Unamuno. Aresti's teaching was that if we wanted to get to the truth about Basques, if we wanted to revive our city, we had first to experience Bilbao's hell.

The young writers of my generation came of age to Aresti's images, made real in the sounds of his trepidant anthem, "Oskorria." They brought us to our feet:

Irrintzi bat entzun dugu	We heard a war cry
ezpataren aurrean.	marching before a sword.
Oskorria zabaltzen da	A red dawn is breaking
euskaldunen lurrean.	in the land of the Basques.

Twilight and dawn were one in his song—the dusk of Franco's regime and ETA's inaugural martyrdom. Ancestral voices echoed in this twilight, a crisis of Christianity tempered only by new Red beliefs. The presence of the proletarianized working classes rising from the nocturnal glare of molten metal in blast furnaces on the Nervión's Left Bank was inescapable in Aresti's Bilbao imaginary. For him, such a red sky prophesized the dawn of a new era, both the red sky at night, the "sailor's delight," and the red sky in the morning, "sailors take warning." By the late 1960s, Oskorri, a Bilbao music group, had named itself after Aresti's poem and was singing his lyrics.

Cover of Oskorri's record with Aresti's lyrics.

As Aresti became the indispensable author for my generation, so did Bilbao turn into a main literary reference. Aresti began a publishing house in Bilbao, while young writers and cultural militants from Donostia-San Sebastián began one of their own; Aresti agreed to transfer the rights of his editorial, including his own works, to his younger colleagues in exchange for a small, second-hand car. As Rikardo Arregi and Ramon Saizarbitoria were driving the car from Donostia-San Sebastián to Bilbao, they had a fatal accident in which Arregi died. A desolate Aresti, a father figure to them, wrote that it was him who should have died instead; he dedicated the first part of his next book of poems to Saizarbitoria, and the second part to Arregi: "In this city of Dante/ Euzkadi is, / Rikardo, / my cross." Arregi was leading a campaign for Basque literacy and was a noted essayist who wrote on topics such as socialism and Christianity. That very year Saizarbitoria would publish *Egunero hasten delako* (Because it begins everyday), considered the first truly modern Basque novel, one that embraces the modern subject's malleable and universalizing creativity. Death on the road was not only for ETA activists such as Etxebarrieta; it could also be the destiny of a writer, his risks no less devastating, his death no less real. The day Arregi died on the road to Bilbao, July 20, 1969, was the day Neil Amstrong and Buzz Aldrin landed on the moon. It was that old Bilbao moon.

A revival in Basque literature followed. Literary narration became a crucial arena for creating new subjectivities free of the traditional moralisms of culture and politics. The inescapable dilemmas of Basque society—caught between Spanish fascism and ETA's violence, traditional Christianity and modern agnosticism, sexual repression and new liberties—called for a field of knowledge best treated in the novel. While revealing the paradoxical pitfalls of "action," literature allowed the ambiguities needed for a new cultural imagination. Txillardegi, Saizarbitoria, Anjel Lertxundi, Arantza Urretabizkaia, and other writers published novels. They were followed by Bernardo Atxaga who became the internationally best-known writer of this generation. His *Obabakoak* (Those of Obaba) depicts an imaginary place traversed by wild white boars and people gone mad because a lizard has entered their heads through an ear while they were sleeping in the grass. By inserting one text within another, mixing reality and dream, Atxaga's narratives perplex the reader and call for an acceptance of the magical reality of folk stories—the very status of reality is questioned, along with the impossibility of language to capture it. Atxaga wrote most of the various stories that make up his novel during the 1970s and 1980s while living in Bilbao and returning regularly to his rural hometown where his mother lived. Of Bilbao, he said, "It is my city, my motherland in one way, or two ways, or three ways." Atxaga found a voice for the culture's imaginary world submerged as a spectral presence in his contemporary literary society. As Aresti and Otero and Oteiza had to descend into Bilbao's "hell" before finding in Arantzazu a mountain escape, Atxaga's "Obaba" became an inevitable return to place for Basque literature through the crucible of the industrial city—a literary paradise of sorts.

It was early June 1975, and in Bilbao's Cruces hospital a forty-one-year-old moribund Aresti was cursing death and singing his prophetic song "Oskorria"—"a red dawn is breaking in the land of the Basques." Two days later, I was one of those carrying his casket at the cemetery in Derio. We distributed his best-known poem with which Basques identified the most, "I will defend my father's house." I had visited him at the hospital earlier that week when he seemed to be recuperating from his liver surgery. He was delighted when I told him I was going abroad to study anthropology, and he showed me one of the two books he was reading—an anthropological study of kinship systems. Like many of my generation, I had become a writer under his influence, and his death became a mandate to write. I learned from who else but him that Bilbao is a Dantesque city and I found inspiration from him to give my book a Dantean structure. Given the impact of his writing on my generation, Steer's words in *The Tree of Gernika*—describing the impact of bombs at the cemetery of Derio splitting the tombs asunder—seemed also written for Aresti: "Buried? No, it was resurrection day in Derio."

The Subject: Zero and the Infinite

If not Unamuno's Subject (agonic, histerical, finitist), what model should we accept for the post-metaphysical Subject needed to rebuild the new city? The transformation of a pleasure-seeking individual into a subject calls for an appropriate theory that goes beyond the designation of the subject as "experience," "morality," or "ideology." For those of my generation who have struggled with the horizons provided by politics, religion, or philosophy, the formalization of the subject derived from post-Cantorian thought, anchored in the notions of zero and the infinite, and from psychoanalysis, becomes pivotal. The technical aspects of this body of theory are beyond the scope of this book, but its consequences are central to the view taken here—for the true Architect taken here, the maker of the new Bilbao, modeled after Plato's Ideal City, is no other than "the Subject—this Minotaur bereft of any Theseus."

Zero is the first and fundamental number. Zarra's *non*-goal was his best performance ever. The *huts* (error, void) forced on the opponent is what fills the fronton with glory in the game of jai alai. It was the *failure* of their antagonism that made the interaction between Prieto and Aguirre historic. Oteiza's *dis*-occupation of Euclidean forms and his aesthetics of *huts* (voids) were his crowning achievement. The elliptical plaza's *de*-centering finds its form as infinite revolution, and it is

Modern mathematics redefined the concept of number on the basis of zero or the empty set. To say that zero is a number is the foundation of Frege's entire edifice. By starting with zero, there was no privileging of "one," a conceptual decision that would not allow Frege to fall back on the idea of "the All" as proceeding from "the One." The ontological and subjective consequences of such "dissipation of the One" are far-reaching, for it marks "a lavishing without measure of infinities. . . . Unbinding from the One delivers us to the unicity of the void and to the dissemination of the infinite" (Alain Badiou, *Number and Numbers*, 14-15). The existence of zero is "absolutely inaugural" in that it "ensures the possibility of separating any extension of a concept whatsoever" (Badiou, *Number*, 22). Zero and infinity are in the end "declarations" that cannot be supported by a final argument and are fragile in their historicity. And yet the world of modern thought is nothing other than the effect of these axiomatic injunctions, absolutely necessary for current science and knowledge. Humanity is not obligated to this knowledge; only a decision makes it real. The problem of infinity concerns art, religion, and culture in general, but the modern subject as such in particular.

the bertsolari's *ellipsis* that makes her sing endlessly of life. The flying queen of Basque traditional mythology is "nourished by the *no,*" a nod to current theories of feminine subjectivity as characterized by the *not-all.* What these all have in common is *subtraction.*

If Oteiza found himself "without sculpture," "Aresti stripped his poetry of any traces of *literature*" and proclaimed his own "resignation from poetry." In Otero, one sees a "destruction" of his poetic language as the years go by. Like Aresti, he expresses a preference for oral poetry over literature. Gehry's building of symptomal torsions follows their steps by producing a sort of auto-immolation of architecture. Like Zarra, the soccer forward refusing to score, they *end* their art for the sake of its re-creation in a different framework by subtraction.

For my generation, truth meant enacting *de*-conversion. Expelled from Paradise, we were outcasts in a world that was not the result of new knowledge but rather of a sudden *dis*belief—a denial of belief in the big Other of religion, to be followed by other similar denials in other domains. Disbelief opened space for new thought and the possibility of a new subject. The deconverted experiences that there is no secret and nothing to gain from the alleged omnipotence of the big Other. De-conversion is one more aspect of subtractive thought, one that is not mere "destruction" or negation of the status quo, but rather the *affirmative* part of negation. The new wager becomes a break with the old, abandons traditional representations, rebels against the oppressive status quo, formalizes a new conception of life and reality. The very weakness of the subtracted position—the lack of belief, the lack of commitment, the lack of partisanship, the lack of sacrifice—becomes its strength, a conviction born of losing other convictions. It is the disbelief *after* belief, the de-conversion *after* conversion that becomes the event—in Badiou's words, "whoever is the subject of truth . . . knows that, in effect, he bears a treasure, that he is traversed by infinite power."

But what can an ethnographer do with the notion of infinity? A song, a *bertso,* a play, a desire, an elliptical form are all measures of infinity. My generation thought of the infinite in terms of origin, omnipotence, a divine being—not as mere conceptual and subjective property. In time, many came to realize that our understanding of infinity in terms of a personal God was a "fundamental fantasy." But still, the infinite could not disappear from desire, for "desire is nothing but that which introduces into the subject's universe an incommensurable or infinite measure." This is a desire that, following Lacan, resides in "the body as distinct from the organism inasmuch as it is not a biological real but rather a form." No longer able to

The Lacanian conception of the "subject" of thought and desire, as both lack and excess, provides the intellectual horizon of our times. Lacan's conception is based on responding to the Fregean question about what constitutes the sequence in numbers; for him the "nothing" and "excess" that allows the very genesis of the progression of numbers is precisely "the function of the subject" (Jacques-Alain Miller quoted in Badiou, *Number,* 24). The contribution of psychoanalysis to current thought is to subtract axiomatically the Subject from the despotism of number. There are however significant differences in current formulations of the subject. For Lacan and Žižek, it is the subject of the unconscious agency of the signifier—"it coincides with its own impossibility; it 'is' nothing but the void opened up by the failure of its representations. . . . In Lacanian theory the subject is nothing but the impossibility of its own signifying representation—the empty place opened up in the big Other by the failure of this representation" (Žižek, *Sublime Object,* 208). For Badiou, however, "this impossibility is simply what can be known of the subject from within the existing situation. Becoming a subject is in every case exceptional, the result of an operation in which language and signification enjoy no special privilege" (Hallward, *Badiou,* 144). The division of the subject can be approached by way of the symptom or by way of creation. What is at stake here is the Pascalian opening—a truth whose veracity is the wager of the subject who decides.

believe in religious transcendence, not surprisingly many of my generation decided to surrender their lives to the political cause—"giving your life" for political freedom was a way to repeat that *infinitizati on* of desire. Martyrdom was a thousand times preferable to the loss of infinity for the many former seminarians and priests who entered ETA.

There is a romantic notion of infinity and a contemporary notion of infinity. Poetic writing is one paramount expression of the sublime romantic infinity, as in Otero's 1941 unpublished poem to a Bilbao woman, Beatriz, with whom he fell in love when she was fifteen (she provided me with this copy in 2006):

LA luna, esa otra enamorada	THE moon, that other one in love
. . . Navega por tus ojos	. . .She navigates by your eyes
queriendo conseguir los infinitos	trying to reach the infinite
horizontes de paz . . .	horizons of peace . . .

The infinity that Otero sees in the lilylike candor of his beloved's gaze is romantic infinity—or romantic eternity, as when Unamuno wrote of the "eternal moon" and the moon being a "mirror of eternity." One could even add that infinity is *the* romantic concept *par excellance.*" What is at stake in contemporary culture (art, religion, politics, marriage) is the *banal* reality of axiomatized infinity. A purely subtractive notion of infinity does not imply a sublime intuition of experience but means simply that "we are infinite because we think infinitely." When Garazi, a five-year-old child insistently asks, "Daddy, why do we *have* to die?" she is confronted with the dialectics between finitude and the infinite that is inaugural to the subject; for the child's "eternal love" the discovery of mortality becomes shattering. The infinite is not captured in any ideal form, but "transits through form." This implies a full laicization of an infinity without aura.

The crisis undergone by my generation in its religious, ethical, or artistic practices is related to modern thought's challenge for "another articulation of the finite and the infinite." Feminine subjectivity has been theorized by Lacanian psychoanalysis as the "*not*-all," a negative that links it with the infinite. The pivotal reversal in current thought consists in that, if traditionally "infinity" was the domain of idealist spiritualism, "today, the main argument for spiritualism, against radical materialism, relies on the irreducibility of human finitude . . . while it is today's forms of radical scientific materialism which keep the spirit of infinity alive." It is ordinary being itself that is infinite for the moderns.

BRIEF ELEGY OF THE MOON
AND SOME TRANSPARENT EYES

THE moon, that other enamored one
—in love with sad things,
soft, tenuous, blue and impossible—
it is for you . . .
She navigates by your eyes
trying to reach the infinite
horizons of peace, where things
show us their unlearned mystery . . .
. . . .
Oh, moon, eternal dreamer,
eternally alone, sad, and cold,
ignored by the world, by the most
beautiful things you love! . . .
All day long
I am thinking of you. All night
I go to the window wondering
how, over my hands, your light falls
and kisses my mouth . . . My soul
becomes, for you, a garden where,
among shadows,
your enchanted tunic goes
. . . .
Moon: imprisoned dove. Iris
sleeping in my mind: you are not
alone.
I know that soft eyes
are watching you, transparent,
as clean as you, so infinite
that, while traveling with you through
the sky
they repeat your candor, oh, moon!

(Author's translation)

ETA declared a definitive end to all violence in 2011. The political
forces backing ETA created a new coalition party, Bildu, which distanced itself from the use of violence and became the second major
political force after winning 25 percent of the Basque vote in municipal elections. Bildu chose Laura Mintegi as its candidate for the Basque
presidency; in an ideological reversal from the line traced for ETA by
the Etxebarrieta brothers, Mintegi declared that "the style of politics"
of former president Aguirre was the new model for her coalition. ETA
is the crucible that tested my generation to the limit, the sword of liberation that became the shackles of a blind love for sacrifice. After
ETA, the formation of a new political subjectivity became a primary
task for my generation.

There is one extraordinary model for such a post-ETA subject—
Yoyes, the nom-de-guerre of María Dolores González Catarín, one
of the teenage girls in ETA's 1970s underground. When her sister was
arrested and tortured in Bilbao, Yoyes was forced into exile in 1974. By
1978, she held one of ETA's highest leadership positions. But the following year she decided to abandon the armed organization and start
a new life in Mexico, where she studied sociology and, in 1982, had a
son. She returned to Paris in 1985 and then settled in Donostia-San
Sebastián with her son and her partner. On September 10, 1986, while
visiting her town during the Basque fiestas, she was shot and killed as a
traitor by her former comrades in front of her three-year-old son.

Yoyes effected a breakthrough. Not only had she given herself
entirely to the "terrorist" cause of Basque independence, she ended
up sacrificing the Cause/Exception itself. If Abraham had been willing to sacrifice his son for the sake of the big Other, Yoyes would not.
Kierkegaard, who wrote the story of Isaac losing his faith in the God
of his idolatrous father, was behind much of Unamuno's existentialist
thinking, and both philosophers were cornerstones to Txillardegi and
Etxebarrieta. What was said of the Danish philosopher—that "Abraham
was not only Kierkegaard's father, who offered his son as a sacrifice, but
Abraham was also Kierkegaard himself, who sacrificed Regine"—could
be applied to Txillardegi's Leturia character and to Etxebarrieta, both of
whom sacrificed what they most loved, Miren and Isabel, for the sake of
the country. In the Miren of his first novel, Txillardegi defined for my
generation the role of woman in relation to revolutionary action—she
is essentially a stand-in for true desire, a kind of symptom who cannot

María Dolores González Cataraín, Yoyes.

satiate the male hero's thirst for the Absolute. Saizarbitoria put an end to this literary legacy with a short story in which its two protagonists Sabine and Polikarpo bury the stolen remains of Sabino Arana, the founder of Basque nationalism, before he switches his desire from the father's sacred relic to his desire for her—"You are my motherland," he tells her. Sabine, like Yoyes, is the real deal who refuses to be reduced to a substitute for a male projection.

Yoyes showed that the glorification of the sacrificial hero was a *masculine* affair. "I don't like the business of heroism," she wrote in her diary. With her decision to challenge ETA, Yoyes faced and rejected the symbolic order of her own former militant big Other as the condition of an autonomous ethics. She wrote that introducing feminist perspectives into the underground organization was a "most urgent task," adding, "What should I do for these men to understand and fully assume that women's liberation is a revolutionary priority?" Not only does she reject the machismo of her comrades, she is afraid that it might infect her as well: "I don't want to become the woman who is accepted because men consider her in some way macho." When the organization repeatedly tried to lure her back to armed activism, she described their efforts as something akin to those of "a spurned husband abandoned by his wife."

In her writings, Yoyes describes the radical changes she experienced in the coordinates of her subjectivity. She had the unique courage to openly take the position that "in the modern ethical constellation . . . one *suspends this exception of the Thing*: one bears witness to one's fidelity to the Thing by *sacrificing (also) the Thing itself*." In both her surrender to and then her overcoming the ethics of martyrdom, Yoyes became ETA's most consequential member. She embodied the Kierkegaardian paradox of "being a martyr without the martyrdom associated with being a martyr."

Yoyes persevered in her new freedom until she was murdered. What Copjec wrote about Antigone applies to her: "Perseverance does not consist in the repetition of a 'pattern of behavior', but of the performance, in the face of enormous obstacles, of a creative act, and it results not in the preservation of the very core of her being—however wayward or perverse—but of its complete overturning. Antigone's perseverance is not indicated by her remaining rigidly the same, but by her *metamorphosis* at the moment of her encounter with the event of her brother's death and Creon's refusal to allow his burial." ETA's refusal to allow Yoyes's own desire for having a child and ordinary family life turned her into an unyielding rebel, but this time not in defiance of Spanish rule but against her former comrades. She persevered by keeping the faith, not to a nationalist allegiance, but to an inner ethical core. Yoyes's drama was, as Butler wrote of Antigone, "a conflict internal to and constitutive of the operation of desire and, in particular, ethical desire." By her decision to oppose ETA, Yoyes, who writes of a feeling of "entombment," made of herself, like Antigone, a figure "between two deaths," or "beyond life and death."

As a prelude to Yoyes's decision, in 1982 the politico-military branch of ETA, rival to Yoyes's military branch, had decided to dissolve itself after a period of questioning the value of armed struggle. As would happen later to Yoyes, hundreds of militants became instant traitors. They understood well the apocryphal doctrine in Judas's gospel: "Betray me if you really love me." When he was eighteen, Onaindia would go to Bilbao to attend social gatherings in which Aresti took part; during the eight years he spent in prison as a member of ETA and later as a citizen involved in Basque politics and culture, he wrote in Basque some ten literary books and translated as many to Basque (including three plays by Brecht), besides many other works in Spanish on politics, history, sociology, and cinema. For Onaindia and many others of our generation who sought a left-wing politics distanced from violence as method, sacrificing their militant lives for the country had been the easy part. Now, when they no longer believed in killing and dying for a country, they were confronted with a "second death" as they turned into enemies of their own nationalist community. Their ideological crucible between Basque and Spanish nationalisms was a repetition of the agonizing impasses inherent to the political interdependencies experienced by Aguirre and Prieto. The killing of Yoyes in 1986, wrote Onaindia, a historic former ETA militant and the secretary of the political party backing the dissolved ETA branch, was "the crisis of all of us who experienced the deception of the collapse of the revolutionary myth." When I met Onaindia the following year he was writing about Hollywood's western films. Onaindia's biography was all about the stark realities of life and death in his search for freedom (he died in a hospital room protected by bodyguards), yet one might add that its truth had the fictional structure of a cinematic western, including the defense of the rule of law as the ultimate guardian of freedom.

"The cowboys have killed Mom," Yoyes's three-year-old son told his family after seeing her ETA comrades shoot at her. Yoyes had forced an evolution of the alternative "Revolution or Death" by showing that ETA had corrupted the empowering revolutionary dilemma into a forced choice that ruled out her subjective freedom. This was comparable to the mugger's alienating dilemma, "Your money or your life," where the alternative resides entirely in the realm of the Other. The radicalness of Yoyes's act consisted precisely in having transformed her understanding of both "freedom" and "death" in the revolutionary dilemma. From her beginning with ETA, "death" had intersected with "freedom" in the revolutionary domain, but for the later Yoyes both terms collided in her own gendered being. As Yoyes resexualized her life, the fusion of love and death took on a different dynamic. By evolving beyond ETA's subject, Yoyes was the Ariadne who unbound the Blind Minotaur.

Yoyes's breakthrough consisted in that she came to see the unconscious link between the political superego, male symbolic castration, and the need for sacrifice—a powerful psychic complex that requires a psychoanalytic reading. Yoyes had become "the man" in ETA by imposing a different subjectivity. She was the one who showed her comrades, who had defined themselves as Gernika's victims, the transposition by which they had turned into executioners themselves. After the Yoyes event, ETA would no longer be the same.

"A fight against death"—that's how Yoyes summed up her life. What Zambrano wrote of archetypal figures such as Antigone, that they "actualize somehow the promise of resurrection," applies to Yoyes. The same ETA militants who assassinated her would soon embrace Yoyes's positions and call for an end to sacrificial politics. Zambrano's play about Antigone's tomb provides an uncanny script of the agon between Yoyes and ETA: "Yes, you had to kill and die," Antigone reproaches her brothers Polynices and Eteocles. "Mortals have to kill, they believe they are not men if they don't kill. . . . You have to kill among brothers out of love, for the good of everyone." But the violent brothers also want reconciliation, and they remind her that they are just "Father's wretched sons"—"Antigone, it all comes from our Father," the blind Oedipus. The brothers insist that they have come to rescue her from the tomb, "because you cannot stay here. This is not your house, it is only the tomb where you have been thrown alive. . . . We will found the city of brotherhood, the new city."

On April 30, 2006, the residents of Deba gathered in the plaza to pay homage to the deceased historic ETA militant Jokin Gorostidi. The bertsolari Jon Lopategi sang a strophe in his memory:

In the patriarchal regime, the actual father never measures up to the Other of the symbolic father; the actual father has to borrow his authority from the second. "Symbolic castration" is the psychoanalytic name for the price one has to pay when one is acting in the name, not of oneself, but of a superior Other he embodies. Lacan came up with the distinction between "feminine" and "masculine" modes of subjectivity on the basis of Kant-inspired female and male modes of failure regarding the "phallic function." He concluded that there is on the female side a fundamental undecidability of the not-all (not all of her is subject to the phallic rule), whereas on the male side all of man is subject to it (with the exception that at least one escapes to the rule). The "feminine" subjectivity, grounded in the premise of the "not-all," relies on an ontological definition of being as plural and partial, in which the objects of desire and drive get highlighted. To the question of why woman does not form an "all," Lacan's answer is that "she is not susceptible to the threat of castration; the 'no' embodied by this threat does not function for her." Copjec, *Imagine*, 35.

Ohore Jokin gudari	Honor to the soldier Jokin
eredu eta gidari.	model and guide.
Eredu eta gidari	Model and guide
ohore Jokin gudari.	honor to the soldier Jokin.
Merituaren sari	Let us praise his work
askatzeko Euskadi.	to liberate Euskadi.
Sortu zintuen herriak	The country that begat you
sortuko ditu berriak.	Will beget new ones.

A heavy silence followed while Jokin's lifelong companion, Itziar Aizpurua, another historic ETA militant and native of Deba, climbed the steps to the platform, carrying his ashes. She placed the urn on a table covered with red roses. Speaking in Euskara, she proceeded to give a vivid account of her dead companion's life as a militant, and of their forty years together. "Strong emotions leave me speechless," she had written to Jokin when they were both in jail. But not that afternoon. We listeners were gripped by the moment, avoiding each other's gazes, our faces distorted with emotion.

Months later, Itziar published a joint autobiography of Jokin and herself. It is the love story of a lifelong romance, beginning with their secret religious wedding and their ETA militancy, when they would sleep with Jokin's huge Astra pistol next to their pillow (the Astras were built in Gernika, but ETA bought them on the international market), and their arrest and trial in Burgos. During the eight years they were jailed under harsh conditions, they were rarely allowed to see each other; on those occasions she would put on makeup and wear a miniskirt for him. They dreamed of having a child, whom they even named Aralar, but only if it would not interfere with their revolutionary struggle. Led by the historic figure Telesforo Monzón and in the company of other militants, they swore at the monastery of Leire, where the first kings of Navarre were buried during the ninth and tenth centuries, "to never give in and forever fight" until the Basque Country had achieved full sovereignty and unity.

When, on June 7, 1968, Txabi Etxebarrieta died in his fateful encounter with the Spanish police, he was on his way to a meeting with Gorostidi. They had spent many hours together, and often while driving Txabi would frequently ask Jokin to sing him boleros by Antonio Machín, such as "Angelitos negros" (Little Black Angels) or "Dos gardenias para ti" (Two Gardenias for You):

Dos gardenias para ti.	Two gardenias for you.
Con ellas quiero decir:	With them I want to say:
Te quiero, te adoro, mi vida.	I love you, I adore you, my life.

As he studied the male and female's relationships to the phallus, Lacan concluded that the castrated one is not the woman, as Freud thought, but it is the man who is completely dependent on the phallic signifier and therefore subjected to symbolic castration. The prohibition of the Father, on the other hand, inaugurates the domain of the superego—the internalization of ideals fashioned by society. The superego is for Lacan "a correlate of castration." Lacan, *On Feminine Sexuality*, 7. In the original scenario of castration, the boy, not the girl, is subjected to the father's prohibition. Castration is enacted for boys as a prohibition coming from a "beyond"—the law that inaugurates the superego. It is this cruel superego that is always thirsty for sacrifice and that affects masculinity in particular. "Feminine" and "masculine" are not substantive gendered realities nor are they trapped in any binary logic, rather they involve two subjective modalities.

The romantic singing of Machín's sensuous voice was a major presence in the radio culture of Franco's Spain and a key emotional component in the sentimental education of Spaniards during the dictatorship. By the 1960s, with television and new musical tastes, including the new Basque protest song, Machín's era was coming to an end. But he was still popular in Bilbao, and Etxebarrieta sometimes asked Gorostidi to join him in singing Machín's balads. After all, while defining themselves as revolutionaries, "both were in love." Che Guevara was their guerrilla hero, but the prerevolutionary Cuban mulatto Machín's boleros were a perfect expression of their sentimental lives with song such as "Cuando tú me besas" (When you kiss me), "Anoche hablé con la luna" (Last night I talked to the moon), or "Espérame en el cielo" (Wait for me in heaven).

Both Gorostidi and Aizpurua had been deeply impacted by Etxebarrieta's death. Gorostidi conversed with him in dreams. Thirty-eight years later, as Gorostidi's remains were being honored in Deba's plaza, it appeared that he and Etxebarrieta were having their final rendezvous—the one that had not taken place in 1968 because of the tragic road incident. ETA had just declared, once again, a much-anticipated ceasefire, and it seemed that this time the clandestine organization that had defined my generation politically was finally coming to an end. Offering up her man's ashes could also be seen as Aizpurua's tribute to ETA's beginning and end, the sacrificial weight in ashes of more than forty years.

That urn of ashes in Aizpurua's hands brought me back to London during the Burgos Trial in December 1970, when Gorostidi, like Onaindia, was given two death sentences by Franco. Onaindia had been the last one to testify in front of the military court that would condemn them to death—ETA's goals, he stated, were national liberation and a classless society. He then declared himself a "prisoner of war," shouted "Long Live a Free Euskadi," and began singing in the company of Gorostidi and the rest of the condemned comrades the "Basque Soldiers' Song" as some members of the military tribunal rose to brandish their sabers.

It was there in London where I met Wilson during his hunger strike in Trafalgar Square. Gorostidi and Onaindia's portraits were among those of the six condemned men on display in the massive London protest. Since then, Gorostidi's face had remained indelible in my memory. There we were again in the presence of that face, sing-

Gorostidi and Onaindia standing at center and right on the top row.

ing the song that summed up his life and death, and echoing with the drama of the Burgos Trial:

Eusko gudariak gara	We are Basque soldiers
Euskadi askatzeko.	to free Euskadi.
Gerturik daukagu odola	We are ready
bere aldez emateko.	to shed our blood for her.

But now, though, since the recent ceasefire, it was the need to shed blood for the Mother Country that had become problematic even for Gorostidi. Onaindia had disavowed sacrificial politics and pushed ETA's political-military branch into disarming by 1983, thus creating a painful rift within ETA's military followers who, like Gorostidi, believed that its activism was still necessary. This militant belief had gone as far as justifying Yoyes's murder in 1986. But now, two decades later, Gorostidi had declared himself in favor of political negotiation to end the armed struggle. Gorostidi's ashes were not only bringing to completion Etxebarrieta's legacy; they were also perhaps calling for a reconciliation with Onaindia and Yoyes.

A large banner in the plaza proclaimed: "The best homage, victory." The dominant slogan was "Independence!" One speaker compared Gorostidi to the IRA leader Bobby Sands, who had died in a hunger strike, observing that IRA militants were also "terrorists" and thanks to them Northern Ireland was achieving sovereignty. We could expect the same for Euskadi, he said, thanks to the lives of militants like Jokin.

Faced with both the ashes of Gorostidi and the ashes of ETA, our question was how to turn them into seeds of freedom, not fascism, for, as Benjamin observed, every fascist movement is a failed revolution. At one point, the loudspeakers began playing Laboa's song "Stardust," with lyrics written by Lete:

Izarren hautsa egun batean	One day, the stardust
bilakatu zen bizigai:	became vital matter:
hauts hartatikan uste gabean	from that stardust unexpectedly
noizbait ginaden gu ernai.	at some point we were born.

Ashes to stardust. "We are stardust"—Joni Mitchell had sung at the Isle of Wight concert I attended thirty-five years earlier. In traditional Basque culture, various ritual settings require the power of ashes. Gorostidi's remains were in the best of that ritual tradition, his ashes an invitation to life.

Itziar spread Jokin's ashes by the sea, over the rocks where they used to walk in the evenings. Daily she visits those rocks at nightfall to be with him. "Jokin, I've gone to bring you a rose," she wrote to him at one point. "I kissed the rose and left it at the sea, hoping that the tide would raise it until it reaches you, with the warmth of my kiss in it." But not all could be roses and kisses; at one point, "unawares, I did something I couldn't avoid: I raised my arm and with my fist clenched I sang for you *Eusko gudariak,* like in Burgos, with the sea and the moon as witnesses." It was always the presence of that old moon, described as the goddess of ancient Basque pagan religion from Strabo to Caro Baroja, turned more recently into Brecht's and Lauaxeta's green moon, telling forever the story of life's transformation through birth, death, and rebirth—for the "story of the Moon . . . is the story of death and resurrection."

"The world tells you lies, heart / lies covered in glitter"—began the opening song "Antzinako bihotz" (Ancient Heart) in a concert by Paco Ibáñez and Imanol at Bilbao's packed Arriaga Theater in the Spring of 1999. Ibáñez was the indispensable, censored singer of the resistance to Francoism, standing and accompanied by a strapless guitar resting on his left leg raised on a wooden chair. His lyrics were those of the main Spanish poets, his gritty voice, either intimate or vibrant, a presence in all the student protests of the 1960s and 1970s, while also capable of a sellout concert at the Olympia of Paris. Imanol was a former dancer and ETA militant who began his musical career extolling the revolutionary struggle, including a song dedicated to Txabi Etxebarrieta; he became a pariah to the Basque nationalist public after singing for Yoyes at her funeral and ended up in self-exile before dying in 2004; one of his last records, with Karlos Giménez on the piano, was a haunting version of Saint John of the Cross's Canticle: "Where have you hidden, beloved . . . I went out calling, but you were gone."

   Ibáñez singing in Spanish and Imanol in Basque have been two iconic singer/songwriters for my generation. The 1999 Bilbao concert, presenting a jointly produced album with Basque songs entitled *Oroitzen* (Remembering), and with a cover designed by Oteiza, was a sort of reckoning with our past. The opening song began slowly, intimately, in a near whisper. Ibañez's worn voice trembled and was sustained by Imanol's harmonizing baritone on a higher note. The song warns the heart against the seductions of this world, and the duos rendition built to the crescendo. The final strophe of the song (with lyrics by Federico Krutwig and music by Lete) is a summary of and still a manifesto for my generation:

CD *Oroitzen* (1999) by Imanol and Paco Ibáñez with cover designed by Oteiza.

Jainko gorde hoiek	All you Gods, in hiding
ez zaituztet gurtzen nik.	I don't worship you.
Zuek ere hilkorrak zarete	You too are mortals
eta ezerezera segurki zoazte	and you surely going to nothingness
ezer ez baizerate.	for you are nothing.

The defiance against all Gods constituted my generation, a defiance by now turned into irony. ETA was our Blind Minotaur in a labyrinth of political desire. Picasso's archetypal images of Ariadne and the Minotaur, *Guernica*'s broken sword, and the rose *are* us. But Ariadne and the Minotaur are finally unbound. ETA's ashes covered with roses in the plaza of Deba made us realize that the collapse of the big Others is the transformative experience of our generation. From that stardust we are reborn.

CD *Barne Kanta* (1994) by Imanol and Karlos Giménez with cover by Chillida.

The Body

I went to visit Ramón, a retired politician who received me in his house brandishing the book he'd been re-reading again, *The Body,* a title he pronounced for me in English. This is the U.S. theologian John Robinson's Pauline study by which man's hope for his "body" of sin and death "lies in the resurrection of the body" proclaimed by Paul's belief that "your bodies are members of Christ" (Cor. 6:15) and his gospel of "the new corporeity of the Body of Christ." Surprised, I asked how a politician like him, who had occupied the highest leadership positions in his Basque Nationalist Party, could be reading this kind of stuff. He told me that these were authors he had read during his adolescence, while he was still a practicing Catholic, under the influence of who else but the Jesuit Bengoa. Ramón was one of several people I was struck by in Bilbao not only by the urgency of St. Paul's declaration "Christ is resurrected" in their lives, but also by the radical transformations in their current understanding of this foundational Christian event.

At age fifteen, Ramón had led a strict life of discipline, annual "spiritual exercises," and a weekly sacramental religious practice under Bengoa's aegis. At age nineteen he experienced a "deep religious crisis" and confessed to the town priest that he no longer believed in God. He read radical theologians such as Dietrich Bonhoeffer, Paul Tillich, and Robinson—authors who gave him inner "tranquility" by claiming that true Christianity has to do with taking care of *this* world. After considering and then discarding the option of joining ETA, he decided to devote his life to party politics. But given the rough and tumble world of politics, after realizing that "those people you trust, people you have mythified, as you get to know them up close you realize they fail," he despaired and fell into a crisis.

At forty, the idealist Ramón concluded that "man fails" and "man by himself is not enough." He returned to the radical theologians, *The Body* in particular. For them, he told me, a *resurrected* body "is not what they taught us. The flesh is not resurrected. What remains alive is Jesus's way of understanding society, of understanding and behaving, a true revolution—a message mostly for the poor and the destitute. God is not an abstract thing; love is something you have to show in concrete behavior towards your neighbor." Ramón concluded, "What Saint Paul says is that we are all *one body* with Jesus and that we all will be saved together." His position challenged my liberal intellectual tendency to see belief in resurrection as an escape into the spiritual and the symbolic; for him it all had to do with his own experience of the traumatic *real* of his own life and society.

I met Sara in Bilbao. She is a doctor, psychoanalyst, and mother, a radiant woman in her mid-fifties. She had married a former priest and social activist and gone to live in a town on Bilbao's Left Bank. The marriage collapsed. She remarried and moved into Bilbao. "Bilbao was changing as my inner life was changing—simultaneously," she told me in her native Euskara. Sara spoke about "the enjoyment of the city." "No, we haven't lost those worlds," she replied to my question about the past religious and political worlds of our generation. "I believe in the human being, in the life we possess. And that new generations will continue remaking the world in conditions that will be satisfying." Sara had been involved in catechesis and social work during her teenage years and almost went to South America as a missionary with her ex-husband.

At one time, she was close to ETA, "the figure of Jesus Christ, jailed and suffering," and although she is an atheist who distanced herself long ago from that world of religious and political sacrifice, she baptized her son. "What matters is life," she told me. "We talk of the fear of dying, but in fact what we are afraid of is *living*. That is why I experience resurrection, because I have the hope of going forward, to continue understanding, and give my children something to live for." Her father had just died, and she felt "a great sadness. But he is in me," she said. I felt fortunate to be listening to this woman who reminded me how we have been "at the edge of many things. Learning how to walk that line has been hard." She personified the new Bilbao.

I run into Rafa, an old friend of mine I hadn't seen in years. He was a psychologist and colleague during the year I taught at the University of the Basque Country in the early 1980s. We made an appointment, and I met him in a hotel near his Indautxu apartment a few days later. I was in for a surprise. Rafa had been through an existential crisis, as a result of which he had turned to Zen. He had published several books on Zen and been conferred the title of Zen master. My first reaction was that Zen must operate as a private fetish in Rafa's life. But soon I realized that Rafa was a different man from the one I used to know, transformed by a reality he could hardly talk about—an ecstatic experience that put him at the edge and made him view life as if from another dimension.

Rafa's crisis occurred soon after he obtained his tenure at the university. "It was a frightening crisis. July 15, 1987. I had gone to Medina de Pomar with my family. A week earlier I had passed the tenure exam at the university. I thought I had reached the climax, belonged to the university's elite. I was exhausted. As I was walking by the Cabrio I had my first panic attack. I was by myself. I knew the symptoms from the books: my heart began to palpitate, I felt completely at a loss, all I could do was visit a psychiatrist. I began taking medication." He would not tell even his wife about his crisis. He called a Zen friend who suggested a book by Karlfried Dürckheim on meditation. "He told me that fear was driving me and I wagered like Pascal. I didn't want to return to belief, but to *experience*." After he'd lost all urge for academic climbing, Rafa was assigned a class on industrial psychology in Bilbao's School of Engineering. What he'd been teaching was essentially spirituality, he said, but his classes were full and the students devoured the spiritual texts he had them read.

Rafa, who'd taught Freudian psychoanalysis for many years, reads neurosis in positive terms as "something that is attempting to change." "Desire is infinity," he stressed. "It has a spiritual dimension. Freud and Lacan are perhaps the most promising authors for a new spirituality. Eric Fromm says it in his book *Zen Bouddhism and Psychoanalysis*—that if we were to follow Freud's project of expanding consciousness, we would arrive at mystical stages. What happens is that desire might be reduced to such a material level that it becomes neurosis. The limits put on desire become a torment." I couldn't follow Rafa when he talked about his ground being not belief, but "experience beyond thought," while making references to various mystics. A key word for him is *liberation*.

I asked him, "Don't you think that atheism is the most spiritual thing we did?" "Yes, yes, yes," he replied eagerly. Rafa would fully agree with the theologian Thomas Altizer's view that "the death of God is the deepest event in modern apocalypticism, apart from which there is no possibility whatsoever of a truly new world." Rafa embraces such a death of God as absolutely redemptive. At one point, Rafa quoted the Spanish poet Claudio Rodríguez—"And my body could not hold so much resurrection"—and tried to explain the resurrection of the empty body in the forms of love and energy, for "energy cannot fool you; it is as much bodily as it is mental."

Had I not known Rafa before, his story would have left me mostly indifferent. But as I looked at my friend, his eyes, face, body appeared to me transfixed by an inhuman being that had overtaken him. A sword had cut through his inner core and left him utterly indigent, convinced beyond doubt of the truth of his new subject.

On another stroll through Bilbao, I recognized Xabier Gereño—a pivotal figure in Bilbao's revival of Euskara since the 1960s, one of the city's best-known writers who had authored more than a hundred novels and plays. He had organized in Bilbao the Festival of the Basque Song the years 1964, 1966, and 1967, as well as helped record local musicians. It had been a work of resistance in a dictatorial period in which, as happened to him, you could be jailed for receiving a letter with a stamp featuring Picasso's *Guernica*. After having being a member all his life of left-wing Basque political parties, he ended up voting for the Spanish Popular Party as a protest against ETA's terrorism. I'd never met him before but remembered that he had written a complimentary review of my first book of poems. He told me he was taking a bus to a residential home for elderly people in Deusto where he had resided since he turned sixty-five and after the death of his wife. He had decided to live at the residence because he didn't want to be a burden on his children. I visited him there. In his eighties by then, rather than living the bourgeois life of Bilbao's middle class and enjoying his status as a consecrated author, Xabier was organizing plays, showing movies, and directing a choir for his elderly companions. He

had given up writing, except poems for his fellow elderly residents—
"they are depressed and need comfort; I write to cheer them up." He
introduced me to a few of the old people living at the residential home.
One of them was on the eve of his hundredth birthday. "I have never
felt better," the man told me; he'd frequent the chapel and pray and
feel God's solace. Another man in his mid-eighties, Marcelino, while
recounting his life concentrated on one aspect—how good his dead
wife had been to him. After her death, he had gone to La Palanca to
a prostitute once but he could hear his wife's voice saying, "Don't do
it, Marcelino!" He paid the woman and left without doing anything.
Women in their eighties told me stories about how they flirted with the
men, but seducing them wasn't easy.

Xabier Gereño.

Xabier was baffled by my interest in his life and kept introducing me to his fellows until I insisted that it was he I wanted to
interview. I asked him whether there was some religious motivation
behind his dedication. No, he said, he was agnostic. As our conversation veered from politics to culture to thought, "I believe in infinity,"
Xabier told me with conviction. He had been an accountant for forty
years; he tried to demonstrate infinity for me on a piece of paper that
he covered with numbers and fractions. The play they were performing
at the residence under his direction was entitled *Hotel Paradise*—based
on their own experiences as tourists in various hotels worldwide.

At one point, he took me to his room; there was a photo of his
deceased wife on his desk. "I kiss her every night," he said. "We had a
wonderful marriage; she was, like me, very happy." A passionate music
lover, Xabier began humming and then singing for me in Italian "E
lucevan le stellae," Cavaradossi's farewell to life in the opera *Tosca*. He
wasn't singing the aria in search for a lost time or a desire for understanding, but as the compulsive memory in imperfect tense of a lover's
remembrance, the melody that allowed him to relive his happy life
with his wife.

And the stars were shining
How sweet the earth smelled . . .
Never have I loved life more!
He died in May 2011.

It was late February 1999, and there wasn't a more beautiful tree in all
Bilbao. I was climbing the seventy concrete steps of Bi Etxeak (Two
Houses) thinking of the interview I was about to have with Joanna,
when the quiet splendor of an orange tree in full bloom in the garden

hit me. I'd barely noticed Bilbao's more than twelve thousand trees, most of them limes, maples, and planes that line and soften the city's streets. But I couldn't ignore the radiance of this one that seemed to reverberate through the city.

Bi Etxeak is a small municipal center of two adjoining houses run by nuns for terminally ill AIDS patients. "People come here to die," Enkarna, the nun in charge of the center who arranged the interview for me, said at the door. HIV-AIDS became an epidemic in the 1980s as the result of the estimated ten thousand heroin junkies in the Basque Country. She spoke of "the generosity" the youths show as they embrace their deaths and how she cries and laughs with them, accompanies them "down to the well" of their despair—making reference to the deep *pozzo* of Dante's Inferno. After they die and are relieved from "the night of the world," Enkarna sings for them in a religious ceremony: "Go to the Light, don't stop, go!" She turns their lives into initiation voyages visualized as Dantean descents and ascents, darkness and light, taking place at Bi Etxeak at the top of seventy steps of concrete as if they were Led Zeppelin's "Stairway to Heaven."

Joanna, a woman in her mid-thirties with an easy smile, welcomed me before we sat down together at a table to talk. She told me of the abuse she had taken from the men she'd lived with, and of her stay as a young girl in a boarding school run by nuns where she was sent so her mother was free to work as a prostitute. Later, her mother's clients began to pursue her instead. Joanna was only a teenager, and she began to work in one of the clubs, "initially just for drinks." Then she entered her mother's trade. She became a heroin junkie. She had two children who were taken away from her by the local authorities. After a decade of HIV and AIDS, she was told she had heart lymphoma. She was relieved to think that the end was near and she could stop struggling. Her mother would not let her come home, so Joanna was brought to Bi Etxeak to die.

But new drugs had become available and she recovered. She was feeling fine now. She told me repeatedly, "I should've been dead by now, but I am alive again." I was talking to a resurrected woman. As someone returned from the dead, there was evident joy, an air of *amor fati* and innocence, in Joanna's broad smile. She talked of how the sexual services she'd provided in the past were not so different from those a nurse might offer a patient. Prompted by her new friendship with Enkarna, she even compared those services to the ones the nuns offer the moribund. Similar to other complex women such as Eva Perón and Marilyn Monroe, Joanna embodied the duality of whore and nun. *Ay, si yo te contara* (oh, if I were to tell you) is the common starting point when a prostitute is asked to tell her life story.

An expert in the arts of seduction, Joanna explained to me how attraction is provoked by that initial eye contact with a potential client, and then the broad smile that reveals all her power, a smile saying, when too much has transpired already, "I know that you know me, I know you." "It is all play with the eyes and the mouth," she observed. "It is all theater," she went on, "but at one point you fall in love and that's the end of everything." That's always the danger in the game, she insisted—the play of love becoming *real*. You are "pretending" to like him until you really do and then the game is over and you are facing the abyss—waiting for the "special client" to show up. When he appears at the door, all others are discarded. *"This happens,"* she emphasized. Professionalism requires not letting the game turn into reality.

Joanna told me about an affair she'd had with a client at the end of her career—a Galician lover, a doctor with whom she'd fallen utterly in love, who had to leave Bilbao with his family as a result. "It wasn't mere sex or play but true love," she said with emphasis. There were others whose mouths reminded her of him. "Can't you see my hands trembling?" she asked as if to counter my skepticism. Her eyes became teary and she was visibly moved. She grew silent. All she'd wanted was to live that love story forever. "I am a woman of excesses," she summed herself up. "I have a problem taking the middle ground."

Joanna's friend and confidant, the nun Enkarna ("Sister Death" had brought the two women together and made them close friends) spoke to me of love in no less passionate terms. She had devoted her entire life to Jesus. Listening to her speak, I was reminded of Thomas Mann: "Isn't it grand, isn't it good that language has only *one* word for everything we associate with love—from utter sanctity to the most fleshly lust?" This was Bilbao, the city where "love was worthwhile."

It was in Berlin that Brecht wrote his ironic song about a Bilbao he had never visited. It was in Berlin that, on April 26, 1937, Hitler celebrated his birthday with a military parade while, as a present to him, the Condor Legion headed by von Richthofen was burning and machine-gunning Gernika. The writer Anjel Lertxundi told me about a lecture he gave in Berlin on the presence of Gernika in Basque poetry. At the end, he played a recording of Lauaxeta's poem "Agur Euzkadi" (Goodbye, Euskadi, written at dawn before he was executed by a firing squad), sung by Antton Valverde. He saw many of the listeners were moved, but one hieratic woman of about fifty especially caught his attention. As he finished, the woman rose to tell her story. She was a teenager and a student of art when she bought a reproduction of the painting *Guernica* to hang on her wall. That night her loving father came to her bedroom to kiss her goodnight as usual, but when he saw the painting he tore it apart and left the room, slamming the door. She inquired about her father's strange reaction; nobody at home had an answer. Later she discovered that he had been one of the German pilots leading a squadron in the bombing of Gernika. She faced him with her discovery, assuming that he'd be ashamed and that his bizarre reaction could only be explained by the horror of the memory. The father was in fact proud of having participated in the murderous raid. The daughter left home and never returned.

Three older women from Gernika were seated in front of her in the Berlin auditorium. They were about ten when Gernika was bombed; the German woman had not yet been born. Addressing them, she concluded: "It is the first time I am making this confession. I owed it to you."

Aresti opened his prophetic *Maldan behera* with two epigraphs from Nietzsche and Christ—both affirmers of life. The descent in which "downhill tumbles / this naked body of mine" is a necessary symbolic death before the rising up in a mad state of joy, *maldan gora* ("uphill"). Otero's 1958 book of poems, *Ancia,* opens with the epigraph, "Under all the invocations of death . . . the emphasis is on the value and price of life." Etxebarrieta's poem with the line "Perhaps . . . / I am cruel—for committing suicide" has the epigraph "Resurrexit / sicut dixit." Basque nationalists, mindful of the Irish rebellion and the Easter Uprising, in 1932 began celebrating the Day of Resurrection as their annual date for the *Aberri Eguna* (Day of the Homeland). In the final statement of his "Experimental Proposal," Oteiza sums up the mission of the artist with cryptic words: "I return from Death. What we tried to bury grows here." This "return from Death" is a symbolic axiom for my Bilbao generation.

Belief in resurrection was Paul's historic creation. It is also the centerpiece of my generation's religious loss—one could not be modern and believe in it. Nietzsche was the thinker we needed for overcoming transcendence and affirming life. Now, decades later, a group of authors influenced by contemporary philosophy and psychoanalysis allow us to put Nietzsche in a new perspective—in part by comparing him to Paul. Even if ultimately a fiction, these materialist authors argue that belief in resurrection provides a paradigm of the founding power of an event to create a new subject of truth. "Death" and "life" in this discussion "are thoughts, interwoven dimensions of the global subject" whereby "body" and "soul" are indiscernible; resurrection for Paul has to be of the *body* of the entire divided subject.

But if the Christian narrative is reduced to the fiction of resurrection, and if we are concerned with the pure secularity of a universal culture, why care for this fable? "That the event (or pure act) invoked by antiphilosophers [such as Paul, Pascal, or Nietzsche] is fictitious," replies Badiou, "does not present a problem"; what matters is the fidelity of the subject to a truth that, while based on an event which always takes place in a given situation, is for all. For my generation, which knows that it is impossible to believe in the resurrection of the Crucified, the scandal is having to face the reality that we are still products of the cultural revolution brought about by Christianity. Despite the provocative centering of thought on a fable, it is one that retains in modern thinking, as Badiou insists, a *theoretical* import of the greatest magnitude. What is remarkable in the current situation is that rigorously atheist thinkers are the best intellectual allies for Bilbao's radical Christians.

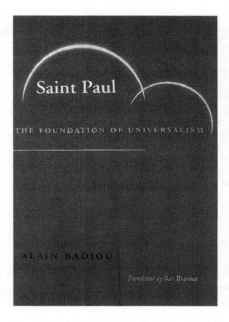

Cover of the book by Alain Badiou, *Saint Paul* (2003).

"This is all Zarathustra," Aresti told me after reading the book of poems I wrote in London about my generation's loss of Paradise. That *Adam's unfinished poem* was also the beginning of this book. But who was really the Zarathustra who came "like a thief in the night" and who took possession of many of us? Zarathustra was no metaphor or hyperbole; it was a literary figure, yet a fiction as real as Dante's, embodying a truth we could no longer avoid. The death of God meant the world had no purpose or value. The only thing that remained standing for me were Blake's prints and watercolors at the Tate Gallery—his sketches for Dante's *Divine Comedy*, his River of Life, his Paradise. When I entered anthropology, the seminal and rigorous work of Gregory Bateson kept alive for me the Platonism of Blake and the eternal forms. It would take me decades to revisit here Nietzsche's law of eternal return, but his eternity is no longer a Paradise lost; for, in Zarathustra's own words, "This life, this is your eternal life." Aresti's *Downfall* had been inspired by the Nietzsche who wrote: "Did I not fall—listen!—into the well of eternity?" Platonic truths are timeless, not because they were there since ever, but because they are created in thought or art or action. Nietzsche's "Ariadne, I love you," is also a declaration of eternity; so is Arrupe's "Hiroshima belongs to eternity."

Dante placed Plato in the first circle of Hell—because he lacked the poet's Christian faith. And yet Dante has been considered the most Platonic of poets. Plato, who called for overcoming the shadows of the cave and the sublunar world with the Sun of the Idea, is the thinker of the Ideal City. My Bilbao generation's attempt to reinvent a new city—a generation that includes disidents and antagonists—is our way to keep fidelity to that Dantesque journey we began long ago ("Midway along the journey of our life / I woke to find myself in a dark wood), a divine comedy that calls for a final canto.

A Broken Hallelujah

It was the night of September 17, 2009, when Sergio and I went to a Leonard Cohen concert in Bilbao—the Cohen who had reemerged after his dark decade of depression and seclusion in a Zen monastery. In our years together in the 1960s in San Felicísimo and later as students (Sergio is an economist), we had both loved Cohen's music. He was now returning in his very lateness, joking that in his previous tour, when he was in his sixties, he was "just a kid with a crazy dream." The moment he stepped up to the microphone and began singing "Dance Me to the End of Love" it was déjà vu for Sergio and me. Soon he was singing his classic "Hallelujah!" In our religious period, "hallelu-jah!" had been a regular punctuation of the ritual cycle. After we were expelled from the convent, Sergio and I both struggled with depres-sion. Here we were again inside that dark song with its many familiar-ities and echoes from those times. We listened spellbound to Cohen's hoarse voice rising slowly in its simplicity amid the chorus of over-

Ticket for Leonard Cohen's Bilbao concert.

flowing female voices. In its fusion of the erotic and the spiritual, it was the cry of a "very cold and very broken hallelujah":

> even though it all went wrong,
>
> I stand here before the Lord of Song,
>
> with nothing on my tongue but Hallelujah.
>
> Hallelujah. Hallelujah.

It was anything but a final harmony, for "love is not a victory march." Cohen's "Anthem" summed it up: "There is a crack in everything, / that's how the light gets in." The haunting "Take This Waltz" followed, based on a poem by Lorca, Lauaxeta's poet, both of them felled by a firing squad, both captive to the moon's erotics: "Oh I want you, I want you, I want you . . . / On a bed where the moon has been sweating." Cohen's waltz echoed with Maurice Ravel's, the quintessential French composer, "a mixture of medieval Catholicism and satanic impiety," born to a Basque mother in the French coastal village of Ciboure, less than a hundred miles from Bilbao. It was the song we needed to realize that "an apocalyptic enactment of ending is thus ultimately and finally an ecstatic celebration of total joy."

Dante tells the absurd story of his Beatrice. Love is folly—like revolution, like sanctity. "Beatrice is Blake's City, yet a Woman; the new Jerusalem, beautiful as a bride adorned to meet her husband." Bilbao is also Blake's City, yet a Woman. Bilbao is Gehry's architecture, yet Marilyn Monroe. Blake's Dionysian Christianity recognizes that the principle of exuberance is one aspect of the human condition, a social phenomenon in which we all participate collectively as one body, that our suffering comes from the excess of life.

At the entrance to Cohen's concert hall, they were selling T-shirts printed with the words "I'm Your Man"—one of his signature songs about a man so overtaken by passion, so indigent in his loss of self, that he is ready to stop wanting, ready finally to experience the ablation of desire. Cohen's "Hallelujah" could only emerge from a radical experience of the Fall and the belief, a la Kierkegaard and Benjamin, that the past can be redeemed by the present through existential repetition. It was also Clarice Lispector's hallelujah: "It's with such intense joy. It is such an hallelujah. 'Hallelujah,' I shout, a hallelujah that fuses with the darkest human howl of the pain of separation but is a shout of diabolical happiness." It was Beckett, known as the writer of despair but also "of the obstinacy of love," concluding: "Farewell to farewell . . . Grace to breathe that void. Know happiness." In old age, the second innocence, *sero te amavi*, late I loved thee. It was the broken hallelujah of my generation, a hymn to Bilbao's resurrection.

Endnotes

Initial number refers to page on which reference is found.

BOOK I: HELL

Return to Bilbao: A Carnival Morning

9. "lowest hell": Aresti, *Obras Completas*, I, 553.

10. "those who have not smelled the odor of sanctity": Van Hensbergen, *Guernica*, 324.

10. "Why not climb up this blissful mountain here": Alighieri, *Inferno*, I, 77–78.

10. renders the subject into a work yet to be completed: Zupančič, *The Shortest Shadow*, 19.

10. "Ariadne was the one great conundrum": Gere, *Knossos and the Prophets of Modernism*, 47.

10. "Love is to be reinvented, that is clear": Rimbaud, *Rimbaud*, 281.

10. "was indissolubly an artistic, existential": Badiou, *In Praise of Love*, 77–78.

11. "it constitutes a dimension of the real": Butler, *"The Force of Fantasy,"* 108.

11. defining traits of "my generation": For a discussion of the performative nature and ethical dimension of autographical writing, see Loureiro, *The Ethics of Autobiography*.

12. Gehry's Bilbao "shipwreck": Gehry quoted in Spalding, *"Bilbao."*

12. "Beatrice is Blake's City, yet a Woman": Brown, *Apocalypse*, 168.

12. "Midway along the journey of our life": Alighieri, *Inferno*, I, 1–3.

Revolution or Death

13. "Why does history take this course?": Agamben, *Potentialities*, 154.

13. agreement with the United States: The Pact of Madrid was signed between Franco's Spain and the United States in 1953. This trade and military alliance between the two nations, which ended Spain's isolation from the international community after having sided with Hitler and Mussolini during World War II, was part of the U.S. policy of containment during the Cold War.

13. the most genuine of prophets: See Batista, *Madariaga*, 81.

14. "my heart needed something Absolute"; "more beautiful than the object"; "when you reach the goal"; "Now I understand the fascination": Álvarez Enparantza, *Leturia-ren egunkari ezkutua*, 117–19.

14. borrows from his mentor Unamuno: Txillardegi, the writer who gave the name ETA to the organization and became its most influential ideologist until the middle 1960s, in 1955 wrote a prize-winning essay on Kierkegaard's influence on Unamuno. His first lecture, in 1957, was on Unamuno. On the pivotal influence of the "anti-Basque" Unamuno on Basque thinkers of this resistance period, see Azurmendi, *Bakea gudan*.

14. "he denies to thought the capacity": Álvarez Enparantza, "Unamuno eragille," 73.

14–15. "I have to ask not"; "Miren needs me"; "I am guilty, yes"; "And what is love?": Álvarez Enparantza, *Leturia-ren*, 137, 139, 142, 136.

15. "We have to offer resistance by all means": Documentos, 1, 197.

15. the first bomb attacks: Batista, *Madariaga*, 79.

15. "We cannot avoid recognizing"; "that we are in 1961, and not in 1936": Documentos, 1, 235, 396.

16. the primacy of the person over nation and state: "The person is above the nation in the sense that man has more QUALITY, intrinsically, than the nation. The rights of the nation above the individuals come, in the last instance, from the demands of the COMMON GOOD to the service of the PERSON. Besides, the nation is nothing without the persons who integrate it. We are, thus, personalists to the extent that we grant PRIMACY to the human person. Not to the nation, and even less to the artificial STATE." Documentos, 1, 260.

16. "conceptually, the modern State": Documentos, 1, 78.

16. the state should always be "underneath" the people: ETA's founders were influenced by authors such as Maritain, whose contention was that "political philosophy must get rid of the word, as well as the concept, of Sovereignty." Maritain's proposal was the possibility of "a World State" predicated upon "a universal basis." This was obviously diametrically opposed to the veneration of the state shown by the fascist writers of the times. See Pradera, *El estado nuevo*.

16. The paradigm of war: Badiou, *The Century*, 34.

16. "What we tried to bury grows here": Oteiza, *Oteiza's Selected Writings*, 244.

Gernika: A Birthday Present for Hitler

17. "Telegram from Guernica": Reprinted in Rankin, Telegram, 2.

17. Steer's report provoked an outcry around the world: A frequently quoted number is that some 1,654 people died that day, a number questioned by other sources. For an overview of the debate on the contested number of dead, see Irujo, El Gernika de Richthofen, 239–80; for a different view that questions radically the mythical use of "Basque genocide" to justify ETA's violence, see Molina, "Lies of Our Fathers."

18. Hitler's birthday was also postponed to the same Monday: Irujo, El Gernika de Richthofen, 17.

18. "Your fight in Spain was a lesson to our opponents": Quotation in Thomas and Witts, Guernica, vii.

18. "an experimental horror": Quotation in Rankin, Telegram, 106.

18. In his autobiography: Elosegi, Quiero morir por algo.

19. "Why did the destruction of Gernika become": Vilar, La guerra civil española, 81–82. Italics in original.

19. "The world ended tonight": Holme quoted in Rankin, Telegram, 119.

19. history stopped with the Spanish Civil War: Orwell, Collected Essays, 2, 256.

19. "In the half-century to come": Miller, Timebends, 395.

20. "They summed up for us the fate of Bilbao": Steer, The Tree, 370.

20. "Excrement of God!": Quoted in Steer, The Tree, 311.

20. "Let the spirit go to luminous heaven": http://klasikoak.armiarma.com/idazlanak/L/LauaxetaSolteak044.htm.

20. "Oh Lord, please grant me this death": http://klasikoak.armiarma.com/idazlanak/L/LauaxetaSolteak044.htm.

21. "the moon is the material embodiment": Nandorfy, The Poetics of Apocalypse, 45.

21. "there is a green moon": García Lorca, Collected Poems, trans. Jerome Rothenberg, 249.

21. "Green, I want you green": García Lorca, "Sleepwalking Ballad," Collected Poems, trans. Will Kirkland and Christopher Maurer, 555.

21. "The moon turned into all blood": Unamuno, El Cristo de Velázquez, 25, 17, 28. Author's translations.

21. six sketches that were the start of Guernica: Viejo-Rose, Reconstructing Spain, 140.

21. the corrida, and the Minotaur: Van Hensbergen, Guernica, 45.

24. In its final version, Guernica: For a combination of geographical and historical perspectives on Gernika, see Raento and Watson, "Gernika, Guernica, Guernica."

24. "as though [they] were alive"; "when they scratch it a drop of blood": Quoted in van Hensbergen, Guernica, 52–53.

24. the dark forces of violence and evil: Gere, Knossos, 152.

24. "vision and touch are reconciled": Florman, Myth and Metamorphosis, 46.

24. the failure of such a synthesis: Bulls and blindness are recurrent motifs in Bataille's essay "Rotten Sun," where he distinguishes between two different suns—the higher one an "abstract object" at which one cannot gaze fixedly, and the blinding sun at which one can stare. The sun you don't look at is perfectly beautiful. The one you scrutinize can be a horror. Bataille observes that in mythology the slain bull, as in Picasso's Guernica, is also the blinding sun.

25. foundational discipline underneath Basque nationalism: See Zulaika, Del cromañón al carnaval: los vascos como museo antropológico.

25. scientific thought began to assert the permanence of race: See Blankaert, "On the Origins of French Ethnology," 6. Among other new scientists inspired by such positivism were Swedish anatomist Anders Retzius and Paul Broca, who, in 1859, founded in Paris the Société d'Anthropologie. They too were interested in Basque skulls, and in 1869 a 300-page and a 550-page volume were published in Paris on the Basque race.

25. found a prime candidate in the Basques: In 1886 a Basque Society was founded in Berlin; between 1886 and 1896 seventeen issues of its journal, Euskara, were devoted to Basque studies. Eminent linguists from Germany, France, and Spain contributed to the journal. See de Pablo, "The Basque Country Through the Nazi Looking Glass, 1933–1945." Under Hitler, between 1933 and 1945, no fewer than thirty-five German publications dealt with Basque linguistics and history. Some referred to the race question. Others considered the Basques a sacred people. Perhaps the most salient book was by Ziesemer, The Country of the Basques: Sketches of the Land of the Oldest Europeans, which vascologist Gerhard Bähr called the first monograph on the Basque Country conceived according to the ideology of the Third Reich. During the Spanish Civil War, most German publishing on the Basques ceased, and after the war, German publications focused on Nazi contributions to Franco's regime. See de Pablo, "The Basque Country," 236–45.

25. "the happiest people in the world": Rousseau, The Social Contract, 158–59.

25. the authors of the U.S. Constitution: Adams, A Defense of the Constitutions of Government of the United States of America.

26. the Basque government's empty offices in the Hotel Carlton: The Hotel Carlton (1926), the work of local architect Manuel María de Smith, was conceived as a top-quality hotel for the new urban Bilbao of the twentieth century. The modernist French-style Hotel Carlton was where the Basque government installed its headquarters while raising a defensive army. The building has a basement, lower and ground floors, and six floors of rooms, and a porch topped with a terrace. Its most outstanding

interior feature is an oval-shaped hall with glass windows. Rankin, *Telegram*, 135.

26. *"Here at least there was moonlight"*: Steer, *The Tree*, 331, 366–367.

26. *Haunted by the memory of his dead wife*: For a captivating portrait of Steer, see Rankin, *Telegram*.

26. *"it was cold, approaching dawn"*: Steer, *The Tree*, 368.

27. *"The Dawns are heartbreaking"*: Rimbaud, *Rimbaud*, 135.

27. *"under the onset of a great emotion"*: Steer, *The Tree*, 370.

27. *"Come see your city"*: Alighieri, *Purgatory*, 6, 109–14.

27. *"But I couldn't do anything"*: Figuera Aymerich, *Belleza Cruel*, 32.

27. *headed for a decade of exile in Chile*: Madariaga's Chilean family branch went back as far as 1656. He also had kinship connections in Argentina and other South American countries, as well as in southern Spain (Seville). Longstanding relations in Great Britain were also a part of his family tradition.

27. *loved ones still in the Basque Country*: See Legarreta, *The Guernica Generation*.

28. *"a grave mistake"*: Roosevelt quoted in Stone and Kuznick, *The Untold History of the United States*, 85.

28. *The word Gernika became taboo*. Vilar, *La guerra civil*, 165.

28. *"The outcome of the Spanish war"*: Orwell, "Looking Back on the Spanish War," 262–63.

28. *"loyalties are political loyalties to the Basque children"*: Cloud, *Basque Children*, 51.

28. *"We very much regret that enemy:"* Ibid., 44–47.

29. *raising their fists*: Ibid., 61.

Aita Patxi/von Richthofen: The Cross and the Trash

29. *While von Richthofen was directing the bombs*: Hitler had sent aircraft under the command of General Hugo Sperrle with von Richthofen as his chief of staff. Mussolini provided an army division—forty thousand men—to Franco's rebel forces, headed by General Mancini. But Italian and Francoist forces had been embarrassingly defeated in the Battle of Guadalajara, near Madrid, in the first days of March 1937, and Franco needed a quick military triumph to restore the morale of his forces and supporters, and his own image as leader. This was possible in the North with the vital advantage of Sperrle's aircraft. Thus von Richthofen's Condor Legion was handed the plan for Bilbao's conquest. The Legion's role was to provide support for the infantry, which was made up of Italians and Spaniards. Von Richthofen made an agreement with the commander of the infantry forces, Colonel Vigón, whereby the air force would be entirely under German command. The day-to-day ground operations would adjust to the air force's capabilities; the infantry and air force would share a strict schedule; and there would be two batteries on the ground under German control. Furthermore, the Condor Legion was not subject to the command of the Army of the North headed by General Mola, but only to General Franco, who was headquartered in Salamanca. For his role as commander of the Condor Legion, von Richthofen rose to the grade of general by September 1938 and would stand next to Franco in Madrid on May 19, 1939, during the victory celebration. In July 1941 he was awarded the most exclusive of titles, the Knight's Cross with Oak Leaves, and in February 1943 he was promoted by Hitler to become Germany's youngest field marshal.

29. *"is capable of experiencing its own destruction"*: Benjamin, *Illuminations*, 242.

30. *"I have gone to Otxandio"*: Quoted in Maier, *Guernica*, 103–4, 118–19, 120–22, 124–27. Author's translation.

31. *"DEATH AND RESURRECTION. It was exactly"*: Aita Patxi, "Mi odisea Pasionista." Unpublished manuscript, 6–10. Author's translation.

32. *the essential gap inside the same symbol*: Besides the cross, a historian could also establish other symbolic comparisons between the Germanic mythology of the God of the sky "Thor" and the Basque God of the sky "Ortzi," or between the Oak of Gernika and the Oak Leaves that were added to the Iron Cross as the highest military decoration during World War II, or between the Basque traditional *lauburu* swastika and the German swastika. See Santiago de Pablo, "El *lauburu*," 109–53.

33. *repeating Lenin in their partisan universality*: "Lenin's wager . . . is that universal truth and partisanship . . . are not only not mutually exclusive, but condition each other: in a concrete situation, its UNIVERSAL truth can only be articulated from a thoroughly PARTISAN position—truth is by definition one-sided." Žižek, *Repeating Lenin*, 26.

36. *Dostoyevsky's mock execution*: Frank, *Dostoevsky*, 177.

36. *"learned the next day that the Asturian"*: Preston, *The Spanish Holocaust*: 440.

36. *"A saint's business, to put it clearly"*: Lacan, *Television*, 15.

36. *"The psychoanalyst truly wants to be shit"*: Quoted in Regnault, "Saintliness," 121.

36. *"bitten harder and deeper"*: Quoted in Regnault, "Saintliness and the Sainthood," 124.

Hiroshima, Mon Amour

37. *Crete, at the turn of the twentieth century*: The discoveries resulted in the reaffirmation of a Cretan mythology at

whose center was the labyrinth with the half-man, half-bull Minotaur—killed by Theseus with the help of Ariadne, who gave him a skein of thread so he could find his way out of the labyrinth.

37. *"One day there will be associated with my name"*: Nietzsche, *Ecce Homo*, 96–97.

37. *that most U.S. top military commanders opposed*: "Six of the United States's seven five-star officers who received their final star in World War II—Generals MacArthur, Eisenhower, and Arnold and Admirals Leahy, King, and Nimitz—rejected the idea that the atomic bombs were needed to end the war." Stone and Kuznick, *The Untold History*, 177.

37. *"This is the greatest thing in history"*: Truman, *Memoirs by Harry S. Truman*, 465.

38. *"If Dante had been with us on the plane"*: Tibbets quoted in Stone and Kuznick, *The Untold History*, 167.

38. *"Hell no, I made it like that"*: Truman quoted in Stone and Kuznick, *The Untold History*, 179.

38. *"We in America"*: Mumford, "Gentlemen: You Are Mad!" 5.

38. *Jesuits were intrinsic to Bilbao's religious fabric*: Already in 1552 Saint Ignatius had sent Francisco de Borja to Bilbao to ascertain the possibility of establishing a Jesuit convent there—something that did not happen until 1604 after overcoming much local opposition. For a history of the Jesuit order's installation in Bilbao and its relationship to local businesses, see Otazu and Díaz de Durana, *El espíritu emprendedor de los vascos*, 439–615.

38. *Arrupe had joined the order*: Arrupe would ultimately become the second Basque superior general of the Company of Jesus and, many believe, the most consequential since Ignatius of Loyola, its founder. His influence was deemed a complete renewal of the order, "a true and authentic refoundation." La Bella, ed., *Pedro Arrupe*, 24.

39. *would later marry Oppenheimer*: Monk, *Robert Oppenheimer*, 285–86.

39. *"From Spain to Los Alamos was a short step"*: Dyson, "Oppenheimer," 19.

39. *Gernika signaled the beginning of the atomic era*: Oppenheimer wrote of the bomb that "we think of it as an instrument of strategic bombing, for the destruction of lives and of plants, principally in cities. It is the decisive, even if perhaps not the final, step in the development that may have started with Guernica, that was characterized by the blitz against London, by the British raids on Hamburg, by our fire raids in Tokyo, and by Hiroshima." Monk, *Robert Oppenheimer*, 585.

40. *"I was in my room with another priest at 8:15"; "We heard a formidable explosion"; "The suffering was frightful"*: Arrupe, *Essential Writings*, 46, 40, 43.

40. *by the Cardoner River*: On his way to the Holy Land, Loyola sat with his eyes towards the river, when "the eyes of his understanding were opened and though he saw no vision . . . [he experienced] an elucidation so bright that all these things seemed new to him": Loyola, *A Pilgrim's Journey*, 39.

40. *"the transcendental importance"* of that *"sort of Pentecost"*: Arrupe, *Essential Writings*, 120–21.

40. *"We were to witness more horrible scenes"*: Ibid., 45.

40. *"In turning around to say Dominus Vobiscum"*: Ibid., 46, 50.

41. *They answered very mysteriously*: Ibid., 50.

41. *"we soon began to raise pyramids"*: Arrupe, *Essential Writings*, 51.

41. *"refuses a redemption which is confined"*: Altizer, *The New Apocalypse*, 194.

41. *"It was 8:10"*: Quoted in La Bella, *Pedro Arrupe*, 18.

41. *"My God, why have you forsaken yourself!"* Jürgen Moltmann quoted in Vitoria, *El Dios Cristiano*, 61.

41. *"God's kenosis on the cross"; "the one of God's self-limitation"; "Why Gernika?"*: Vitoria, *El Dios Cristiano*, 63, 65, 25.

Wigs and Bullets

42. *"This same air power had made"*: Aguirre, *Escape Via Berlin*, 29. Aguirre's sister Encarna was killed during that bombing; his brother Juan was arrested by the Gestapo. Aguirre's friend, Lluis Companys, the exiled president of Catalonia, was captured and thrown into a Paris prison. At the close of the Civil War in the spring of 1939, Aguirre and Companys traveled together over the mountains of Catalonia into France when everything was lost. Aguirre tried to console his sobbing friend while passing the endless lines of his countrymen escaping on foot, homeless and hungry, and while recalling Companys's sick son interned in a sanatorium in Belgium. Companys was turned over to Franco and shot. Removing his shoes before the firing squad, he died barefoot, so that he might feel the protection of the Catalan earth and the people who had elected him.

42. *"the promised land"; "continent which . . . attained a marvelous"; "felt like bending down and kissing"*: Aguirre, *Escape Via Berlin*, 294, 285, 296.

42. *He moved to New York*: There he wrote *From Gernika to New York, Passing through Berlin*. The English translation is titled *Escape via Berlin*. Aguirre arrived in New York with his wife and two children in December 1941 and stayed for the next four years, writing and teaching at Columbia University. Jacques Maritain and other writers of the time were among his closest friends and advisors.

43. *Franco's days were numbered*: Aguirre combined his pro-Basque activities with his dedication to the creation of a European federalist movement (led by Konrad Adenauer and Alcide de Gasperi). The movement was officially launched in The Hague in May 1947,

with Aguirre named to its Honorary Committee.

43. "He is already in his casket": Quoted in Martin de Ugalde, "José Antonio de Aguirre y Lecube," 58.

43. "With the liberation [of Europe from fascism]": Leizaola, "Mauriac ante el féretro," 292.

44. "is like an internal miniature"; its passion for the real: Badiou, *The Century*, 22, 48–57.

44. "Aguirre dies and ETA is born": Batista, *Madariaga*, 78.

44. "a new era of violence will result": Aguirre, *Escape via Berlin*, 369.

44. could not destroy the spirit of the Basque people: Ibid., 371.

47. "was the appropriate antidote to Arana's racism": Batista, *Madariaga*, 83–84.

47. Basques had helped many Jews escape the Nazis: Batista, *Madariaga*, 85. See also Ott, *War, Judgment, and Memory in the Basque Borderlands, 1914–1945*.

47. that would jeopardize Israel's relationship with de Gaulle's France: Batista, *Madariaga*, 87.

48. "place Basque legality before Spanish or French legality": Madariaga quoted in Ibid., 99.

The Tragic Subject: Etxebarrieta

48. the abertzale (patriotic) left: See Lorenzo Espinosa, *Txabi Etxebarrieta: Armado*, 107.

48. "'Stand up, the oppressed of the world'": Quoted in Lorenzo Espinosa, *Txabi Etxebarrieta: Armado*, 249.

49. "forgive me"; "Perhaps. . .": Lorenzo Espinosa, *Txabi Etxebarrieta: Poesía*, 147, 63. Author's translation.

49. "Bilbao is an act": Lorenzo Espinosa, *Txabi Etxebarrieta: Poesía*, 70.

49. "Wretched whoever has a motherland": Ibid., 76.

49. "I'd like to be buried in you": Ibid., 87.

49. "I don't know how to fill your absence." Ibid., 114.

50. "equations that I never learnt how to solve"; "the turbid authorities of the bodies": Etxeberrieta, *Poesía*, 102, 101, 103.

50. "Where the sea is the turbid breakwater": Ibid., 106.

50. "To satiate myself with the sea": Ibid., 93–94. Author's translation.

50. "everything Machado and Lorca said": Ibid., 151.

50. stronger than even his impending death: Ibid., 113.

50. "You are my only unequivocal feeling." Ibid., 78.

50. he would trade it all to simply be her lover: Ibid., 120.

51. "Was a word from her missing": Echevarría, *Memoria lírica*, 243.

51. "displace their existential center"; "there is a short step from irrationalism to fascism": Lorenzo Espinosa, *Txabi Etxebarrieta: Poesía*, 162, 163, 165.

51. "and are not 'in themselves'"; "a romantic idea in the irrational sense"; "suffering is the road to consciousness": Álvarez Enparantza, "Unamuno eragille," 80, 78, 78.

54. "laced with pseudo-profound banalities": Eagleton, *Sweet Violence*, 25.

54. "would walk down from Sarriko": Lorenzo Espinosa, *Txabi Etxebarrieta: Armado*, 236.

54. "Peace in War": Unamuno, *Paz en la Guerra*.

54–55. "We are for a radical and total change"; "our militants have been arrested armed once and again": Quoted in Lorenzo Espinosa, *Txabi Etxebarrieta: Armado*, 118, 98, 96.

55. let herself be caught rather than killing: Iriarte, *Borrokaren Gorrian*, 151–52.

55. a text he wrote: Estudio Histórico del País Vasco 1839–1959 ("Historic Study of the Basque Country 1839–1959")

in Etxebarrieta, *Los vientos favorables*, 49–211.

55. "lethal without spilling blood": Benjamin, "Critique of Violence," 249.

55. "naïve simple-mindedness": Etxebarrieta, *Los vientos favorables*, 125.

55. "I feel death among my fingers": Lorenzo Espinosa, *Txabi Etxebarrieta: Poesía*, 131.

56. "I know I am going to die in a few hours": Lorenzo Espinosa, *Txabi Etxebarrieta: Armado*, 231–32.

56. he let himself be killed: Uriarte, *Mirando atrás*, 90.

56. "the country needs me and I will offer myself for her": Lorenzo Espinosa, *Txabi Etxebarrieta: Armado*, 271.

56. "at bottom I always thought that he was obsessed": Onaindia, *El precio de la libertad*, 322.

56. would have been enough to avoid the breakup: Lorenzo Espinosa, *Txabi Etxebarrieta: Armado*, 100.

57. about 40 percent were from the Bilbao area: Unzueta, *Los nietos de la ira*, 181. Unzueta, a key ideological and operational leader in ETA's pro-working-class faction after Etxebarrieta, signed his writings with the name "Bilbao."

58. Basquists, anticapitalists, and atheists: Sarrionandia quoted in Etxeberria, *Bost idazle*, 299.

58. Dostoyevsky's influence on their work: See Etxeberria, *Bost idazle*, 18, 206.

58. "It is mythical violence that demands sacrifice": Žižek, *Violence*, 199–200.

59. "an apologist for political terrorism": See Judt, *Past Imperfect*, 125–26.

59. "the singular universality of the Basques"; "against the fascist troops, Basques": Sartre, "Prefacio," 28, 23–24.

59–60. *"an act always misunderstands itself"; "spoke of the inability of any revolution to free the subject"*: Lacan quoted in Roudinesco, *Jacques Lacan*, 341, 343.

60. *Even the trees of Campo Volantín*: Echevarría, *Memoria lírica*, 189.

61. *"deep emotion"; "take revenge on what happened to the father"*: Molina Aparicio, *Mario Onaindia (1948–2003)*, 48, 84.

A Journey into Black Waters

62. *colored the sentimental education*: See Baroja, "Elogio sentimental del acordeón." Prior to his literary career, Baroja worked as a rural doctor in Zestoa. One of Lastur's barrios belongs to that municipality.

62. *"What is the wound of a parturient woman?"*: Onaindia, *Mila Euskal-Olerki Eder*, I, 38.

62. *"the bilbaino Oteiza"*: Eugenio d'Ors quoted in Muñoa, *Oteiza*, 95.

63. *"It is not the emotions themselves"*: Louise Bourgeois quoted in *Louise Bourgeois*, directed by Cajori and Wallach.

64. *taken to an old spa turned Passionist seminary*: The building operated as a spa between 1867 and 1904; from 1911 to 1965, the former spa became the Passionists' convent school.

64. *Carlos, who years later would be killed by ETA*: See Zulaika, *Basque Violence*.

67. *all basic education in the hands of the religious orders*: There is a story in my neighboring town of Deba (Itziar and Lastur belong to its municipality) that sums up the educational dilemmas of my generation. The Ostolaza brothers migrated at the turn of the twentieth century to Cuba and Mexico and, having prospered there by making straw hats, shared their wealth with Deba by converting (in 1927) their inherited farmhouse into a public secondary four-year school and public library. The first class included thirty-five twelve-year-old boys. The library had 4,200 volumes, donated mostly by the Ostolazas (Urdangarin, "Ostolaza anaiak"). The school and library remained open until the Spanish Civil War, when they were forced to close. The new conservative regime targeted the Ostolaza brothers' school because, they being liberals, the school they funded was considered a source of moral danger. The conservatives established the Mont-Real College in Deba instead, run by the San Viator religious order. After José Manuel's death in Mexico City in 1954, his younger sibling, Francisco, created an endowment to reopen Deba's Ostolaza School a few years later. During the sixties this school provided basic instruction in various technical skills. It was too late for me, though my two younger brothers would study there. In spring of 1960 my mother sent me to Deba's religious school of the San Viator order and from there to the seminary.

67. *"the most beautiful word in the French language."* Sartre, *Saint Genet*, 87.

67. *"Though saintliness is my goal"*: Genet, *The Thief's Journal*, 53.

68. *"challenges the human condition in its totality"; "the outdated game of Saintliness"*: Sartre, *Saint Genet*, 87, 203.

68. *"I am a sick man"*: Dostoevsky, *Notes from the Underground*, 1.

Maldan Behera (Downfall)

69. *"If you want to write me"*: Aresti, *Obra Guztiak*, II, 52. Author's translation.

72. *"Since my spirit today"*: Aresti, *Obra Guztiak*, 184. Author's translation.

72. *Since my winged soul*: Aresti, *Obra Guztiak*, 260.

72. *Nietzschean serpents and eagles*: See extended comments on these aspects in Sarasola, "Hitzaurrea"; Arkotxa, "Imaginaire et Poesie dans MALDAN BEHERA de Gabriel Aresti"; and Kortazar, "El poeta Gabriel Aresti."

72. *"If you ever think of me"*: Quoted in Kortazar, *El poeta Gabriel Aresti (1933–1975)*, 7.

73. *"A world like a mutilated tree"*: Otero, *Ancia*, 56; Baland and St. Martin (eds. and trans.), *Miguel Hernández and Blas de Otero*, 159.

73. *"Land / gnawed by war"*: Baland and St. Martin (eds. and trans.), *Miguel Hernández*, 242–43.

73. *Words with the prefix des (less)*: *desgajado* (disconnected), *desarraigado* (rootless), *deshelado* (defrosted), *desamar* (to un-love), *desamparo* (helplessness), *deshace* (undoes), *desesperar* (to despair), *desazón* (disease), *desamarrado* (untied), *desconsuelo* (distress), *desgarrar* (to tear), *desfloradas* (deflowered), *desaladas* (wings clipped), *despojo* (remnants), *desmayo* (fainting), *descarriado* (misdirected). See Alarcos Llorach, *Blas de Otero*, 50–51.

73. *"the glare of your factories"; "So much Bilbao in my memory"*: Otero, *Que trata de España*, 20. *Sea* is both male and female in Spanish, and Otero changes from one to the other.

73. *"in truth you don't deserve my word"*: Otero, *Poemas vascos*, 89.

73. *"Gernika is for Aresti a wound that can never be forgotten"*: Arkotxa, "Arestiren hiri mitikoak," 70.

73. *Aresti and Otero sought transcendence downward*: For a cultural semantics of transcendence downwards, see James W. Fernandez, "The Dark at the Bottom of the Stairs."

74. *"mind immersed in blackness"*: Words of his friend Azaola, quoted in Germán Yanke, *Blas de Otero con los ojos abiertos*, 30.

74. *"dreadful crisis of belief"*: Aldekoa, *Munduaren neurria*, 36.

74. *"stranded objects" in Santner's use*: Santner describes them as "psychic perturbations, as a symptomatic torsion of one's being in the world, or what I have called signifying stress." Santner,

"Miracles Happen," 89. See also Santner, *Stranded Objects* and *On the Psychotheology of Everyday Life*.

74. *"accursed city and one buried deep within my breast"*; *"to breathlessness"*: Otero, *Poemas Vascos*, 99, 105.

74. *"a recumbent wax figure"*: Viar, *La mirada del vigilante*, 111.

75. *"not even Dante could have / imagined."* Aresti, *Obra Guztiak*, I:552.

Hell Is Too Sweet

75. *"We could in no way start now"*: Quoted in Douglass and Zulaika, *Basque Culture*, 429.

75. *Garbage, Scurvy, Vomit . . .*: For these and dozens of other musical groups, see López Aguirre, *Historia del Rock Vasco* (The History of Basque Rock).

75. *influenced by international youth culture*: See Urla, "We Are All Malcolm X!"; and Kasmir, "From the Margins."

77. *"Where the radical rocker sees the police"*: Aresti, quoted in Douglass and Zulaika, *Basque Culture*, 440.

77. *entitled it Flowers in the Dustbin*: Moso, *Flores en la basura*.

77. *"When you listen to the Sex Pistols"*: Quoted in Marcus, *Lipstick Traces*, 1.

77–78. *"we were connecting brutally"*; *"they were straightforward"*: Moso, *Flores*, 67, 49.

78. *"Life must hurt"*: Huelsenbeck quoted in Marcus, *Lipstick Traces*, 27.

A Family Photograph in Winter City

79. *controlled half of all Bizkaian industrial output and most of its banking*: See Glas, *Bilbaos Business Elite*. Gecho is a town on the Nervión's Right Bank, ten miles from downtown Bilbao. By the 1960s, Neguri was made up of about five hundred families. They lived in single-family units and in spacious apartments on the riverfront avenues. There were hardly any bars or shops in Neguri; the meeting places were private clubs. The community was staunchly pro-Franco. Money, class superiority, Catholicism, and disdain for intellectual activities were its core values.

79. *it was an oligarchy in its pure state*: See Ibarra, "Prólogo."

79. *"those who oppress us are as Basque as are we"*: Quoted in Morán, *Los españoles que dejaron de serlo*, 303.

80. *"that provoked the greatest urbanization catastrophe"*: Quoted in Agirreazkuenaga, "Javier Ybarra," 366.

80. *"the important thing [was] the new city"*: Ibid., 371.

80. *"gifts from the State"*: Ibid., 385.

80. *"the City Hall of the projects"*: Ibid., 365.

82. *Euskara of Ibarrangelua*: A fishing town on the Bizkaian coast.

83. *recognized he was a "good man"*: Agirreazkuenga, "Javier Ybarra," 354.

84. *"sacrificial ritual, Abraham planning"*: Ybarra e Ybarra, *Nosotros, los Ybarra*, 37.

85. *it was the same ETA leader who ordered the killings*: Agirreazkuenaga, "Javier Ybarra," 353.

85. *with whom I had built a discotheque and organized rock concerts*: See Zulaika, *Basque Violence*, 343–47.

Autobiography and Murder

87. *"rock 'n' roll had essentially been born out of the turmoil"*: McAnuff quoted in Wilkerson, *Who Are You*, 424. Frank Rich wrote: "In the apocalyptic year of 1969, *Tommy* was the unwitting background music for the revelation of the My Lai massacre, the Chicago Seven trial, the Charles Manson murders." Quoted in ibid., 426.

87. *"My life began with a huge atomic bomb"*: Quoted in Wilkerson, *Who Are You*, 477.

87. *Guernica is in fact an iconic reference for Townshend*: Townshend, *Who I Am*, 72. And also Smith, *Just Kids*, 20.

87. *about our most intimate "rebirth"*: Townshend, *Who I Am*, 146.

87. *the "stomping ground" of the musical group The Who*: Ibid., 514.

88. *writer or terrorist, there seemed to be no other alternative*: One of the leading Basque authors, Sarrionandia, was arrested as an ETA activist and, after years in prison, escaped to live in exile to this day. Many authors regularly acknowledge that they began writing as a form of militancy. See Etxeberria, *Bost idazle*, 91, 209.

88. *Pink Floyd's "Wish You Were Here"*: Woodworth, *The Basque Country*, 271–75.

91. *an unpredictable passage à l'act*: For a further discussion, see Zulaika, "Excessive Witnessing."

The Ghost of Madness: Writing the Ruins

92. *"a voluntary obliteration of the self"*: Foucault quoted in Copjec, *Imagine There Is No Woman*, 58.

92. *the Blakean poem I wrote on the myth of paradise*: Zulaika, *Adanen poema amaigabea*.

92. *"by external signs instead of on their own interior resources"*: Quoted in Ràfols, "Writing to Seduce and Seducing to Write About It," 258.

93. *"Stephen has slain the Minotaur within himself"*: Fortuna, "The Art," 208.

93. *escape Hegel's "bad infinity"*: Bad infinity is the infinity of the infinite, of the transcendent God who alone is God, whereas true infinity is the infinity of the finite. In the preface to his *The Phenomenology of Spirit*, a book that articulates the end of religious transcendence in a deeper way than Nietzsche's Zarathustra, Hegel writes of having experienced "That death [which] is the painful feeling of the Unhappy

Consciousness that *God Himself is dead.*" In the unhappy self-alienation the Spirit is capable of "mere belief," whereas later "pure insight" takes over and directs itself against belief, for "pure insight. . . is . . . without any content . . . by its negative attitude towards what it excludes it will make itself real and give itself a content." Hegel, *Phenomenology*, 561. Blake himself went through something like this struggle between belief and insight when he had a conversion experience, as a result of which he rebelled against the belief in a tyrant God, whom he identified with Satan, and abandoned the contents of Christian faith to search for a new mythology of his own; Blake's view of God as Satan (the reduction of infinite universe to individual Selfhood) runs parallel to Hegel's notion of "bad infinity." See Altizer, *The New Apocalypse*, 43.

93. *but rather a process and a project*: For the paradoxes of the converted having to do with the problematic relationship between the autobiographical narrative and self-identity, see de Man, *Allegories of Reading*; Nehamas, *Nietzsche*; Sartre, *Les Mots*.

93. *I tried at Deusto to mend with Wittgenstein's Tractatus*: Typical discussions were: Is Wittgenstein's thesis that "objects make up the substance of the world" (2.021) a "necessary truth"? And if so, then what kind of truth is it? And if such a substance can only be *shown*, then what type of categorization is this?

93. *and that was their "antiphilosophy"*: What characterizes antiphilosophy, sums up Badiou, is "the ability to despise mathematics, reducing it, in regard to what is morally serious and existentially intense, to a mere child's game." See Badiou, *Wittgenstein's Antiphilosophy*, 71. In this view, mathematics is not real thinking concerned with being itself but mere calculation.

93–94. *"not a paradise" but "a cancerous growth"; "so much sin"*: Quoted in Monk, *Ludwig Wittgenstein*, 416, 439, 416.

94. *"between saintliness and suicide"*: Bosteels, "Translator's Introduction," Badiou, *Wittgenstein's Antiphilosophy*, 53.

94. *"psychotic ferocity"; "There is no sense except the sense of desire"*: Lacan quoted in Ibid., 42, 50.

94. *the psychoanalytic term psychosis*: Badiou, *Wittgenstein's Antiphilosophy*, 166.

94. *"the paranoid certitude of he who believes"*: Badiou quoted in Bosteels, "Translator's Introduction," Badiou, *Wittgenstein's Antiphilosophy*, 52.

94. *to write of "intellectual terrorism"*: "Even the very Exact Sciences were terribly non-exact, fluctuating, capricious and absurd. Mathematics without laws, axioms, definitions, or rules, stuffed only with theorems and corollaries. . . . This intellectual terrorism entered our brain and took hold of it in some fold like a cyst." Lasa, *Memory Dump (1960–1990)*, 117.

94–95. *so long as it upholds its own impossibility*: See Juaristi, *Miguel de Unamuno*, 417; Juaristi, *El chimbo expiatorio*, 105.

95. *our lives will always be failures*: This is the world of Kant's categorical imperative of the will and the demand to realize the highest good. Kant introduces the postulate of immortality of the soul to open up a field beyond death and make possible for the subject a relationship to a *second death*. The field between these two deaths is the "purgatory of desire." This is also the point of view of the Last Judgment. Zupančič, *The Shortest Shadow*, 252.

95. *in the end "delirium is an interpretation"*: "Given that everyone's 'me-I' (*moi-je*) is delirious, one can assume that delirium is an amplification of what each one has in himself, which can be written thus: 'delirIum' (*delireje*)," wrote Jacques-Alain Miller.

Psychoanlytic transference, and the knowledge that derives from it, "is equivalent to the beginning of a delirium," Miller observed, adding about his teacher that "[i]n this sense, there are not many of us who think that Lacan is not delirious"—a view he extends to Freud and Newton ("who devoted more time to alchemy than to mathematics"). Miller, "The Invention of Delirium," 22, 23.

95. *intense identification with Don Quixote*: See Unamuno, *Vida de don Quijote y Sancho*.

95. *"These fragments I have shored"*: Quoted in Juaristi, *Miguel de Unamuno*, 452–53.

95. *"We can all approach these two terms"; "If psychosis didn't exist"*: Miller, "The Prisons of *Jouissance*," 51.

96. *but I myself am in the frame.* Žižek, *Less Than Nothing*, 702–8.

96. *"The Poet makes himself a seer"*: Rimbaud, *Rimbaud*, 377.

96. *"it is not necessary to consider them as error or malady"*: Miller, "The Prisons," 48–49.

96. *define themselves as "a monstrosity"*: Lispector, *The Passion According to G. H.*, 9.

96. *"the act of seeing [was] ineffable"; "the essence of numbers"*: Lispector, *The Stream of Life*, 73, 24.

97. *"what will be already is"; "manufacture the future"; "in writing, I deal with the impossible"*: Lispector, *The Stream of Life*, 28, 55, 59.

97. *"a world wholly alive has a Hellish power"*: Lispector, *The Passion*, 14.

97. *"not madness, but a desperate attempt to escape madness"*: Žižek, *Less Than Nothing*, 331 n. 9.

97. *"state of grace"; "the body is transformed"; "achieving a higher"*: Lispector, *The Stream of Life*, 71, 72, 43.

97. *"we are always saved"*: Lispector, *The Passion*, 139.

97. *"an artifice through which there arises"*: Lispector, *The Stream of Life*, 13.

97. *"I saw her there in all her glory crowned"*: Alighieri, *Paradise*, XXXI: 71–72.

A Pietà

97. *Oteiza sculpted fourteen apostles*: "I left Bilbao in January of 1935 to see up close some of the American megalithic statuary and to study the muralism of Mexican painters," Oteiza wrote in the prologue to his 1952 book on pre-Colombian statues. "But it has taken me fourteen years to return." Having returned in 1948, he remained in Bilbao until late 1951. He began his artistic work in Madrid in 1929, influenced by the European contemporary movements of Cubism, Russian Constructivism, De Stijl, and the Bauhaus. When asked why he built fourteen, rather than twelve, apostles, Oteiza said, "Forgive me. There was no room for more." He arrived at the number fourteen by adding to the twelve apostles Paul and Judas Iscariot.

97. *"aggressive and monstrous giants that chew"*: Plazaola, "La escuela vasca de escultura," 342. The Vatican's Museum of Modern Religious Art now has copies of these censored pieces.

98. *and spent most of the summer with them*: Muñoa, *Oteiza*, 187.

98. *the mother with a dead child*: On the basis of Picasso's first etching in his *The Dream and Lie of Franco* that preceded *Guernica*, Oteiza interpreted Picasso's horse as "a moving Pietà prehistoric and Basque, of horse and dead man, we must think of a secret Pietà of horse and Picasso dead, a Pietà of horse and miliciano dead, a Pietà of horse and *gudari* [Basque soldier] dead." Oteiza, "La significación vasca del 'Guernica,'" 4–5.

99. *which found expression in Dante*: "O lady of virtue, through you and you alone / mankind surpasses all that is contained

/ within the close sphere of the circling moon." Alighieri, *Inferno*, II, 76–78.

99. *Beatrice took Dante to the sphere above the moon*: Singleton, *Journey to Beatrice*, 128–29.

99. *earlier "female" pagan divinities*: Built in the early century in the pastoral mountainous region of Urbia, in the province of Gipuzkoa, Arantzazu was erected as a bastion against rural witchcraft and pagan cults.

99. *"the current folkloric and linguistic data"*: Caro Baroja, *Los pueblos del norte de la península ibérica*, 200.

99. *represented by the figure of Ariadne*: "In the case of Ariadne signs on coins suggest a connection with the moon. . . . Knossos coins bear witness to a star in the labyrinth, to the lunar nature of Ariadne." Kerényi, *Dionysos*, 104–6.

100. *his painting of Christ on the cross*: See Blanco Aguinaga, *El Unamuno contemplativo*, 358.

100. *"only your lunar light tells us"*: Unamuno, *El Cristo de Velázquez*, 22.

100. *"man who philosophized . . . under the moon"*: Clavería, "Don Miguel y la luna," *Temas de Unamuno*, 165. Italics in original.

100. *"The moon in the sky"*: Aresti, *Obra Guztiak*, I, 520.

101. *"the mothers of ETA activists suffer much"*: Quoted in Iriarte, *Borrokaren gorrian*, 277.

101. *"I gathered myself in front of her body"*: Quoted in Batista, *Madariaga*, 30.

102. *It was a moment of "mystical lucidity"*: Ibid., 53.

Bilbao Dantesque: Painting a River Downstream

102. *"rivers . . . are dyed in noble blood"*: Ibarruri, *Speeches & Articles*, 126.

102. *"You are, Nervión, the history of the town"*: Unamuno, *Obras Completas*, 6, 506.

102. *"Nothing in the world is more magnificent"*: Reprinted in the magazine *Bilbao* 35 (1994), 4.

102. *famed "Protestant ethics" thesis*: Julio Caro Baroja referred to the Weberian thesis to point out that it did not apply to hard-working Basque Catholics. Caro Baroja, *The Basques*, 184–85. Eduardo Glas dwelled on the hypothesis of a Jesuit work ethic by remarking how piety and business go hand in hand within Bilbao's business elite and pointing out the crucial role of the Jesuit education provided by the University of Deusto, as well as by the Deusto Business School. Glas, *The Basque Business Elite*, 134, ff. Glas's conclusion is that "Jesuit moral teaching helped encourage Basque business activities." Ibid., 139. Andreas Hess has insisted on the crucial role of higher education and the worldliness of Jesuit teaching. Hess, "Is It Justified to Speak of a Jesuit Work Ethic in the Basque Country?" See also Azaola, "El viaje a Vasconia de Max Weber." But it is the work of Otazu and Díaz de Durana, *El espíritu emprendedor de los vascos*, that gives a full historical background of the Jesuit influence upon Bilbao's entrepreneurial mentality. Already in the seventeenth century there was a fierce ideological battle between the Jansenists and the Jesuits. The Basque cleric Saint-Cyran, abbot of Port Royal, was with Cornelius Jansen the founder of the rigorous doctrine known as Jansenism, which insisted on the depravity of human nature always burdened with original sin and redeemable only through the predestination of God's grace given only to a few. To this "pessimist" view of human nature the Jesuits contrasted a more optimistic and morally probabilistic one that was deemed as "lax" by their opponents. One charge against the Jesuits was that they approved of "usury." Otazu and Díaz de Durana, 542. Saint-Cyran furiously attacked Jesuit "opportunism," but it was Pascal's defense that contributed the most to Jansenism's expansion. One of Saint-Cyran's ideas was that "money is the lord of the world and God's greatest

enemy." Ibid., 551. Although a son and brother of merchants, he considered business to be a burden. If Jansenism had a decisive influence in the French Basque city of Bayonne, Jesuits ruled in Bilbao, and their teaching of a more positive view of business fit better, in the opinion of some, with the optimism of Bilbao's successful local aristocracy. Still, the Jansenists' rigorous influence affected the Jesuit order as well, and works such as Pascal's *Thoughts* were read in Bilbao by business entrepreneurs like José Antonio de Ibarra, the founder of the most prominent Bilbao mining and industrialist dynasty. Jansenism had a pedigree in Bilbao's "old type bourgeoisie," described as "impregnated with humanism, believer, educated, fond of meditation and introspection, heir to a long tradition of moral austerity, linked to money, but only as a mere instrument." Taveneaux quoted in Otazu and Díaz de Durana, 553. Blasco Ibáñez's view in his novel *El Intruso* was that the Jesuits provided a nefarious influence on Bilbao's society by their intrusion into wealthy households through spiritual guidance of the wives. In terms of business mentality, however, the Jesuits supported the city's entrepreneurial spirit, "praising the virtues of work against the aristocratic conception of life symbolized by Madrid." Caro Baroja quoted in Glas, *Bilbao's Modern Business Elite*, 138.

103. *Bilbao was a port before it was a city*: See Ossa Echaburu, *Bilbao, puerto antes que villa.*

104. *including off Newfoundland*: See Kurlansky, *Cod.*

104. *one of Europe's most important trade routes*: See Douglass and Bilbao, *Amerikanuak*, 58.

104. *Bilbao's iron went to Great Britain*. Glas, *Bilbao's Modern Business Elite*, 55.

104. *more of the social elite than the working class*: Arpal, "El Bilbao de la industrialización."

104. *use to repay Hitler's favors*: Muñoz-Rojas, *Ashes and Granite*, 113.

105. *Basque Country's first Socialist Association (1886)*: Bilbao would also become an early focus of the Spanish Socialist Party, as well as the Spanish Communist Party. In 1890, thirty thousand workers took part in a strike. After the Russian Revolution of 1917, the majority of the miners of the Left Bank joined the Spanish Communist Party. The city also produced the reactionary response (with Basque overtones) to proletarianism.

105. *unemployment was above 20 percent*: See Rodríguez, "Planning and Revitalization of an Old Industrial City."

105. *the Spanish government proposed a plan for restructuring*: Colectivo Autónomo de Trabajadores de Euskalduna, *La batalla de Euskalduna*, 27.

105–6. *the last link uniting the right and left riverbanks*: With the exception of the "hanging bridge" or suspension bridge in Portugalete.

106. *"Our strength doesn't come from heavens"*: Colectivo, *La Batalla*, 13–14. Emphasis added.

106. *the cloistered monk in Zenarrusa*: Zenarrusa is a monastery twenty miles from Bilbao.

106. *"much like the tides get high with the full moon"*: Lorenzo Espinosa, *Txabi Etxebarrieta: Poesía*, 172.

109. *producing ruins as a precondition*: See Zulaika, "The Ruins of Theory and a Theory of Ruins."

109. *true learning has to come from this Theology of Hell*: Benjamin quoted in Buck-Morss, *The Dialectics of Seeing*, 176.

109. *Paul Klee's Angelus Novus*: Benjamin, *Illuminations*, 257–58.

BOOK II. PURGATORY

Shackles and Swords: A Lover's Passion

111. *"Sir, in my heart there was a kind of fighting"*: Shakespeare, *Hamlet*, Act V, Scene II:4–6.

111. *"Bilbo . . . from Bilbao in Spain"*: The Compact Edition of the Oxford Dictionary, vol I: 215.

111. *"The mind is its own place"*: Milton, *Paradise Lost*, 235.

112. *"If I go down, I am not going by myself"*: Decker, "What Price Guggenheim?," 39.

112. *"the brink of absurdity"*: Richardson, "Go, Go, Guggenheim," 21.

113. *try the casino model*: "[W]hatever happens is good for the museums. Like casinos, they cannot lose, and that is their curse." Adorno, "Valéry Proust Museum," 177.

114. *its proximity to the city's auction markets*: See Sullivan, "Inside Trading," 257.

114. *auction-based international art community*: No other museum director had previously dared to auction off masterpieces from a major museum's permanent collection. When the Basques signed a contract that gave Krens, in addition to the franchise fee, $50 million for new acquisitions, he wanted to spend it at Sotheby's. The Basque partners rejected the idea. It was also in an auction house (Sotheby's in Vienna) that Krens bought some works by Beuys for Bilbao, which, after being exhibited in New York, were found to be fakes. See Decker, "Can the Guggenheim Pay the Price?"

114. *"this whole 'degraded' landscape"*: Jameson, "Postmodernism," 54.

118. *"chronicle of a seduction"*: Zulaika, *Crónica de una seducción.*

118. *"deal of the century"*: Bradley, "The Deal of the Century."

118. *skeptical of a krensified model*:
See Zulaika, "Desiring Bilbao: The
Krensification of the Museum and Its
Discontents."

The Sword and the Wound:
Virgins and Prostitutes

118. *four plazas in different locations*: The
current plaza of Vista Alegre was built
at the end of the nineteenth century. It
burned down in 1961, two months after
Hemingway's death, and a similar one
for fifteen thousand spectators was built
five months later. See Sáiz Valdivielso
and Sáiz Bernuy, *Bilbao: Toros y toreros*.

119. *a woman forty years younger than he.*
Mandel, *Hemingway's* The Dangerous
Summer, 62.

119. *he frequented them*: Hemingway was
in Bilbao during the summers of 1925,
1926, 1927, 1929, and 1933. Jimenez,
Hemingway eta euskaldunak, 37, 38, 294.

119. *wrote of the city's raw ugliness*: Baker,
Hemingway: The Writer as Artist, 147.

119. *"Bilbao, a city that he loved"*:
Hemingway, *Death in the Afternoon*, 198.

119. *priest Andrés Untzain, was buried*:
When Hemingway visited the cemetery,
he was most probably in the company
of José María Uzelay, whose painting
of Hemingway and Juan Dunabeitia,
another of the writer's close Basque
friends in Cuba, now hangs in Bilbao's
Museo de Bellas Artes. See Jimenez,
Hemingway eta euskaldunak, 321.

119. *"the original moment of truth, or
of reality"*: Hemingway, *Death in the
Afternoon*, 174.

119. *echoing the power of Picasso's painted
allegories*: Baker, *Hemingway*, 258.

120. *"There is no translation for this word"*:
Hemingway, *The Old Man and the Sea*, 61.

120. *"the bull of moon and honey"*: Vicente
Aleixandre, quoted in Museo de Bellas
Artes de Bilbao, *Taurus*, 13.

120. *Writing was tauromachy for Michel
Leiris*: See Leiris, *Mirror of Tauromachy*

121. *"There is no longer the passion it once
created"*: There is a decline in public
attendance, and some bullrings have
ceased operations. Bullfighting is
currently immersed in a growing debate
as to the legitimacy of such "art" in
contemporary Europe, many arguing
that it is a shame for Spain to still abide
by such a "barbarous" practice. In
the summer of 2010, bullfighting was
forbidden in Barcelona, a decision that
was seen as combining new sensibilities
as well as politics. The Bilbao feria of
2010 was considered a "success" by the
organizers because attendance at Vista
Alegre's bullring had gone done down
"only" 5 percent.

121. *"más cornadas dan las mujeres"*:
Hemingway, *Death in the Afternoon*, 103.
In Spanish in the original.

121. *but she replies with cornadas (acts
of goring)*: Pamplona was the place
where not only matadors get gored but,
Hemingway observed cryptically, where
the Jesuit founder "Loyola got his wound
that made him think" and forced his
conversion. Hemingway, *Death in the
Afternoon*, 274–75.

121. *The wound has been viewed as
Hemingway's truth*: Comley and Scholes,
Hemingway's Genders, 8.

121. *As in hunting, this type of possessive
passion*: See Zulaika, *Caza, símbolo y eros*.

121. *"mockery of love and death"*:
Bergamin, *La claridad del toreo*, 11.

121. *"marked by an irreducible failure"*:
Žižek, *How to Read Lacan*, 65.

121. *impasses of the macho erotic model*:
Hemingway's own brand of anti-
sentimentalism was branded by critics
as "infected by a queer kind of maudlin
emotion, which sounds at once neurotic
and drunken" to the point that "the
whole thing becomes a little hysterical."
Max Eastman, quoted in Strychacz,
Hemingway's Theaters, 146–47.

121. *These bulls were brought from where
else*: The *sokamuturra* would take place
around 8 a.m., at the nexus of the

night's end for the revelers and the
beginning of the new fiesta day. The city
hall, concerned about the dangers of
excessive "carnivalization" of the fiesta
posed by the bull, moved the running of
the bulls from the street to the bullring
and later eliminated it altogether.

122. *"The way a bull breaks loose"*:
Alighieri, *Inferno*, XII: 22–25.

122. *writing an ethnograpahy on them*:
Zulaika, *Caza, símbolo y eros*.

122. *"exactly like a dream"; "absolutely no
control whatsoever"*: Zulaika, *Caza*, 139.

123. *"the orgiastic, Dionysian element . . .
flows and boils"*: Ortega y Gasset, "A
'Veinte Años de la Caza Mayor,'" 235.

123. *"the hunter has more than a little of
Don Juan"*: Delibes, *El libro de la caza
menor*, 83.

123. *affects the bullfighter's identity*: The
hysterical woman's classical question
is, Is my love for this man *mine*, or is it
simply an echo of the love *he* wants from
me?

123. *almost feminine, sexless figure*: He is
the opposite of the soldier with a gun
and wearing boots—footwear being
the key fetish of military dress. Such
a "feminine" aura of the bullfighter
has been frequently represented in
art. Picasso himself depicted a *torera*
modeled after the *Sleeping Ariadne* in his
Minotauromachy. See Museo de Bellas
Artes, *Taurus*, 350. One of Picasso's
paintings was *La mujer torero*. But it is
in his remarkable *Minotauromachy*, the
etching that directly antecedes *Guernica*,
where we see the female matador on a
horse with her breasts bared.

123. *impostor who represents what he is
not*: In a psychoanalytic reading, the
matador can be taken as a signifier of
"symbolic castration." It is the phallic
sword that condenses the matador's
displaced erotic killing potency. "In
the traje de luces a bullfighter is on
display in a bejeweled garment that both
conceals and reveals his body, including
his sexual organs." Comley and Scholes,

Hemingway's Genders, 109. We might say that the matador's phallus displays the paradox of castration, whereby "the phallus, the signifier of enjoyment, had simultaneously to be the signifier of 'castration', that is to say, *one and the same signifier had to signify enjoyment as well as its loss.*" Žižek, "Courtly Love," 97. Hemingway wrote a great deal about male homosexuality among bullfighters.

123. *Bilbao is also starkly androgynous*: This perspective is further expanded in Zulaika, "Is Bilbao a Woman?"

123. *as were the following three rulers*: While María Díaz de Haro was heiress to both Bilbao and the Seigneury of Bizkaia, her uncle, Diego López de Haro, seized power from her and then conferred upon Bilbao its foundational charter as villa (town) in the year 1300. He was known as "The Intruder" for having usurped his niece's birthright. After papal mediation, Don Diego agreed that upon his death the dominion would return to María. She took charge in 1310 and reaffirmed Bilbao's charter, conferring upon the city a monopoly on the trade from and to Burgos in Castile, thereby ensuring that Bilbao would become an important seaport. She was followed as ruler of Bizkaia first by her niece María, who died in childbirth, and then by her daughter Juana and her granddaughter María.

123. *preceded the earliest development of the town*: Other bridges were built between the city's Seven Streets and Old Bilbao. In the 1920s and 1930s, two drawbridges were built in front of the City Hall and in Deusto, followed by the La Salve Bridge. Beyond Deusto there were no bridges. There are twelve kilometers of right and left riverbanks from the city to the sea, their isolation uncompromised by any link with the one exception of the hanging bridge in Portugalete. More recently, the river has been crisscrossed by several new bridges (Rontegi, Euskalduna, Zubizuri).

123. *constantly mixed and identified, in his work*: See Blanco Aguinaga, *El Unamuno Contemplativo*, 276.

124. *the source of the neurotic's erotic impasse*: Freud, "The Most Prevalent Form of Degradation in Erotic Life," in Sigmund Freud, *Collected Papers*, IV, 210.

124. *one of the most glamorous plazas for prostitution*: Already in 1894 there were 2,305 prostitutes in the city. The hygienic regulations were drastic; syphilis and other venereal diseases were by then "practically endemic." González García, "La prostitución en Bilbao," 234.

124. *La Palanca became an isolated and marginal space*: For a study of the evolution of prostitution in Bilbao, see Vázquez and Sanz, "Estudio sociológico de la prostitución en Bilbao," unpublished manuscript, 1985.

124. *a prime space for urban gentrification*: See Vicario and Martínez Monje, 2003.

125. *El Correo, under the banner of "relax"*: Currently *El Correo* advertises daily several hundred prostitutes, 80 to 90 percent of whom are immigrants. According to Emakunde's 2007 study, there were 1,820 prostitutes working in the Basque community. The profits earned by such advertising are substantial. In 2001 the earnings of just one Spanish newspaper were estimated at 450 million pesetas, or about $3 million. Pisano, *Yo puta*, 29.

125. *"the possibility that Big Brother is not watching"*: Žižek quoted in Zabet Patterson, "Going On-line," 116.

126. *there were several convents and churches in Old Bilbao*: The convent of the Franciscans, on San Francisco Street, at one time housed more than a hundred religious men. In 1889 the Order of the Claretians came to San Francisco's barrio. Another of the churches, built in the late seventeenth century, was the Merced, managed by the Mercedarian cloistered nuns. In Naja Street, the convent of the Congregation of the Servants of Jesus was constructed at the

end of the nineteenth century. Also in La Palanca there was another convent on Concepción Street that lost its site to the railroad going from Bilbao to Tudela; it was reestablished in the mining zone in 1861. See Izarzelaia, *Los barrios altos de Bilbao*.

126. *"exhausted from fighting"*; *"a seafaring Virgin"*: Mañaricua, *Santa María de Begoña en la historia espiritual de Vizcaya*, 114, 338.

126. *attachment to the Virgin Mother's distant figure*: See Zulaika, *Terranova*, for the occupational logic of such distant attachments.

126. *the vassal projects his idealized wishes*: Žižek, "Courtly Love," 90.

126. *"the inaccessibility of the object"*: Jacques Lacan, *The Ethics of Psychoanalysis*, 151.

126. *the same condition that forbids its obtainment*: Žižek, "Courtly Love," 96.

126. *as religious fundamentalism and Carlist insurrection*: The incompatibility between these two sensibilities was apparent on the occasion of the "coronation" of the Virgin of Begoña in 1900 and again in 1903 when the Vatican declared Her patroness of Bizkaia. The great festivities organized to celebrate the declaration were opposed by Bilbao's city hall, which declined to contribute money to honor the new patroness and even boycotted the solemn procession.

The Dominatrix

128. *the headdress replicating the shape of the horn*: In more recent times, in the 1970s and 1980s, the cartoonist Juan Carlos Eguillor produced the figure of Miss Martiartu, with a hairdo in the shape of two large horns. She became a popular cartoon figure in various newspapers, an heir to the horned hairdos of ladies of the sixteenth century. Eguillor's drawings of the word *Bilbao* frequently include a horn crossing

the letter A—as if he were suggesting that the entire city had been cuckolded.

128. *the actual women depicted in the painting*: There is a Basque writer, Mirande, who has given expression to this phallic woman under the symbol of the malevolent, castrating moon. The moon "acquires a mythical dimension because of its personification," and furthermore "it contaminates all the other images." Arkotxa Scarcia, "La mirada malévola de la luna en la *Ahijada* de J. Mirande (1925–1972)," 320.

130. *men have a phallus, women are the phallus*: See Lacan, "The Significance of the Phallus."

130. *to throw combs to Mari of Anboto*: Anboto is a mountain thirty minutes away from Bilbao.

131. *"cold-maternal-severe"*: Deleuze, "Coldness and Cruelty," in Deleuze and von Sacher-Masoch, *Masochism*, 51.

131. *"the tyranny and cruelty that constitute"*: Von Sacher-Masoch quoted in Paglia, *Sexual Personae*, 436.

131. *"the formula of masochism is the humiliated father"*: Deleuze, "Coldness," 60–61.

131. *"furious hunger for maternity"*: Unamuno quoted in Blanco Aguinaga, *El Unamuno comtemplativo*, 159.

131. *femininity is projected into the role of the mother*: It is the alliance between the son and the oral-stage mother that gives ground to the masochistic experience: the two masculine and feminine "impulses constitute one single figure; femininity is posited as lacking in nothing and placed alongside a virility suspended in disavowal." Deleuze, "Coldness," 68. It is not so much identification with the mother that characterizes the masochist, but that "masochism proceeds by a twofold disavowal, a positive, idealizing of the mother (who is identified with the law) and an invalidating disavowal of the father (who is expelled from the symbolic order)." Ibid., 68. In

the constellation of masochism, characterized by disavowal, waiting, fetishism, and fantasy, not only does the victim consent to the contract but he has to persuade and train his torturess to perform her part of the pact. In submission to the "phallic" woman or the religious master, the servant stages and creates his own bondage in a pact that is essentially formal and bound by his world alone, while accepting captivity as protection from his own sexual autonomy.

132. *But was it also arousal and erotic pleasure?*: See Largier, *In Praise of the Whip: A Cultural History of Arousal.*

132. *"is the opposite of what might be expected"*: Deleuze, "Coldness," 88.

132. *"sadomasochism's punitive hierarchical structure"*: Paglia, "Scholars in Bondage," 56.

132. *"eroticism . . . is assenting to life up to the point of death"*: Bataille, *Death and Sensuality*, 5.

132. *exposed to eroticized images of saints*: The main model for our devotional life was Saint Gabriel of Our Lady of Sorrows—a young, handsome, amorous Italian motherless youth from a well-to-do family in Assisi who, after a life of dance and romance, joined the Passionist Order as a result of a repeatedly deferred promise of conversion if he were to survive a grave illness. Gabriel Possanti died in 1863 of tuberculosis at the age of twenty-five and was canonized as a saint in 1926. For incisive comments on the erotic dimension of his figure, see Paglia, *Vamps and Tramps*, 197–200.

132. *"Do not think that I have come to bring peace"*: This was also Chesterton's most damning conclusion: "Christianity is a sword which separates and sets free." Chesterton, *Orthodoxy*, 139.

133. *"but precisely because sexuality competes"*: Žižek, *Less Than Nothing*, 441.

In the Name of the Father

134. *"the original sin was one against God the Father"*: Freud, *Totem and Taboo*, 154. This is a sin that, since it required Christ's sacrifice of his own life, drives one "to conclude that the sin was murder. The law of talion, which is so deeply rooted in human feelings, lays it down that a murder can only be expiated by the sacrifice of another life: self-sacrifice points back to blood-guilt." Jones, *Dostoyevsky*, 208.

134. *"He has never been the father"; with the origin of the superego*: Lacan, *The Ethics of Psychoanalysis*, 177, 307.

134. *the bond between father and son becomes binding*: See Lacan, *On the Names-of-the-Father*, 78–81.

136. *Basque society is staunchly "patriarchal"*: See Teresa del Valle et al., *Mujer vasca*; del Valle, *Modelos emergentes en los sistemas y las relaciones de género*; del Valle, *Andamios para una nueva ciudad*; Bullen, *Basque Gender Studies*; Esteban, *Reproducción del cuerpo femenino*; Díez Mintegui, "Female Labour, Participation and Gender Relationships."

136. *reading of the Bible was hopelessly patriarchal*: See Bernabé, "Biblia."

137. *"The World as Labyrinth: Knossos"*: Ortiz-Osés, *Antropología simbólica vasca*, 26.

138. *one of them his autobiography*: Ortiz-Osés, *Mitología cultural y memorias antropológicas*, 40.

138. *"the loss of the (external) father coincides"*: Ibid., 37.

138. *truth, in its "weakness," accepts castration*: "The love of truth is the love of this weakness whose veil we have lifted, it's the love of what truth hides, which is called castration." Lacan, *The Seminar of Jacques Lacan*, vol. 17, *The Other Side of Psychoanalyis*, 52. "Castration is universal in that it affects access to enjoyment for every speaking being, regardless of position, woman or

295

man. . . . Castration means that language is not-whole, precisely." Badiou, "The Subject and Infinity," 213. Castration is thus stripped of its horror by the veiling effect of the love of truth. It is not the plenitude of truth but its subtractive dimension that deserves philosophical love—"the love of truth is the *love of castration.*" Badiou, "Truth: Forcing the Unnameable," 130.

140. *their struggle as a "crisis of adolescence"*: Etxebarrieta, *Los vientos favorables*, 136.

A Broken Sphere

141. *did not emerge from a vacuum*: An Association of Basque Artists was founded in Bilbao as early as 1911. A Museum of Fine Arts was conceived and approved in 1908 and opened in 1914, and a Museum of Modern Art was completed by 1924. In 1945, the two museums were merged in a building next to Casilda Park. These museums reflected the artistic interests of the newly prosperous and cosmopolitan middle class that resulted from the city's industrial wealth at the turn of the century. It was in Paris that Bilbaoan artists discovered modernity. Despite being a conservative anglophile city, Bilbao "facilitated the education of a number of artists, enabling them to visit Impressionist Paris and return with a certain spirit, although tempered, of the revolutionary ideas emanating from the French capital. These artists were essential in the establishment of cultural events and institutions." Viar, "The Guggenheim Bilbao," 98–99.

143. *"failure is a sign that the composer is dealing with the Real"*: Žižek, *Less Than Nothing*, 604 n. 45.

143. *writings as a development parallel to his*: Oteiza, "Art Today, The City, and Man," 316.

143. *"in the not uncommon process of finding"*: Cronin, *Samuel Beckett*, 147.

143. *"I'm horribly tired and stupefied"*: Beckett quoted in Cronin, *Samuel Beckett*, 441.

143. *"that failure is the inevitable outcome of all attempts"*: Cronin, *Samuel Beckett*, 554, 572.

143. *"writing has nothing more to assert"*: Badiou, "The Writing of the Generic," 263–64. Italics in original.

143. *"is conical and consequently implies culmination"*: Quoted in Cronin, *Samuel Beckett*, 96.

144. *"through a veritable intellectual and artistic mutation"*: Badiou, "The Writing of the Generic," 264, 266. Italics in original. The modification had to do with a "chance" that, under the signifier of "happiness," "saved Beckett from falling back on the secret schemas of predestination." Ibid., 266.

144. *"where one would expect serenity and maturity"*: Said, *On Late Style*, 12.

144. *the initiative that became the Cubo (Cube)*: The Center would have combined a museum with workshops for artists, a public library, an auditorium, etc. It was to be an "experimental" center as much as a museistic one. It would display the world's avant-garde artists, and the Basque avant-garde would be second to none. It would embrace the great aesthetic movements, but without ignoring what Oteiza had been labeling for decades "Basque anthropological aesthetics."

145. *"a figure of lateness itself, an untimely"*: Said, *On Late Style*, 14.

146. *"For me Oteiza is like Le Corbusier"; "Oteiza is the greatest sculptor alive"*: Muñoa, *Oteiza*, 253, 252.

147. *and Bilbao, curated by Badiola*: See the exhibit's catalog *Oteiza: Propósito Experimental.*

147. *"In no way did we feel Oteiza's disciples"*: Badiola, "El lugar de la controversia: Múltiples relaciones del arte y lo político en el País Vasco," unpublished paper presented at the conference "Beyond Guernica and the Guggenheim: Relations between Art and Politics from a Comparative Perspective," May 2, 2013, Center for Basque Studies, University of Nevada, Reno.

147. *"I don't know what you are doing"*: Badiola, "El lugar de la controversia."

147. *"the space conquered in these"*: Richard Serra, "Notes on Jorge Oteiza." Originally published in *El País*, Madrid, February 2003. Reprinted in *Oteiza: Mito y Modernidad*, 367.

147. *show fidelity to the Thing by first sacrificing it*: Žižek, *The Fragile*, 154.

Easy Rider: From Sacrament to Spectacle

148. *a book he completed in Bilbao in 1952*: Oteiza discovered the pre-Columbian "fantastic statuary left by an unknown people" in the city of San Agustín (Colombia) after migrating to South America in 1935. In 1928 there had been a major exhibition of pre-Columbian art in Paris; Bataille, Métraux, and Rivet contributed essays for the occasion. Krauss, *The Originality of the Avant-Garde and Other Modernist Myths*, 55. Oteiza would later write a book-length essay on the imposing prehistoric statues in the Colombian Andes. Oteiza, *Interpretación estética de la estatuaria megalítica americana*. A key chapter was entitled "The Statue as Agustinian Sacrament": "On coming in contact with their statues. . . . these men became bewitched, deified," Oteiza wrote while extolling as the "maximum creation" of the culture "the symbolic Eucharist of their stones or sacred forms: sacrament of transfiguration through the statue." Oteiza, *Oteiza's Selected Writings*, 134. These pre-Columbian people identified with jaguars—but not as mere metaphor; theirs was a sacramental identification, Oteiza contended. As with bread and wine for churchgoers, for art lovers a statue can be a metaphor or, as for Oteiza, a sacrament. It not only signifies but *affects*

what it signifies. These are surprising formulations to come from a modernist avant-garde artist who was anything but a pious man.

148. *"Have you been in Bilbao? . . ."*: Muschamp, "The Miracle in Bilbao," 54.

149. *"because of their sense of sacrifice"*: Zambrano, *Las palabras del regreso*, 44.

149. *"almost everything I thought of or looked at"*: Quoted in Hughes, "Masterpiece Theater," 8.

152. *"Guernica's presence in the Casón had transformed"*: Van Hensbergen, *Guernica*, 308–9.

152. *"Here it is now, in the Neolithic Casón"*: Josep Lluís Sert, quoted in ibid., 309.

155. *"I've never had / another life but hers"*: Oteiza, *Selected Writings*, 486.

157. *"I ANDROCANTO and continue"*: *Androcanto*: a neologism by Oteiza; its first component, *andro*, echoes the address to Arantzazu's Madonna as Andra Mari (Lady Mari). Oteiza, *Poesía*, 243.

Euskadi Fantôme

157. *"Transgression does not negate an interdiction"*: Quoted in Clifford, "On Ethnographic Surrealism," 126. Leiris wrote a book entitled *Afrique fantôme*. For a full ethnographic background of the notion of "Euskadi fantôme," see Zulaika, *Del Cromañón al Carnaval*.

159. *"the operation of a triumphant ego"*: Deleuze, "Coldness," 126.

159. The word *desencanto* (disenchantment) summed up: See Vilarós, *El mono del desencanto*.

160. *"Here woman rules, period"*; *"planning the escape from his particular Alcatraz"*: Terol, *Técnicas de la mujer vasca*, 197.

Urban Processions

161. *Bilbao's jobless were 28,606*: Throughout the 2000–2010 decade,

unemployment stayed below 10 percent. In early 2013, while the unemployment rate in Spain overall was 26 percent, it was 16 percent in the Basque Country.

The Actor's Labyrinth

166. *"In each action, in each either/or, it is the Minotaur"*: Lipus, "Minotauroa Labirintoan" unpublished manuscript, Bilbao, 2003, 1.

166. *"what a lesson in humility, a tremendous creator"*: The notion of "subjective destitution" as equivalent to excrement has been a standard allegory since Luther.

Happy End in Mahagonny Paradise

167. *in Kafe Antzokia*. Kafe Antzokia is the café-theater that leads Bilbao's efforts at reviving Euskara by organizing language courses and offering cutting-edge musical entertainment. See Urla, "Kafe Antzokia."

167. *this is actually happening*: Pete Townshend, quoted in Marcus, *Lipstick Traces*, 1.

168. *Mahagonny goes to its doom*: Weill's music was described by Adorno as "music with a smoldering vividness and, at the same time, a mortally sad and faded background, music with a circumspect sharpness which, by means of its leaps and side-steps, makes articulate something that the song's public would prefer not to know about." Quoted in Jarman, *Kurt Weill*, 112. Weill deliberately distorts the melodies in overt dissonances and "shows the stupidity of the modulation," a modulation that, rather than producing emotional involvement, "collapses into an abyss of nothingness." Quoted in ibid., 114.

168. *"arching tune shaking off the churlishness of the verse"*: Ross, *The Rest Is Noise*, 190.

168. *"It was fantastic!"* These are songs consisting of "two contrasted halves" in which the first half employs the simplest, obsessively repetitive melodic patterns, then moves to the cadence of the lyrical melodic line, which takes place ambiguously against a flat accompaniment—"Together the melody and the accompaniment undermine, and consequently neutralize, one another. The emotional ambiguity and the sense of ironic objectivity produced by this fusion of romantic and anti-romantic gesture lies at the heart of the peculiar fascination exerted by Weill's music of the 1920s and 1930s." Jarman, *Kurt Weill*, 115, 119. For both Brecht and Weill, the ideological and the formal are the two elements that must be fused in order to create something new.

169. *"had constructed out of America a fabulous"*: Frederic Ewen, *Bertolt Brecht*, 113.

169. *"the most modern of capitalisms"*: Reprinted in the magazine *Bilbao* 35(1994): 4.

170. *"totally influenced by 'Pirate Jenny'"*: Dylan, *Chronicles*, 272–76.

170. *a direct quote from Brecht*: Ross, *The Rest Is Noise*, 194.

171. *the fabulous riches and green pastures of capitalism*: In the first play Brecht staged in Berlin in 1922, *Drums in the Night*, the setting included a "childish-like" Berlin "with an illuminated moon that glowed now and then," while a placard proclaimed, "Don't Stare So Romantically." Ewen, *Bertolt Brecht*, 108.

Streets of Love

177. *the gift's logic of arbitrary donation*: Contemporary authors (Derrida, Badiou, Marion) link the logic of the gift with the theme of *immanent grace* understood in non-religious terms as "a formal, wholly secularized conception of grace" (Badiou, *Saint Paul*, 66). Grace is what "suspends the conditions of an ordinary, causal temporality with the display of an

unconditional and unconditioned gift." Adam Miller, *Badiou, Marion and St Paul: Immanent Grace*, 63–64. Such a gift is excluded by the rules of the capitalist economy, it appears as exception or subtraction—as *lack* that appears as infinite excess. What these authors establish are the logical links between "the graciousness of the gift," "the immanence of givenness," and its "actual infinity."

Here Comes Everybody

177. *on "affordable luxury" at the Architecture School*: The talk had a definite purpose—to promote a product and a book by a firm whose aim was to sell electric installations by the Italian firm BTicino.

177. *the need for squandering wealth and public display*: See Basurto Ferro, Rodríguez-Escudero Sánchez, and Velilla Iriondo, *El Bilbao que pudo ser*.

180. *belonging to the same company with different names*: Oysho, Maximo Dutti, Bershka, Stradivarius, Zarahome (all of which had at least two shops). Outside of Bilbao's Gran Vía, there were more Zara shops in the big shopping malls of MxCenter, Artea, Zubiarte, and Bilbondo.

180. *elite shunned the ostentatiousness of luxury*: Eduardo Glas studied the family fortunes of two dozen Bilbao families and concluded that rarely was their wealth used for speculation or personal profit. Expenditures on jewelry, clothing, and furniture were 1.2 percent of the total, about half of what Parisian businessmen spent at the time. The Bilbao business elite, during the 1850–75 period, lived rather modestly. Glas, *Bilbao's Modern Business Elite*, 152–71.

181. *"the master of us all"*: Blume, *The Master of Us All*.

181. *in the early 1930s while staying at the Hotel Carlton*: Arzalluz, *Cristóbal Balenciaga*, 105–11.

181. *Franco's wife had been Balenciaga's client since 1933*: Coco Chanel preceded Balenciaga in dressing Bilbao and San Sebastián's high bourgeoisie, after she opened her first couture house near the Biarritz casino in 1915 in the wave of luxury and consumerism that took over the Côte des Basques during the First World War. Balenciaga met Chanel in San Sebastián's casino in September 1917, when she was there to show her winter collection. That same year Balenciaga opened his own shop. Ibid., 18.

181. *"Modernity, the time of Hell"*: Buck-Morss, *The Dialectics of Seeing*, 97.

184. *object produced by the phantasmagoria of commodities*: For women in particular, fashion displaces their sexuality and fecundity into the sex appeal of the clothes they wear. Their "continuous effort to be beautiful" derives in the end "from the weakness of women's social position," in which age and decay become fateful punishment.

184. *praying daily in a nearby church*: According to his apprentice, designer André Courrèges, Balenciaga would daily leave the atelier to pray in the church. Ellis Miller, *Cristóbal Balenciaga*, 22. His workplace was described as permeated by an "atmosphere . . . comparable to that of a convent," where people talked in hushed voices and walked on tiptoe. Jouve, *Balenciaga*, 10.

184. *"the idea of fashion is antipathetic to the idea of sainthood"*: Barthes, *Mythologies*, 47.

184. *"mourning, all black, sad beyond belief"*: The *vendeuse* Florette Cherlot quoted in Blume, *The Master*, 82.

184. *his "pessimism" was noted by writers*: Ballard, *In My Fashion*, 115; Beaton, *Glass of Fashion*, 267.

184. *"c'est la vie d'un chien [it's a dog's life]"*: Glynn, "Balenciaga and la vie d'un chien."

184. *"I said [to the Germans] he might as well take all the bullfighters"*: Quoted in Blume, *The Master*, 61.

184. *"the great rule that elimination is the secret of chic"*: Quoted in Miller, *Cristóbal Balenciaga*, 42.

184. *"simplicity dramatically presented"*: Ibid., 44.

184. *"the black is so black that it hits you like a blow"*: Quoted in ibid., 42.

184. *the couturier was not a decorator but a builder*: Blume, *The Master*, 19.

184. *"create classical, timeless models"*: Miller, *Cristóbal Balenciaga*, 49, 51.

185. *"derived much pleasure from"*: Ibid., 37.

185. *Spanish/Basque traditional designs*: Diana Vreeland wrote: "His inspiration came from the bullrings, the flamenco dancers, the loose blouses the fishermen wear, the cool of the cloisters." Quoted in Arzalluz, *Cristóbal Balenciaga*, 194. For the Basque influences in his designs, see ibid., 229.

185. *Balenciaga found himself in a desfase (gap)*: Miller, *Cristóbal Balenciaga*, 84.

185. *"A woman, she is not a cube"*: Emmanuelle Khahn quoted in ibid., 53.

187. *defined at below 900 euros per month*: Gil, "One out of every four bilbainos lives 'on the edge' and under the threat of poverty," 6.

188. *the new industries' technological innovation*: See Galarraga and Gallastegui, "Bilbao: Transformación económica." Zamudio opened in 1985. In 1998 it had 81 companies operated by 2,950 employees; in 2002 it had 120 companies and 5,260 employees.

188. *the value of the apartments around it had risen 74 percent*: Vicario and Martínez Monje, "Another 'Guggenheim Effect'?" 2388.

Play It Again, Joe

189. *including Bilbao in the past*: Anthropologist Olatz González showed how pelota has been for centuries the Basque game par excellence and the

fronton the most representative public space; it also became an extraordinary source of metaphors and cultural performances in the traditional society. González, *Pelota vasca.* A century ago, Bilbao had as many as eight *frontones*; the last one remaining, the Euskalduna, closed in August 1959. Since then it has been the absence of a fronton in Bilbao that was most remarkable until March 5, 2011, when the Fronton Bizkaia was inaugurated in the barrio of Mirivilla.

189. *A variant of pelota known worldwide is jai alai*: In Euskara, *jai alai* means "happy festival." When Orson Wells produced the BBC documentary on the Basques, "the aboriginals of Europe," he focused his camera on the frontier between Spain and France and also on a fronton to ask: "What is a Basque?" More recently, filmmaker Julio Medem chose the fronton for his movie *Basque Pelota: The Skin Against the Stone,* an exploration of the current Basque political impasse.

189. *action and subjectivity—a quality space*: The cultural notion of "quality space" was developed by James Fernandez in "The Mission of Metaphor." But intrinsic to the *n continua* of this deep space is their paradoxical or *excessive* nature in the Fregean sense—the continua are not simply the well-ordered series of a symbolic universe but also display the internal gap of scoring, which in Basque is defined as *huts* (void or error). For a further analysis of the fronton's subtractive strategy, see Zulaika, "Un golpe de pelota jamás eliminará el azar."

193. *"loss of meaning that Zen calls a satori"*: Barthes, *Empire of Signs,* 4.

193. *"the wisdom of all the sages . . . consists not in the satisfaction"*: Beckett, *Proust,* 7.

193. *the potlatch-like need for loss*: The classical study of the logic of the potlatch is Mauss, *The Gift.*

BOOK III. PARADISE

"The Word Is Out That Miracles Still Occur . . ."

195. *"'Have you been to Bilbao?' In architectural circles"*: Muschamp, "The Miracle in Bilbao," 54.

195. *the Fish Gallery*: It was later renamed the Arcelor Gallery.

196. *"the reincarnation of Marilyn Monroe"*: Muschamp, "The Miracle in Bilbao," 54. Emphasis added.

196. *"what twins the actress and the building"*: Ibid.

197. *"The miraculous occurrence"*: Ibid.

197. *"combination of sensuality and spirituality"*: Banner, *MM-Personal,* 45.

197. *"radioactive nation-building"*: Masco, *The Nuclear Borderlands,* 25.

197. *"became a mirror to me"*: Miller, *Timebends,* 382.

197. *". . .past Reno, Pyramid Lake"*: Ginsberg, *Collected Poems,* 507.

197–98. *"gift of life"*; *"Being with her, people want not to die"*; *"sheer cultural terrorism"*; *"is more powerful than the atomic bombs"*: MacCannell, "Marilyn Monroe Was Not a Man," 27, 116, 126, 114.

198. *Benjamin's "Angel of History"*: Benjamin, *Illuminations,* 257–58.

198. *"to raise the possibility of a purely feminine"*; *"a kind of breakdown"*; a new kind of *"intersubjective imagination"*: MacCannell, "Marilyn Monroe Was Not a Man," 117, 116, 122.

198. *protagonist of The Who's 1969 rock opera*: Decorated with images of the saint and preceded by incense-swinging acolytes, a giant sculpture of St. Marilyn flaunting the iconic *The Seven Year Itch* skirt is led down the aisle among the afflicted, who are waiting to touch her and be cured. Tommy is pushed under the icon to touch Marilyn and be cured, and he topples it over, smashing the icon to pieces. The idol had to be broken and

"Marilyn has now been elevated to the level of an immortal goddess," (De Vito and Tropea, *The Immortal Marilyn,* 5), a symbol ever to be adored from afar. Tommy is cured. Her "curative powers" spring from her dual role as *The White Whore and The Bit Player*: "The Whore is Marilyn as she appears to the world, and the Nun is Marilyn's own sad image of herself." Ibid., 103). Tom Eyen's *The White Whore and the Bit Player* is a roman à clef depiction of Marilyn's life. Warhol depicted her best as Saint Marilyn of Sorrows.

198. *"the use of his senses"*: Townshend, *Who I Am,* 147.

198. *"confounded by my blindness"*; *"restore my eyes"*; *"Beatrice drove out every speck"*: Alighieri, *Paradise* XXVI: 1, 14, 76–78.

198. *"the chapel"*: Van Hensbergen, *Guernica,* 327.

199. *"I have always been, since my student days"*: Miller quoted in Meyers, *The Genius and the Goddess,* 143.

199. *"like a kind of sinfulness:"* Miller, *Timebends,* 294.

199. *"true miracle on 34ᵗʰ Street"*; *"a vision of paradise"*; *"that might have been dreamed up by Jean Genet"*; *"transformed into a lily"*: Muschamp, "Nature and Artifice in Bloom," *New York Times,* April 5, 1996.

200. *"a religious ceremony"*; *"a transfiguration"*; *"an event is nothing other than a transubstantiation"*; *"a miracle has taken place"*: Sartre, *Saint Genet,* 319, 472, 316, 310.

200. *"Platonic idealism"*; *"reproducing what might be called"*; *"each creature is the word incarnate"*; *"the magical action of analogy"*; *"I even tried, me too"*; *"Harcamone is a rose"*: Ibid., 469, 399, 475, quoted in 324, quoted in 396.

200. *"there is a close relationship between flowers"*: Genet, *The Thief's Journal,* 9.

200. *"[a]n intimate and intense relationship"*; *"[t]he rose is the feminine flower"*; *"[i]ts perfume is an insane*

mystery"; "the rose isn't it": Lispector, *The Stream*, 40, 45.

200. "thinking of the medieval clerk"; "was cast into an artificial medieval world": Sartre, *Saint Genet*, 471, 470.

200. "Plato's poet": Singleton, *Dante's Commedia*, 70

200. "it is art": Sartre, *Saint Genet*, 474.

201. "The whole of Dante's work suggests that": Gilson, *Dante and Philosophy*, 69.

201. "You are the part of myself that a spiritual essence has shaped": Quoted in Gilson, *Choir of Muses*, 79.

201. an inspiration behind Gehry's masterpiece: Arata Isozaki, one of the three contenders for the Bilbao Guggenheim project, explicitly stated that his building for the MoCA Museum in Los Angeles (1984) was inspired by the impact that Marilyn Monroe's body had in the early 1960s. Gilbert-Rolfe, *Frank Gehry*, 69. It is a fact that while working on the Bilbao museum, Gehry studied medieval carvings of folds in cloth; skirts and other feminine forms could similarly have inspired him. Ibid., 229.

201. "the astounding paradox of what is called": Auerbach, *Mimesis*, 191.

201. "insisted that she be read—as a figure": MacCannell, "Marilyn Monroe," 116. Emphasis in original.

201. "the incarnate body of Christ in Beatrice": Altizer, *The Contemporary Jesus*, xvii.

201. "signifies not only itself but at the same time another": Auerbach, *Mimesis*, 555.

202. "into present reality"; "Here revealed truth and its poetic form are one": Auerbach, *Dante*, 154, 100.

202. dangerous jungle amid unsophisticated natives: A contrary critical opinion of Gehry's work is provided by Hal Foster. He finds the building and site to be disconnected, their spaces mystifying. Foster, "Master Builder." In either Muschamp's "miracle" or Foster's failed "Potemkin architecture," the implied premise is that Bilbao is an unlikely venue for hosting the masterpiece of the turn of the millennium.

Maialen's Bilbao Song

203. *The exhibition center had opened in April 2004*: Bilbao's Feria de Muestras (Trade Exhibition) has exhibited the products of local industries since 1941. BEC is the new headquarters of the Feria de Muestras and also the place for international competitions and cultural events.

203. "An abyss opens before you": English translation by Xabi Paia.

204. "rapid movement of images": For a discussion of the "argument of images," see Fernandez, "The Mission of Metaphor."

204. elisions and the absence of rhetorical links: Lekuona wrote that the images are juxtaposed by (a) "a relative abundance of elisions and 'pregnant' constructions"; (b) "an exceptional absence of rhetorical-grammatical means for linkage"; (c) "a somewhat careless logical-chronological order in the succession and disposition of narrative elements"; and (d) "a somewhat apparent lack of relation or logical cohesion between images and the theme of the song." Lekuona, *Literatura oral vasca*, 23.

204. where instead of the sentence we have the sounddance: Brown, *Closing Time*, 63.

204. the soul of everyelsebody rolled into its oleseleself: Joyce, *Finnegans Wake*, 329.

204. Apur dezagun katea: Aresti, *Obra guztiak I*, 472.

204. "In the buginning is the woid": Joyce, *Finnigans Wake*, 378.

205. As Lekuona reminded us, by subtraction: For a philosophical rendering of the subtraction of the generic subset, see Hallward, *Badiou*, xxxi.

206. a window to his most intimate world: See Zulaika, "Bertsolariak and Writers: An Old Tale of Fathers and Sons."

206. situations in which speech was undesirable: "Communication is undesirable, not because of fear, but because communication would somehow alter the nature of the ideas." Bateson and Bateson, *Angels Fear*, 80.

206. "symbol of Basque social equality": Steer, *The Tree*, 62.

206. the first to wear one in the Spanish parliament: The day arrived when, requested by the president of the Republic, Prieto also had to wear a top hat to the Parliament, the top hat being an invention of John Hetherington that Prieto found "loathsome." Prieto, *De mi vida*, 75–76.

207. She made berets fashionable: Arzalluz, *Cristóbal Balenciaga*, 109. I owe this information to Miren Arzalluz.

208. rare case of revival from near extinction: When I was a student in Bilbao, schooling in Basque was forbidden and official use of Euskara suppressed. In the 1970s, only 7 percent of Bilbaoans could still speak their native tongue. Currently 18 percent of the Bilbao population knows Euskara, but among 16–24 year-olds, 53 percent know it. Two-thirds of all Bilbao children are now schooled in both Spanish and Basque. According to the latest figures, 37 percent of Basques overall know Euskara. Among youths 15–17 years old, 67 percent are fluent in it; among people 18–29, 58 percent are fluent; with people 30–45, 28 percent are fluent; above 46 years of age, the percentage goes down to 26 percent (http://www.euskara.euskadi.net). What worries promoters of Euskara is that overall only 13 percent of Basques use it as their daily language.

208. most decisive aspect of "the miracle in Bilbao": For a comprehensive and insightful discussion of Euskara's revival in an era of counterterrorism, see Urla, *Reclaiming Basque*.

The Snake, the Spider, and the Rose

210. *"My body is my sculpture"*: Quoted in Bal, *Louise Bourgeois' Spider,* 61. Emphasis added.

210. *"a woman weaving a man"*: Lispector, *The Passion,* 81.

210. *she marks their ending by being ritually burnt*: Marijaia is the invention of artist Mari Puri Herrero, who has made it annually since 1978. She created the figure of an older woman who, she told me, had been longing to have fun for many years and finally was allowed to do so.

212. *Miller called her "a flower of iron"*: Miller, *Timebends,* 481.

212. *Steer found rose petals scattered*: Steer, *The Tree,* 244.

212. *"the rose embodies the chief spiritual implications"; "the flower of Beatrice, but of Beatrice exalted"*: Seward, "Dante's Mystic Rose," 515, 517.

212. *Such visions of Dante, or Blake*: As Frye writes, Blake's has "a great deal in common with the theory of anagogy, which underlies the poetry of Dante." Frye, *Frye on Milton and Blake,* 204.

212. *the object is not mere symbol or allegory*: In the fourfold theory of meaning of Dante's times, beyond the literal, the allegorical and the moral meaning of texts, there was the *anagogical*—the "spiritual" sense that went beyond the previous three. One of the great admirers of Dante was Samuel Beckett, who objected to his allegories, to then add that, "because he was an artist and not a minor prophet, [Dante] could not prevent his allegory from becoming heated and electrified into anagogy." Beckett, *Proust,* 60. Beckett also wrote about Proust that only art can decipher "the baffled ecstasy that he had known before the inscrutable superficies of a. . . . flower. . . . when the mystery, the essence, the Idea, imprisoned in matter, had solicited the bounty of a subject passing by within the shell of his

impurity, and tendered, like Dante . . . an incorruptible beauty." Ibid., 57.

212. *"shades of Disneyland"*: Richardson, "Go, Go, Guggenheim," 21.

213. *not fall into the trap of a Disneyfied architecture*: See Zukin, *Landscapes of Power,* ch. 8.

213. *so real that it is the reincarnation of Marilyn*: The buildings by Gehry and Bourgeois work subjectively on the viewer through the principle of sublimation, by which an object is raised "to the dignity of the Thing": "To raise an object to the dignity of the Thing is not to idealize it, but, rather, to 'realize' it, that is, to make it function as a stand-in for the Real." Zupančič, *The Shortest Shadow,* 77. Such "real" is the blind spot in reality, its internal split, and the task of sublimation is to sustain that gap whereby reality separates from itself. Passions and drives create new gaps in reality. And so do Bourgeois's sculptures and Gehry's buildings. In this precise sense, they are *realizations*—the "stand-in for the Real."

213. *Hegel's reversal of crucifixion to redemption*: The Phenomenology of Spirit ends with the crucifixion as "the Calvary of Absolute Spirit," every actualization of consciousness into self-consciousness being a repetition of crucifixion and resurrection. Hegel, *The Phenomenology of Spirit.*

213. *"is nothing but 'the universalization of the crucifixion'"*: Žižek, "Dialectical Clarity Versus the Misty Conceit of Paradox," 267.

213. *"in Hegel and Blake alike"*: Altizer, *The Contemporary Jesus,* xxi.

213. *"this beautiful Rose of joy"*: Alighieri, *Paradise,* XXXII: 126.

213. *Gehry at the top of his Bilbao architecture*: Gilbert-Rolfe, *Frank Gehry,* 21.

The Architecture of Labyrinths

214. *"If we willed and dared an architecture"; "us into the labyrinth of the infinite"*: Harries, "Nietzsche's Labyrinths," 35, 41.

214. *"Oh Ariadne, you are yourself the labyrinth"*: Quoted in Gere, *Knossos,* 47.

215. *"the circularity of the bullring, if occupied"*: Oteiza quoted in Arana, *Oteiza y Unamuno,* 68.

215. *other radial streets that forced the ellipse*: Carmen Abad brought this point to my attention.

216. *the planners' and architects' imaginations*: The entire grid was still organized around a *center* and along a longitudinal axis, with the streets of Recalde, Elcano, and Ercilla turning into the radii springing from the irradiating center, but still the two surrounding avenues of Urquijo and Mazarredo, adapting to the bending river, shaped the periphery of the enlargement into an *ellipse* that expanded the inner elliptical form of Plaza Moyúa.

216. *"The layout of a city"*: Quoted in Ward, *Cities of God,* 42.

216. *from the "closed world" to "the infinite universe"*: Koyré, *From the Closed World to the Infinite Universe.* Still, this kind of infinity is a property of the global space and does not break with the premise that being as such makes a Whole; after Cantor the infinite can be local and characterize a singular being and not be a property of the global universe. *See* Badiou, *Logic of Worlds,* 11.

216. *Oteiza and Chillida did to circular stele*: The stele are the traditional upright stone pillars, typically three to five feet tall, in the form of a round disc resting on a trapezoidal "shoulder." Chillida's first abstract sculpture was *Ilarik*—a funerary stela deconstructed by turning its biplanar structure into a three-dimensional form. Close to *Ilarik* in Donostia-San Sebastián is his three-piece *Wind Comb*, powerful iron tentacles

in elliptical shapes, the supreme expression of my generation's struggle with "the wind of freedom." Chillida's later *Homage to the Horizon* in Gijón is also an ellipse —"the horizon is not circular, it is elliptical," he explained. Oteiza's text that accompanied his winning submission to the São Paulo Biennale, the "experimental proposal" that summed up his artistic project, ended with a note on "funerary stele."

216. *from its "third" dimension*: Repetition for Kierkegaard is the "second" time, in which "'second' means not a second time but the infinite which belongs to a single time, the eternity that belongs to an instant, the unconscious that belongs to consciousness, the 'nth' power." Deleuze, *Difference and Repetition*, 8.

216. *"the emergence of the ellipse"*: Lacan, *Ecrits*, 797 n. 295.

217. *symptoms that inscribe the excess*: The mathematical formulation of such "excess" consists in that the multiple elements of a set that are said to "belong" to it are themselves composed of subsets that are also "included" parts in the set—this set of the parts is *in excess of* the set itself. The logical consequences of this excess are far reaching.

217. *and the object is one of "torsion"*: Badiou, *Theory of the Subject*, 124.

217. *"the true . . . is never reached except by twisted pathways."* Lacan quoted in ibid., 121. Besides its topological use, the concept of "torsion" is also employed in algebra—the contorted element that interrupts repetition, a qualitative excess, a finitude that blocks repeatable infinities—"Torsion functions as the border-limit of algebra. Torsion is perverse: subject." Ibid., 154.

217. *the bilbo-shackle and the bilbo-sword*: This is reminiscent of Hegel's story of the *shell* (mystical, idealist)—equivalent to the sword—and the *kernel* (materialist)—equivalent to the shackles. Hegelian thought is engaged in the dialectic of the One and the multiple, the finite and the infinite. The "leap"

from the quantitative to the qualitative requires that the subject overcome the shackles. The sword makes the multiple proceed from the One, for there is no dialectic without division. Philosophers write about "the topological status of truth" as if truth were a surface having to do with the passing from the global study of a topos to its local limit.

217. *the origin of the modern museum with the guillotine*: Hollier, *Against Architecture*, xiii.

217. *They function as the escape fantasy for people's desires*: See Hollier, *Against Architecture*, x.

220. *"the architect who has most challenged"*: Betsky, *Building Sex*, 184.

220. *"architecture without the grid"*: Gilbert-Rolfe, *Frank Gehry*, 84.

220. *"reinvents location through dislocation"; "formalism of formlessness"*: Ibid., 18, 111.

220. *"a shipwreck"*: Gehry quoted in Spalding, "Bilbao,"

Painting Paradise

220. *the Renaissance Italian painter Arcimboldo*: In my assessment of Ameztoy's work, I benefitted from conversations with Adelina Moya.

222. *his paintings had become sacred icons with healing powers*: Ameztoy, *Sagrado-Profano*, 15.

222. *"In the history of art late works are the catastrophes"*: Adorno, *Essays on Music*, 567.

The Last Supper

223. *you will be greeted by Puppy's fifty thousand pansies*: The sculpture is supported by a metallic structure that has four floors and an internal irrigation system. The structure is covered with soil and protected by a perforated geo-textile mantle; the flowers that make up the skin of the spectacular dog are

inserted into holes in this mantle and replaced every six months with new ones. *Puppy*'s change of skin requires the installation of a scaffolding; the discarded flowers are offered as gifts to museum visitors.

224. *"Saint Marilyn of the Sorrows"*: Danto, *Andy Warhol*, 40.

224. *Puppy is "a very spiritual piece"*: Solomon, "Puppy Love," 15.

224. *"Abstraction and luxury are the guard dogs"; Sacred Heart on Bilbao's Gran Vía*: Koons, *The Jeff Koons Handbook*, 37, 144.

224. *irony is modernity's baptism by fire*: Kierkegaard, *The Concept of Irony*, 338.

225. *a series of over one hundred Last Supper works inspired by Leonardo*: A reproduction of *The Last Supper* was hanging in Warhol's home while he was eating Campbell's soup daily. His mother had a prayer card with the image of Leonardo's painting that she kept in her Bible and which Warhol kept after her death. His mother lived with him in New York for twenty years, and Andy could not leave their apartment until they both kneeled down and prayed; he lived under her intense piety for almost forty of his fifty-eight years. Daggett Dillenberger, *The Religious Art of Andy Warhol*, 21.

225. *Warhol was seeking a transubstantiated culture*: Romaine, "Transubstantiating the Culture: Andy Warhol's Secret."

226. *"a zone of transfiguration"; "Warhol underwent an artistic change"*: Danto, *Andy Warhol*, 2, 145.

226. *the Last Supper, was what most mattered spiritually to Arrupe's Jesuit group*. Faced with the question of how the post-Christian, post-Holocaust, and secular Death-of-God theologies have given way to the postmodern return to religion, Žižek replies that the death of God "paradoxically opens the space for the new authentic postmetaphysical religion, a Christianity focused on Agape." Žižek, "Dialectical Clarity Versus the Misty Conceit of Paradox," 255.

226. *he staged a play entitled The Last Supper*: Amestoy directed a film, *Kisses*, for which Etxebarrieta wrote the script; Etxebarrieta staged Ibsen's *An Enemy of the People* with Ignacio's help; Amestoy staged Brecht's *Galileo Galilei* with Etxebarrieta's assistance. Eventually Ignacio dropped his business studies to study journalism and devote himself to writing plays. He was stunned when he heard of his friend's death by the roadside in a confrontation with the police.

227. *Aita (Dad), a name the father then repeats in disbelief*: Etxebarrieta, whose father died when he was thirteen, did in fact write a poem "To my *Aita*" that laments the death that "took his eyes and his voice" and concludes "Ay, father! I miss you." The Etxebarrieta family house in the coastal town of Ispaster had been turned into the Spanish police station. Lorenzo Espinosa, *Txabi Etxebarrieta: Poesía*, 109.

The Passion for the Real

228. *"Solidarity of Basque Workers"*: The first general assembly was held in 1929 in the industrial town of Eibar. Bengoa's father, who lived in the next town, was involved in ELA and the turbulent politics of those Republican years. By the time the civil war broke out in 1936, ELA had fifty thousand members.

228. *instructing Catholic youths in Marxist doctrines*: He translated, among other texts for "the militancy" (not for publication), Gors's *Socialism and Revolution* (1967).

229. *he was in charge of the links between his organization*: Lorenzo Espinosa, *Txabi Etxebarrieta: Armado*, 126.

230. *not an abstract son of God but "the Liberator"*: Sobrino, *Jesus, the Liberator*, 7.

231. *only 4 percent of them are practicing Catholics*: *El Correo*, March 26, 2013.

231. *"two-thirds of the youths between fifteen and twenty-four"*: Pérez-Agote and Santiago, *La nueva pluralidad religiosa*, 21. These authors mention three waves of secularization in Spain. The first occurred at the end of the nineteenth century and early twentieth, with the socialist masses in Bilbao its main expression. Religion was seen as the enemy against which modernity must fight. A second wave occurred after the 1960s with the new economic development and access to the consumer society and its "more secularized" disinterest in religion; people generally identified themselves as Christian but no longer practiced religion. And there is now a third wave characterized by agnosticism and atheism.

232. *"identifying the biblical God as Satan"; "is in part a radical and prophetic reaction"*: Altizer, *The New Apocalypse*, 6, 105.

232. *"most deeply Christian when [their] language is most"*: Ibid., 63.

232. *"Christianity is, at its deepest core, already atheist"*: Žižek, *Less Than Nothing*, 112.

232. *"not only is Christianity . . . the only truly consistent atheism"*: Ibid., 116.

232. *"Listen to my prayer You, God who does not exist"*: Unamuno quoted in Arana Cobos, *Oteiza y Unamuno*, 38.

232. *the exclusion of non-Europeans from the Last Supper*: In 1999 alone, over eight hundred thousand Moroccans were denied entry into Spain.

234. *"He had to pay dearly for this"*: Arrupe was shunned in public by the conservative Pope John Paul II, who preferred the company of the corrupt Father Maciel Degollado, who showered the Vatican with cash.

234. *"Sacraments, as they are lived today"*: Segundo, *The Sacraments Today*, 9, 13.

235. *missionaries produced by the Basque region*: From the middle of the nineteenth century until the 1960s, in a society of about two million people more than ten thousand Basque men and women went as missionaries to South America alone. See Álvarez Gila, *Misiones y misioneros vascos en Hispanoamérica, 1820–1960*. Orders such as the Franciscans and Passionists recruited mostly in rural towns; the Jesuits recruited in urban areas. Bilbao is Jesuit territory.

235. *his masters Rahner and Xabier Zubiri*: Ellacuría studied with Rahner, the most influential theologian at Vatican Council II, and with Xabier Zubiri, the great Spanish metaphysician whose main collaborator he became and whose bridging of Pauline theology and modern philosophy on ideas such as "God," "nature," and "grace" is articulated in his ground-breaking *Naturaleza, Historia, Dios*. Ellacuría was ordained a priest in Bilbao in 1961; he spent four decades of his life in El Salvador. The encounter with Monsignor Óscar Romero, assassinated in 1980 by a right-wing paramilitary group, had great influence on him. See Sobrino, "Monseñor Romero y la fe de Ignacio Ellacuría," 19. "Liberation" was not only a spiritual category, but it had to do with the injustices of the capitalist system and political repression. From the evangelical perspective that the poor are the embodiment of Jesus, Ellacuría developed critical assessments regarding the nation, private property, bourgeois marriage, and in general the capitalist culture of consumption. Violence had to be redeemed, but only by oneself assuming it as martyrdom. See Hernández Pico, S.J., "Ellacuría, ignaciano."

236. *the realization of God's kingdom in history*: Ellacuría operates similarly with Rahner's "supernatural existential" (a substantive that combines the reference of human existence, rather than essence, while it stresses its a priori character). According to this category, grace is not an additional layer of human nature but a radicalization of its potentiality. Beyond the level of individual subjectivity, the openness to the transcendental applies to the totality of historical reality.

236. *"Even if I consider myself an atheist":* Iriarte, *Borrokaren gorrian*, 396.

236. *riddled with bullets and beheaded:* Castellón and Dolijanin, *Pakito Arriaran*, 94–98.

237. *"I am a happy man":* Quoted in ibid., 153.

237. *"an extraordinary woman":* Mazariego Zetino, *La otra cara de la Guerra*, 88.

237. *organizing mountain hospitals:* When the opposition won in El Salvador and the former guerrillas took part in the new government, things did not become easier for Laura. She was uncomfortable with the winners' politics. She left her comrades in El Salvador and returned to the farm where she was born to care for her ill mother (which she did for the next eleven years). Back home, she became involved once again in the Basque political struggle and was accused of having links to ETA; after years of legal harassment from the Spanish legal system, the charges against her were dismissed. When I met her, her mother had just died and she admitted to being depressed. Soon she returned to El Salvador in a mission to revamp the nation's psychiatric system with monies granted by the Basque government.

The Monstrosity of Love

237. *"love is a trap, a delusion":* Esteban, *Crítica del pensamiento amoroso*, 53.

237–38. *"Love is the only moment of madness"; "blind" for love; "how stupid of me!"; "I have asked myself frequently"; "a point of mystery in desire":* Ibid., 256, 373, 278, 360, 241.

238. *"I have always been scared of love"; "love is very important"; "Love is a delusion"; "It is fundamental to point out":* Ibid., 379, 412, 410, 229.

238. *the couple becomes an atadura; "desamor"; "very liberating when you get out of the fix"; uncertainty as to whether one is really in love; a relationship of dependence; discussions as whether*

one *"believes" in love; "we women are oppressed"; even seductiveness:* Ibid., 281, 357, 242, 219, 420, 405, 366, 408, 448.

238. *a unique field of knowledge; "sexual fluidity"; the state of enjoying the love one already has; men's "emotional illiteracy"; "the changes have been very abrupt":* Ibid., 216, 208, 215, 233, 447, 296

238. *awareness of the force of fantasy and its traps:* Ibid., 442.

239. *"the deepest epiphany":* Altizer, *The New Apocalypse*, 19.

240. *the commandment to enjoy:* "Nothing forces anyone to enjoy (*jouir*) except the superego. The superego is the imperative of jouissance—Enjoy!" Lacan, *On Feminine Sexuality*, 3.

241. *"love is giving what you do not have":* Lacan, *Ecrits*, 516.

241. *Hegelian "negation of negation":* See Žižek, *On Belief*, 80. Žižek illustrates this "negation of negation" with Hitchcock's *Vertigo* when Scottie and Madeleine experienced that there was no real difference between the first "authentic" passionate love and the second "artificial" manipulative one—both were equally "artificial" and "authentic."

241. *"lost the loss itself":* Žižek, *Less Than Nothing*, 787.

242. *"Love fits through desire like a camel":* Badiou, "What is Love?" 190. While desire is captive to its object as cause, love is not. Both the body of desire and the body of love are the same one, yet love deals with a different body in its attempt to expand it beyond the limitations of a particular narcissistic object of desire. The nonamorous encounter between the sexes is masturbatory—takes place in the interior of only one sexuated position, hence the maxim that, from the viewpoint of the original disjunction of love, "there is no sexual relationship." Love is the supplement of such lack, for "the lovers as such enter into the composition of *one* loving subject, who *exceeds* them both." Badiou, *Ethics*, 43. For Badiou, love is

"a giving of permission to be multiple," and "beyond seduction or the serious mediation of marriage, a medium to have access to the superhuman." Badiou, *In Praise of Love*, 278, 4.

242. *"I have . . . kept nothing for myself":* Quoted in Michalski, *The Flame of Eternity*, 136.

Forgiveness

243. *He also co-wrote the Falange's anthem:* Areilza, *Así les he visto*, 48.

243. *a best-selling novel:* Cercas, *Los soldados de Salamina*.

243. *"miraculously saved from the firing squad":* Areilza, *Así les he visto*, 48.

243. *"infrahuman," "barbarian":* Quoted in Anasagasti and Erkoreka, *Dos familias vascas*, 157.

243. *"heroism is properly the act of the infinite"; "victory over death . . . is both anonymous and nonreligious":* Badiou, "The Figure of the Soldier," 42, 49.

244. *"To understand, we say, is to forgive":* Jankélévitch, *Forgiveness*, 84.

244. *"Enemies, there is no enemy!":* See Derrida, *The Politics of Friendship*.

244. *"reasons for forgiveness abolish the raison"; "Forgiveness inaugurates a vita nuova":* Jankélévitch, *Forgiveness*, 107, 98–99.

245. *"the sin of doubting the forgiveness of sins":* Garff, *Soren Kierkegaard*, 544.

245. *"resuscitates dead people":* Jankélévitch, *Forgiveness*, 149.

245. *"Bilbao is a city redeemed by blood":* Areiza, quoted in Anasagasti and Erkoreka, *Dos familias vascas*, 146–48.

246. *"honors the memory of a man":* Leizaola, *Conversaciones*, 138.

246. *some jailed members of the organization asked:* See Pascual Rodríguez, *Los ojos del otro*.

246. *two opposing poles of the conditional and unconditional:* This brings us

to Derrida's point that there is true forgiveness only where there is the unforgiveable and to its brutal *aporia*—that "forgiveness forgives only the unforgiveable." Derrida, *On Cosmopolitanism and Forgiveness*, 32.

246. *for Blake forgiveness was Christianity's only novelty*: At this point, Blake's work fits uneasily with the theological and political outlook of Dante's "system"— Christianity was only forgiveness for Blake, the opposite of Dante's belief in eternal Hell. Blake's "Proverbs of Hell" subvert the dichotomy of moral values and make of Hell and Heaven complementary states. In contrast to Dante's Mariology, Blake scorned virginity as a perverse fetish.

246. *"a forgiveness without power"*: Derrida, *On Cosmopolitanism*, 57, 59.

Jai Alai in New York

247. *Prieto gave impetus to the idea*: See Molina and Rojo, *Historia del túnel de Artxanda (1900–2002)*, 24.

247. *What most mattered for Prieto was his city; "there is already no other power"; "an ardent and patriotic regenerationist faith in Spain"*: Quoted in Sáiz Valdivielso, *Crónica*, 65, 129, 143.

248. *Bastida gave the salary he received from Madrid*: Foraster Bastida, Bastida Díaz-Tejeiro, and Pérez de la Peña Oleaga, *Ricardo de Bastida*, 44.

248. *"What a tragedy it is for me not to have religious faith"*: Quoted in Sáiz Valdivielso, "Prólogo," in Prieto, *Pasado y futuro de Bilbao*, ix.

248. *"To my most beloved friend"*: Prieto wrote that even though "he was a fervent Catholic, me a recalcitrant unbeliever," he had never minded his friend's attempts at converting him until the last hour, for, "such [was] his tenderness! And so immense his charity!" Foraster Bastida et al., *Ricardo de Bastida*, 51.

248. *"Bilbao, city of iron, that forged chains"*: Prieto quoted in Sáiz Valdivielso, *Crónica*, 53.

249. *"a wound I will never be able to close"*: Quoted in Leizaola, *Conversaciones*, 102.

249. *"innate goodness" and the "magical force"; Aguirre's "exceptional qualities"; "because José Antonio was a few weeks older"*: Quotes from Leizaola, *Conversaciones*, 110–11, 112, 102.

249. *the pathos of their singular political complicity*: Historian José Luis de la Granja summed it up best: "Their lives, so different yet so parallel in some respects, constitute an example we must bear in mind for the current times. They were political rivals capable of understanding each other and of reaching transcendental agreements in autonomic and governmental issues during the tragic circumstances of the Civil War and exile. . . . We are confronted with two unequaled figures who no longer belong exclusively to their parties, for they are patrimony of Basque society and form part of Bilbao's historic memory." Granja, "Aguirre y Prieto."

249. *"a sort of prietista avant la lettre"; "the project of a co-federal [Spanish] State"*: Mees, *El profeta*, 168, 151.

249–250. *"today we know that the Spanish problem cannot"*: Aguirre quoted in Mees, *El profeta*, 90.

250. *"the waning state"*: Barbería, "El Estado menguante," *El País*, May 3, 2005.

251. *untouchable democratic constitution*: Unconcerned with the strong rejection that its claims to exclusive constitutional sovereignty elicit among Basques and Catalans, it is still a state that in the twenty-first century can censor on grounds of unconstitutionality the reform of a statute approved by a large majority of the Catalan Parliament, or force arbitrarily the closure of the only Basque-language newspaper, *Egunkaria*, and even brutally torture its director and board members under false pretenses of links to terrorism, or can currently keep

in prison the very politicians who forced ETA's final ceasefire.

251. *"Does the State exist after the Nation-State?"; "constituted by a historic conglomerate of flows and functions"*: Rubert de Ventós, *De la identidad*, 72, 145.

251. *"are parts, rather than antagonists, of each other's history:"* Said, *Freud and the Non-European*, 53.

252. *Basque territories have their own fiscal autonomy*: See Zubiri, *The Economic Agreement*, and Aguirreazkuenaga and Alonso Olea, eds., *Basque Fiscal Systems*.

253. *an option that was quite minoritarian until recently*: According to the Centro de Estudios de Opinión, in June of 2005 Catalans in favor of an independent state were 13,6%, in favor of a federal state were 31,3%, and 40,8% favored an autonomous community. In 2013, the corresponding numbers were 54,7%, 22,1% and 15,7%.

253. *"Catalonia has passed from being a pro-autonomy region"*: Antoni Segura's intervention at the "Fiscal Systems & The Crisis" conference held at the University of Nevada, Reno, on March 26–28, 2014.

A Red Dawn Is Breaking

253. *"We remain hardly half a dozen"*: Quoted in Sáiz Valdivielso, *Crónica*, 78.

254. *"the army is the only fundamental thing of value in Spain"*: Unamuno quoted in Juaristi, *Miguel de Unamuno*, 431.

254. *"Despairing is he who knows very well that he has nothing"*: Quoted in Juaristi, *Miguel de Unamuno*, 443–45.

254. *his writings allowed my agnostic generation to retain humanistic*: Oteiza is a case in point. See Arana Cobos, *Oteiza y Unamuno*. Both Unamuno's and Oteiza's existential stance could be described as "Christian atheism," religion being for both "a thing of the heart." Oteiza describes his as the vision of a man outside of Christianity but with a sincerely Christian solution; for both,

religion and art are alternative responses to the ultimate "tragic sense of life." Both develop a sacramental view of art—in Oteiza in a deliberate interpretation of statues as "eucharist"; in Unamuno with poems that are silent embodiments of the Word. Saint Paul being for both writers a key model, Unamuno and Oteiza made sustained apologies of *the fool* in their work, in particular by invoking the figure of Don Quixote.

254. *"faith is passive, feminine, the daughter of grace"*: Unamuno, *The Agony of Christianity*, 74.

255. *a female beauty that could only be idealized*: I owe this point to Juan Arana.

255. *"the modern atheist thinks he knows that God is dead"*: Žižek, "For a Theologico-Political Suspension of the Ethical," 28.

255. *"but does the chicken know?"*: Žižek, *The Parallax View*, 351.

255. *"situating one's pain at the precise point where others"*: Kierkegaard quoted in Garff, *Soren Kierkegaard*, 192.

255. *"the ironic nothingness"*: Kierkegaard quoted in ibid., 193.

256. *"being abandoned by God is the most God can give us"*: Žižek, *Less Than Nothing*, 111.

256. *the resurrection of the humiliated body has already taken place*: The Christ of "why have you forsaken me?" is the Christ who has become fully human in his own impotence, "the point at which the radical gap that separates God from man is transposed into God Himself." Žižek, *On Belief*, 145–46. The truth was that one had to find God in abjection, not in spiritual elevation, for it is "(w)hen I, a human being, experience myself as cut off from God, at that very moment of the utmost abjection, I am absolutely close to God, since I find myself in the position of the abandoned Christ." Ibid.

256. *Since I am a poet*: Aresti, *Obras Completas*, 1, 474–75. Author's translation.

256. *universalism that, while extolling European civilization, was blind*: Unamuno's "universalism" recalls Freud's critique of Egypt's monotheism in which "all the people" becomes a particularized universal that includes everyone conquered or conquerable by the Egyptian empire, but with the exception of Egypt itself—a universal that is based on the mutual *exclusion* of conquerors and conquered. Freud opposed to it a different type of universal based on Jewish monotheism, which is not of the particularized type because there are no special criteria for belonging to it (their God is the God of all)—such an "all" originates from nothing, a case in which the election of the Jews by God must constitute *an immanent exception*, that is, not an exception to the all but within the all. See Freud, *Moses and Monotheism*. The socialist Rubert de Ventós argued against defenders of the Spanish state who proclaim its "alleged universalism with arguments and for reasons that are, in the end, nationalists"; to which he adds, "I, on the other hand, pretend to defend *nationalism for universalist reasons.*" Rubert de Ventós, *Nacionalismos*, 51.

256. *"City raised against my Basque Country"; "A moon beam comes through:"* Aresti, *Obra Guztiak*, II, 142. Author's translation.

257. *"We heard a war cry"*: Sung by the music group Oskorri. Author's translation.

257. *his next book of poems*: Aresti, *Harrizko herri hau* (1970).

257. *"In this city of Dante:"* Aresti, *Obra Guztiak*, II, 372. Author's translation.

258. *"It is my city, my motherland in one way"*: Etxeberria, *Bost idazle*, 27.

258. *submerged as a spectral presence*: Such stories are *"more real than reality*: they are 'true', although, of course, they 'didn't really take place'—their spectral presence sustains the explicit symbolic tradition." Žižek, *The Fragile Absolute*, 65.

259. *an anthropological study of kinship systems*: Fox, *Kinship and Marriage*.

259. *"Buried? No, it was resurrection day in Derio"*: Steer, *The Tree*, 304.

The Subject: Zero and the Infinite

259. *"the Subject—this Minotaur bereft of any Theseus"*: Badiou, *Theory of the Subject*, 36.

260. *"nourished by the no"*: Barandiarán, *Diccionario*, 166.

260. *characterized by the "not-all"*: See footnote for page 261 below on *the notion of infinity*.

260. *"Aresti stripped his poetry of any traces of literature"; "resignation from poetry"*: Aldekoa, *Munduaren*, 75; Aresti, *Poemak*, I, 548.

260. *In Otero, one sees a "destruction" of his poetic language*: Following the transition from his existential poetry to his social poetry, there is a new "anti-literary prejudice that presides the new style of Blas de Otero," in Yanke's commentary. "What lies behind the anti-literary prejudice is, clearly, the conviction that ethics should prevail over aesthetics, that one cannot be a 'poet,' although yet a 'literate,' without committing yourself to a social class." Yanke, *Blas de Otero*, 75.

260. *and the possibility of a new subject*: In modern exemplary autobiographies (Montaigne, Descartes, Rousseau, Kierkegaard, Nietzsche, Unamuno, Sartre), the new models of subjectivity typically re-deploy the rhetoric of secular conversion in which the place of God is taken by the intellectual or authorial vocation of the writer.

260. *the affirmative part of negation*: Schoenberg's music not only "destroyed" the tonal system, observes Badiou, it also "subtracted" a dodecaphonic system in a new musical framework indifferent to tonality. Applied to violence, his point is that, even if we cannot exclude all its forms, still, "violence is not, as has been

said during the last century, the creative and revolutionary part of negation. The way of freedom is a subtractive one." Badiou, "Destruction, Negation, Subtraction."

260. *the lack of sacrifice*: The subject comes to realize that the role of such sacrifice is to disavow the impotence of the big Other, that sacrifice is not offered in order to profit from it, "but to fill in the lack *in the Other*, to sustain the appearance of the Other's omnipotence or, at least, consistency." Žižek, "Christianity Against the Sacred," 56.

260. *"whoever is the subject of truth"*: Badiou, *Saint Paul,* 54. The metaphor Badiou uses for this power is *grace*—a term Copjec rescues from Kant but subverts its ultimate meaning of "infinity of failure" by intersecting it with Freud's notion of the superego.

260. *"desire is nothing but that which introduces into the subject"*: Zupančič, *The Shortest Shadow,* 251.

260–61. *"the body as distinct from the organism inasmuch as"*: Miller, "The Prisons of *Jouissance*," 40.

261. *Martyrdom was a thousand times preferable to the loss*: For the substitution components of religion in Basque politics, see Sáez de la Fuente Aldama, *El Movimiento de Liberación Nacional Vasco.*

261. *Unamuno wrote of the "eternal moon" and . . . a "mirror of eternity"*: Unamuno, *Obras Completas*, IV, 311; *Antología poética,* 148.

261. *"the romantic concept par excellence"*: Badiou, *Conditions,* 108.

261. *the banal reality of axiomatized infinity*: It is the post-Greek, post-Christian notion of the infinity of being itself, a consequence of modern mathematics, that presents the greater challenge to contemporary thought. The medieval Christian God was, in the end, finite because its basic ontology of being was also finite. Even the new "infinite universe" of the Copernican revolution, to the extent that it is conceived as the being of the One-universe, is still "nothing other than a depunctualized God" and far from "the essential infinity of being." Badiou, *Being and Event,* 144. From Descartes to Kant, a new anxiety affected the finitist position: could it be that, if infinity belongs to nature, this predicate could also be applied to the presentation of the pure *multiple*? Not until Cantor's formulation did thought axiomatize the true infinitization of being—one that presupposes "the vertigo of an infinity of infinities." Ibid., 145–46. Crucial to this concept of infinity is the ontological decision itself, for "without such a decision it will remain forever possible for being to be essentially finite." Ibid., 148.

261. *"we are infinite because we think infinitely"*: Hallward, *Badiou,* 67.

261. *"transits through form"*: Badiou, *Being and Event,* 155. In Hegelian thought, the finite is what remains the same within itself by repeating itself, much as for Freud and Lacan desire is affected by the compulsion to repeat itself—this is the "bad infinite" of a repetitive series ad infinitum. But there is a difference, observes Hegel, between the result and *the act itself* of repetition; it is this act of self-surpassing that is the subjective ground of the infinite immanent to the movement of the finite.

261. *"another articulation of the finite and the infinite"*: Badiou, *Being and Event,* 155. Regarding the "sacramental crisis" in religion, art, and culture, this is how Kierkegaard wrote about marriage: "[its] aesthetic quality consists in its infinity, the apriority of love . . . it consists in the unity of contradictions exemplified by love: it is sensuous and yet spiritual; it is freedom and yet necessity; it is in the moment . . . in the present tense, and yet it has in it an eternity." Kierkegaard, "The Aesthetic Validity of Marriage," 61. Similarly Badiou: "The problem then resides in inscribing this eternity within time. Because, basically, that is what love is: a declaration of eternity to be fulfilled or unfurled as best as it can be within time: eternity descending into time." Badiou, with Nicolas Truong, *In Praise of Love,* 47. It is precisely the articulation of these ideas of infinity that has been transformed in modern thought.

261. *"not-all," a negative that links it with the infinite.* The notion of infinity has affected the Lacanian theory of the "feminine" subjective position as *"not-all"*: "The not-whole becomes the equivalent of that which, in Aristotelian logic, is enunciated on the basis of the particular. There is an exception. But we could, on the contrary, be dealing with the infinite. Then it is no longer from the perspective of extension that we must take up the not-whole (*pas-tout*). When I say that woman is not-whole and that that is why I cannot say Woman, it is precisely because I raise the question of a jouissance that. . . . is in the realm of the infinite." Lacan, *On Feminine Sexuality*, 103. Noteworthy about Lacan's thinking, including his tying the theme of "castration" to the theme of finitude, is that the logical issues underlying his formula of sexuation—"all," "exception," "not-whole"—are closely related to the modern mathematical notions of the finite and the infinite.

261. *"today, the main argument for spiritualism"*: Žižek, "Psychoanalysis This Side of the Hermeneutic Delirium," 145.

Ashes and Roses

262. *she ended up sacrificing the Cause/ Exception itself*: "In contrast to this ('masculine') universality of the struggle for power that relies on the ethical figure of Woman as its inherent exception, the ('feminine') ethical act proper involves precisely the suspension of this exception: it takes place in the intersection of ethics and politics, in the uncanny domain in which ethics is 'politicized' in its innermost nature, an affair of radically contingent decisions, a gesture that can no longer be accounted for in terms of fidelity to some pre-existing Cause, since it redefines the

very terms of this Cause." Žižek, *The Fragile Absolute*, 155.

262. *"Abraham was not only Kierkegaard's father"*: Garff, *Soren Kierkegaard*, 256.

264. *"You are my motherland"*: Saizarbitoria, *Gorde*, 464. The relevance of Sabine's character was pointed out to me by Mari Jose Olaziregi; see her "Worlds of Fiction," 175.

264. *the glorification of the sacrificial hero was a masculine affair*: Aretxaga summed up the conundrum posed by Yoyes to ETA: "Hero, traitor, martyr— Yoyes was everything that, from the cultural premises embedded in nationalist practice, a woman could not be. Moreover, Yoyes was a mother. In the nationalist context, the models of hero, traitor or martyr and the model of the mother are mutually exclusive. It is precisely, I believe, the synthesis of these models in the person of Yoyes which made her 'treason' much more unbearable than that of other ex-militants." Aretxaga, "The Death of Yoyes," 158.

264. *"What should I do for these men"; I don't want to become the woman"*: Garmendia et al., *Yoyes desde su ventana*, 57.

264. *"a spurned husband"*: Ibid., 166.

264. *"in the modern ethical constellation"*: Žižek, *The Fragile Absolute*, 154.

264. *"being a martyr without the martyrdom associated"*: Garff, *Soren Kierkegaard*, 636.

264. *"Perseverance does not consist in the repetition"*: Copjec, "The Tomb of Perseverance," 258.

265. *"a conflict internal to and constitutive"*: Butler, *Antigone's Claim*, 47.

265. *he wrote in Basque some ten literary books*: See Gojenola, *Mariorenak*.

265. *"the crisis of all of us who experienced the deception"*: Quoted in Molina Aparicio, *Mario Onaindia*, 175.

266. *the alternative resides entirely in the realm*: Lacan, *The Four Fundamental Concepts*, 209–15.

266. *love and death took on a different dynamic*: Yoyes was confronting a "second death" that went beyond that of an initial revolutionary formula and could only be justified in ethical terms. The "death drive" that guided Yoyes's new subjectivity no longer views death in the same manner of biological fatality leading to nihilism and belonging ultimately to the romantic heritage that turns the body's limits into a sort of transcendence. Paradoxically, it is by *not* achieving its goal that the death drive obtains its satisfaction—that is, the elimination of death. Yoyes's new perspective in regard to her body was closer to "psychoanalysis, where the body is conceived not 'biopolitically' as the seat of *death* but, rather, as the seat of *sex*." Copjec, *Imagine*, 29.

266. *they had turned into executioners themselves*: See Zulaika, "Tropics of Terror."

266. *"actualize somehow the promise of resurrection"*: Zambrano, *La tumba de Antígona*, 20–21.

266. *"Yes, you had to kill and die"*: Ibid., 63.

266. *"because you cannot stay here"*: Ibid., 68–71.

267. *"Strong emotions leave me speechless"*: Aizpurua, *Jokin Gorostidi*, 55.

267. *"to never give in and forever fight"*: Ibid., 276.

267. *"Dos gardenias para ti"*: Ibid., 39.

268. *"both were in love"*: Ibid., 37.

268. *Gorostidi conversed with him in dreams*: Ibid., 84.

269. *various ritual settings require the power of ashes*: See Zulaika, *Basque Violence*, 331–32, and Aretxaga, *Los funerales del nacionalismo radical vasco*.

270. *"unawares, I did something I couldn't avoid"*: Aizpurua, *Jokin Gorostidi*, 376.

270. *"story of the Moon . . . is the story of death and resurrection"*: Cashford, *The Moon*, 25.

271. *the collapse of the big Others*: One aspect of such collapse is the "unilaterality," which, according to the leader Arnaldo Otegi, has become ideologically the "key factor" of an "authentic political and mental revolution," which has taken place within the political arm of ETA known as the *abertzale* left and which was rewarded by the Basque electorate. Having come to terms with the failure of a frontal and military antagonism against the State, unilaterality implies relinquishing the dependence from both the State and ETA for the sake of giving form to a new political community. Munarriz, *El tiempo de las luces*, 108, 146.

The Body

271. *"the new corporeity of the Body of Christ"*: Robinson, *The Body*, 10.

272. *belief in resurrection as an escape into the spiritual*: See for example Benjamin's view of the Baroque allegorists in Buck-Morss, *The Dialectics of Seeing*, 175.

274. *"the death of God is the deepest event in modern apocalypticism"*: Altizer, *The Contemporary Jesus*, 14.

274. *authored more than a hundred novels and plays*: For an analysis of Gereño's work, see Cillero Goiriastuena, "The Moving Target."

275. *allowed him to relive his happy life with his wife*: See Barthes, *A Lover's Discourse*, 216–17.

276. *terminally ill AIDS patients*: During its first six years in the middle 1990s, it took in 103 patients, of whom 40 died. In one of the two houses resided ten patients; the four nuns who took care of them lived in the other.

277. *estimated ten thousand heroin junkies in the Basque Country*: It is estimated that about a hundred thousand people died as the result of the heroin epidemic

in Spain, and about ninety thousand survive with substitutes such as methadone. See Jesús Rodríguez, "La epidemia invisible," *El País Semanal*, June 25, 2006.

277. *"I know that you know me, I know you"*: O'Brien, *Leaving Las Vegas*, 99.

277. *"Isn't it grand, isn't it good that language"*: Quoted in Nehamas, *The Art of Living*, 19.

278. *a lecture he gave in Berlin on the presence of Gernika*: It is published in Lertxundi, *Eskarmentuaren paperak*, 101–3.

278. *"Resurrexit / sicut dixit"*: Espinosa, *Txabi Etxebarrieta: Poesía*, 63.

278. *final statement of his "Experimental Proposal"*: The text examines the development of his latest artistic process. Critics such as Santiago Amón consider this text to be the only manifesto of any real depth in Spain between 1939 and the 1960s.

279. *"are thoughts, interwoven dimensions of the global subject"*: Badiou, *Saint Paul*, 68.

279. *resurrection for Paul has to be of the body of the entire divided subject*: These ideas are initially inspired by Rudolf Bultmann's theory of demythologization. Anthropological thinking is relevant to them as they revisit Jewish views of the person in the Bible as being holistic and quite different from the Greek dualist view of "soul" and "body." The corporality of such a resurrected Jesus radically transcends any spacio-temporal condition, "therefore, it has not—*nor cannot have*—any of the physical qualities that constituted his mortal body." Torres Queiruga, *Repensar la resurrección*, 22, 77, 38. "Resurrection no longer belongs to this world we can observe. That is why it could be said that properly it is not a 'historic event,' like so many others that happen in the world and that we can observe and verify, but it is a 'real event' that has happened in reality." Pagola, *Jesús*, 418–19. See also Bernabé, "Yo soy la resurrección," 29.

279. *why be concerned with this fable?*: The fundamental answer from current thinkers has to do with the constitution of the subject itself—an identity-less subject "suspended to an event whose only 'proof' lies precisely in its having been declared by a subject." Badiou, *Saint Paul*, 5. Paul's new Christian subject will not depend on any communitarian grasp or statist generality or legal category. It will be founded on an *event* that commands a declaration. Truth, the singularity of such an event, is essentially subjective, commands a fidelity, and is offered to everyone independent of the state of a situation, for "the messianic vocation is the revocation of any vocation." Agamben, *The Time That Remains*, 23.

279. *"That the event (or pure act) invoked by antiphilosophers"*: Badiou, *Saint Paul*, 108.

279. *a theoretical import of the greatest magnitude*: "Its bearing, in a mythological context implacably reduced to a single point, a single statement (Christ is resurrected), pertains rather to the laws of universality in general. This is why it can be called a *theoretical* break, it being understood that in this instance 'theoretical' is not being opposed to 'practical,' but to real. Paul is a founder, in that he is one of the very first theoreticians of the universal." Badiou, *Saint Paul*, 118.

279. *Adam's unfinished poem*: Zulaika, *Adanen poema amaigabea*.

279–80. *the seminal and rigorous work of Gregory Bateson*: See *Steps to an Ecology of Mind* and *Mind and Nature*.

280. *"This life, this is your eternal life"*; *"Did I not fall—listen!—into the well of eternity?"* Quoted in Michalski, *The Flame of Eternity*, 188, 136.

280. *"Hiroshima belongs to eternity"*: Quoted in La Bella, *Pedro Arrupe*, 18.

281. *even though it all went wrong*: Quoted in Simmons, *I'm Your Man*, 338.

281. *"a mixture of medieval Catholicism and satanic impiety"*: Ricardo Viñes, quoted in Nichols, *Ravel*, 22.

281. *"an apocalyptic enactment of ending"*: Altizer, *The Contemporary Jesus*, 13.

281. *"Beatrice is Blake's City, yet a Woman"*: Brown, *Apocalypse*, 168.

282. *"It's with such intense joy. It is such an hallelujah"*: Lispector, *The Stream of Life*, 3.

282. *"of the obstinacy of love"*: Badiou, *In Praise of Love*, 82.

282. *"Farewell to farewell . . . Grace to breathe that void"*: Beckett, *Ill Seen Ill Said*, 86.

282. *In old age, the second innocence*: Brown, *Love's Body*, 205–6.

HALF PRICE BOOKS®

Half Price Books
3860 LA REUNION PKWY
DALLAS, TX 75212
OFS OrderID 7555427

Thank you for your order, Heidi Cloutier!

Thank you for shopping with Half Price Books! Please contact service84@hpb.com. if you have any questions, comments or concerns about your order (114-7619806-3765030)

Visit our stores to sell your books, music, movies games for cash.

SKU	ISBN/UPC	Title & Author/Artist	Shelf ID	Qty
S215830744	9781935709589	That Old Bilbao Moon: The Passion and Resu. Zulaika, Joseba	WDHIS 13.5	1

SHIPPED STANDARD TO:
Heidi Cloutier
20 EVELYN PL
LANCASTER MA 01523-3114

ORDER# **114-7619806-3765030**
AmazonMarketplaceUS

Bibliography

Adams, John. *A Defense of the Constitutions of Government of the United States of America.* 1787. Reprint, New York: Da Capo Press, 1971.

Adorno, Theodor W. *Essays on Music.* Edited by Richard Leppert. Berkeley: University of California Press, 2002.

———. "Valéry Proust Museum." In *Prisms.* Translated by Samuel Weber and Sherry Weber Nicholsen, 175–77. Cambridge: MIT Press, 1981.

Agamben, Giorgio. *The Time That Remains: A Commentary on the Letter to the Romans.* Translated by Patricia Dailey. Stanford: Stanford University Press, 2005.

———. *Potentialities: Collected Essays in Philosophy.* Stanford: Stanford University Press, 2005.

Agirreazkuenaga, Joseba. "Javier Ybarra Bergé." In *Bilbao desde sus alcaldes: Diccionario biográfico de los alcaldes de Bilbao y gestión municipal en la Dictadura*, edited by Joseba Agirreazkuenaga and Mikel Urquijo. Bilbao: Ayuntamiento de Bilbao, 2008, 341–389.

Agirreazkuenaga, Joseba, and Alonso Olea, Eduardo, eds. *Basque Fiscal Systems: History, Current Status, and Future Perspectives.* Reno: Center for Basque Studies, 2014.

Aguirre, José Antonio de. *Escape Via Berlin: Eluding Franco in Hitler's Europe.* 1944. Reprint, Reno: University of Nevada Press, 1991.

———. *Obras Completas.* Donostia: Sendoa, 1981.

Aizpurua, Itziar. *Jokin Gorostidi: Autobiografia.* Tafalla: Txalaparta, 2006.

Alarcos Llorach, Emilio. *Blas de Otero.* Oviedo: Clarin, 1997.

Aldekoa, Iñaki. *Munduaren neurria: Arestiren ahots biblikoaz.* Irun: Alberdania, 1998.

Alighieri, Dante. *The Portable Dante.* Translated and edited by Mark Musa. New York: Penguin Books, 1995.

Altizer, Thomas J. J. *The New Apocalypse: The Radical Christian Vision of William Blake.* Ann Arbor: Michigan University Press, 1967.

———. *The Contemporary Jesus.* Albany: State University of New York Press, 1997.

Álvarez Enparantza, José Luis. *Huntaz eta Hartaz.* 2nd ed. Donostia: Elkar, 1983.

———. "Unamuno eragille." In *Gertakarien Lekuko*, 71–80. Donostia: Haranburu, 1985.

———. *Leturia-ren egunkari ezkutua.* 2nd ed. Durango: Leopoldo Zugaza, 1977.

Álvarez Gila, Óscar. *Misiones y misioneros vascos en Hispanoamérica, 1820–1960.* Bilbao: Labayru Ikastegia, 1998.

Ameztoy, Vicente. *Sagrado-Profano: Santoral de Remelluri, Paraiso y otras obras.* Donostia: Gipuzkoako Foru Aldundia, 2000.

Anasagasti, Iñaki, and Josu Erkoreka. *Dos familias vascas: Areilza-Aznar.* Madrid: Foca, 2003.

Arana Cobos, Juan. *Jorge Oteiza: Art as Sacrament, Avant-Garde and Magic.* Reno: Center for Basque Studies, in press.

———. *Oteiza y Unamuno: Dos tragedias epigonales de la modernidad.* Alzuza: Fundación Museo Oteiza, 2012.

Areilza, José María de. *Así les he visto.* Barcelona: Planeta, 1974.

Aresti, Gabriel. *Obra Guztiak. Obras Completas.* Introduction by Ibon Sarasola. 2 vols. Donostia: Kriselu, 1976.

Aretxaga, Begoña. *Los funerales del nacionalismo radical vasco: Ensayo antropológico.* Donostia-San Sebastián: Baroja, 1988.

———. *States of Terror: Begoña Aretxaga's Essays.* Edited by Joseba Zulaika. Reno: Center for Basque Studies, 2005.

Arkotxa, Aurelia. "Arestiren hiri mitikoak." *Hegats* 15/16 (1995): 65–78.

———. *Imaginaire et Poesie dans* Maldan behera *de Gabriel Aresti.* Donostia: Gipuzkoako Foru Aldundia, 1993.

———. "La mirada malévola de la luna en la *Ahijada* de J. Mirande (1925–1972)." In *Breve historia feminista de la literatura española (en lengua catalana, gallega y vasca).* Edited by Iris M. Zavala. Barcelona: Anthropos, 2000.

Arpal, Jesús. "El Bilbao de la industrialización: Una ciudad para una élite." *Saioak* 2, no. 2 (1978): 31–68.

Arrupe, Pedro. *Essential Writings.* Edited by Kevin F. Burke, S.J. New York: Orbis Books, 2005.

Arzalluz, Miren. *Cristóbal Balenciaga: The Making of a Master (1985–1936).* San Sebastián: Nerea, 2011.

Atxaga, Bernardo. *Obabakoak.* Translated by Margaret Jull Costa. New York: Pantheon Books. 1992.

Auerbach, Eric. *Dante: Poet of the Secular World.* Translated by Ralph Manheim. Chicago: University of Chicago Press, 1961.

———. *Mimesis.* Translated by Willard R. Trask. Princeton: Princeton University Press, 1953.

Azaola, José Miguel de. "El viaje a Vasconia de Max Weber." *Bidebarrieta* (II Symposium: Arte, Patrimonio Monumental y Ciudad) (1997): 189–222.

Azurmendi, Joxe. *Bakea gudan: Unamuno, historia eta karlismoa.* Tafalla: Txalaparta, 2012.

———. *Espainolak eta Euskaldunak.* Donostia: Elkar, 1992.

Badiola, Txomin. "Beyond Guernica and the Guggenheim: Relations Between Art and Politics from a Comparative Perspective." Paper presented at the University of Nevada Center for Basque Studies, May 2, 2013.

———. "El lugar de la controversia: Múltiples relaciones del arte y lo político en el País Vasco." Paper presented at the University of Nevada Center for Basque Studies, May 2, 1913.

Badiou, Alain. *Conditions.* Translated by Steven Corcoran. New York: Continuum, 2008.

———. "Destruction, Negation, Subtraction: On Pier Paolo Pasolini." Lecture delivered at the University of California, Los Angeles, January 2007.

———. "The Figure of the Soldier." In *Philosophy for Militants.* Translated by Bruno Bosteels, 41–59. London: Verso, 2012.

———. *Being and Event.* Translated by Oliver Feltham. New York: Continuum, 2005.

———. *Ethics: An Essay on the Understanding of Evil.* Translated by Peter Hallward. London and New York: Verso, 2001.

———. *Number and Numbers.* New York: Polity Press, 2008.

———. *Saint Paul: The Foundations of Universalism.* Translated by Ray Brassier. Stanford: Stanford University Press, 2003.

———. *The Century.* Translated by Alberto Toscano. Malden, Mass.: Polity Press, 2007.

———. *Theory of the Subject.* Translated by Bruno Bosteels. New York: Continuum, 2009.

———. *Deleuze: The Clamor of Being.* Translated by Louise Burchill. Minneapolis: University of Minnesota Press, 2000.

———. *Wittgenstein's Antiphilosophy.* London: Verso, 2011.

Badiou, Alain, with Nicolas Truong. *In Praise of Love.* Translated by Peter Bush. New York: New Press, 2012.

Baker, Carlos. *Hemingway: The Writer as Artist.* Princeton: Princeton University Press, 1956.

Bal, Miekel. *Louise Bourgeois' Spider: The Architecture of Art-Writing.* Chicago: University of Chicago Press, 2001.

Baland, Timothy, and Hardie St. Martin, eds. and trans. *Miguel Hernández and Blas de Otero: Selected Poems.* Boston: Beacon Press, 1972.

Ballard, Bettina. *In My Fashion.* Salt Lake City: David McKay Company, 1960.

Banner, Lois. *MM-Personal: From the Private Archives of Marilyn Monroe.* New York: Abrams, 2010.

Barandiarán, José Miguel de. *Diccionario ilustrado de mitología vasca. Obras Completas,* I. Bilbao: La Gran Enciclopedia Vasca, 1972.

Barbería, José Luis. "El Estado menguante." *El País,* May 3, 2005.

Baroja, Pío. "Elogio sentimental del acordeón." In *Paradox.* Madrid: Espasa-Calpe, 1906.

Barthes, Roland. *A Lover's Discourse.* New York: Hill and Wang, 1978.

———. *Mythologies.* Translated by Annette Lavaers. New York: Hill and Wang, 1972.

———. *Empire of Signs.* New York: Hill & Wang, 1982.

Basurto Ferro, Nieves, Paloma Rodríguez-Escudero Sánchez, and Jaione Velilla Iriondo. *El Bilbao que pudo ser: Proyectos para una ciudad, 1800–1940.* Bilbao: Diputación Foral de Guipúzcoa, 1999.

Bataille, George. *Death and Sensuality: A Study of Eroticism and the Taboo.* New York: Ballantine Books, 1969.

———. *Visions of Excess: Selected Writings, 1927–1939.* Edited by Allan Stoekl. Minneapolis: University of Minnesota Press, 1985.

Bateson, Gregory. *Steps to an Ecology of Mind.* New York: Ballantine Books, 1972.

———. *Mind and Nature: A Necessary Unity.* New York: E.P. Dutton, 1979.

Bateson, Gregory, and Mary Catherine Bateson. *Angels Fear: An Investigation into the Nature and Meaning of the Sacred.* London: Rider, 1988.

Batista, Antoni. *Madariaga: De las armas a la palabra.* Barcelona: RBA, 2007.

Beaton, Cecil. *Glass of Fashion.* London: Doubleday, 1954.

Beckett, Samuel. *Proust.* New York: Grove Press, 1970.

———. *Ill Seen Ill Said.* In *Nohow On.* New York: Grove, 1996.

Begin, Menachem. *The Revolt.* New York: Nash Publishing, 1951.

Benjamin, Walter. *Illuminations.* New York: Schocken, 1969.

———. "Critique of Violence." In *Selected Writings.* Vol. 1, *1913–1926.* Cambridge: Harvard University Press, 1996.

Bergamín, José. *La claridad del toreo.* Madrid: Turner, 1987.

Bernabé, Carmen. "Biblia." In *10 Mujeres escriben teología.* Edited by Mercedes Navarro, 13–62. Estella: Editorial Verbo Divino, 1998.

———. "Yo soy la resurrección." In *Y vosotras: Quién decís que soy yo?,* edited by Isabel Gómez-Acebo, 279–326. Bilbao: Desclée de Bouver, 2000.

Betsky, Aaron. *Building Sex: Men, Women, Architecture, and the Construction of Sexuality.* New York: William Morrow and Company, 1995.

Blanco Aguinaga, Carlos. *El Unamuno contemplative.* Barcelona: Laia, 1975.

Blankaert, Claude. "On the Origins of French Ethnology: William Edwards and the Doctrine of Race." In *Bones, Bodies, Behavior: Essays on Biological Anthropology,* edited by George W. Stocking, 18–55. Madison: University of Wisconsin Press, 1988.

Blasco Ibáñez, Vicente. *El intruso.* Valencia: Prometeo, 1914.

Blume, Mary. *The Master of Us All: Balenciaga, His Workrooms, His World.* New York: Farrar, Strauss, Giroux, 2013.

Bosteels, Bruno. "Translator's Introduction." In Alain Badiou, *Wittgenstein's Antiphilosophy.* London: Verso, 2011.

Bowers, Claude. *My Mission to Spain: Watching the Rehearsal for World War II.* New York: Simon and Schuster, 1954.

Bradley, Kim. "The Deal of the Century," *Art in America* (July 1997) 85 (7): 48 (10).

Brantlinger, Patrick. "'Dying Races': Rationalizing Genocide in the Nineteenth Century." In *The Decolonization of Imagination: Culture, Knowledge and Power,* edited by Jan N. Pieterse and Bhikhu Parekh, 43–56. London: Zed Books, 1995.

Brown, Norman O. *Apocalypse and/or Metapmorphosis.* Berkeley: University of California Press, 1991.

———. *Closing Time.* New York: Random House, 1973.

———. *Love's Body.* New York: Vintage Books, 1966.

Buck-Morss, Susan. *The Dialectics of Seeing: Walter Benjamin and the Arcades Project.* Cambridge: MIT Press, 1989.

Bullen, Margaret. *Basque Gender Studies.* Reno: Center for Basque Studies, 2003.

Butler, Judith. *Antigone's Claim: Kinship Between Life and Death.* New York: Columbia University Press, 2000.

———. "The Force of Fantasy: Feminism, Mapplethorpe, and Discursive Excess." *Difference: A Journal of Feminist Cultural Studies* 2, no. 2 (1990): 105–25.

Butler, Judith, Ernesto Laclau, and Slavoj Žižek. *Contingency, Hegemony, Universality: Cotemporary Dialogues on the Left.* London: Verso, 2000.

Caja de Pensiones. *Oteiza: Propósito Experimental.* Madrid: Caja de Pensiones, 1988.

Cajori, Marion, and Amei Wallach. *Louise Bourgeois: The Spider, the Mistress and the Tangerine.* Zeitgeist Films, 2008.

Cardenal, Ernesto, and Dorothée Solle. *Oración por Marilyn Monroe.* Managua: Editorial Nueva Nicaragua, n.d.

Caro Baroja, Julio. *Los pueblos del norte de la península ibérica (análisis histórico-cultural).* Madrid: Consejo Superior de Investigaciones Científicas, 1943.

———. *The Basques.* Translated by Kristin Addis. Reno: Center for Basque Studies, 2009.

Cashford, Jules. *The Moon: Myth and Image.* New York: Four Walls Eight Windows, 2003.

Castellón, Ricardo, and Nicolás Dolijanin. *Pakito Arriaran: De Arrasate a Chalatenango.* Tafalla: Txalaparta, 2008.

Castells, Manuel. *The Power of Identity.* Malden: Blackwell, 2004.

Cavanagh, Michael. "Walking into the Light: Dante and Seamus Heaney's Second Life." *South Carolina Review* 32, no. 1 (1999): 119–31.

Cercas, Javier. *Los soldados de Salamina.* Barcelona: Tusquets, 2001.

Chesterton, G. K. *Orthodoxy.* San Francisco: Ignatius, 1995.

Cillero Goiriastuena, Francisco Javier. "The Moving Target: A History of Basque Detective and Crime Fiction." PhD diss., University of Nevada, Reno, 2001.

Clavería, Carlos. *Temas de Unamuno.* Madrid: Gredos, 1970.

Clifford, James. "On Ethnographic Surrealism." In *The Predicament of Culture: Twentieth-Century Ethnography, Literature, and Art.* Cambridge: Harvard University Press, 1988.

Cloud, Yvonne. *The Basque Children in England: An Account of Their Life at North Stoneham Camp.* London: Victor Gollancz, 1937.

Colectivo Autónomo de Trabajadores de Euskalduna. *La batalla de Euskalduna: Ejemplo de resistencia obrera.* Madrid: Editorial Revolución, 1985.

Comley, Nancy R., and Robert Scholes. *Hemingway's Genders.* New Haven: Yale University Press, 1994.

Copjec, Joan. "The Tomb of Perseverance: On Antigone." In *Giving Ground: The Politics of Propinquity.* Edited by Joan Copjec and Michael Sorkin, 233–66. London and New York: Verso, 1999.

———. *Imagine There Is No Woman: Ethics and Sublimation.* Cambridge: MIT Press, 2003.

Cronin, Anthony. *Samuel Beckett: The Last Modernist.* New York: Da Capo Press, 1999.

Danto, Arthur. *Andy Warhol.* New Haven: Yale University Press, 2009.

de Man, Paul. *Allegories of Reading.* New Haven: Yale University Press, 1979.

de Pablo, Santiago. "El *lauburu*: Política, cultura e identidad nacional en torno a un símbolo del País Vasco." *Memoria y Civilización* 12 (2009): 109–53.

———. "The Basque Country Through the Nazi Looking-Glass, 1933–1945." In *War, Exile, Justice and Everyday Life, 1936–1946,* edited by Sandra Ott, 226–49. Reno: Center for Basque Studies, 2011.

De Vito, John, and Frank Tropea. *The Immortal Marilyn: The Depiction of an Icon.* Lanham, Maryland: Scarecrow Press, 2007.

Decker, Andrew. "Can the Guggenheim Pay the Price?" *ARTnews* 93 (January 1994): 142–49.

———. "What Price Guggenheim?" *Village Voice,* June 23, 1992, 39–42.

Deleuze, Gilles. "Coldness and Cruelty." In Gilles Deleuze and Leopold von-

Sacher Masoch, *Masochism*. New York: Zone Books, 1989.

———. *Difference and Repetition*. New York: Columbia University Press, 1994.

Delibes, Miguel. *El libro de la caza menor*. Barcelona: Destino, 1964.

Derrida, Jacques. *Gift of Death*. Chicago: University of Chicago Press, 1995.

———. *On Cosmopolitanism and Forgiveness*. London and New York: Routledge, 2001.

———. *The Politics of Friendship*. Translated by George Collins. London and New York: Verso, 1997.

Díez Mintegui, Carmen. "Female Labour, Participation and Gender Relationships: Analysis of Rural and Urban Environments." *RIEV* 40, no. 2 (1995): 271–87.

Dillenberger, Jane Daggett. *The Religious Art of Andy Warhol*. New York: Continuum, 1998.

Documentos. Donostia: Hordago, 1979–81.

Dostoyevsky, Fyodor. *Notes from the Underground*. New York: Dover Publications, 1992.

Douglass, William A., and Jon Bilbao. *Amerikanuak: Basques in the New World*. Reno: University of Nevada Press, 1975.

Douglass, William A., and Joseba Zulaika. *Basque Culture: Anthropological Perspectives*. Reno: Center for Basque Studies, 2007.

Dylan, Bob. *Chronicles*. New York: Simon and Schuster, 2004.

Dyson, Freeman. "Oppenheimer: The Shape of Genius." *New York Review of Books*, August 15, 2013, 18–19.

Eagleton, Terry. *Sweet Violence: The Idea of the Tragic*. Malden, Mass.: Blackwell, 2003.

Echevarría, Germán. *Memoria lírica: Oroitzapen lirikoa (Poemas, 1964–2002)*. Leioa: Servicio Editorial, Universidad del País Vasco, 2003.

———. "Bilbao-Song." In *Zurgai*. Bilbao: Diputación de Vizcaya, 2009.

Eguillor, Juan Carlos. "Euskadi Sioux." In *Disidencias otras (1972–1982): Poéticas y acciones artísticas en la transición política vasca*, edited by Fernando Golvano. San Sebastián: Koldo Mitxelena Kulturunea, 2004.

Elosegi, Joseba. *Quiero morir por algo*. Barcelona: Plaza y Janés, 1977.

Esteban, Mari Luz. *Crítica del pensamiento amoroso*. Barcelona: Bellaterra, 2011.

———. *Reproducción del cuerpo femenino: Discursos y prácticas acerca de la salud*. San Sebastián: Ed. Gakoa, 2001.

Etxeberria, Hasier. *Bost idazle*. Irun: Alberdania, 2002.

Etxebarrieta, Jose Antonio. *Los vientos favorables: Euskal Herria 1839–1959*. Edited by José María Lorenzo Espinosa and Mikel Zabala. Tafalla: Txlaparta, 1999.

Ewen, Frederic. *Bertholt Brecht: His Life, His Art, and His Times*. London: Calder and Boyars, 1970.

Feingold, Michael, and Frank McGuinness, trans. "Bilbao Song," by Berthold Brecht. In Marianne Faithful, *The Seven Deadly Sins*. Compact disc. 1998.

Fernandez, James W. "The Dark at the Bottom of the Stairs." In *Persuasions and Performances: The Play of Tropes in Culture*, 214–38. Bloomington: Indiana University Press, 1986.

———. "The Mission of Metaphor." In *Persuasions and Performances: The Play of Tropes in Culture*, 28–70. Bloomington: Indiana University Press, 1986,

Figuera Aymerich, Ángela. *Belleza Cruel*. Barcelona: Lumen, 1958.

Florman, Lisa. *Myth and Metamorphosis: Picasso's Classical Prints of the 1930s*. Cambridge: MIT Press, 2000.

Foraster Bastida, José Ramón, María Elisa de Bastida Díaz-Tejeiro, and

Gorka Pérez de la Peña Oleaga. *Ricardo de Bastida: Arquitecto*. Bilbao: Colegio Oficial de Arquitectos Vasco-Navarro, 2002.

Fortuna, Diane. "The Art of the Labyrinth." In *Critical Essays on James Joyce's* A Portrait of an Artist as a Young Man, edited by Philip Brady and James F. Careus, 187–212. New York: Simon and Schuster, 1998.

Foster, Hal. "Master Builder." In *Design and Crime and Other Diatribes*, 27–42. London: Verso, 2002.

Foster, Thomas C. *Seamus Heaney*. Boston: Twayne Publishers, 1989.

Fowlie, Wallace. *A Reading of Dante's Inferno*. Chicago: University of Chicago Press, 1981.

Fox, Robin. *Kinship and Marriage: An Anthropological Perspective*. Harmondsworth: Penguin, 1977.

Frank, Joseph. *Dostoevsky: A Writer in His Time*. Edited by Mary Petrusewicz. Princeton: Princeton University Press, 2010.

Freud, Sigmund. "The Most Prevalent Form of Degradation in Erotic Life." In Sigmund Freud, *Collected Papers*. Edited by James Strachey. Translated by Joan Riviere. 5 vols. New York: Basic Books, 1959.

———. *Moses and Monotheism*. London: Hogarth Press, 1939.

———. *Totem and Taboo*. New York: W. W. Norton, 1950.

Frye, Northrop. *Frye on Milton and Blake*. Edited by Angela Esterhammer. Toronto: University of Toronto Press, 2005.

Galarraga, Xabier, and Mari Carmen Gallastegui. "Bilbao. Transformación económica: Del barro al ordenador personal." *RIEV* dossier, "Bilbao y sus transformaciones," 49, no. 1 (2004): 77–106.

García Lorca, Federico. *Collected Poems*. Edited by Christopher Maurer. Revised bilingual edition. New York: Farrar, Straus and Giroux, 2002.

Garff, Joakim. *Soren Kierkegaard: A Biography.* Princeton: Princeton University Press, 2000.

Garmendia, Elixabete, et al. *Yoyes desde su ventana.* Pamplona: Garrasi, 1987.

Genet, Jean. *The Thief's Journal.* Translated by Bernard Frechtman. New York: Grove Weidenfeld, 1964.

——. *The Miracle of the Rose.* Translated by Bernard Frechtman. New York: Grove Weidenfeld, 1966.

——. *Prisoner of Love.* Translated by Barbara Bray. Hanover, NH: Wesleyan University Press, 1989.

Gere, Cathy. *Knossos and the Prophets of Modernism.* Chicago: University of Chicago Press, 2009.

Gil, Lorena. "Uno de cada cuatro bilbainos vive 'al limite' y bajo la amenaza de la pobreza." *El Correo,* December 19, 2007, 6.

Gilbert-Rolfe, Jeremy, with Frank Gehry. *Frank Gehry: The City and Music.* London and New York: Routledge, 2001.

Gilson, Étienne. *Choir of Muses.* Translated by Maisie Ward. London: Sheed and Ward, 1955.

——. *Dante and Philosophy.* Translated by David Moore. New York: Harper, 1963.

Ginsberg, Allen. *Collected Poems 1947–1997.* New York: Harper Collins, 2006.

Glas, Eduardo. *Bilbao's Modern Business Elite.* Reno: University of Nevada Press, 1997.

Glynn, Prudence. "Balenciaga and la vie d'un chien." *The Times,* August 3, 1971.

Gojenola, Manu. *Mariorenak.* Donostia: Hiria, 2013.

Gómez-Acebo, Isabel, ed. *Y vosotras, ¿Quién decís que soy yo?* Bilbao: Desclée de Bouver, 2000.

Gondra, Patxi. "Mi odisea Pasionista (Memorias de Aita Patxi, 1937–1939)." Unpublished manuscript.

González Abrisketa, Olatz. *Pelota vasca: Un ritual, una estética.* Bilbao: Muelle de Uribitarte, 2005. Published in English as Basque Pelota: A Ritual, an Aesthetic. Reno: Center for Basque Studies, 2012.

González García, Sonia. "La prostitución en Bilbao: Último tercio del s. XIX y primeros decenios del XX." *Vasconia* 35 (2006): 221–37.

Gors, André. *Socialism and Revolution.* Garden City, N.Y.: Anchor Books, 1967.

Granja, José Luis de la. "Aguirre y Prieto: Vidas paralelas." *Diario Vasco,* October 1, 2006.

Guasch, Anna María, and Joseba Zulaika, eds. *Learning from the Bilbao Guggenheim.* Reno: Center for Basque Studies, 2005.

Hallward, Peter. *Badiou: A Subject to Truth.* Minneapolis: University of Minnesota Press, 2003.

Harries, Karsten. "Nietzsche's Labyrinths: Variations on an Ancient Theme." In *Nietzsche and 'An Architecture of Our Minds,'* edited by Alexandre Kostka and Irving Wohlfarth, 35–52. Los Angeles: Getty Research Institute, 1999.

Harrison, Robert Pogue. *The Body of Beatrice.* Baltimore and London: The Johns Hopkins University Press, 1988.

Heaney, Seamus. *Preoccupations: Selected Prose, 1968–1978.* New York: Farrar, Strauss and Giroux, 1980.

——. "Envies and Identifications: Dante and the Modern Poet." *Irish University Review* 15, no. 1 (1985): 5–19.

——. *The Redress of Poetry.* New York: Farrar, Strauss and Giroux, 1995.

——. Translation of Dante's Canto II. In *Dante's Inferno.* Edited by Daniel Halpern. Hopewell, N.J.: Eco Press, 1993.

Hegel, G. W. F. *The Phenomenology of Spirit.* Translated by A. V. Miller. Edited by J. N. Findlay. Oxford: Oxford University Press, 1977.

Hemingway, Ernest. *Death in the Afternoon.* New York: Charles Scribner's Sons, 1947.

——. *The Old Man and the Sea.* New York: Charles Scribner's Sons, 1952.

——. *The Dangerous Summer.* London: Hamish Hamilton Ltd., 1985

Hernández Pico, Juan. "Ellacuría, ignaciano." In *Ignacio Ellacuría: Aquella libertad esclarecida,* edited by Jon Sobrino and Rolando Alvarado, 245–73. Santander: Sal Terrae, 1999.

Hess, Andreas. "Is It Justified to Speak of a Jesuit Work Ethic in the Basque Country? Variations on a Weberian Theme." *Max Weber Studies (Ingenta)* 7, no. 1 (January 2007): 89–96.

Hilbert, David. "On the Infinite," In *From Frege to Gödel: A Source Book in Mathematical Logic, 1879–1931,* edited by Jean van Heijenoort. Cambridge: Harvard University Press, 1967.

Hollier, Denis. *Against Architecture: The Writings of George Bataille.* Cambridge: MIT Press, 1989.

Hughes, Robert. "Masterpiece Theater." *New York Review of Books,* March 4, 1993, 8–14.

Ibarra, Pedro. "Prólogo." In Alejandro Gaytan de Ayala, *De Neguri a Lausanne: Memorias de transición (1977–1980).* Bilbao: Editorial Rampas de Uribitarte, 2012.

Ibarruri, Dolores. *Speeches & Articles (1936–1938).* New York: International Publishers, 1938.

Iriarte Bikila, Joxe. *Borrokaren gorrian.* Tafalla: Txalaparta, 1999.

Irigaray, Luce. *Marine Lover: Of Friedrich Nietzsche.* New York: Columbia University Press, 1991.

Irujo, Xabier. *El Gernika de Richthofen.* Gernika: Gernikako Bakearen Museoa Fundazioa, 2013.

Izarzelaia, Arturo. *Los barrios altos de Bilbao.* Bilbao: Aldauri Fundazioa, 2001.

Jameson, Fredric. "Postmodernism, or The Cultural Logic of Late Capitalism." *New Left Review*, 146 (1984), 53–91.

Jankélévitch, Vladimir. *Forgiveness*. Chicago and London: University of Chicago Press, 2005.

Jarman, Douglas. *Kurt Weill: An Illustrated Biography*. Bloomington: Indiana University Press, 1982.

Jimenez, Edorta. *Hemingway eta euskaldunak zerbitzu sekretuetan*. Zarautz: Susa, 2003.

Johnson, Terry. *Insignificance*. In *Plays: One*. London: Methuen Drama, 1993.

Jones, Malcolm V. *Dostoyevsky After Bakhtin: Readings in Dostoyevsky's Fantastic Realism*. Cambridge: Cambridge University Press, 1990.

Jouve, Marie-Andrée. *Balenciaga*. Paris: Assouline, 1997.

Joyce, James. *A Portrait of the Artist as a Young Man*. Edited by John Paul Riquelme. New York: W. W. Norton, 2007.

———. *Finnegans Wake*. London: Faber and Faber, 1939.

Juaristi, Jon. *El chimbo expiatorio (La invención de la tradición bilbaina, 1976–1939)*. Bilbao: El Tilo, 1994.

———. *Miguel de Unamuno*. Madrid: Taurus, 2012.

Judt, Tony. *Past Imperfect: French Intellectuals, 1944–1956*. Berkeley: University of California Press, 1992.

Kasmir, Sharryn. "From the Margins: Punk Rock and the Repositioning of Ethnicity and Gender in Basque Identity." In *Basque Cultural Studies*, edited by William A. Douglass et al., 178–204. Reno: Basque Studies Program [Center for Basque Studies], 1999.

Keating, Michael. *Plurinational Democracy: Stateless Nations in a Post-Sovereignty Era*. Oxford: Oxford University Press, 2001.

Kerényi, Carl. *Dionysos: Archetypal Image of Indestructible Life*. Translated by Ralph Manheim. Princeton: Princeton University Press, 1976.

Kierkegaard, Soren. "The Aesthetic Validity of Marriage." In *Either/Or*, 3–157. Translated by Walter Lowrie. 2 vols. Princeton: Princeton University Press, 1944.

———. *The Concept of Irony (With Constant Reference to Socrates)*. New York: Harper and Row, 1965.

Koons, Jeff. *The Jeff Koons Handbook*. London: Thames and Hudson, 1992.

Kortazar, Jon. "El poeta Gabriel Aresti." *Cuadernos de Alzate* 43 (2010): 68–101.

———. *El poeta Gabriel Aresti (1933–1975)*. Bilbao: BBK, 2003.

Koyré, Alexandre. *From the Closed World to the Infinite Universe*. Baltimore: John Hopkins University Press, 1957.

Krauss, Rosalind E. *The Originality of the Avant-Garde and Other Modernist Myths*. Cambridge: MIT Press, 1986.

Kurlansky, Mark. *Cod: The Biography of the Fish That Changed the World*. New York: Walker and Company, 1997.

La Bella, Gianni, ed. *Pedro Arrupe, General de la Compañía de Jesús: Nuevas aportaciones a su biografía*. Bilbao: Mensajero 2007.

Lacan, Jacques. "The Significance of the Phallus." In Jacques Lacan, *Ecrits: The First Complete Edition in English*. Translated by Bruce Fink, 575–84. New York: W. W. Norton, 2006.

———. *The Seminar of Jacques Lacan*. Vol. 11, *The Four Fundamental Concepts of Psychoanalysis*. Edited by Jacques-Alain Miller. New York: W. W. Norton & Company, 1998.

———. *The Seminar of Jacques Lacan*. Vol. 17, *The Other Side of Psychoanalyis*. Edited by Jacques-Alain Miller. Translated by Russell Grigg. New York: W. W. Norton, 2007.

———. *The Seminar of Jacques Lacan*. Vol. 20, *On Feminine Sexuality: The Limits of Love and Knowledge, 1972–1973*. Edited by Jacques-Alain Miller. New York: W. W. Norton & Company, 1999.

———. *Television*. Translated by Dennis Hollier, Rosalind Krauss, and Annette Michelson. New York: W. W. Norton, 1990.

———. *The Seminar of Jacques Lacan*. Vol. 7, *The Ethics of Psychoanalysis*. London: Routledge, 1992.

———. *On the Names-of-the-Father*. Translated by Bruce Fink. Malden, MA: Polity, 2013.

Laclau, Ernesto, and Chantal Mouffe. *Hegemony and Socialist Strategy: Towards a Radical Democratic Politics*. London: Verso, 1985.

Largier, Niklaus. *In Praise of the Whip: A Cultural History of Arousal*. Translated by Graham Harman. New York: Zone Books, 2007.

Lasa, Mikel. *Memory Dump (1960–1990)*. Leioa: Euskal Herriko Unibertsitatea, 1993.

Legarreta, Dorothy. *The Guernica Generation: Basque Refugee Children of the Spanish Civil War*. Reno: University of Nevada Press, 1984.

Leiris, Michel. *L'Afrique fantôme*. Paris: Gallimard, 1950.

———. *Mirror of Tauromachy*. Translated by Paul Hammond. London: Atlas, 2007.

Lekuona, Manuel de. *Literatura oral vasca*. San Sebastián: Colección Kardaberaz, 1935.

Leonardo Aurtenetxe, Jon. "Segunda industrialización, urbanismo y crisis. El Bilbao de los años 1960–80." In *Bilbao, Arte eta Historia. Bilbao, arte e historia*, vol. 2, 235–251. Bilbao: Diputación de Bizkaia, 1990.

Lertxundi, Anjel. *Eskarmentuaren paperak*. Irun: Alberdania, 2009.

Lesser, Wendy. *His Other Half: Men Looking at Women Through Art*. Cambridge: Harvard University Press, 1991.

Lipus, Ander. "Minotauroa labirintoan." Unpublished manuscript, 2003.

Lispector, Clarice. *The Passion According to G. H.* Translated by Ronald W. Sousa. Minneapolis: University of Minnesota Press, 1988.

———. *The Stream of Life.* Translated by Elisabetz Lowe and Earl Fitz. Minneapolis: University of Minnesota Press, 1989.

López Aguirre, Elena. *Historia del Rock Vasco.* Vitoria-Gasteiz: Aianai Kultur Elkartea, 2011.

Lorenzo Espinosa, José María. *Txabi Etxebarrieta: Armado de palabra y obra.* Tafalla: Txalaparta, 1994.

———. *Txabi Etxebarrieta: Poesía y otros escritos 1961–1967.* Tafalla: Txalaparta, 1996.

Loureiro, Angel G. *The Ethics of Autobiography: Replacing the Subject in Modern Spain.* Nashville: Vanderbilt University Press, 2000.

Loyola, Ignatius. *A Pilgrim's Journey: The Autobiography of Ignatius of Loyola.* Translated by Joseph N. Tylenda, S.J. Wilmington, Del.: Michael Glazier, 1985.

MacCannell, Dean. "Marilyn Monroe Was Not a Man." *Diacritics* 17 (Summer 1987): 114–27.

———. "The Bilbao Effect: Ethical Symbolic Representation." In *The Ethics of Sightseeing,* 159–66. Berkeley: University of California Press, 2011.

———. "The Fate of the Symbolic in Architecture for Tourism: Piranesi, Disney, Gehry." In *Learning from the Guggenheim*, edited by Anna Guasch and Joseba Zulaika, 21–36. Reno: Center for Basque Studies, 2005.

Maier, Klaus. *Guernica: La intervención alemana en España y el "Caso Guernica."* Madrid: Sedmay Ediciones, 1976.

Mañaricua, Andrés Eliseo. *Santa María de Begoña en la historia espiritual de Vizcaya.* Bilbao: La Editorial Vizcaína, 1950.

Mandel, Miriam B. *Hemingway's* The Dangerous Summer. Lanham, MD: Scarecrow Press, 2008.

Marcus, Greil. *Lipstick Traces: A Secret History of the Twentieth Century.* Cambridge: Harvard University Press, 1989.

Martínez, Gaspar. *Confronting the Mystery of God: Political, Liberation, and Public Theologies.* New York: Continuum, 2001.

Masco, Joseph. *The Nuclear Borderlands: The Manhattan Project in Post-Cold War New Mexico.* Princeton: Princeton University Press, 2006.

Mauss, Marcel. *The Gift: Forms and Functions of Exchange in Archaic Societies.* London: Routledge, 1990.

Mazariego Zetino, Manuel, et al. *La otra cara de la guerra: Salvar vidas.* San Salvador: Fundabril, 2012.

Mees, Ludger. "The *Völkisch* Appeal: Nazi-Germany, the Basques and the Bretons." In *War, Exile, Justice and Everyday Life, 1936–1946,* edited by Sandra Ott, 251–83. Reno: Center for Basque Studies, 2011.

———. *El profeta pragmático: Aguirre, el primer lehendakari (1939–1960).* Irun: Alberdania, 2006.

Menchaca, Antonio. *Las cenizas del esplendor: Memorias de la Marquesa de Avendaño.* Madrid: Espasa, 1987.

Meyers, Jeffrey. *The Genius and the Goddess: Arthur Miller and Marilyn Monroe.* Urbana: University of Illinois Press, 2009.

Michalski, Krzysztof. *The Flame of Eternity: An Interpretation of Nietzsche's Thought.* Princeton: Princeton University Press, 2007.

Miller, Adam. *Badiou, Marion and St Paul: Immanent Grace.* New York: Continuum, 2008.

Miller, Arthur. *The Misfits.* New York: Dell, 1961.

———. *Timebends: A Life.* New York: Grove Press, 1987.

Miller, Jacques-Alain. "The Invention of Delirium." *Lacanian Ink* 34 (2009): 6–27.

———. "The Prisons of *Jouissance.*" Translated by Barbara P. Fulks. *Lacanian Ink* 33 (2009): 36–55.

Miller, Lesley Ellis. *Cristóbal Balenciaga.* London: B. T. Batsford, 1993.

Milton, John. *Paradise Lost.* Edited by Merritt Y. Hughes. New York: Hacket, 1933.

Molina, Fernando, and Juan Carlos Rojo. *Historia del túnel de Artxanda (1900–2002).* Bilbao: Diputación Foral de Bizkaia, 2002.

Molina Aparicio, Fernando. *Mario Onaindia (1948–2003): Biografía patria.* Madrid: Biblioteca Nueva, 2012.

———. "Lies of Our Fathers: Memory and Politics in the Basque Country under the Franco Dictatorship, 1936–68." *Journal of Contemporary History* 2014, Vol. 49(2): 196–319.

Monk, Ray. *Ludwig Wittgenstein: The Duty of Genius.* New York: Free Press, 1990.

———. *Robert Oppenheimer: A Life Inside the Center.* New York: Doubleday, 2012.

Monroe, Marilyn. *Fragments: Poems, Intimate Notes, Letters.* Edited by Stanley Buchthal and Bernard Comment. New York: Farrar, Straus and Giroux, 2010.

Morán, Gregorio. *Los españoles que dejaron de serlo: Euskadi, 1937–1981.* Barcelona: Planeta, 1982.

Moso, Roberto. *Flores en la basura: Los días del Rock Radikal.* Algorta: Hilargi Ediciones, 2003.

Munarriz, Fermin, *El tiempo de las luces: Entrevista con Arnaldo Otegi.* Bilbao: Baigorri, 2012.

Munford, Lewis. "Gentlemen: You are Mad!" *Saturday Review of Literature,* March 2, 1946, 5–6.

Muñoa, Pilar. *Oteiza. La vida como experimento.* Irun: Alberdania, 2006.

Muñoz-Rojas, Olivia. *Ashes and Granite: Destruction and Reconstruction in the Spanish Civil War and Its Aftermath.* Brighton: Sussex Academic Press, 2011.

Muschamp, Herbert. "Design Review: Nature and Artifice in Bloom," *New York Times*, Arts Section, April 5, 1996, 1.

———. "The Miracle in Bilbao." *New York Times Magazine,* September 7, 1997, 54–59, 72, 82.

Museo de Bellas Artes de Bilbao. *Taurus: Del mito al ritual.* Bilbao: Museo de Bellas Artes, 2010.

Nandorfy, Martha J. *The Poetics of Apocalypse: Federico García Lorca's Poet in New York.* London: Bucknell University Press, 2003.

Nehamas, Alexander. *Nietzsche: Life as Literature.* Cambridge: Harvard University Press, 1985.

———. *The Art of Living.* Berkeley: University of California Press, 1998.

Nichols, Roger. *Ravel.* New Haven: Yale University Press, 2011.

Nietzsche, Friedrich. *Ecce Homo: How One Becomes What One Is.* Translated by R. J. Hollingdale. London: Penguin, 1992.

O'Brien, John. *Leaving Las Vegas.* New York: Grove Press, 1995.

Olaziregi, Mari Jose. "Worlds of Fiction: An Introduction to Basque Narrative." In *Basque Literary History,* edited by Mari Jose Olaziregi, 137–200. Reno: Center for Basque Studies, 2012,

Onaindia, Mario. *El precio de la libertad: Memorias (1948–1977).* Madrid: Espasa, 2001.

Onaindia, Santiago. *Mila Euskal-Olerki Eder.* 2 vols. Bilbao: La Gran Enciclopedia Vasca, 1976.

Ortega y Gasset, José. "A 'Veinte Años de la Caza Mayor' del Conde de Yebes," *Obras Completas, VI (1941–1946).* Madrid: Revista de Occidente, 1973.

Ortíz-Osés, Andrés. *Antropología simbólica vasca.* Barcelona: Anthropos, 1985.

———. *Mitología cultural y memorias antropológicas.* Barcelona: Anthropos, 1987.

Ortiz-Osés, Andrés, and Franz-Karl Mayr. *El matriarcalismo vasco: Reinterpretación de la cultura vasca.* Bilbao: Universidad de Deusto, 1980.

Orwell, George. "Looking Back on the Spanish War." In *The Collected Essays, Journalism and Letters of George Orwell.* Vol. 2, *My Country Right or Left 1940–1943.* Edited by Sonia Orwell and Ian Angus, 262–63. New York: Harcourt, Brace & World, 1968.

———. *Collected Essays.* London: Heinemann Group, 1961.

Ossa Echaburu, Rafael. *Bilbao, puerto antes que villa.* Bilbao: Real Sociedad Vascongada de los Amigos del País, 1994.

Otazu, Alfonso de, and José Ramón Díaz de Durana. *El espíritu emprendedor de los vascos.* Madrid: Silex, 2008.

Oteiza, Jorge. "Art Today, The City, and Man." In *Oteiza's Selected Writings,* 294–322. Reno: Center for Basque Studies, 2004.

———. "La significación vasca del 'Guernica.'" *Deia* 29 (January 1978): 4–5.

———. *Ejercicios espirituales en un túnel.* San Sebastián: Hordago, 1984.

———. *Interpretación estética de la estatuaria megalítica americana.* Madrid: Ediciones de Cultura Hispánica, 1952.

———. *Quousque tandem . . . ! Ensayo de interpretación estética del alma vasca.* Zarautz: Auñamendi, 1963.

———. *Itziar: Elegía y otros poemas.* Pamplona: Pamiela, 1992.

———. *Oteiza's Selected Writings.* Edited by Joseba Zulaika. Translated by Frederick Fornoff. Reno: Center for Basque Studies, 2003.

———. *Poesía.* Edited by Gabriel Insausti. Alzuza: Fundación Museo Jorge Oteiza, 2006.

Otero, Blas de. *Ancia.* Madrid: Visor, 1984.

———. *Ángel fieramente humano.* Buenos Aires: Losada, 1960.

———. *Poemas vascos.* Bilbao: Ayuntamiento de Bilbao, 2002.

———. *Que trata de España.* Madrid: Visor, 1967.

Ott, Sandra. *War, Judgment, and Memory in the Basque Borderlands, 1914–1945.* Reno: University of Nevada Press, 2008.

Paglia, Camille. "Scholars in Bondage: Dogma Dominates Studies of Kind." *Chronicle of Higher Education,* May 20, 2013.

———. *Sexual Personae: Art and Decadence from Nefertiti to Emily Dickinson.* New Haven: Yale University Press, 1990.

———. *Vamps and Tramps: New Essays.* New York: Vintage, 1994.

Pagola, José Antonio. *Jesús: Aproximación histórica.* Madrid: PPC, 2007.

Panero, Leopoldo María. *Poesía Completa (1970–2000).* Burgos: Visor, 2001.

Pascual Rodríguez, Esther. *Los ojos del otro: Encuentros restaurativos entre víctimas y ex miembros de ETA.* Santander: Sal Terrae, 2013.

Patterson, Zabet. "Going On-line: Consuming Pornography in the Digital Era." In *Porn Studies,* edited by Linda Williams. Durham: Duke University, 2004.

Pérez-Agote, Alfonso, and José Santiago. *La nueva pluralidad religiosa.* Madrid: Ministerio de Justicia, 2009.

Pisano, Isabel. *Yo puta: Hablan las prostitutas.* Barcelona: Plaza y Janes, 2001.

Plazaola, Juan. "La escuela vasca de escultura." In *Cultura vasca,* J. M. Barandiarán et al. 3 vols., vol. 2, 331–55 San Sebastián: Erein, 1978.

Pound, Ezra. *The Cantos of Ezra Pound.* New York: New Directions, 1996.

Pradera, Victor. *El estado nuevo.* Madrid: Cultura Española, 1935.

Preston, Paul. *The Spanish Holocaust: Inquisition and Extermination in Twentieth-Century Spain.* New York: W. W. Norton & Company, 2012.

Prieto, Indalecio. *De mi vida: Recuerdos, estampas, siluetas, sombras.* Mexico: El Sitio, 1965.

———. *Pasado y futuro de Bilbao: Charlas en Méjico.* Bilbao: El Sitio, 1980.

Raento, Pauliina, and Cameron Watson. "Gernika, Guernica, *Guernica*? Contested Meanings of a Basque Place." *Political Geography* 19 (2000): 707–36.

Ràfols, Wifredo de. "Writing to Seduce and Seducing to Write About It: Graphocentrism in Don Juan Tenorio." *Revista Hispánica Moderna* 50 (1997): 253–64.

Raguer, Hilari. *Aita Patxi: Prisionero con los gudaris.* Barcelona: Claret, 2006.

Rankin, Nicholas. *Telegram from Guernica: The Extraordinary Life of George Steer, War Correspondent.* London: Faber and Faber, 2003.

Regnault, Francois. "Saintliness and the Sainthood." *Lacanian Ink* 33 (2009): 114–25.

Richardson, John. "Go, Go, Guggenheim." *New York Review of Books*, July 16, 1992, 18–22.

Rimbaud, Arthur. *Rimbaud: Complete Works, Selected Letters.* Edited with an introduction by Wallace Fowlie. Chicago: University of Chicago Press, 1966.

Robinson, John A. T. *The Body: A Study in Pauline Theology.* Philadelphia: Westminster Press, 1977.

Rodríguez, Arantxa. "Planning and Revitalization of an Old Industrial City: Urban Policy Innovations in Metropolitan Bilbao." In *Local Economic Development in Europe and the Americas,* edited by Christophe Demazière and Patricia Wilson. London: Mansell, 1996.

Romaine, James. "Transubstantiating the Culture: Andy Warhol's Secret." *Regeneration Quarterly* 5, no. 3 (1999): 1–7.

Ross, Alex. *The Rest Is Noise: Listening to the Twentieth Century.* New York: Picador, 2007.

Roudinesco, Elisabeth. *Jacques Lacan.* Translated by Barbara Bray. New York: Columbia University Press, 1997.

Rousseau, Jean-Jacques. *The Social Contract.* Translated by Rosse Harrington. New York: Knickerbocker Press, 1893.

Rubert de Ventós, Xavier. *Nacionalismos: El laberinto de la identidad.* Madrid: Espasa, 1994.

———. *De la identidad a la independencia.* Barcelona: Anagrama, 2000.

Sáez de la Fuente Aldama, Izaskun. *El Movimiento de Liberación Nacional Vasco: Una religión de sustitución.* Bilbao: Desclée de Brouwer, 2002.

Said, Edward W. *On Late Style: Music and Literature Against the Grain.* New York: Pantheon Books, 2006.

———. *Freud and the Non-European.* New York: Verso, 2003.

Saizarbitoria, Ramon. *Egunero hasten delako.* Donostia: Kriselu, 1969.

———. "Asaba zaharen baratza." In *Gorde nazazu lurpean,* 401–64. Donostia: Erein, 2000.

Sáiz Valdivielso, Alfonso. *Crónica de un corazón.* Barcelona: Planeta, 1984.

———. "Prólogo." In Indalecio Prieto, *Pasado y futuro de Bilbao: Charlas en Méjico,* i–xi. Bilbao: El Sitio, 1980.

Sáiz Valdivielso, Alfonso, and Covadonga Sáiz Bernuy. *Bilbao: Toros y toreros.* Bilbao: Area de Cultura y Turismo del Ayuntamiento de Bilbao, 2000.

Santner, Eric L. "Miracles Happen: Benjamin, Rosenzweig, Freud and the Matter of the Neighbor." In Slavoj Žižek, Eric L. Santner, and Kenneth Reinhard, *The Neighbor: Three Inquiries in Political Theology.* Chicago: University of Chicago Press, 2005.

———. *Stranded Objects: Mourning, Memory, and Film in Postwar Germany.*

Ithaca and London: Cornell University Press, 1990.

———. *On the Psychotheology of Everyday Life: Reflections on Freud and Rosenzweig.* Chicago: University of Chicago Press, 2001.

Sarasola, Ibon. "Hitzaurrea." In Gabriel Aresti, *Poemak I,* 11–99. Donostia: Kriselu, 1976.

Sartre, Jean Paul. *Saint Genet: Actor and Martyr.* Translated by Bernard Frechtman. New York: George Brazilier, 1963.

———. "Prefacio." In Gisèle Halimi, *El proceso de Burgos.* Caracas: Monte Ávila Editores, 1972.

———. *Les Mots.* Paris: Gallimard, 1964.

Segundo, Juan Luis. *The Sacraments Today.* New York: Orbis Books, 1974.

Serra, Richard. "Notes on Jorge Oteiza." Originally published in *El País,* Madrid, February 2003. Reprinted in *Oteiza: Mito y Modernidad.* Bilbao: Guggenheim Bilbao Museum, 2004.

Seward, Barbara. "Dante's Mystic Rose." *Studies in Philology* 52, no. 4 (October 1955): 515–23.

Shakespeare, William. *Hamlet.* In *Complete Works of William Shakespeare.* New York: Thomas Y. Crowell, 1903, 594–619.

Singleton, Charles S. *Dante's* Commedia: *Elements of Structure.* Baltimore and London: The Johns Hopkins University Press, 1954.

———. *Journey to Beatrice.* Baltimore and London: The Johns Hopkins University Press, 1958.

Smith, Patti. *Just Kids.* New York: HarperCollins, 2010.

Sobrino, Jon. *Jesus, the Liberator: A Historical-Theological View.* New York: Orbis Books, 1993.

Sobrino, Jon, and Rolando Alvarado, eds. *Ignacio Ellacuría: "Aquella libertad esclarecida."* Santander: Sal Terrae, 1999.

Solomon, Deborah. "Puppy Love." *New York Times Magazine*, June 25, 2000, 15.

Spalding, Jill, "Bilbao: A Cultural Congregation," *Travel + Leisure,* February, 1998.

Steer, George. *The Tree of Gernika.* 1938. Reprint, London: Faber and Faber, 2009.

Stone, Oliver, and Peter Kuznick. *The Untold History of the United States.* New York: Gallery Books, 2012.

Strychacz, Thomas. *Hemingway's Theaters of Masculinity.* Baton Rouge: Louisiana State University Press, 2003.

Sullivan, Nancy. "Inside Trading: Postmodernism and the Social Drama of *Sunflowers* in the 1980s Art World." In *The Traffic of Culture: Refiguring Art and Anthropology,* edited by George Marcus and Fred Myers, 256–301. Berkeley: University of California Press, 1995.

Summers, Anthony. *Goddess: The Secret Lives of Marilyn Monroe.* New York: Macmillan, 1985.

Taussig, Michael. "Maleficium: State Fetishism." In *Fetishism as Cultural Discourse,* edited by Emily Apter and William Pietz, 217–47. Ithaca: Cornell University Press, 1993.

Terol, Oscar. *Técnicas de la mujer vasca para la doma y monta de maridos.* Madrid: Santillana, 2010.

The Compact Edition of the Oxford Dictionary. vol. I. Oxford: Oxford University Press, 1971.

Thomas, George, and Max Morgan Witts. *Guernica: The Crucible of World War II.* New York: Ballantine Books, 1975.

Torres Queiruga, Andrés. *Repensar la resurrección: La diferencia Cristiana en la continuidad de las religiones y de la cultura.* Madrid: Trotta, 2003.

Townshend, Pete. *Who I Am.* New York: Harper, 2012.

Truman, Harry. *Memoirs by Harry S. Truman: 1945 Year of Decisions.* Old Saybrook, Conn.: Konecky Associates, 1999.

Ugalde, Martin de. "José Antonio de Aguirre y Lecube." In José Antonio de Aguirre y Lecube, *Obras Completas*. Vol. 1. Donostia: Sendoa, 1981.

Unamuno, Miguel de. *The Agony of Christianity.* Translated by Kurt F. Reinhardt. New York: Frederick Ungar, 1960.

———. *The Tragic Sense of Life in Men and Nations.* Translated by Anthony Kerrigan. Princeton: Princeton University Press, 1972.

———. *Obras completas.* Edited by Manuel García Blanco. 5 vols. Madrid: Aguado, 1958.

———. *Paz en la guerra.* Edited by Manuel Basas. 1897. Reprint, Bilbao: El Correo Español, 1986.

———. *Vida de don Quijote y Sancho.* Madrid: Espasa-Calpe, 1961.

———. *El Cristo de Velázquez.* Madrid: Espasa-Calpe, 1963.

Unzueta, Patxo. *Los nietos de la ira: Nacionalismo y violencia en el País Vasco.* Madrid: El País/Aguilar, 1988.

Urdangarin, Carmelo. "Ostolaza anaiak." *Deba* (Winter 1999): 18–23.

Uriarte, Teo. *Mirando atrás: De las filas de ETA a las listas del PSE.* Barcelona: Ediciones B, 2005.

Urla, Jacqueline. "Kafe Antzokia: The Global Meets the Local in Basque Cultural Politics." *Papeles del CEIC* (Centro de Estudios sobre la Identidad Colectiva, Universidad del País Vasco) 10 (2003): 1–17.

———. "We Are All Malcolm X!: Negu Gorriak, Hip-Hop, and the Basque Political Imaginary." In *Global Noise: Rap and Hip-Hop Outside the USA*, edited by T. Mitchell, 171–93. Middletown, Conn: Wesleyan University Press, 2001.

———. *Reclaiming Basque: Language, Nation, and Cultural Activism.* Reno: University of Nevada Press, 2012.

Valle, Teresa del. *Andamios para una nueva ciudad: Lectura desde la antropología feminista.* Madrid: Cátedra 2007.

———. *Modelos emergentes en los sistemas y las relaciones de género.* Madrid: Narcea, 2002.

Valle, Teresa del, et al. *Mujer vasca: Imagen y realidad.* Barcelona: Anthropos, 1985.

van Hensbergen, Gijs. *Guernica: The Biography of a Twentieth-Century Icon.* New York: Bloomsbury, 2004.

Vázquez Antón, Carmele, and Rosa Andrieu Sanz. "Estudio sociológico de la prostitución en Bilbao." Unpublished manuscript, 1985.

Viar, Javier. "The Guggenheim Bilbao, Partner in the Arts: A View from the Fine Arts Museum of Bilbao." In *Learning from the Bilbao Guggenheim,* edited by Anna María Guasch and Joseba Zulaika, 97–109. Reno: Center for Basque Studies, 2005.

———. "La mirada del vigilante." Unpublished manuscript.

Vicario, Lorenzo, and P. Manuel Martínez Monje. "Another 'Guggenheim Effect'? The Generation of a Potentially Gentrifiable Neighbourhood in Bilbao." *Urban Studies* 40, no. 12 (2003): 2383–400.

Viejo-Rose, Dacia. *Reconstructing Spain: Cultural Heritage and Memory After Civil War.* Brighton: Sussex Academic Press, 2011.

Vilar, Pierre. *La guerra civil española.* Barcelona: Editorial Crítica, 1986.

Vilarós, Teresa. *El mono del desencanto. Una crítica cultural de la transición española (1973–1993).* Madrid: Siglo XXI, 1998.

Vitoria, F. Javier. *El Dios Cristiano.* Bilbao: Universidad de Deusto, 2008.

Wahl, Francois. "The Subtractive." Preface to Alain Badiou, *Conditions*, vii–xliv. New York: Continuum, 2008

Ward, Graham. *Cities of God.* London and New York: Routledge, 2000.

Weber, Max. "Letter to My Mother." Reprinted in *Bilbao,* June-December, 1994, 31–36.

Wilkerson, Mark. *Who Are You: The Life of Pete Townshend.* London: Omnibus Press, 2009.

Wittgenstein, Ludwig. *Tractatus Logico-Philosophicus.* Translated by D. F. Pears and B. F. McGuinness. London: Routledge, 1961.

Yanke, Germán. *Blas de Otero con los ojos abiertos.* Bilbao: Bilbao Vizcaya Kutxa, 1999.

Ybarra e Ybarra, Javier de. *Nosotros, los Ybarra: Vida, economía y sociedad (1974–1902).* Barcelona: Tusquets, 2002.

Zambrano, María. *La tumba de Antígona.* Madrid: Siglo XXI, 1967.

———. *Las palabras del regreso.* Edited by Mercedes Gómez Blesa. Salamanca: Amarú Ediciones, 1995.

Ziesemer, Wilhelm. *Das Land der Basken. Skizzen aus der Heimat der ältesten Europäer.* Berlin: Hobbing, 1934.

Žižek, Slavoj. "Christianity Against the Sacred." In Slavoj Žižek and Boris Gunjevic. *God in Pain: Inversions of Apocalypse,* 43–71. New York: Seven Stories Press, 2012.

———. "Courtly Love, or, Woman as Thing." In *The Metastases of Enjoyment: Six Essays on Woman and Causality.* London: Verso, 1994.

———. "Da Capo senza Fine." In Judith Butler, Ernesto Laclau, and Slavoj Žižek, *Contingency, Hegemony, Universality: Contemporary Dialogues on the Left,* 213–62. London, New York: Verso, 2000.

———. "Dialectical Clarity Versus the Misty Conceit of Paradox." In Slavoj Žižek and John Milbank, *The Monstrosity of Christ: Paradox or Dialectic?,* 234–306. Edited by Crestin Davis. Cambridge: MIT Press, 2009.

———. "For a Theologico-Political Suspension of the Ethical." In Slavoj Žižek and Boris Gunjevic. *God in Pain:*

Inversions of Apocalypse, 7–41. New York: Seven Stories Press, 2012.

———. "Psychoanalysis This Side of the Hermeneutic Delirium." *Lacanian Ink* 34 (2009): 139–51.

———. *For They Know Not What They Do: Enjoyment as a Political Factor.* London: Verso, 2002.

———. *How to Read Lacan.* London: Granta Books, 2006.

———. *Less Than Nothing: Hegel and the Shadow of Dialectical Materialism.* London: Verso, 2012.

———. *On Belief.* London and New York: Routledge, 2001.

———. *Repeating Lenin.* Zagreb: Arkzin, 2001.

———. *Sublime Object of Ideology.* London: Verso, 1989.

———. *The Fragile Absolute.* London: Verso, 2000.

———. *Violence: Six Sideways Reflections.* New York: Picador, 2008.

———. *The Parallax View.* Cambridge: MIT Press, 2006.

Žižek, Slavoj, and John Milbank, John. *The Monstrosity of Christ: Paradox or Dialectic?* Edited by Crestin Davis. Cambridge: MIT Press, 2009.

Žižek, Slavoj, and Boris Gunjevic. *God in Pain: Inversions of Apocalypse.* New York: Seven Stories Press, 2012.

Zubiri, Ignacio. *El sistema del concierto económico en el contexto de la Unión Europea.* Bilbao: Círculo de Empresarios Vascos, 2000.

———. *The Economic Agreement between the Basque Country and Spain.* Bilbao: Ad Concordiam, 2014.

Zubiri, Xabier. *Naturaleza, Historia, Dios.* Madrid: Editora Nacional, 1942.

Zukin, Sharon. *Landscapes of Power: From Detroit to Disney World.* Berkeley: University of California Press, 1991.

Zulaika, Joseba. *Basque Violence: Metaphor and Sacrament.* Reno: University of Nevada Press, 1988.

———. "Bertsolariak and Writers: An Old Tale of Fathers and Sons." In *Voicing the Moment: Improvised Oral Poetry and Basque Tradition,* edited by Samuel G. Armistead and Joseba Zulaika, 245–61. Reno: Center for Basque Studies, 2005.

———. "Desiring Bilbao: The Krensification of the Museum and Its Discontents." In *Learning from the Bilbao Guggenheim,* edited by Anna María Guasch and Joseba Zulaika, 149–70. Reno: Center for Basque Studies, 2005.

———. "Excessive Witnessing: The Ethical as Temptation." In *Witness and Memory: The Discourse of Trauma,* edited by Ana Douglass and Thomas Vogler, 89–107. New York: Routledge, 2003.

———. "On the Seduction of Architectural Miracles." *Neon* (Nevada Arts Council) (Summer 1998): 14–16.

———. "The Ruins of Theory and a Theory of Ruins: On Conversion." *Revista de Antropologia Social* 15 (2007): 173–92.

———. "Tropics of Terror: From Guernica's 'Natives' to Global 'Terrorists.'" *Social Identities* 4, no. 1 (1998): 93–108.

———. "Un golpe de pelota jamás eliminará el azar." In Olatz González Abrisqueta, *Pelota vasca: Un ritual, una estética,* 409–29. Bilbao: Muelle de Uribitarte, 2005.

———. "Is Bilbao a Woman? From Picasso to Gehry, Ariadne's Lunar Labyrinth," *Bidebarrieta* 21 (2010): 9–28.

———. *Adanen poema amaigabea.* Donostia: Kriselu, 1975.

———. *Caza, símbolo y eros.* Madrid: Nerea, 1992.

———. *Basque Violence: Metaphor and Sacrament.* Reno: University of Nevada Press, 1988.

———. *Crónica de una seducción: El Museo Guggenheim Bilbao.* Madrid: Nerea, 1996.

——. *Del cromañón al carnaval: Los vascos como museo antropológico*. San Sebastián: Erein, 1996.

——. *Terranova: The Ethos and Luck of Deep-Sea Fishermen*. Philadelphia: Ishi, 1981.

Zupančič, Alenca. *The Shortest Shadow: Nietzsche's Philosophy of the Two*. Cambridge: MIT Press, 2003.

Acknowledgments

During the twenty years of research I did for this book I interviewed, tape-recorder in hand, hundreds of Bilbainos. I am grateful to each one of them for sharing with me their views of Bilbao and much else. Nothing has been harder than leaving out many of their stories. It is my hope that, even if most of them will disagree with some aspects of my narrative, still they might feel that this is also their book. The list that follows includes most of the people I interviewed: Carmen Abad, Joaquín Achúcarro, Joseba Agirreazkuenaga, Alex Agirrezabal, Ignacio Agreda, Xabier Aierdi, Amadeo Aizpitarte, Marifer Aizpitarte, Ana Laura Aláez, Miren Alcedo, Kepa Altonaga, Antton Mari Aldekoa-Otalora, José Allende, Andoni Alonso, Oscar Álvarez Gila, José Luis Álvarez Enparantza, Josu Amezaga, Marisa Amigo, Ignacio Amestoy, Vicente Ameztoy, Álvaro Amman, Esti Amorrortu, Rosa Andrieu, Ramon Arana, Iñaki Aranbarri, Ibon Aranberri, Iñaki Aranguren, Ibon Arbulu, Pilar Aresti, Begoña Aretxaga, Mikel Arizaleta, Gregorio Arrien, Manu Arrue, Federico Arruti, Josean Arza, Miren Arzalluz, Anttone Arzeluz, Iñaki Arzoz, Amparo Arzua, Lourdes Arzua, Marta Astorqui, Agustin Atxega, Kepa Aulestia, José Luis Aurroecoechea, Iñaki Azkarraga, Jon Azua, Imanol Azkue, Carlos Bacigalupe, Rikardo Badiola, Txomin Badiola, Luis Badosa, Ana Bañuelos, José Julián Baquedano, Iñaki Barcena, Josune Barrena, Valentin Bengoa, Ion Bilbao, Sabin Bikandi, Marta Brancas, José Luis Burgos, Ignacio Cacho, Segundo Calleja, Rafael Canales, Iñaki Cano, Adolfo Carrión, Begoña Cigarán, Ofa Bezunartea, Pedro Crespo, Evaristo Churruca, Francis Díaz, Santiago Díez, Juanjo Dorronsoro, Alfonso Dubois, Gonzalo Dúo, Germán Echevarría, Guadalupe Echevarría, Xabier Egaña, Begoña Eguren, Miguel Elizondo, José Elorrieta, Javier Elzo, Santiago Eraso, Tasio Erkizia, Anton Erkoreka, Jesús María Erquicia, Manu Erzilla, Mari Luz Esteban, Teo Etxaburu, Agustin Etxebarria, Gotzone Etxebarria, José Ramón Etxebarria, Jon Mikel Euba, Pedro Feijóo, Alicia Fernández, Isabel Fica, Alberto Flor, Soledad Frías, Santiago Gabilondo, Ángel Gago, Mari Karmen Gallastegi, Alberto Garai, Víctor Garaigordobil, Román Gárate, Javier García Egocheaga, Begoña Gardeazábal, Elixabete Garmendia, Frank Gehry, Xabier Gereño, Manu Gojenola, Ramón Goldazarena, Mertxe Gómez, Mikel Gómez Uranga, Sonia Gonzalez, Olatz Gonzalez Abrisketa, Manuel González Portilla, Karmele Goñi, José María Gorordo, Fausto Grossi, Ana Gurruchaga, Ander Gurrutxaga, Mari Puri Herrero, Andreas Hess, Kepa Ibaibarriaga, Iñigo Ibarra, Pedro Ibarra, Petxo Idoiaga, Juan Infante, Natalia Infante, Iñaki Insausti, Paskual Intxausti, Iñaki Iriarte, Jose Angel Iribar, Jose Anjel Irigarai, Iñaki Irigoien, Xabier Irujo, Miriam Ispizua, Amaia Iturbide, Juantxu Iturralde, José Luis Iturrieta, Arturo Izarzelaia, Javier Izquierdo, José Manuel Izquierdo, Edorta Jimenez, Koldo Jones, Begoña Juaristi, Julita, Aintzane Kamara, Guruzne Kareaga, Khalid, Xabier Kintana, Thomas Krens, Erramun Landa, Eugenio Landa, Ana Larrañaga, Koldo Larrañaga, Carmela Lasallette, Jesus Mari Lazkano, Mauri Lazkano, Juan Lejarraga, Jon Leonardo, Anjel Lertxundi, Roberto Lertxundi, Alberto Letona, José Luis Lizundia, José Ignacio López de Arriortúa, Julen Madariaga, Julia Madrazo, Joxe Mallea, Ander Manterola, Cristina Martínez, Gaspar Martínez, José Ignacio Maturana, Xabier Mendiguren Bereziartu, Asier Mendizabal, José Luis Merino, Pilar de Miguel, Inés Miján, Fernando Molina, Miguel Monfort, Manu Montero, Morquillas, Roberto Mosso, Abel Muniategi, Antoni Muntadas, Vidal de Nicolás, José Antonio Nielfa, Mikel Noval, Lorea Oar-Arteta, Mikel Ocio, José Mari Odriozola, Miren Odriozola, Carlotta Olaizola, Jaime Oráa, Carmen Oriol, Ángel Ortiz Alfau, Julen Ortiz de Murua, Andrés Ortiz-Osés, Jon Ortuzar, Rafael Ossa Echaburu, Pablo Otaola, Jorge Oteiza, Josemari Otxoa, Chusa Padrones, Jakue Paskual, Celina Pereda, María Pereda, Asier Pérez, Iñaki Pérez, Juan Carlos Pérez, Alfonso Pérez-Agote, Ámparo Pimiento, Txema Portillo, José Alberto Pradera, Teresa Querejazu, Agustín Ramos, Rafa Redondo, Josu Rekalde, Julen Rekondo, Javier Retegi, Juan Carlos Rodríguez, Pilar Ros, José de la Rosa, Ixiar Rozas, Eduardo Ruiz, José Ignacio Ruíz Olabuenaga, Izaskun Sáez de la Fuente, Mercedez Sáinz, Covadonga Sáiz Bernuy, Alfonso Sáiz Valdivielso, Javier Salazar, Manuel Salgado, Patxi Sampedro, José Ángel Sánchez Asiaín, Pilar Santamaría, Jon Sarasua, Periko Solabarria, Patrick de la Sota, Ramón de la Sota, Aurora Suárez, Lourdes Subinas, Roman Sudupe, Rafael Suso, Maribel Tellitu, Oscar Terol, Tito, Ana Txurruka, José Ángel Ubieta, Pedro Ugarte, Mitxel Unzueta, Juan Antonio Urbeltz, Ibon Urgoiti, Juan Ignacio Uria, Iñaki Uriarte, Teo Uriarte, Arantza Urkaregi, Víctor Urrutia, Iñaki Urruzola, José Antonio Urteaga, Teresa del Valle, Ana Venegas, Josu Venero, Roberto Velasco, Iñaki Viar, Javier Viar, Juan Ignacio Vidarte, Gabriel Villota, Javier Vitoria, Germán Yanke, Borja de Ybarra, Javier de Ybarra, David Zabala, Javi Zabala, Gemma Zabaleta, Iñaki Zabaleta, Xabier Zabalo, Ramon Zallo, Juanjo Zearreta, Begoña Zuaznabar, Iñaki Zumarraga, Ángel Zurita.

The process for editing the text owes the most to the thoroughly creative work of Elisa Adler who rewrote many of my sentences. Kirk Robertson and William Douglass's incisive work forced me to get rid of some of my theoretical and rhetorical excesses. I also benefited from Sandra Ott, Garazi Zulaika, Daniel Montero, and Cameron Watson's editing, and from Margaret Dalrymple's careful copyediting and Kimberly Jo Daggett's and Joannes Zulaika's editorial assistance. Mark Kurlansky, David Brent and Dean MacCannell read and made encouraging remarks about earlier drafts of the manuscript. Their contributions to this text are much appreciated.

Many colleagues and friends have contributed to this book. Teresa Querejazu introduced me to many people. In Bilbao I enjoyed a constant support from Pello Salaburu, Pedro Ibarra, Anttone Arzelus, Begoña Zuaznabar, and Teo Etxaburu. Anton Erkoreka took days off to show me the mines of Berruelo, the town in the province of Palencia from where people migrated to Bilbao's Left Bank. Javier Viar opened the doors of the Museum of Fine Arts and spoke to me about Basque art and the city. Javier Echeverría spent hours trying to explain to me the mathematics of infinity. Bernardo Atxaga was most generous with his time in sharing with me his knowledge of Bilbao. Alfonso de Otazu invited me for lunch many times while talking to me about Bilbao's industrial history.

Xabier Egaña did various paintings on Bilbao's river thinking of this book. Many days José Mari Zabala accompanied me through Bilbao's streets while he took thousands of photographs of the city. Anna María Guasch helped me organize a conference on "Learning from the Guggenheim-Bilbao." Izaskun Etxaniz compiled for me databases on Bilbao. Koldo San Sebastián, Germán Echevarría, Joseba Agirreazkuenaga, Goretti Etxaniz, and Manu Gojenola read earlier versions of the manuscript and made significant corrections and incisive observations. I owe special gratitude to the friends and family members from Itziar. My sincere thanks to them all. They are not responsible for the shortcomings of my book.

Iñaki Uriarte, Jose Luis Agote, Goretti Etxaniz, Germán Echevarria, and Daniel Montero were most generous in providing me the photos. I am most thankful to them.

The Center for Basque Studies at the University of Nevada, Reno, has provided me shelter and ideal conditions for work. I thank my colleagues, visiting scholars, graduate students, and librarians for their daily interaction and support. Kate Camino's administrative assistance has made my life much easier. Daniel Montero has patiently and skillfully guided the production of the book at every stage and produced the cover. The design was done by Jose Luis Agote. Many thanks to them all.

Index

relationship with father, 64–65, 134, 164, 205–6
voyage to the black waters, 61–68
Zulaika, Miguel, 62–65, 97, 108, 122, 134, 164, 205–6. See father
Zulaika, Xalbador, 88
Zupančič, 283n.10, 290n.95, 301n.213, 307n.260
Zurita, Carlos, 115